CW00672889

"Julie Morris's *Introduction to Sociology* book I would have wanted in my undergr students where they are through familiar and podcasts, this work introduces the most important sociological concepts in a way that is rigorous, accessible, and entertaining. Even better, this book is a great intro to comedy for sociologists and a great intro to sociology for comedy scholars."

Stephanie Brown, *Visiting Assistant Professor of Communication and Media Studies at Washington College*

Introduction to Sociology Through Comedy

Questioning society and one's place in it is a common theme in both comedy and sociology. Understanding and subverting hierarchies and norms, exploring deviance and taboos, and relating lived experience to broader questions all hold a crucial place for them both.

Introduction to Sociology Through Comedy teaches foundational sociological concepts using comedy, first considering the history of sociology before employing examples from comedians – including standalone comedy bits, sketches, characters, and scenes – to illustrate a specific theory, concept, or social phenomenon. The profession of comedy is then used as a case study for the application of sociological concepts, such as impression management, social stratification, racial segregation, deviance, and stigma, allowing readers to gain familiarity with the concepts while simultaneously practicing their application.

This book explains why we laugh by applying theories of humor, which will bolster students' understanding of sociological principles by forcing them to question their own assumptions – helping them to put why they laugh into sociological terms.

Julie Morris is a sociologist and statistician living in Anchorage, Alaska. She earned a PhD in Sociology from the University of Washington (UW) in Seattle, WA. Her sociological research focuses on the relationship between social support and mental and physical health, and her work has been published in academic journals, including *Birth*, *Journal of Women's Health*, and *The Lancet*. She previously taught courses on sociology, statistics, and demography at UW and Western Washington University in Bellingham, WA.

Introduction to Sociology Through Comedy

Julie Morris

Routledge
Taylor & Francis Group

NEW YORK AND LONDON

Designed cover image: Matthew Jungling, Unsplash

First published 2024
by Routledge
605 Third Avenue, New York, NY 10158

and by Routledge
4 Park Square, Milton Park, Abingdon, Oxon, OX14 4RN

Routledge is an imprint of the Taylor & Francis Group, an informa business

Library of Congress Cataloging-in-Publication Data
Names: Morris, Julie (Sociologist), author.
Title: Introduction to sociology through comedy / Julie Morris.
Description: New York, NY : Routledge, 2024. | Includes bibliographical references and index.
Identifiers: LCCN 2023052368 | ISBN 9781032745060 (hardback) | ISBN 9781032644387 (paperback) | ISBN 9781003469537 (ebook)
Subjects: LCSH: Sociology. | Sociology--Humor. | Comedy--Social aspects.
Classification: LCC HM585 .M669 2024 | DDC 306.4/81--dc23/eng/20231113
LC record available at https://lccn.loc.gov/2023052368

ISBN: 978-1-032-74506-0 (hbk)
ISBN: 978-1-032-64438-7 (pbk)
ISBN: 978-1-003-46953-7 (ebk)

DOI: 10.4324/9781003469537

Typeset in Sabon
by KnowledgeWorks Global Ltd.

Access the Support Material: www.routledge.com/9781032644387

To my family, who were the first ones to make me laugh,

and to James, who keeps it going.

Contents

Acknowledgments

There are so many people to thank for the completion of this project. I want to thank my editor at Routledge, Michael Gibson, for supporting this project. Thank you for bringing this book to life. Great thanks are owed to Gabriella Jones-Monserrate. Gabi, you believed in this project from the start and saw its potential more clearly than even I could. You added so much to its depth and structure and brought to light its potential for levity and empathy. I am so thankful for all your tremendous contributions. I owe thanks to my sociological mentors: Drs. Andrea Bertotti Metoyer, Jerald Herting, and Hedwig Lee. Thank you for showing me how to see the world through a new lens and doing so with joy and endless humor.

I owe special thanks to my husband, James, for believing in me, supporting me, and making me laugh every single day. You inspire me to be the best version of myself and give me the love, space, and encouragement to follow my passions. I owe the most thanks to my amazing mom, Dr. Sharon Morris. Our comedic sensibilities may not overlap in the slightest but you believed in me anyway. You did more to bring this book to light than I ever could have imagined or for which I could ever hope to repay. I want to thank my dad, Dr. Jack Morris, for teaching me that jokes are shared experiences that bring people together at the end of a nice meal. To my brother, Michael Morris, thank you for instilling a love of comedic television in me from a young age.

I want to thank my amazing family and friends who read early drafts of this book, including my cousin, Scott Morris, and my dear friends, Drs. Nina Cesare and Michael Esposito. Your feedback and encouragement were instrumental to this project. I owe thanks to my wonderful friends, Drs. Anne Fast and Batool Zaidi. You supported me from the start and this project would have never gotten off the ground without you. Thank you to all my other amazing friends and family who were so encouraging throughout this process.

Above all else, I want to thank everyone who shared their personal stories with me about the ways comedy changed their lives. Thank you for sharing with me how comedy brought you joy or gave you hope. This book is for you.

Preface

In 2010, I was an undergraduate student in sociology at Gonzaga University in Spokane, Washington. I spent the summer after my junior year interning at a documentary film company called the Media Education Foundation in Northampton, Massachusetts, which analyzed pop culture and mass media through a critical sociological lens. Here, I shared a small apartment with my cousin Scott. We grew up not knowing each other very well. Scott grew up in a suburb of New York City, while I grew up 4,500 miles away in a small town in Alaska. Scott was several years older than me and already a working professional. But we quickly discovered we had an identical sense of humor. Our connection was largely built on what made us laugh.

One of the first things that made us laugh together that summer was a bit of standup comedy by Kumail Nanjiani from a set he performed at Comix NY in 2008. We found the clip on YouTube and watched it dozens of times, whenever we needed a pick-me-up, whenever we had friends over, or for no reason at all. In the bit, titled "Cheese," Nanjiani reacts to recent events in the news about a new drug rising in popularity in the Midwest, called "cheese." He explains the drug is a cocktail of Tylenol® PM and heroin. Nanjiani starts the bit with an air of fear and anxiety about a new, scary drug targeting our nation's youth. The audience – whether watching live at Comix NY or watching later on YouTube – are compelled to share in that fear. Then, Nanjiani flips the script. He goes on an extended riff about the absurdity of labeling something a "new drug" (and the resultant news coverage stoking public fear) when the main ingredient is heroin, a drug that already exists.

How to break down the selection of stories covered by the evening news and the intentional way those stories were framed was exactly what I was learning to do as a sociologist and as an intern at the Media Education Foundation. Nanjiani did this by pointing out the absurdity of the idea that cheese was a new drug sweeping the nation because, as Nanjiani identifies, cheese is not even a new drug. The news sensationalized the wrong problem; by focusing on Midwestern party drugs, the media diverted attention away from larger-scale public threats tied to heroin and the opioid crisis. This clip was a turning point for me. Nanjiani was speaking like a sociologist. It was the beginning of my journey in learning how to analyze the news and mass media through a sociological and critical lens.

Here, Nanjiani highlights sociological skills which we will dig into later in the book. For example, Nanjiani's bit explores symbolic interactionism. **Symbolic interactionism** refers to how we interact with one another based upon shared understandings of words and symbols.[1] It matters if something is called a "new drug" that is "sweeping the nation." That influences how we understand the issue, how we prioritize it, and what emotional responses we have to such information. Also, Nanjiani engages the sociological imagination. The **sociological imagination** is understanding how one's personal experiences relate to broader society, which is accomplished by seeing the world through the lens of an outsider.[2] Breaking apart *how* and *why* news stories are told the way they are – such as to stoke fear for political or advertisement-revenue reasons – is an exercise in one's sociological imagination. Sociology allows one to be a savvy consumer of media and information.

Comedy allows us to practice these sociological skills. Sociology and comedy are symbiotic. Comedy rests on shared understanding between the audience and the comic.[3] The laugh often comes from the surprise, which is usually something the audience recognizes to be true but did not expect. A good comedian uses the comedic form to guide the audience into a certain way of thinking. It is both a comedian's and a sociologist's job to be a tour guide for our own reality. This is what Nanjiani does in this bit.

Notes

1 Blumer, H. (1986). *Symbolic Interactionism: Perspective and Method*. University of California Press.
2 Mills, C. W. (2000). *The Sociological Imagination*. Oxford University Press.
3 *Good One: The Lucas Brothers' History of Western Philosophy*. (2019, February 24). https://podcasts.apple.com/ie/podcast/the-lucas-brothers-history-of-western-philosophy/id1203393721?i=1000430481890

Introduction

Society is built on a shared set of norms and values that are taught from a young age.[1] These norms are outlined by the interpretation of mass lived experience through the controlled lens of popular culture and geographical tradition. This book will define sociology theories of mass culture and deviance and explain how social values stem from the dominant social class and compel coercion through demonization of the "other." It is in the interest of the dominant group for people not to question society and not to question themselves.

Yet, comedians have long been challenging the status quo (although, as this book explores, not *all* comedians). Questioning society and one's position in it is a common thread in both comedy and sociology. This includes understanding hierarchies and **in-group** and **out-group** statuses. In-groups refer to the groups to which an individual belongs; out-groups refer to the groups to which a person does not belong.

Consider how comedians may joke about members of their own audience or joke about themselves, which are forms of crowd work. **Crowd work** occurs when a comedian engages directly with their audience. Crowd work can take many forms (e.g., a general query to the whole audience or a one-on-one conversation with a specific member of the audience) and can be used to varying ends (e.g., to poke fun at oneself or at a member of the audience, to connect with the audience, or to challenge the audience's way of thinking). To poke fun at an audience member, for example, a comedian may play off the shared assumptions held about their assumed group memberships. Knowing what these commonly held beliefs are, and knowing how a crowd will respond to them, is a sociological exercise. It is also a sociological exercise to know the norms of the space. Consider, for example, how being poked at by a comedian in a comedy room likely feels different than being poked at by your boss during an important meeting. The norms and expectations of the space are different.

While we just discussed crowd work being used to "poke fun" at someone, crowd work – at its core – is used to connect with the audience. It breaks down the "fourth wall" and allows the comedian to learn more about their audience and tailor their material specifically for them. When comedians use crowd work, every show is different. This is not much different from teaching sociology. When teaching sociology, it is important to understand your

DOI: 10.4324/9781003469537-1

classroom of students – for example, what they value and what references resonate with them – and tailor your material to suit their goals and learning styles. You can use crowd work to teach your students social norms. When professors engage with students like comedians, every lecture is different.

Students respond to this style of engagement. In my own experience teaching sociology, I turned to comedy to teach sociological theories which were not always easily digestible to my students. I played standup clips in class, discussed comedians during lectures, and used laugher as a relief valve to connect with my students when they went through tough times. My students latched onto the comedic examples in ways they never did to other examples. Laughing together in the classroom made my students more engaged and made us all more connected to each other. In short: using comedy made me a better professor (and it was a lot of fun).

Once I realized this connection between comedy and sociology, my urge to connect the two grew stronger. I was looking for a resource to help me in the classroom that provided a list of examples I could use throughout the semester to teach sociological theories; and that described historical, cultural, and social phenomena through the lens of comedy as a profession. That book did not exist at the time, so I decided to write it myself. To write this book, I listened to countless hours of interviews with comics, watched and listened to standup specials, read comedic histories, memoirs, and articles written by preeminent sociologists and journalists covering comedy.

This book is for students who want to use comedy to understand sociology. The book explains why we laugh by applying theories of humor, which will bolster students' understanding of sociological principles by forcing them to question their own assumptions. In short, it will help students put *why* they laugh into sociological terms.

Notes on Methodology

In my career, I have always been drawn to sociological theories and research that reinforce the idea that having a community that understands you is associated with positive mental health outcomes. My own sociological research primarily focuses on how social support and community context translate to mental health outcomes, including clinical depression and depressive symptoms. As a sociologist, I see how feeling heard, seen, and connected to others are healing forces. I see those forces come alive in comedy.

I approached writing this book the same way I would approach a new piece of sociological research: I turned to the experts. My research for this book consists of reading comedic histories and articles by sociologists, journalists, and comedy scholars, reading memoirs of prominent comedians, listening to interviews with comedians (both prominent and up-and-coming), and watching and listening to standup specials spanning decades.

This is a sociological and historical text but it is intentionally not built exclusively on peer-reviewed academic work. I call on "experts" using a wide definition – one largely based on comedic perspective versus a specific set of accolades. To explain this rationale, I will introduce a point made by *Vulture* editor and comedy critic Jesse David Fox regarding a paradox inherent in the field of comedy critique.[2] As detailed with incongruity theory, an important component of comedy is surprise. As acknowledged by Fox, what surprises him as someone who watches roughly one hundred comedy specials per year for work, will not be the same thing that surprises someone who only watches two comedy specials per year. A comedic bit that Fox identifies as an overused trope may be brand new to someone watching at home. The laugher and surprise the person watching at home feels are not any less valid because a critic thinks the bit is historically overdone. For this reason, this book engages with not only critiques of comedy, but also critiques of those critiques.

My relationship to comedy has changed throughout the writing of this book. I confronted my own narrow understanding of what comedy is and who performs it. I *thought* I knew comedy. Throughout this process, I learned that my understanding of comedy was narrow and largely White, male, and elite. It consisted primarily of comedians who played to sold-out shows in large arenas and made jokes that resonated with people young and old from coast-to-coast.

Many people share this experience with comedy. I began my research with books on comedic history. Like most broadly shared historical narratives, the history of comedy often focuses on the figures who had access to big opportunities and mainstream success. A core example of one of these opportunities is the chance to perform on *The Tonight Show*, which was a career-maker for comedians for decades. It was also an opportunity that was almost entirely, and explicitly, reserved for White men.

As my knowledge of comedy grew deeper, it also grew wider. There are amazing books, articles, and interviews chronicling the history of trailblazing comics who made their paths for success and absolutely changed the landscape of comedy. In many ways, my research for his book mirrors the narrative it seeks to tell. As you navigate this book and weave between comics who play to big arenas, those who perform in laundromats, and those who come to you exclusively through your phone, I hope you will see that history of comedy is a history of our world and that comics with the most novel things to say are often the most silenced.

The Comedy Timeline

This book moves through various eras of comedy's history. As the book mimics the flow of a sociology course by building on sociological ideas, it is not organized chronologically. However, the chronological history of comedy is important as it allows the reader to see and understand the ways social norms evolve over time, as exemplified by changing comedic perspectives, venues, platforms, and performances. To ground readers in time and space as the book moves back and forth through comedy history, I will refer regularly to a visual timeline.

Table I.1 and Figure I.1 highlight prominent comedians and comedic moments, organized by era. Table I.1 notes these moments in slightly more detail, while the graphic allows for a quick reference of where a comedian or

Table I.1 Comedy Timeline by Era and Medium

Borscht Belt, Chitlin' Circuit, and Theaters	*Alternative, Def Comedy Jam, and Sitcoms*

1951 *I Love Lucy* premieres on CBS.	1990 Series premiere of *Seinfeld* on NBC.
1955 Phyllis Diller begins her standup career at age thirty-seven.	1990 Series premiere of *In Living Color* on Fox.
1956 Redd Foxx records his first (of many) comedy LPs: *Laff of the Party: Volume 1.*	1991 Launch of the network Comedy Central.
1957 Premiere of *Tonight Starring Jack Paar* on NBC (rebranded as *The Jack Paar Show* in 1959).	1992 Premiere of *Def Comedy Jam* on HBO.
	1994 Janeane Garofolo joins the cast of *Saturday Night Live* on NBC.
Late Night TV, Comedy Clubs, and Records	1994 Margaret Cho gets her own sitcom, *All-American Girl* on ABC.
1961 Lenny Bruce first arrested for obscenity.	*The Digital Boom*
1961 Dick Gregory debuts at Chicago's Playboy Club and appears on *The Jack Paar Show.*	2003 Dane Cook releases his first comedy CD and DVD, *Harmful If Swallowed*, after building his fanbase on MySpace.
1961 Nipsey Russell packages a late-night talk show, *Point of View.* No network will back a show with a Black host.	2003 *Chappelle's Show* premieres on Comedy Central.
1962 Moms Mabley becomes first woman to headline at Carnegie Hall.	2005 The video sharing platform YouTube launches.
1962 Johnny Carson replaces Jack Paar. Show is rebranded as *The Tonight Show.*	2006 Bo Burnham posts his first song on YouTube, called "My Whole Family."
1963 Bill Cosby releases his first comedy album, *Bill Cosby Is a Very Funny Fellow...Right!*	2006 The micro-blogging video platform Twitter launches.
1967 Joan Rivers performs on *The Ed Sullivan Show* while pregnant.	2007 Netflix launches streaming service.
1972 The Comedy Store opens in West Hollywood, California.	2009 Marc Maron launches his podcast, *WTF with Marc Maron.*
SNL and Richard Pryor	2014 Standup set by Hannibal Buress about Bill Cosby's sexual assault allegations goes viral on YouTube.
1975 *Saturday Night Live* premieres on NBC.	2016 The social media platform TikTok launches.
1978 The Belly Room opens at The Comedy Store.	2016 *Atlanta* premieres on FX.
1979 The 1979 Comedy Strike begins.	2018 *Insecure* premieres on HBO.
	2018 Hannah Gadsby's *Nanette* lands on Netflix.
The Comedy Boom	2021 *Ziwe* premieres on Showtime.
1982 The Comedy Cellar opens in NYC.	2021 Bo Burnham's *Inside* launches on Netflix.
1983 Eddie Murphy stars in *Trading Places.*	
1984 Series premiere of *The Cosby Show* on NBC.	

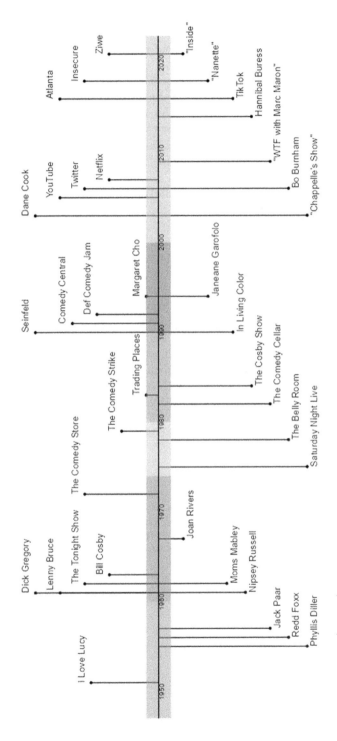

Figure I.1 Comedy Timeline

comedic moment is situated in history. Versions of the graphic (Figure I.1) will be used throughout the book to situate a comedian or comedic moment in history and will specifically call out the era of discussion in the graphic's title and color blocking.

As you move through the book, you will gain understanding of the items on the timeline and build their comedic historical knowledge piece-by-piece. By the end of the book, you can refer to this timeline to recall knowledge, visualize comedy's historical trajectory, and aid their predictions about comedy's future. The construction of this timeline was based on multiple historical texts, specific influential comedians, and media productions.[3]

The book uses this timeline to showcase the evolution of comedy throughout history as it evolved in style and in response to the introduction of new platforms. This is exemplified through relevant comedic standup bits, sketches, song lyrics, movie and television scenes, and interview quotes spanning decades. From these examples and the corresponding historical context each chapter provides, the book concludes in a note on how comedy can promote representation, acceptance, and inspire hope. Like sociologists, comedians use their sociological imagination to depict the world through a new lens. They speak to emotional truth and – as can be seen in comedy's evolution over time – shepherd in real social change. By learning the history and sociological significance of the comedy we consume, I hope this book helps you better understand yourself and the world. I hope readers will use the tools taught in this book – of sociological dissection and analysis – to consider their own relationships with comedy. Some attribute the following quote to Mark Twain, others to E.B. White, that "analyzing humor is a bit like dissecting a frog: You learn how it works but you end up with a dead frog."[4,5] I hope you enjoy your dead frog.

Notes

1 Ritzer, G. (2013). *Introduction to Sociology*. SAGE.
2 *10 Years Covering Comedy with the New York Times's Jason Zinoman* (2022, March 24). https://podcasts.apple.com/cl/podcast/10-years-covering-comedy-with-the-new-york-timess/id1203393721?i=1000555092932
3 Federman, W. (2021). *The History of Stand-Up: From Mark Twain to Dave Chappelle*. Independent Artists Media.
4 Calisher, C. H. (2008). What is funny and what is not? *Croatian Medical Journal*, 49(1), 120–127. https://doi.org/10.3325/cmj.2008.1-120
5 Van, J. (1991, April 27). *Comic Relief*. Chicago Tribune. https://www.chicago tribune.com/news/ct-xpm-1991-04-28-9406160010-story.html

1 History of Sociological Theory

This chapter provides an overview of foundational sociological theorists and their core contributions to the field. This chapter covers two main eras – classical sociology and contemporary sociology. Classical sociological theorists include Karl Marx, Georg Simmel, Max Weber, Émile Durkheim, Thortein Veblen, and W.E.B. Du Bois. Contemporary sociology comprises three core sets of theories: structural/functional theories, conflict/critical theories, and inter/actionist theories. Theorists include Robert K. Merton, Friedrich Engels, Ralf Dahrendorf, Mary Wollstonecraft, bell hooks, Patricia Hill Collins, Kimberlé Crenshaw, Eduardo Bonilla-Silva, Eve Kosofsky Sedgwick, Jean Baudrillard, George Herbert Mead, and Charles Horton Cooley. Throughout this book, we call back to the theories introduced in this chapter. We practice applying their sociological frameworks to the social world by analyzing comedic examples.

Classical Sociology

Karl Marx

Karl Marx (born in Trier, Germany, 1818) was a German philosopher whose theories focused on macro issues, particularly those related to capitalism. Marx understood that under the social structure of capitalism, the means of production (i.e., factories and tools) were owned entirely by one group of people (the **bourgeois** or capitalists).[1] Therefore, everyone else (the **proletariat** or workers) could only make money by selling their labor. This allowed capitalists to **exploit** their workers for their labor, paying only a small share of the money earned by selling the factory's goods back to the proletariat (whose labor produced it) and keeping a large share for themselves (even though they contributed very little labor to the process).

Capitalism refers to an economic system based on the private ownership of vehicles of industry. In other words, the means of production – the materials and factories, for example – are owned by individual actors. They are incentivized to maximize their own profit. Goals under a capitalist system include ever-increasing revenue generation and business growth. Competition between companies can result in an "arms race" of lowering, and lowering,

DOI: 10.4324/9781003469537-2

prices to edge out the competition. Such competition under the capitalist system pummels the wages of workers lower and lower. The capitalists want to make more money for themselves by doing more business, but to do more business, they need to further exploit workers.

The capitalist system prioritizes speed and efficiency. Workers are arranged in factories to focus on one specific task; they experience **alienation** from the finished product and from other workers. Marx understood that this alienation under capitalism separated the proletariat from the experience of being human. Our humanity comes from our ability to think, create, and interact. Capitalists saw workers as machines and treated them accordingly. Capitalism's survival is strengthened by its alienation of workers from each other and by limiting their ability to think and connect. The structure of capitalism keeps workers in the dark from the true levels of exploitation they face.

Marx understood that how capitalism "really" works is hidden by the sets of ideologies capitalists put forward. They lie to workers; tell them capitalism *benefits* them. This results in a **false consciousness** of workers. Their reality is one of the lies created to keep them in a cycle of exploitation. The propagation of these ideologies allows capitalists to continually decrease wages and increase the demands of the job. Marx posited that once the proletariat understood the exploitation and alienation they faced under the capitalist system (i.e., once the façade of capitalism was lifted) – what Marx dubbed **class consciousness** – they would rise up and tear the system down.

Marx predicted a global expansion of capitalism. **Globalization** refers to the vast interconnection of people, media, and cultures across the globe. Globalization stems from developments in technology, communication systems, economic markets, and the speed and affordability of international travel. As Marx would have predicted, to find the cheapest labor, companies may build production facilities and hire workers in countries with cheaper labor costs. This is a key feature of modern globalization. Even if you live in the United States, you may buy a shirt produced in Indonesia, for example. If you look in the average American closet, you will likely see countless items that were produced in countries where wages are lower, and goods can be produced cheaper, than in the United States.

In addition to goods, globalization is marked by expansion of culture, media, and ideologies across geographic boundaries. Consider, for example, how brands are also increasingly global. Brands from the United States – such as Coca-Cola, McDonald's, and Starbucks – are found across the globe and influence the consumption habits and health status of people all over the world. Media is another area of global expansion. Media produced in the United States is aired on radios, televisions, and movie theaters across the globe. This can influence the style (e.g., clothing and hairstyles), speaking habits (e.g., learning slang or English language), and beliefs on, or understanding of, identity and behaviors (e.g., sex and sexuality).

Marxist theorists are critical of globalization. They believe it creates false needs. People living in a country with a different lifestyle may watch a television show set in the United States and want to emulate what they see on the screen (e.g., a big house, fancy clothes, or an expensive car). However, they may live in a country which does not have access to those items. They are being sold a lifestyle they cannot access. Regardless of access, Marxists would argue that they should not desire to be pawns in the capitalist system selling them items they do not need. Globalization, to Marxists, is an expansion of capitalism's ability to make the rich richer by lying to, and exploiting, more people.[2]

Georg Simmel

An influential scholar in the areas of culture and social interaction was Georg Simmel (born in Berlin, Germany, 1858). Simmel's work focused on two key elements of social interaction: forms and types. The **forms** of interaction refer to how social structure dictates the way individuals of different positions interact with one another. Consider interactions between a boss and an employee. There are social structures in place which dictate the form of the interactions, above and beyond the individual personalities.

Similarly, Simmel understood an interaction is dictated by the **types** of people engaging in it, above and beyond individual personalities. "Types" here refers to features of one's social identity, such as their sex, gender, race and ethnicity, social status, or intersections therein. Consider, again, a boss and an employee. There is a natural power imbalance impacting the *form* of their interaction. If the employee is undocumented (in Simmel's words, a feature of their *type*), that status further impacts the social interaction. An employee who is undocumented, not by any feature of their personhood or personality, but purely by their status, may have less security in their position and have fewer opportunities for advancement than an employee who is documented. To sum up Simmel's view, social interaction is less about people's personalities, and more about the relative positions and power of the individuals, as determined by our social structure.

Max Weber

While Marx's core focus was on the role of the economy in society, macro social theorist Max Weber (born in what is now Erfurt, Germany, 1864) studied how myriad social factors operated in society to impact social life. His core focus was on the relationship between the economy and religion. His book *The Protestant Ethic and the Spirit of Capitalism* (1904) proved foundational for this area of study by providing a detailed analysis of religion's role in communities across space and time.[3] Weber's research led him to the conclusion that religion bolstered the capitalist system and aided in the construction of global economies.

Weber was informed by the work of Karl Marx. He agreed that capitalists used false narratives to exploit and alienate workers. Weber added to this body of work theories about how religion was a part of this process. Weber saw religion as both (1) a mode by which capitalist messages (false narratives) could be disseminated and (2) a means of distraction from the problems caused by capitalism. For example, as detailed in his book, Protestants believed economic success was a "sign" from God that they were good, worthy, and would make it into Heaven. The **Protestant work ethic,** as detailed in Weber's book, was the idea that to live piously, you must work hard and live simply. This script – the actions one must take to get into Heaven – also fits the bill for what it meant to be a productive worker under the system of capitalism. Marx was similarly critical of religion – calling it the "opium of the people."[4]

Weber's core contribution to the field of sociology was not simply about the relationship between religion and the economy but about the underlying processes which allow such a relationship to form. One of those processes was **rationalization.** Social structures – such as capitalism – are *rational* in the sense that they are constantly trying to find the most efficient means of achieving their goals.

Weber's concept of the "iron cage" ties to his views on rationalization.[5] The **iron cage** refers to how the emphasis on efficiency and rationality in capitalist social structures stifles freedom and creativity. Individuals are – metaphorically – trapped inside a cage. Behavior and ideas are drastically limited and homogenized. Individuals feel pressure to meet the excessive demands placed upon them. It is hard to break free from the iron cage because the myth is touted, within capitalist societies, that rationality and efficiency are worthy goals which benefit everyone.

Weber noted it is *rational* for capitalists to integrate their beliefs into other domains of social life, like religious tenets. It is also *rational* to further exploit workers – driving down wages or increasing labor demands – to make more profit. Later in the book, we will discuss rationalization in a factory using an example from *I Love Lucy* and discuss rationalization in other domains of social life, including the decline of local news. We will also use examples from comedic history to showcase what it looks like to "break free" from rationalization, including how comedy became less scripted, more fractured, and more personal when we discuss the alternative comedy movement.

Another process was the division of majority and minority groups.[6] As detailed by sociologist Louis Wirth (born in Gemünden, Germany, 1897), a **majority group** is a group that holds a dominant position due to its relative abundance of status, power, or wealth – all of which *they* have defined as worthy. A **minority group,** conversely, is a group that is excluded from a dominant position in society due to their relative lack of the necessary status, power, or wealth that the majority group deems as worthy.[7] Social theorists distinguish majority and minority groups not based on size (for example, a numerical majority as representing 51 percent or more of the population) but on the power they can exercise on others. Even if there were fewer capitalists than proletariat, the capitalists had more power. We will cover many examples in the book which consider who has power, and why, and call back to Weber's definitions.

Émile Durkheim

Unlike Marx and Weber, who were quite critical of social structures, Émile Durkheim (born in Épinal, Lorraine, France, 1958) was more laudatory of the impact of social structures on people's lives. He believed it was *positive* that social structures impose norms and values on individuals. Otherwise, as Durkheim believed, people would submit to their sins and passions at the expense of society and civility. Durkheim believed things would get *Lord of The Flies-y* quickly if it were not for social norms and rules keeping people in check.

People *need* rules and limits. The norms regulating behavior are what Durkheim called **social facts**. Durkheim saw a society's shared beliefs about good and evil, its **collective conscience**, as the most important social fact for fostering a functional society. For example, beliefs opposing murder, assault, and theft are parts of the collective consciousness of many societies, and Durkheim saw these shared beliefs as beneficial for the preservation of a collective society. From this, Durkheim argued that **deviance** is functional for society.[8] What Durkheim means here is that defining and penalizing "bad" behaviors encourage individuals to avoid those behaviors. If we do not define theft as "bad," then what would stop people from stealing?

Durkheim's most well-known work was *Suicide* (1897), which provided an analysis of suicide rates using a sociological perspective.[9] Prior research on suicide tended to focus on individual factors. Durkheim's focus on the social factors of suicide was novel. Through this study, Durkheim effectively demonstrated that seemingly individual circumstances (e.g., suicide) can be explained by social phenomena. This proved the importance of sociology as a field of study and repositioned the onus of responsibility from the individual to society.

For example, Durkheim identifies four types of suicide. The most prominent is *anomic suicide*. Anomic suicide stems from experiencing **anomie** – the lost or listless feeling that results when individuals are unsure of their purpose and direction in life. Anomie is a social problem. It occurs when there is a breakdown of collective norms or expectations that give individuals guidance for what is expected of them. Durkheim saw anomie as an increasing and modern problem. He saw **social integration** – strong connections between individuals and their social groups – was imperative for a functional and happy social life.

Previously, when individuals tended to work on either the farms or the factories, there was more commonality in human experiences and, thus, more consensus of social norms and expectations. This is **mechanical solidarity**, the solidarity of people based upon having similar experiences and sharing a collective conscience.[10] Solidarity comes from people living relatively homogenous lives. However, as people started having more diverse experiences as labor became more divided, their days had different structures and they faced different challenges. Solidarity became less mechanical and more organic. Individuals with diverse jobs, resources, and expertise must rely on one another more to meet their needs. They become interdependent. **Organic solidarity** refers to a social order wherein solidarity comes from individuals needing to depend upon one another's specialization.

As experiences, beliefs, and social norms are more varied, there is a decline in the shared collective conscience. To Durkheim, this decline of the collective conscience has a negative impact on society as there was less collective agreement on, and control of, "deviant" acts. However, as we will discuss throughout the book, "deviant" behaviors are not necessarily or inherently bad or dangerous. Indeed, definitions of "deviant" behaviors extend far past murder, assault, and theft. Many behaviors are labeled and penalized as deviant based upon homophobic, racist, xenophobic, and misogynistic viewpoints. We will discuss how definitions of "deviant" behaviors are not innate or static; they vary by place, culture, and time. As such, we can use a sociological lens to assess *how* and *why* those behaviors became labeled as deviant – and how they are tied to preservation of social hierarchies and concentration of power.

Thorstein Veblen

Thorstein Veblen (born in Cato, Wisconsin, 1857) was a foundational theorist in how people signal their position in the social hierarchy. In his book *The Theory of the Leisure Class* (1899), Veblen describes how wealthy individuals show off their resources through two primary means: conspicuous leisure and conspicuous consumption. **Conspicuous leisure** refers to activities such as playing rounds of golf or lingering over fancy lunches which signal that a person does not need to be constantly engaging in work. Instead, they have the means to engage in leisure. However, in the era before social media (this book was written in 1899), these activities were difficult to broadcast widely. Therefore, people began to signal their wealth through expensive goods – such as luxury cars or designer clothing. This is **conspicuous consumption**. But, as Veblen notes, conspicuous consumption is easier to "fake" than conspicuous leisure. Individuals of lower means can follow the consumption patterns of the wealthy through buying used or knock-off items.

William Edward Burghardt (W.E.B.) Du Bois

Early sociology was largely dominated by White male perspectives. Thanks to the efforts of pioneering sociological thinkers, sociology was improved upon through the inclusion of more theoretical perspectives. W.E.B. Du Bois (born in Great Barrington, Massachusetts, 1868) was the first scholar to bring race studies into the field of sociology. Three of Du Bois's most well-known works were *The Philadelphia Negro* (1899), *The Souls of Black Folk* (1903), and *Black Reconstruction in America* (1935).

The Philadelphia Negro provided an analysis of the experiences of Black and African American people in Philadelphia in the late 1800s.[11] Through extensive research, Du Bois's work detailed all areas of social life in Black communities, including family, education, employment, religion, and police contact, among others. Du Bois highlighted the painful and omnipresent effects of racism and discrimination. While most of the blame for racism was attached to White folks and institutions, Du Bois also noted areas where, he believed, Black folks were contributing to the system of racism. For example, Du Bois noted that many Black families would leave their neighborhood to seek healthcare from White physicians rather than from Black physicians. This negatively impacted the professional and financial livelihood of Black physicians and their families.

From his extensive research, Du Bois built a theoretical framework around the color line. The **color line** refers to the barriers separating Black and White folks, both in the United States and abroad. These barriers took three forms: physical, political, and psychological. The physical barrier refers to the visual differentiation between Black and White folks based on skin color. The political barrier referred to the political and legal restrictions imposed upon Black folks which limited full citizenship and rights of personhood, such as voting rights. The psychological barrier refers to how these physical and political limits impact how Black people may take on the viewpoint of their oppressors and begin to see themselves as "the other" or as "less than" when it comes to their abilities, values, and dreams.

In his next major work, *The Souls of Black Folk,* Du Bois sought to show Black folks that they could break free from the way White folks saw them and begin to see themselves with a new and better light. He wanted Black folks to break free from the psychological barriers limiting their potential. Consider how this effort to inform Black folks about the true nature of their position as a catalyst for radical change parallels Marx's ideas around the proletariat revolution.

Another sociological contribution of Du Bois's work is that of **double consciousness**. Du Bois notes that Black folks hold their identities as Black folks and as Americans simultaneously. White folks have defined being "American" as being White, so the identities of being Black and being "American" are thought of as separate identities by the majority group. Black Americans, therefore, must juggle what it means to be both Black and American in ways that White folks do not need to consider. Du Bois discusses how it may feel like a juggling act to break down barriers while holding onto one's traditions and culture. To break down barriers is not to become more like a White American. It is to widen the definition of what it means to be an American, so "Black" and "American" are not exclusive identities.

Contemporary Sociology

Classic theories established the foundations of sociology. New waves of theorists expanded upon the classic theories to usher in a broader and more nuanced field of study. Contemporary sociological theories fall into three main areas: structural functional theories, conflict/critical theories, and inter/actionist theories.

Structural/Functional Theories

The focus of **structural/functional theories** are social structures and their intended and unintended functions (hence the name *structural/functional theories*). These theories were influenced by Durkheim. Recall, Durkheim had a positive view of social structures imposing limits on "deviant" behavior. In this view, structures such as police departments and U.S. Immigration and Customs Enforcement (ICE) are essential for maintaining order and control in a society. An important tenet of structural/functional theories is the belief that if a social structure exists, then it is assumed to be functional. When a structure is assumed to be functional, it becomes difficult to change or to impose limits on its power or reach. Consider the adage, *"If it ain't broke, don't fix it."* Structural/functional theories tend to believe that if a social structure exists, then it *ain't broke.*

Robert K. Merton

Robert K. Merton (born in Philadelphia, Pennsylvania, 1910) contributes to structuralist/functionalist theories through defining a social structure's *functions*. To Merton, functions are the observable and positive impacts of a social structure which allow it to adapt in effective ways. For example, following the attempted "shoe bombing" incident of 2006, the Transportation Security Administration (TSA) heightened screening requirements at airports to include the removal of shoes for individuals passing through security checkpoints.[12] In Merton's view, the positive function of the TSA (screening passengers for potential threats at airport security checkpoints) was adaptable to new threats (potential shoe bombings), highlighting its ability to survive under new conditions.

However, structuralist/functionalists like Merton also understand that social structures also have **dysfunctions**. Dysfunctions are the observable and negative impacts of a social structure which limit its ability to survive. For example, after the heightening of TSA screening procedures at airport security checkpoints, the airport screening process became longer and more burdensome for all passengers, creating long lines and confusion for the screening process, and this, in turn, amplified frustrations toward the organization as a whole.[13]

To help us weigh the relative functions and dysfunctions of a social structure, Merton detailed two additional functions: **manifest functions** and **latent functions**. Manifest functions are the positive *intended* impacts of a social structure, while latent functions are its positive *unintended* impacts. However, what is positive for one thing (or one group) may be negative for something (or someone) else. These unanticipated consequences can ultimately threaten the survival of social structure if it becomes contested by an outside group.

Structural Theories

The focus of structural theories are social structures themselves. Unlike structural/function theories, structural theories do not lend attention to the structure's functions. Structural theorists concern themselves with both political structures – such as those dictating voting rights – and physical structures – such as security checkpoints at border crossings.

Karl Marx's theories fit within the area of structuralism due to his focus on how the capitalist social structure dictated the lives of individuals based on their social class. A collaborator of Marx who went on to define and expand the area of structuralism was Friedrich Engels (born in what is now Wuppertal, Germany, 1820). Engels's primary interest was in the social structures which defined the lives of, and relationships between, women and men. Engels saw both capitalism and patriarchy as the social structures responsible for the subjugation of women in society. Specifically, Engels believed that the social emphasis on property ownership was responsible for men restricting the rights of women. By prohibiting women from owning property, there was more opportunity for men to own that property. This theoretical framework was built upon the White experience. Yet, you can extend the same theoretical framework of structuralism to the subjugation of Black, Brown, and Indigenous peoples by White people. The desire of property ownership among White men encouraged the creation and maintenance of social structures which subjugated the livelihood of members of other social groups.

Based on this framework, Engels believed the "answer" to women's subjugation in society was to abolish the ownership of private property. Without the goal of private property ownership, Engels believed, there would no longer be incentives to maintain capitalist and patriarchal social structures. Engels's beliefs were somewhat misguided. His work alluded to societies founded on "primitive communism" which he believed existed prior to the existence of capitalism. However, such societies did not actually exist. Yet, the contribution of his thinking to structuralist theories remained important. Future scholars would build upon Engel's framework of considering how social structures create and maintain inequality. Modern feminist theorists, for example, expand on this idea.

Throughout the book, we will engage a structuralist lens to social issues. We will explore what structures may exist below the surface to dictate the organization of social life and reify social inequalities. Identifying and critiquing these structures are at the heart of the field of sociology. Sociologist Peter L. Berger (born in Vienna, Austria, 1929) defined the goal of structuralism – and I would argue, all areas of sociology – as **debunking**.[14] To debunk is to break apart the false narratives put forward by those in power which aim to hide their true intentions or means. For example, rules designed to "protect women" are, often, actually designed to control women's autonomy, or rules designed to "protect children" are, often, designed to control the rights of another, or an overlapping, group – such as LGBTQ+ people. Examples of the latter include policies restricting the ability of same-sex couples to adopt a child, or the enactment of House Bill 1557 in Florida (commonly referred to as the "Don't Say Gay" bill), which imposed limits on the instruction of sexual orientation and gender identity in public schools.[15,16]

Conflict/Critical Theories

Conflict Theory

Conflict theory is an extension of Marx's work. Conflict theorists believe that society is held together by **conflict** and **coercion**. In unequal societies – like those that exist under capitalism – what keeps individuals "in line" and thwarts rebellion are coercive forces like the police, the courts, or the prison system. This line of thinking is in direct opposition to structural/ functional theories, which believe that society is held together by consensus and cohesion.

An important conflict theorist is Ralf Dahrendorf (born in Hamburg, Germany, 1929). Dahrendorf's work gives weight to the beliefs of structural/ functionalists (i.e., society is built on consensus) and conflict theorists (i.e., society is built on conflict). He believed both consensus *and* conflict are present in society, and therefore, sociology needs theories of both elements.[17] One of the foundational elements of Dahrendorf's work is the assertation that power resides in **positions of authority** (such as the position of a Supreme Court Justice), not the inherent power of a particular *person* holding that position. The powerful influence of institutions enforces compliance to rules and social norms. Individuals disadvantaged in society, such as those facing economic hardship or racial discrimination, would rebel if not for the coercive forces of these institutions. But, as Dahrendorf acknowledges, there is an opportunity for conflict between individuals in those positions of power and those over whom they have authority.

To understand such a conflict, consider how even peaceful protestors acting within their constitutional rights may be arrested, by turning to the civil rights movement marches of the 1960s or the Black Lives Matter marches of 2020. Thousands of protestors, including children, were arrested during the civil rights movement marches. One of the most notable figures to be arrested during these marches was Dr. Martin Luther King, Jr.[18] In the Black Lives Matter marches, *The Hill* reported that 17,000 protesters were arrested in just a two-week span – most for low-level offenses such as breaking curfew.[19]

Members of the civil rights movement or Black Lives Matter are what conflict theorists would call **conflict groups**.[20] These groups form based on their own consensus of beliefs that are at odds with the views of the ruling powers. These groups may use protest or other forms of rebellion (e.g., labor strikes) to fight for social change. These visible efforts are also avenues to recruit new members, and the movement can keep going even if the group meets resistance from authority. For example, even if some protestors in a movement are arrested, thwarting their individual efforts (at least temporarily), new members may be called to action – jumping in to replace them in the movement. Conflict groups are powerful agents of social change. We will later discuss a conflict group in comedy and the power of their labor strike.

Critical Theory

Critical theory follows much of the same thought as conflict theory but focuses on culture – versus the economy – as the main driver of social inequality. To Karl Marx, the economy shapes culture. To critical theorists, however, this causal relationship goes in the reverse direction; culture shapes the economy.

Critical theorists believe we are *controlled* by culture; in the same way, Marx believed we are controlled by capitalism and economic forces.

Recall from our discussion of Max Weber, he studied how myriad social factors – not just the economy – operated in society to impact social life. While his primary focus was religion, he also studied the impact and importance of culture. Weber defined **culture industry** as the social structure which controls social life. The culture industry provides a mechanism to sell products and lifestyles. The culture industry is *rational*. It benefits capitalists and serves to homogenize people through the promotion of a particular set of products or ideals.[21] **Mass culture** is the resulting shared set of values and ideals held by people in a society, based upon shared exposure to the same cultural media.

Critical theorists are critical of mass culture for its falseness and repressiveness. **Falseness** refers to how mass culture creates "false realities." Reality television provides clear examples of false realities. It purports to be a real look into real people's lives but it is highly edited, written, and produced. There is very little "real" about it. Similar arguments can be made for commercials and advertisements. They show you images of "what your life could look like" if you purchase a certain product. But most products are not particularly revolutionary or life-altering.

Repressiveness refers to how mass culture's falseness serves to maintain the status quo. Just as Marx described religion the "opium of the people" for how it pacified and sold individuals on ideals which support capitalism, so too is mass culture the opium of the people. It pacifies and sells individuals on false narratives which serve capitalism. Consider how a commercial may market you something based on *"Unhappy with your life? Buy this product!"* and consider how that would differ from a message that asks you to consider how social structures may be responsible for challenges in your life like low wages, unsafe housing, or discrimination based upon personal features such as your sex, race, sexuality, or physical appearance.

Feminist Theory

Mary Wollstonecraft (born in London, England, 1759) is largely considered to be the first prominent feminist thinker. However, at the time of Wollstonecraft's writing, her work was largely ignored in academia, a social structure run almost entirely by, and for, men. Wollstonecraft lays out her feminist framework win her book, *A Vindication of the Rights of Woman* (1792). In the book, Wollstonecraft explains that men and women are not innately differently. It is different socialization and unequal access to resources which result in our society's sex-based hierarchy. Wollstonecraft points to women's limited access to education as the main driver. She describes a future just society wherein women are treated as rational, capable beings.[22]

While early feminist theorists provided important contributions to the sociology and other fields in the social sciences, many early works were told through the lens of White women's experiences and failed to take Black and Brown women's experiences into account. More recent scholarship in the area of feminist theory engages intersectional lenses to understand the unique experiences of women based upon social status and other features of their identity, including expressions of sex, gender, and sexuality, race and ethnicity, and country of origin.

A scholar at the forefront of this movement is bell hooks (born in Hopkinsville, Kentucky, 1952). hook's books include *Ain't I a Woman?: Black Women and Feminism* (1981) and *Feminist Theory: From Margin to Center* (1984) among countless others. hook's work details the unique and overlapping experiences of sexism and racism experienced by Black women, and details how Black women's experiences and personhood were devalued by society and ignored by mainstream feminist theorists. hooks' work was part of the radical feminist movement, which provides inclusive and nuanced frameworks to describe the experiences faced by women – all women – in society, and calls for dismantling of unjust social structures which serve to subordinate women – and particularly, Black women, women of color, and financially disadvantaged women.

Another hugely important figure in this area of work is Patricia Hill Collins (born in Philadelphia, Pennsylvania, 1948). Her book *Black Feminist Thought: Knowledge, Consciousness and the Politics of Empowerment* (1990) describes the origins of Black feminist thought, which Collins notes was born out of Black women's own experiences, not as a rebuttal to White feminist scholarship. Collins drew inspiration for the book from other Black scholars, writers, and artists – including Audre Lorde (born in New York City, New York, 1934), Angela Davis (born in Birmingham, Alabama, 1944), and Alice Walker (born in Eatonton, Georgia, 1944 and is best known for her Pulitzer Prize-winning book *The Color Purple* (1982)). In *Black Feminist Thought*, Collins discusses how oppression based upon features of one's identity, including race, sex, sexuality, and social status, *intersect* and form a *matrix of oppression*. The **matrix of oppression** refers to the system by which people are denied opportunities and are subjected to discrimination based upon the social-valuation of their overlapping identities.[23] Collins further discusses how Black women's experiences at the center of this matrix provide valuable insight into how mechanisms of oppression operate for other individuals and communities.

Critical Theories of Race and Racism (CTRR)

The sociological study of race traces back to the work of W.E.B. Du Bois but many scholars later adapted Du Bois's work. Not unlike early feminist scholarship which focused primarily on the experiences of White women, early race scholars focused primarily on the experiences of men. Black and Brown women were excluded from these conversations.

Scholars like Kimberlé Crenshaw (born in Canton, Ohio, 1959) helped build more comprehensive understandings of people's experiences based upon features of their overlapping identities. Crenshaw coined the term **intersectionality** to refer to the idea that we cannot separate someone's experiences based on *individual* features of their identity, such as race, ethnicity, sex, gender, sexuality, or social status.[24] These features *intersect*. The way a person is treated in society is based upon intersecting features of their identity, such as their race, sex, gender, religion, age, and social status. Contemporary sociological theorists acknowledge that, as individuals cannot separate features of their identity, nor should sociologists.

An intersectional framework allows us to conceptualize how an individual's overlapping identities shape their experiences and contribute to complex and multifaceted systems of oppression. Crenshaw. In the United States, the social treatment of Black women, Latina women, and Alaska Native or American Indian women may differ wildly from each other. The treatment of those groups may also differ from the social treatment of Black men, Latino men, and Alaska Native or American Indian men, trans people, people who do not speak English, people with a visible physical disability, and more. Intersections of identity matter. The reverse is also true, with individuals who hold multiple socially advantageous identities, such as White, Anglo-Saxon, English-speaking, cisgender men without a disability experience matrixes of power that afford them greater privileges and opportunities than people who hold a less advantageous intersection of identities.

Contemporary scholars in the areas of race and racism embrace intersectional frameworks. An important scholar in the area of **critical theories of race and racism** is Eduardo Bonilla-Silva (born in Bellefonte, Pennsylvania, 1962). One of his most well-known works is his 2003 book *Racism without Racists: Colorblind Racism and the Persistence of Racial Inequality in the United States*. In the book, Bonilla-Silva describes the ongoing, pernicious problem of racism in the United States. He describes that racism is baked into our social structures *systematically*, and therefore, continues whether individuals make racist statements or perform racist acts.[25]

One of the Bonilla-Silva's theoretical contributions from this work is in the realm of **color-blindness**. Color-blindness refers to the notion that people and institutions do not treat people differently based upon their race; they are "color-blind" or "do not see race." However, as Bonilla-Silva explains, the notion of color-blindness is simply a new form of racism. It serves to maintain the status quo by implying everyone is treated equally and allowing White individuals to not question their own White privilege, internal biases, or acts of racism.

Queer Theory

Queer theory holds that there are no stable or unchanging features of identity. Queer theory scholars assert that our gender and sexuality are fluid.

These features are not pre-determined (such as by biological sex) and they can change throughout our lives. Queer theory scholars call for greater flexibility in our language and social constructs to break apart the ties between biological sex, gender, and sexuality and to allow for them to shift over time. Not requiring individuals to place themselves in one of the two checkboxes – "female" or "male" – on a governmental form or survey but instead, offering a more representative and open-ended set of options is progress in line with queer theory frameworks.

Queer theory scholars have been wonderfully successful in deconstructing the false binaries society has placed around people to maintain a certain social order. Consider, for example, the work of Eve Kosofsky Sedgwick (born in Dayton, Ohio, 1950), whose prolific writings helped form the foundations of queer theory. In her work, Sedgwick notes that society defines someone's **sexuality** purely based upon the biological sex of the individuals with whom they want to engage in sexual relationships. However, Sedgwick breaks down this narrow conception and offers a more holistic representation of what sexuality is truly composed, including the amount of sex people want to have, the amount of time they spend thinking about sex, and the degree of emotional connection they like to have with their partners, among others. Using our sociological imagination, we can see that these features identified by Sedgwick are, indeed, a part of what we may define as someone's "sexuality." Yet, the term "sexuality" is generally used in a much narrower and less nuanced context.[26]

Postmodernism

As the name implies, postmodern refers to the era after the modern era. Descriptive, right? Think about it this way: the modern era was framed around rationality, and lifestyles and beliefs were relatively consistent from person to person. Individuality was not "in." In the **postmodern** era, by comparison, there is less emphasis on rationality and greater emphasis on individuality of experiences and beliefs. As an example of this distinction, consider paintings. If you have seen paintings from the modern era, they were most likely direct representations of life: people, animals, houses, fruit. A skilled artist could closely mimic a photograph and that was the goal. If you consider paintings from the postmodern era, however, they tend to be more abstract. You and the person standing next to you may have completely different interpretations of the painting's contents and meaning. Unlike the modern era, wherein the goal was to mimic a photograph, in the postmodern era, the goal was to play with visual structure to convey a mood or feeling. The same is true for other artistic media in the postmodern era, such as films. Films from the postmodern era are less linear and more interpretive than their modern ancestors.

Now, let us move out of art example and move into sociology. In this book, we will consider postmodernism in two ways: (1) we will discuss theories – notably from Jean Baudrillard – which aimed to make sense of so-cial life in the postmodern era and (2) we will note how these theories which sought to make sense of postmodern life were, themselves, representative of the era in which they were created.

Jean Baudrillard (born in Reims, France, 1929) was a French sociologist who saw postmodern life as that which was marked by consumerism. We no longer define ourselves by our labor, but by our consumption behaviors. We will return to this idea when we discuss distinction (Pierre Bourdieu) in consumption. In this view, we – quite literally – wear our identities on our sleeves. Baudrillard understood we live in a world of **hyperconsumption**, which he defined as consuming at rates beyond our needs or means. We will return to this idea when we discuss how lifestyles are sold to us through ad-vertising and social media. Specifically, we discuss it in terms of being sold goods based on unrealistic, or entirely false, realities. This is what Baudril-lard would call a **simulation**, a fake or unrealistic version of a situation or product. Increasingly in the postmodern era, people are inundated with simu-lations. It can be hard to know what is and is not real. When a simulation is indistinguishable from reality, that is known as **hyperreality**. Think about social media. Social media platforms display "real" content but such content is commonly heavily curated or edited, or in some instances, fake entirely. Products and dreams are sold to us based on these simulations. Later in this book, we will expand on Baudrillard's definition of simulations to discuss if they need to be viewed through a negative lens – or if they can be used to convey emotional truths.

In addition to theories aimed at understanding postmodern life – like the framework developed by Baudrillard – theories put forward by theorists in the postmodern era tend to be less rational and linear than theories put for-ward in the modern era. Modern theorists tried to explain how the whole world worked by using one lens or concept which they applied again and again, often in large volumes of work. Postmodern theories tend to be more fragmented and specific; they offer one piece of a large, colorful, and moving puzzle. Postmodernists understand that the world is nuanced, as are indi-viduals' experiences within it. Their theories match that understanding. In this way, postmodernists reject some modern norms and assumptions. For example, postmodernists attempt to reflect the language of the communities they are studying, rather than defining their lives for them.

Inter/actionist Theories

Symbolic Interactionism

Developed by George Herbert Mead (born in South Hadley, Massachusetts, 1863) and Charles Horton Cooley (born in Ann Arbor, Michigan, 1864), **symbolic interactionism** refers to the idea that we interact with each other based on shared meaning of symbols. This shared understanding stems from social norms, popular culture, and historical or cultural traditions.[27] It is through social interaction that people learn about symbols' meanings. Consider symbols related to a religious service. The religious institution *holds* the meaning of its symbols but it is through personal interaction – with family members, fellow worshipers, religious leaders, etc. – that the meaning of those symbols is acquired by a new member.

An important facet of symbolic interactionism is the understanding that individual people have their own ability to think, and thus, the interpretation of a symbol may differ from one person to another or within one person as context shifts. Symbols are not static. They can evolve and change. However, despite the adaptability of symbolic meaning, there remains a root understanding in society of a symbol's meaning which enables understanding and communication between people.

The meaning behind symbols and the process of creating and sharing meaning through social interaction also serve to shape personal identity. We perform our identity. Our manner of dress, our language, and our mannerisms, for example, all serve to convey information to others about our gender, race and ethnicity, religion, social class, or intersections therein.

Mead, importantly, defined the sociological concept of the self. The **self**, according to Mead, is the identity of an individual as defined by oneself. While individual beliefs, preferences, and behaviors may change over the course of one's lifetime, the self is a relatively stable identity. Through **socialization**, individuals learn about social structures, institutions, and groups, and it is only *from* that learning that we understand how our self stands apart from others. In this way, the concept of the self is inherently tied to the concept of distinction. Individuals must first understand how they fit into the larger society and social groups to then distinguish themselves from them.

Rational Choice Theory

Rational choice theorists posit that people act in service of achieving their goals. How people achieve their goals is based upon the set of options available to them. From those options, people choose the best course of action using **rational** thought. In other words, they base their actions based upon what is most logical. Not everyone has access to the same resources. People face two primary **constraints** in the process of reaching goals through rational choices: (1) limited access to resources and (2) restrictions imposed by social structures.[28]

The first of these constraints is straightforward. Your goal may be, for example, to own a nice car. Someone who has a lot of money in their savings account has several options: they could go down to the dealership and pay cash for the car, they could take out a loan to buy the car, or they could steal the car. Given their resources, the most rational choice may be to pay cash for the car, saving them money on a loan's interest payment and saving them potential jail time for theft. Someone with more limited financial resources, however, would have a different set of options. They could take out a loan for the car (if they qualify), they could pick up another job or side hustle to earn additional money for the car, or they could steal the car. The "rational" choice may be less clear here than it was for the person with greater means.

The second of these constraints refers to how the rules or expectations of a social system may limit the options available to a person. This may be time. In the United States, many workplaces are based on a 40-hour workweek. Acknowledging many people work more than 40 hours per week and/or work piecemeal jobs that require a lot of transit and mental juggling, let us start with this basic example. If you work 40 hours per week, you may not have a lot of extra time on your hands to pursue a goal, like writing a novel or training for a marathon. This becomes even more difficult if, on top of your 40-hour workweek, you have caregiving responsibilities. Social structures set expectations about our caregiving responsibilities, which vary by gender, religion, country of origin, and social status, among others.

As we conclude our discussion of rational choice theory, I encourage you to look back on this section and consider how the classic and contemporary sociological theories work together. The field of sociology is always growing and evolving. None of the individual theories discussed here are fully comprehensive or explanatory, but taken together, they help us better understand our social world.

Summary

Sociologists use theories to make sense of the social world. Theories provide a framework for understanding social phenomena. Without such frameworks, we would be unable to organize and synthesize social phenomena into digestible and understandable sets of information. Instead, everything we see and experience would exist in our brains as isolated anecdotes.

This section provides a brief overview of many foundational sociological theorists and their core contributions to the field. Each sociological theory represents a specific era and perspective. The theories build upon one another, expanding the field over time. No individual theory is perfect but they provide a helpful building-block for improved understanding.

This book views comedy through the same lens. If we do not use a sociological framework to understand the evolution of comedy over time, then we would only see pieces of comedy as isolated bits. Instead, we can apply a sociological framework and begin to understand comedy as a social institution with norms, rules, and power structures. Viewing comedy through this frame will bolster our ability to apply sociological theories to myriad other areas of social life.

Throughout the remainder of this book, we call back to the theories introduced in this chapter and practice applying sociological frameworks to the social world through comedy. We will see that comedy, too, represents specific eras and perspectives. Both sociologists and comedians are reflective of the thinking of their time. Even if outdated, they tell us a lot about comedy and sociology today.

In the following chapters, we will dig deeper into core topics of sociology and have opportunities to engage with these theories. We will see their concepts come to life through comedic bits and examples. Further, we will practice thinking like a social theorist by analyzing the field of comedy as another social institution with rules and hierarchies.

Discussion Questions

1-1: Describe what Karl Marx means by the "means of production." What are the "means of production" in today's world? Do you believe the proletariat are still exploited and alienated today, as they were in the time of Marx's writing?

1-2: With a classmate, discuss a real-world example of Max Weber's concept of rationalization you have seen in your lifetime. How do you think this example ties to the iron cage?

1-3: Do you agree with Émile Durkheim that deviance is functional for society? Why or why not?

1-4: Consider how you would update Thorstein Veblen's theories related to conspicuous consumption and conspicuous leisure to incorporate modern-day technologies, such as smartphones and social media.

1-5: With a classmate, discuss the relationship between social media and Peter L. Berger's concept of debunking. Do you think social media is a useful tool for debunking, or does it do more harm than good?

1-6: Describe the distinction between conflict and coercion, according to conflict theorists.

1-7: At the time of Weber's writing of the culture industry and mass culture, radio, magazines, and film were the dominant media. How do you think these media transitions to television and the Internet bolster, or hinder, the power of the culture industry and mass culture?

1-8: Discuss the similarities and differences of Patricia Hill Collins's concept of the matrix of oppression and Kimberlé Crenshaw's concept of intersectionality. Describe can they both be used to understand people's experiences and opportunities.

1-9: Do you agree with Eduardo Bonilla-Silva that color-blindness is not the absence of racism but instead is a new form of racism? Why or why not? Justify your answer.

1-10: Queer theory holds that there are no stable or unchanging features of identity, such as those related to gender and sexuality. George Herbert Mead defined the sociological concept of "the self" as one's identity as defined by oneself, and the self is relatively stable. Explain if and how these concepts can co-exist.

Notes

1 There is a nod to this in Bo Burnham's song "How the World Works" from his 2021 Netflix special *Inside*, discussed later in this book.
2 Goldblatt, D., Held, D., Perraton, J., & McGrew, A. G. (1999). *Global Transformations: Politics, Economics, and Culture*. Stanford University Press.
3 Weber, M. (1904). *The Protestant Ethic and the Spirit of Capitalism* (Abridged edition). Merchant Books.
4 Marx, K. (1970). *Critique of Hegel's Philosophy of Right*, trans. Annette Jolin and Joseph O'Malley. Cambridge University Press, 1843.
5 Weber, M. (1904). *The Protestant Ethic and the Spirit of Capitalism* (Abridged edition). Merchant Books.
6 Weber, M. (1981). *From Max Weber: Essays in Sociology* (H. Gerth, Ed.; Nachdr. d. Ausg. 1958). Oxford University Press.
7 Wirth, L. (1945). The Problem of Minority Groups. In *The Science of Man in the World Crisis* (p. 347–372). edited by R. Linton. Columbia University Press.
8 Durkheim, É. (1893). *The Division of Labor in Society*. trans. by W. D. Halls, intro. by Lewi Coser. Macmillan Publishers.
9 Durkheim, É. (1897). *Suicide*. Routledge & Kegan Paul.
10 Durkheim, É. (1893). *The Division of Labor in Society*. trans. by W. D. Halls, intro. by Lewi Coser. Macmillan Publishers.
11 Du Bois, W. E. B. (1899). *The Philadelphia Negro*. University of Pennsylvania Press.
12 Schaper, D. (2021, September 10). It Was Shoes on, No Boarding Pass or ID. But Airport Security Forever Changed on 9/11. *NPR*. https://www.npr.org/2021/09/10/1035131619/911-travel-timeline-tsa
13 Gumbrecht, J. (2012, June 2). *How Much Do We Really Hate the TSA?* https://www.cnn.com/2012/06/01/travel/tsa-complaints/index.html
14 Berger, P. L. (1963). *Invitation to Sociology: A Humanistic Perspective*. Anchor.
15 Harris, E. A. (2017, June 20). Same-Sex Parents Still Face Legal Complications. *The New York Times*. https://www.nytimes.com/2017/06/20/us/gay-pride-lgbtq-same-sex-parents.html
16 *Florida's New 'Don't Say Gay' Laws: What They Mean for Kids*. (2023, April 20). Time. https://time.com/6273364/florida-dont-say-gay-expansion/
17 Dahrendorf, R. (1959). *Class and Class Conflict in Industrial Society*. Routledge.
18 James, F. (2009, August 11). *Civil Rights Protesters Granted Pardon for 1963 Birmingham Arrests: The Two-Way: NPR*. https://www.npr.org/sections/thetwo-way/2009/08/civil_rights_protesters_grante.html
19 Somvichian-Clausen, A. (2020, October 29). *The Aftermath of the Black Lives Matter Protests—Where Do They Stand Now? – The Hill*. https://thehill.com/changing-america/respect/equality/523416-the-aftermath-of-the-black-lives-matter-protests-where-do/
20 Lewis, C. A. (1956). *The Functions of Social Conflict*. Routledge & Kegan Paul PLC.
21 Adorno, T. W., & Bernstein, J. M. (2020). *The Culture Industry: Selected Essays on Mass Culture* (2nd ed.). Routledge. https://doi.org/10.4324/9781003071297

22 Wollstonecraft, M. (1792). *A Vindication of the Rights of Woman*. J. Johnson, No. 72, St. Paul's Church-Yard.
23 Collins, P. H. (1990). *Black Feminist Thought: Knowledge, Consciousness, and the Politics of Empowerment*. Hyman.
24 Crenshaw, K. (n.d.). *Demarginalizing the Intersection of Race and Sex: A Black Feminist Critique of Antidiscrimination Doctrine, Feminist Theory and Antiracist Politics*. 1989(1), 31.
25 Bonilla-Silva, E. (2003). *Racism without Racists: Color-Blind Racism and the Persistence of Racial Inequality in America*. Rowman & Littlefield Publishers.
26 Sedgwick, E. K. (1990). *Epistemology of the Closet* (Writing in Book edition). University of California Press.
27 Herbert Blumer (1986). *Symbolic Interactionism: Perspective and Method*. University of California Press.
28 Friedman, D., & Hechter, M. (1988). The contribution of rational choice theory to macrosociological research. *Sociological Theory*, 6(2), 201–218.

2 Introduction to Sociological Research

We just discussed foundational sociological theories to help us understand social phenomena and the structure of our world. In this chapter, we begin with comedy's definitions of sociology and comedy and dive deeper into the connection between the two fields. We then explain how you can use scientific methods to conduct your own sociological research. This chapter introduces you to the components of the scientific method, including forming a question, developing a hypothesis, conducting a literature review, collecting data, executing your study, and interpreting and sharing your results.

Defining Sociology

Sociology is the study of how people interact with each other through the constraints placed on them by social structures and institutions. Sociology is also a way of seeing the world, a way to understand our culture and society, and a way to make sense of how our culture and society shape our personal choices. Sociology teaches you to step outside of your own experiences, values, and fears, and to see the world as an outsider.

This is an important skill for a researcher. One must be able to see things as objectively as possible when conducting a study – so you can ask the right questions, select the right measures and analytic strategies, and interpret results appropriately. In this section, we will walk through how to conduct sociological research.

Defining Comedy

Comedy is used throughout the book to highlight sociological concepts, including those related to sociological research. Viewing the world as an outsider is the tool of both sociologists *and* comedians. What, then, is the difference between comedy and sociology? Is it laughter? Well, not all comedy necessitates laughter, and we sometimes laugh in a sociology classroom.

Before I define comedy for the purpose of this book, let us acknowledge how many recent comics are severing the idea that comedy provokes or requires laughter. Instead, much recent comedic work (television, movies, and standup) strives, instead, to provoke a deeper emotional response. *Vulture*

DOI: 10.4324/9781003469537-3

editor Jesse David Fox defines this era as **post-comedy**. Recall the sociological concept of postmodernism. Compared to the modern era, in the postmodern era, there was more room for individuality in how people see and experience the world. Art became less literal and more interpretive. Indeed, this book will discuss the ways comedians have and will always push boundaries to reframe what defines comedy as comedy.

This book engages a broad definition of comedy. This book defines **comedy** as any written, oral, or visual display which presents the world in a nontraditional light. Comedy, according to this definition, is any text or performance that reacts to the zeitgeist by "flipping the script." Flipping the script is what links comedy and sociology. In comedy, the result is often, but not always, laughter and surprise. More fundamental to this book's definition of comedy is that it speaks truth to power and results in the disruption of the status quo. Inherent in this definition is that comedy respects the humanity of all people and is not derogatory or traumatizing. This mirrors the goals of a sociology classroom.

I want to share a quote from Hershal Pandya, a satirical writer who contributes to publications such as *Vulture* and *McSweeney*'s who lives in Toronto, Ontario, Canada. Pandya writes (2017):

> For better or for worse, comedy ... isn't given inherent meaning by the people who make it; it takes on meaning over time as it is consumed and analyzed by audiences. To put it another way, if an artist sketches a fruit bowl in a forest and no one is around to consume it, can it still be considered a subtle depiction of the loneliness of the human condition?[1]

To Pandya, comedy does not exist without reaction. The art form itself is dependent upon audiences reacting to its assumed meaning. Going with Pandya's farcical example: a sketch of a fruit bowl exists as a sketch of a fruit bowl, absent of audience views or reaction. It exists. But its meaning wholly rests on it being seen, interpreted, and emotionally felt by an audience.

A sketch of a fruit bowl can exist in a forest; comedy cannot. Comedy needs an audience to disrupt reality; to convey messages of hope, joy, and light – of pain and sadness – out of the human experience. In this way, comedy is an art form with power and opportunity. Comedy is a performance. Sociology will help us investigate the meaning and impact of that performance.

Recall this book's introduction to crowd work. **Crowd work** is when a comedian engages with the audience. Crowd work is an exercise in symbolic interactionism through identifying or playing with shared understandings. It is also an exercise in social norms. Comedians may poke fun at an audience member – something that may be appropriate in a comedy club, but not another space – or themselves. Crowd work is a part of the performance. Querying the audience allows a comedian to better tailor their jokes for the specific group of people in attendance. We can break these shared understandings apart using a sociological lens. How a comedian tailors a joke for one crowd versus another is a sociological exercise.

This book will break comedy down into its parts as a practice for you to do this in all areas of your life. The Internet, social media, television, films, and advertisements all have a big influence on the lives of many of us. The analysis of comedy – across all these platforms – is not merely a fun exercise. It teaches you to consume media like a sociologist. It teaches you to consider whose voices and stories are being told, and whose are not. It will teach you to question the veracity of what you are seeing on the screen, and subsequently, teach you to question if any falseness is meant to *teach* you something or to *sell* you something.

Before we move forward with our introduction to sociological research methods, we need to begin with a sociological foundation: everything is a performance. Your professor at the front of the sociology classroom is performing. You are performing for your classmates. And comedians perform. We need to remember that throughout the book as we discuss sociological and comedic examples.

To elucidate this point, let us start with an example from comedian and actress Maria Bamford (born in Port Hueneme, California, 1970). In her 2012 Netflix special, *The Special Special Special!*, Bamford breaks from the traditional format by performing her standup set in her living room to an audience of two: her parents. In this special, Bamford's whimsical yet sharp content, her unusual venue, and her tight guest list were not the only features that made her special unique. What is really unique about this special is the way Bamford acknowledges the fact that it is, indeed, a performance. During the special, she takes a break to put in her dog's medical eye drops. Bamford asks her father if he needed to use the bathroom, and when he said yes, the screen cuts to a plain black screen showcasing the text "Pee Break" (à la the classic movie intermission screen). Their delivery pizza arrives. Bamford breaks the fourth wall of a traditional comedy special.

Using a sociological lens, the fact that Bamford broke the script to do things a standard comedy special would never do (like taking a pizza break) allows the audience to see what elements producers usually plan around or hide to make a traditional comedy special happen. Bamford's interruptions were, of course, planned. But they gave the audience a view into the stark contrast of how a lived-in life (with pet's medical needs, peeing, and eating) does not fit into the confines of a traditional comedy special.

It takes a lot of planning and editing to make a seamless and uninterrupted performance. This is something oft discussed around social media. Selfies are curated; someone may take fifty images before posting the best "candid" shot. Instagram posts compose the highlight reel of people's lives. Social media is the front stage of people's lives, and so are standup specials for most comedians. Bamford's scripted airing of her back stage in *The Special Special Special!* reminds audiences of the amount of curation that goes into traditional comedy specials. We will contextualize "front stage" and "back stage" in sociological terms later in this book.

I want to highlight one of my favorite jokes from this special, which contains a very sociological sentiment. Bamford jokes: "I wish that science … would come up with a brain ride where you could take a ride in someone's brain and see all their thoughts and their feelings." She continues, "I know there's a low-tech version just called listening, but I want a ride!"[2] Breaking this joke apart sociologically, we can see how Bamford sets up the audience to be excited about this sci-fi invention. The audience is likely thinking: "Can you imagine?! A ride where you can get inside someone's brain?! Think of the possibilities!" Then, Bamford flips the script and reminds people this already exists: it is called listening. I see this as a core function of what comedy has always had the ability to do: remind people how to listen. Comedy reminds people that no matter how the platforms, messages, and performers change over time, there is no technology or revolution better than human connection.

Listening is an important part of comedy. Something I have thought a lot about during the writing of this book is the notion that one cannot be considered funny without being heard. Before moving on, I want to explore the relationship between listening, comedy, and sociology using one more example: the show *How To With John Wilson* (hereafter referred to as *How To*). *How To* was created by documentary filmmaker John Wilson (born in New York City, New York, 1986) and premiered on HBO in 2020. The show is kind, smart, interesting, and ... *maybe funny?* HBO bills it as a comedy, and I think that is appropriate. I say funny with a question mark because what most viewers take away from the show are honest, heartwarming, and surprising stories about real people. It is funny, but in an empathetic way, not in a laugh-out-loud way.

You almost never see Wilson in the entire series. Wilson carries a camera facing in front of him as he navigates New York City in search of the answers to life's questions. Each episode centers around the pursuit of answering a specific question or exploring a specific topic. Episode titles include pursuits such as "How To Make Small Talk," "How To Cover Your Furniture," and "How To Cook the Perfect Risotto" (all titles featured here appear in season one). The episodes begin with Wilson exploring those topics but the show takes unexpected turns as he follows whatever people, situations, or tangents present themselves before him. He opens doors to explore what is on the other side.

There is a lot of footage that went into the creation of this show. Wilson filmed for years, collecting B-roll of New Yorkers living their lives (it is worth noting: the show got signed releases from everyone who appears on the show). You see some truly wild behavior, like a woman casually placing a pigeon into a Duane Reade bag as if it were a magazine she planned to finish reading later, with Wilson's voiceover adding a narrative structure to the footage. In someone else's hands, I imagine the show would look very different. *How To* depicts unexpected behavior, wild beliefs, and fringe groups of people. It is easy to see how someone might mine such footage for humor by making people the butt of the joke. But Wilson makes the show with such patience, empathy, and wonder that the audience is endeared toward the people on the screen. Wilson mines the humanity out of what would otherwise seem weird, strange, or worthy of derision.

In this, Wilson's comedic perspective shines. What I love about this show is the way it represents the everyday in a new light. This is inherently sociological. Wilson is not trying to prove a personal experience with film-as-evidence (an idea we will return to when we discuss docu-comedy specials). Instead, he is trying to broaden his view of the world. He is trying to uncover life's hidden gems – the mundane, the strange, the tacky – to show life as it really is and highlight the beauty in it. In doing so, Wilson shows unpolished portraits of peoples' lives.

Let us compare that to the approach of popular television reality shows, which can exemplify the sociological concept of falseness. **Falseness** is a term used by critical theorists to define how **mass culture**, such as through television and movies, "false reality." *The Real Housewives* franchise, for example, has been running on Bravo since 2006 and has eleven separate series in the United States alone, including Atlanta, Beverly Hill, New York City, and Orange County. The series follows the lives of rich women as they lead opulent and highly dramatic lives. While the people are "real" in that they play themselves and are situated within their real homes and families, the circumstances in which they find themselves are often fabricated. Said differently: the production team sets them up, amps them up, and heavily edits the footage afterward. The shows feel authentic but they are actually scripted and edited to fit a particular narrative.[3]

Wilson's approach, however, attempts to capture what would normally happen after cameras stop rolling. For example, in the episode of *How To* titled "How To Make Small Talk," Wilson takes a trip to Cancún, Mexico (so he would have some travel-related small talk fodder upon his return to NYC), and there he finds that MTV is filming for spring break. In Cancún, Wilson meets a man named Chris, who presents as a wild and obnoxious party guy who seems a little too old for MTV spring break. This wild, partier image of Chis is all most reality shows or documentaries would capture (and maybe MTV did just that). But Wilson keeps talking to Chris and he eventually learns that Chris is in Cancún processing his grief following a friend's death by suicide. The conversation is honest, vulnerable, and makes the audience question their original judgments of Chris.

We only see the interaction and feel this connection to Chris because Wilson kept the interaction going after even after most reality or documentary film crews would have stopped filming. Wilson spends time with people in their own settings. He understands that everyone has a unique perspective and he aims to let them share it, in their own words, on a platform to which they normally do not have access.[4] Wilson's artistic and comedic perspective is simply to listen and be warmly receptive to whatever people want to share. Wilson listens to people who are normally overlooked, underrepresented, underappreciated, or misunderstood, and he does so with patience and empathy.

Comedy is about breaking down, or breaking wide open, the specifics and absurdities of what we are doing in our everyday lives. So is sociology. Both fields are about asking new questions, letting people speak for themselves, and sharing the answers with broad audiences – whether that be to crowds of drunk people in dark basements or to rooms of academics and students (I'll let you be the judge which goes with the comedian and which goes with the sociologist). Comedy seems like it is about talking (standup *is* one person with a microphone, after all) but I hope this book effectively makes the case that comedy is first and foremost about listening and observing. So is sociological research.

The Scientific Method

We will continue to break apart comedy throughout the book to practice our sociological knowledge and skills. As you hone your skills as a sociologist, you will start seeing the world a little differently. You will start asking more questions and seeking more answers. That is the beginning of sociological research.

Let us start with the scientific method as used in sociology. The **scientific method** refers to developing a theory about how the social world works – usually informed by an observation, paradox, or curiosity – then testing the theory using empirical data. The scientific method has six key parts: (1) ask a question, (2) conduct a literature review, (3) develop a testable hypothesis, (4) collect your data, (5) execute your study, and (6) interpret and share your results.

Throughout the book, we will detail the results of several forms of sociological research study. We will briefly introduce those forms here. But first, let us start with some anecdotes about why we must, first, be very conscious of the questions we ask.

Part 1: Ask the Right Question

Part 1 of sociological research is identifying what topics to study and which questions you seek to answer. There is a lot more bias in this part of the process than we often consider. So let us spend a little time here before moving onto methodology.

Research shows that men reinforce gender stereotypes through humor. Specifically, men lift up the humor of men and belittle the humor of women. The expected role of women in comedy, then, is to appreciate men's jokes. Humor scholars Jimmy Carr and Lucy Greeves note in their book *Only Joking: What's So Funny About Making People Laugh?* (2006) that many men are so opposed to the idea of women being funny that they refuse to let women make them laugh.[5] There are myriad examples from popular culture we could use as examples for men not wanting to acknowledge women's humor. In the early days of *Saturday Night Live*, for example, there are accounts of male actors not being interested in acting in sketches written by the women writers.[6] We can also turn to examples like the statement made by Jerry Lewis (born in Newark, New Jersey, 1926), who, at a comedy festival in 2000, stated that he is not a fan of any female comedians. Martin Short pressed Lewis on this point, saying that he must surely like Lucille Ball, to which Lewis simply and assuredly responded: "No."[7,8]

Research by psychology professors Eric R. Bressler, Rod A. Martin, and Sigal Balshine (2006) concludes that men believe what defines a good sense of humor in women is being a "humor appreciator." While having a good sense of humor in men is being a "humor producer."[9] The body of sociological research on gender and humor highlights that being funny is what's desired and expected of men, and recognizing the humor of men is what's desired and expected of women.[10] Ken Jennings discusses in his book *Planet Funny* (2018) that humor research studies spanning decades had for a long time put forward the conclusion that men are funnier than women. Much of that work found that women do not laugh at sex-based humor (as in humor focusing on the differences between men and women) as much as men do, which was used as a marker of women's inferior sense of humor.[11] However, more recent and more nuanced research studies show that women are simply averse to sex-based humor that makes them "the butt of the joke."[12]

It is important to highlight that most of these earlier studies were conducted by men. The way sense of humor was measured in these earlier, less-nuanced research studies was defined by male-centric understandings of humor. No research is entirely value-free or objective, nor is sociology. When we conduct research guided by our own pre-conceived notions about what humor is or is not, we insert bias into the outcome before we even begin. This has happened in research labs and in comedy clubs alike.

Listening is an important part of comedy. Something I have thought a lot about during the writing of this book is the notion that one cannot be considered funny without being heard. Recall that Bressler and colleagues (2006) found that men believe what defines a "good sense of humor" for men is being a humor producer, while having a "good sense of humor" for women is being a humor appreciator.[13] Let us think about that more specifically as it relates to being *heard*. Consider two scenarios of someone telling a simple street joke in Figure 2.1(a) and (b).

Figures 2.1 (a) and 2.1(b) Who Is Funnier? Comic *(Continued)*

Figures 2.1 (Continued)

Who is funnier? The person on the left may certainly think *they* are funnier, based on evidence that they (a) got a laugh at their joke or (b) have a wild or funny orange juice story that will thrill others. Witnesses to either of these two interactions may think that the person on the left is funnier, too. There just is not a lot of evidence in support of person on the right's humor. This is because person on the right was interrupted and talked over as if their joke was less important than whatever the person on the left had to say.

This is what it means to have your voice silenced. People cannot appreciate what you have to say when someone else speaks over you, when no one else is listening, or when you were not welcomed into the room in the first place. This is something I first thought about when I heard and read multiple pieces from comedians highlighting how Johnny Carson, host of *The Tonight Show Starring Johnny Carson* from 1962 to 1992, changed the game when it came to interviewing comedians on late night. He gave the comedians time and space to tell their stories. He let their stories breathe.

This seems obvious in late night now but it was not at the time (and, today, is still not true for other programs like daytime talk shows). Most late night television hosts at the time did not have the same comedic sensibility. Their job was to keep the conversation flowing by peppering the guest with questions. When the host heard a pause, they jumped in to keep the momentum flowing. The problem with this approach is that interruption kills comedy. Carson, however, knew that when a comedian took a beat, it meant a punchline was coming – not a dead end. Comedy requires patience and patience requires respect and empathy.

Part 2: Conduct a Literature Review

A literature review is a systematic review of related studies. These may include studies in the same general area, those asking similar questions or analyzing the same community but from a different lens. Literature reviews allow you to understand what is known and what is unknown in your area of study.

You would not want to embark on a time- and resource-consuming research study if an identical study was recently conducted by another research. Literature reviews allow you to tailor your research study to build on existing knowledge while filling in important gaps in understanding. You can use this information to develop your research question (informed by what remains unknown) and form your hypothesis (informed by what is already known).

Part 3: Develop a Hypothesis

A hypothesis is a proposed explanation for how a social phenomenon works. Your hypothesis should be informed by your literature review. Even if your exact research question has not been asked in the past, you likely encountered similar work in your literature review which informed your understanding how variables move together. In this step, you will identify your independent (or *cause*) variables and dependent (or *effect*) variables for analysis.

Part 4: Collect Your Data

Now that we have our hypothesis, we can figure out how to best test it. Your first decision is whether your study would best benefit from quantitative or qualitative data. **Quantitative data** is information presented using numbers. Researchers using quantitative data, for example, may statistically analyze information contained in a spreadsheet to understand something about the social world. These data may come from survey responses, vital records (e.g., birth and death records), or social media data, among others. **Qualitative data** is information presented with words. Researchers using qualitative data, for example, may analyze information obtained while interviewing or observing subjects. The researcher may look for overall patterns or themes and write up their findings in a narrative framework. Alternatively, a researcher may choose to use a mixed-methods approach. A **mixed-methods** approach integrates quantitative and qualitative data sources, so a researcher can analyze a topic from multiple angles.

Now that you have decided if your study would best benefit from quantitative data, qualitative data, or mixed-methods, your second decision is how you will *get* those data. There are two primary forms you can select for your study: primary and secondary. **Primary data** refers to data collected by the researcher (such as by conducting qualitative interviews or an ethnography) and **secondary data** refers to data collected by another researcher or organization at a previous time (such as using data collected for a large, national survey conducted the prior year).

Once you have decided on quantitative or qualitative, and primary or secondary, you can move onto the final decision in this step: which data collection method is appropriate for your study. Several data collection methods core to sociological research are outlined below.

Before we discuss data collection techniques, we need to differentiate between populations and samples. Your **population** is everyone you hope to learn something about. If you are conducting a study about standup comedians in Los Angeles, you are (presumably) hoping to learn something about *all* standup comedians in Los Angeles. Even if there are further signifiers within your study – such as all Black women comedians in Los Angeles – your population still represents a large and likely unmanageable group in terms of your time and resources as a researcher (here, your population is all Black women comedians in Los Angeles). So instead of using data from everyone in your population, you may use data from just a sample of them.

A **sample** is a subset of the population, which is generally of a manageable size and allows you to learn something about the population. **Sample size** is the number of individuals included in your sample. A good sample should be representative of your population. **Representative**, in this context, refers to how well your sample matches your population on key indicators. For example, researchers generally strive for samples to match populations on indicators such as race, ethnicity, sex, age, and region or country of origin. If collecting your own data (primary data), you may choose to match your sample on additional indicators which may be important in your analysis. You want to ensure your data allow you to make inferences about your population of interest.

Quantitative

SURVEY RESEARCH

In a survey, respondents answer a battery of questions about their experiences, behaviors, wants, or opinions. It may be in the form of an interview – generally in-person or over the telephone – or in a written questionnaire provided for or mailed to the respondent. Surveys are a very common tool for sociological research for several reasons. First, they can provide a high level of anonymity, which aids in the truthfulness and forthrightness of respondent answers. Second, they can be distributed to many individuals, so is a good tool for researchers who need large sample sizes. Third, they can be distributed to wide and targeted geographic areas (especially if conducted over the phone or distributed through the mail), so respondents can be selected for, or later weighted on, characteristics for which the researcher may want a representative sample.

This means the researcher wants their sample to match, as closely as possible, the underlying population they are studying. For example, if the researcher wants to know something about residents of the United States as a whole, they would want the distribution of their sample (i.e., survey respondents) to match their population (i.e., all residents of the United States) on characteristics such as the age, sex, race, ethnicity, region of residence, religious observation, and political affiliation. Getting such a distribution is much easier to achieve with a survey than with, for example, qualitative interviews or ethnographies.

SOCIAL NETWORK ANALYSIS

In social network analysis, researchers seek to understand the formal and in-formal relationships between social groups. Researchers commonly look at the number of ties (e.g., how many connections does someone have) and the strength of ties (e.g., people you could call in an emergency versus loose so-cial media connections). Researchers may be interested in how whole social groups interact with one another ("socio-centric"; e.g., if and how politicized groups on the Internet interact with groups of differing ideologies or if they primarily exist in an echo chamber), or how individual actors interact with fel-low members of their primary social group ("egocentric"; e.g., the frequency or manner in which connections of the group communicate with one another). Researchers often analyze if features of someone's social identity – such as race, ethnicity, sex, gender, sexuality, religion, and social class – are associated with one's social networks and interactions therein.

CONTENT ANALYSIS

In content analysis, a researcher analyzes media content (e.g., film, television, commercials, music, and visual art) to understand something about the social norms of the culture by which it was created. Researchers interpret, catego-rize, and quantify the words and images presented to understand broader themes. For example, content analysis has been used to examine stereotypic beliefs held about Alaska Native and American Indian people in the United States through the way they are portrayed in film and television.

Qualitative

QUALITATIVE INTERVIEW

In an interview, a researcher asks a respondent to answer a series of open-ended questions which were selected to gather information on a specific topic(s). Interviews may be conducted in-person or over the telephone/video chat. Interviews allow the researcher to ask follow-up questions, probe deeper in certain areas, and/or take the interview in new directions based on a respondent's answers and experiences. A benefit of qualitative interviews is that they grant the interviewee time and opportunity to answer in their own words – as compared to surveys, in which respondents are usually asked to answer from a set of pre-determined responses. Such flexibility makes quali-tative interviews a great data collection technique for complex topics related to experiences and identities.

FIELD RESEARCH

Field research is used to understand the human behaviors and social dynam-ics tied to a particular setting (e.g., courtrooms, public libraries, and comedy clubs). Researchers go out into these spaces and observe elements such as the physical space, how people interact with the space, and how people interact with one another while there. The space is important but it serves as a backdrop for understanding human behavior and dynamics. The goal is to better understand *why* people behave the way the way they do. For example, we will discuss throughout the book why some behaviors are normal and acceptable at comedy clubs that are not in college classrooms. There are three primary forms of field research: ethnography, participant observation, and the case study.

ETHNOGRAPHY

In ethnographic research, researchers embed themselves within a community to observe the natural behaviors, social structures, and social dynamics occurring in those communities. This type of research takes a lot of time to build up trust within the community. People tend to behave differently when being observed by outsiders, so by embedding oneself as an "insider," the ethnographer enhances their chances of observing people acting naturally. Ethnographic research is a great data collection technique for when a researcher wants an in-depth and nuanced analysis of a small community or small number of people. To better understand the social dynamics of local standup comedians, for example, a researcher may go ingratiate themselves in that community.

PARTICIPANT OBSERVATION

In a participant observation study, the researcher participates in the lifestyle, routines, or activities of the group they are studying. This allows the researcher to better understand the challenges or nuances of an experience which may be difficult to see as an outside observer. To better understand the social experience of being a standup comedian, for example, a researcher may go to perform standup comedy at a local comedy club.

CASE STUDY

In a case study, a researcher deeply analyzes one event or person of interest. A researcher may use a variety of data collection techniques within their case study, including qualitative interviews, ethnographic research, or participant observation. Case studies are not widely used in sociological research as they are limited in their generalizability. However, if the goal is to understand the unique circumstances that led to a singular event or unique qualities of an individual, case studies may be an appropriate form of data collection.

Mixed-Methods

HISTORICAL COMPARATIVE RESEARCH

In historical comparative research, a researcher sociologically analyzes historical events across time and space using both quantitative and qualitative data sources. The goal is to identify underlying social processes which are consistent – and which change – across time and place. The goal is to better understand the consistency or variability of social dynamics and social experiences. Researchers use this information to develop robust sociological theories which help to understand a wide range of historical and current events.

Part 5: Execute Your Study

Once you have collected your data, it is time to begin your analysis. But first, you must make a clear plan. Researchers should strive to maximize reliability. **Reliability** refers to the extent to which a study is replicable. If another researcher followed your analytic plan using the same or similar data, would they find the same results? To maximize reliability, you should accurately and fully document your processes, including all data sources and all analytic decisions and processes. Many people think of research as a recipe. If you found a cake recipe online and the author only included half the ingredients and half the steps, would your cake turn out the same? Probably not. So, be clear and detailed to make sure other researchers could follow your recipe and get the same results.

Researchers should also strive to maximize validity. **Validity** refers to how well you measure what you seek to measure. In sociological research, maximizing validity takes very careful consideration. Measuring social dynamics is not the same as measuring a physical indicator, like temperature. Social life is nuanced and messy. Say you are studying whether comedians who are more feminine-presenting receive less favorable audience reactions than comedians who are more masculine-presenting. How do you measure gender presentation? How do you measure the favorability of audience reactions?

The first step to maximize both reliability and validity is to create **operational definitions,** wherein you clearly define how you measure each concept (i.e., variable) used in your analysis. Let us run through some possible operational definitions for the concept of favorability of audience reactions. You could go to a standup show and measure the volume of audience claps and/ or the frequency of audience laughter. Or, after the show, you could survey audience members, asking them to rate their enjoyment of the comedian's set on a five-point scale (e.g., ranging from "Greatly Disliked" to "Greatly Liked"). Without needing to go out to a standup show, you could identify a specific set of comedians, then count their subscribers and views on YouTube. There are countless other ways you could measure this concept. You will notice different operational definitions go together with different data collection techniques. Indeed, your operational data will necessarily be based on the available data. If using secondary data, the available variables may be limited. So you may need to adjust your study design and expectations to fit the data that are available. If collecting primary data, be sure to develop your operational definitions beforehand so you can collect the variable(s) you need.

Your operational definition will also go together with your hypothesis and interpretation. You may have an amazing hypothesis you wish to test. But if you are unable to effectively test it with your data and variable(s), you may need to adjust the wording. To maximize reliability and validity, you need to be very clear about what you are testing and how you are testing it. Remember that it takes time, careful consideration, and repeated adjustment to harness complex data to effectively capture the nuance and complexity of social life (and to then clearly document it).

Part 6: Interpret and Share Your Results

You have now conducted your study and tested your hypothesis. It is now time to consider your findings. If your hypothesis was supported by your research, take time to consider the following questions as you interpret and write up your results: What did you find? Which elements of your findings are consistent with prior research, and which are novel? What does your research contribute to our sociological understanding of this topic?

If your hypothesis was *not* supported by your research, it is important to consider whether you used appropriate data sources, methods, and operational definitions (i.e., consider how effectively you maximized validity in your study). Findings contrary to what was expected based upon your literature review do not necessarily mean you discovered something new or that prior research was incorrect. Instead, it may signal your approach needs some tweaks. This is not to say you cannot find something new or different. Social dynamics can certainly evolve. However, finding unexpected results *does* mean you should carefully check your work before moving forward. We just discussed how social life cannot be fully or easily distilled into a survey, qualitative interview, or day of observation, nor can those forms of data collection be fully or easily distilled into one concept via a perfect operational definition. Prior research provides helpful guardrails for you to see how well you did in maximizing reliability and validity. Use those guardrails.

Once you feel confident in your results – which may take lots of time and tweaks – it is time to write up your findings and share out with fellow sociologists and researchers. Common sharing techniques include drafting a manuscript for publication in an academic journal or presenting at conferences. Sociology is a collaborative field. Get out there, share, learn, and have fun.

Summary

Sociology is the study of how people interact with each other through the constraints placed on them by social structures and institutions. Sociology is also a way of seeing the world, a way to understand our culture and society, and a way to make sense of how our culture and society shape our personal choices. In this chapter, we defined the parallels between sociology and comedy. We discussed how comedians are trained to see the world as outsiders, to listen, observe, and ask the right questions. These are the same skills you learn as a sociologist.

In this chapter, you learned how to use the scientific method to conduct your own sociological research to better understand the world. We discussed how the scientific method as the foundation of sociological research. It provides a framework under which you can develop and test theories about how the social world works. Asking questions and seeking answers is the backbone of both comedy and sociology.

Discussion Questions

2-1: Recall the research (as reported by Ken Jennings in his book *Planet Funny* (2018)) which found men to be "funnier" than women, based upon evidence that women were less likely than men to laugh at sex-based humor. Based on this short description, do you believe such research properly evaluated men's and women's senses of humor? Why or why not? How would you design a study to compare senses of humor across different social groups?

2-2: Do you believe it is possible to be objective in sociological research? Why or why not?

2-3: What steps can a researcher take to improve objectivity in sociological research?

2-4: Discuss how John Wilson's approach on *How To* differs from that of more typical reality television (e.g., the *Real Housewives* franchise). What, if anything, does his approach teach you about methodological choices in sociological research?

2-5: Why is it important to conduct a literature review before conducting your research study?

2-6: With a classmate, discuss the pros and cons of using (a) quantitative data and (b) qualitative data, and a mixed methods approach. Name one pro and one con for each data approach.

2-7: With a classmate, discuss the pros and cons of using (a) primary data and (b) secondary data. Name two pros and two cons for each data source.

2-8: What is the difference between field research, ethnography, and participant observation? Do you see any ethical considerations researchers should consider when conducting these types of research studies?

2-9: Define reliability and validity. Explain how both can be improved through careful design of your study's operational definitions?

2-10: Define the difference between a population and a sample. Why would a researcher use a sample for their research study?

Notes

1 Pandya, H. (2017, May 5). *Comedy vs. Criticism.* Vulture. https://www.vulture.com/2017/05/comedy-vs-criticism.html

2 Brady, J. (Director). (2012, November 28). *Maria Bamford: The Special Special Special!* [Comedy]. Brady Oil Entertainment, Chill, Comedy Dynamics.

3 For this reason, The *Real Housewives* franchise is ripe for satire. Kristen Schaal (born in Longmont, Colorado, 1978) and a group of fellow comedians starred in *The Hotwives*, a parody franchise which had a two-season run on Hulu (2014–2015) with *The Hotwives of Orlando* and *The Hotwives of Las Vegas.*

4 *The Last Laugh: John Wilson Demystifies 'How To with John Wilson.'* (2020, November 26). https://podcasts.apple.com/us/podcast/john-wilson-demystifies-how-to-with-john-wilson/id1456474041?i=1000500431325

5 Carr, J., & Greeves, L. (2006). *Only Joking: What's So Funny about Making People Laugh?* Penguin.

6 Shales, T., & Miller, J. A. (2015). *Live From New York: The Complete, Uncensored History of Saturday Night Live as Told by Its Stars, Writers, and Guests.* Back Bay Books.

7 The opinion that women are not funny has certainly not disappeared in the years since Jerry Lewis' 2000 statement. Comedian and podcaster Adam Carolla (born in Los Angeles County, California, 1964) was vocal about holding the same view. Comedian Jeff Ross (born in Springfield Township, New Jersey, 1965) lambasted him for this view during The *Comedy Central Roast of Alec Baldwin* (2019). Ross roasted Corolla on stage for this view, telling him that, yes, women are funny and Carolla's jokes that night would have been a lot funnier had he hired some women to write them. *"Comedy Central Roasts" The Comedy Central Roast of Alec Baldwin (TV Episode 2019)—IMDb.* (2019, September 15). https://www.imdb.com/title/tt10520800/

8 Nast, C. (2008, March 3). *Who Says Women Aren't Funny?* Vanity Fair. https://www.vanityfair.com/news/2008/04/funnygirls200804

9 Bressler, E. R., Martin, R. A., & Balshine, S. (2006). Production and appreciation of humor as sexually selected traits. *Evolution and Human Behavior*, 27(2), 121–130. https://www.sciencedirect.com/science/article/abs/pii/S1090513805000760

10 Hurley, M. M., Dennett, D. C., & Adams, R. B. (2011). *Inside Jokes: Using Humor to Reverse-Engineer the Mind.* MIT Press.

11 Jennings, K. (2018). *Planet Funny: How Comedy Took Over Our Culture* (First Scribner Hardcover Edition). Scribner.

12 Hurley, Dennett, & Adams, 2011; Jennings, 2018.

13 Bressler, Martin, & Balshine, 2006.

3 Introduction to Foundational Sociological Concepts

This chapter defines core sociological concepts – including the sociological imagination, sociological norms, and the socialization processes. We discuss how sociologists understand our personal identity is formed through interactions with others. This chapter draws on the work of C. Wright Mills, George Herbert Mead, Claude M. Steele, Erving Goffman, Judith Butler, Charles Horton Cooley, Candace West, and Don Zimmerman. Additional concepts include socialization and the generalized other, identity contingencies and stereotype threat, the looking-glass self, gender, gender performativity, and "doing gender." The comedic concept of incongruity theory is discussed to highlight sociological principles. Throughout the book, we will call back to these sociological concepts and continue to practice their application with comedic examples.

Symbolic Interactionism

One of the most important tools in any sociologist's toolkit is the ability to employ the **sociological imagination**. The sociologist C. Wright Mills (born in Waco, Texas, 1916), who coined the term, defined the sociological imagination as understanding how one's personal experiences connect to broader society.[1] Mills saw the sociological imagination as the tool we can use to connect "personal troubles to public issues." People who have a good sociological imagination have the ability to step outside themselves and see the world through a new lens.

Jerry Seinfeld (born in Brooklyn, New York, 1954), one of the most successful comedians of the past century, became known for his comedic material which focused on the absurdity of society expectations and facets of everyday life. I argue that *most* of Seinfeld's best-known bits are examples of viewing the world as an outsider and engaging the sociological imagination. He does so through engaging another sociological concept – symbolic interactionism. **Symbolic interactionism** describes how people interact with one another based upon shared understandings of symbols.[2] Seinfeld's bits commonly question why people behave in certain ways, and/or why objects hold certain value or meaning. *Hello, sociology!*

Let us look at one of the standup bits as an example. In a bit which appeared in the opening of season one of his hit show *Seinfeld* in 1990, in an

DOI: 10.4324/9781003469537-4

episode titled "The Robbery," Seinfeld describes how a driver had recently given him the middle finger during a road rage incident.[3,4] He then digs into the absurdity of the symbol. He notes how absurd it is how, at the mere sight of someone showing you their middle finger, you are supposed to feel negative emotions like guilt, shame, or hurt. Seinfeld wonders why the symbol is a *finger* at all. Couldn't it be any appendage? Perhaps a toe?

At its core, "the finger" does not hold any *inherent* meaning; it only holds meaning because society determined that it has a specific meaning. "The finger" is a great example of symbolic interactionism. Think about how if someone lifts their middle finger and directs it at you, you may have a very different emotional response than if someone lifts their thumb and directs it at you. Seinfeld knows this symbol's meaning and then uses his **sociological imagination** to deconstruct it. He asks *why* "the finger" is so powerful. A toe, for example, takes a lot more work for someone to show during a road rage incident. He takes his personal experience and makes it public.

We just walked through Seinfeld's example of "the finger," but let us go back to even more classic example: *money*. Money, including cash, credit, or cryptocurrency, only works as a means of currency because we all agree it has value. Otherwise, a U.S. dollar is just a piece of cotton fiber with an old dead man on it. Credit and cryptocurrency are, well, *nothing* (and at least you can blow your nose on a dollar bill). Yet, since we all agree money is something of specific value: we exchange goods with each other. Make sense? Congratulations, you now understand the concept of symbolic interactionism.

But the concept gets more complicated when we do not all share the same understanding. Aside from some fringe individuals or sects in the United States who do not believe in money (whether that is in its inherent necessity in society or what its standard should be based upon), most of us pretty much get it. The same is not true when it comes to religion, art, or information presented on various news outlets. This problem is highlighted through a widening bifurcation of what information is decimated, believed, and re-shared according to someone's underlying political ideology and social networks.

Social Norms

Throughout this book, we will discuss how comedians speak and act – often in comparison to how non-comedians speak and act. This book is premised on the idea that paying attention to how comedians speak and act effectively inhibits the learning of sociological concepts. To better understand this point, let us discuss how sociologists define norms. Sociology defines **norms** as the rules and values which provide guardrails for how we live. They guide our behaviors and inform our choices. Central to sociological thinking is the notion that norms are socially constructed and they are learned – not innate laws or biological instincts. Sociologists break norms into *formal* and *informal* categories.

Formal norms are those which are formally codified, such as laws. An example of a formal norm is that we should not kill people. This norm is written into the laws prohibiting homicide. Norms can also be informal. **Informal**

norms are not necessarily written down but are widely known and adopted. These may include proper etiquette for how to greet someone (like when to use a handshake versus a hug) or how to behave at a dinner party (like knowing which fork to use). We enforce these norms through sanctions; the positive rewards or negative punishments incentivizing behavior in compliance with expected norms.

George Herbert Mead – who, along with Cooley, developed the concept of symbolic interactionism – put forward the concept of the generalized other. The **generalized other** refers to the socialization process wherein we learn what society expects of us in different situations and we adapt our behavior to meet those expectations. As children, we learn how to behave in different settings – such as at home, school, the movies, or a dinner party. The most influential agents of socialization are often family members, and Mead calls these individuals "significant others." Once we learn and internalize those expectations, we naturally adapt our behavior as we enter different social situations. We learn social expectations primarily from "significant others" and carry on those expectations to the "generalized other."

Let us consider an example. When you enter an elevator with other passengers, what do you do? Usually, you face the door, make no prolonged eye contact, and say nothing except for perhaps a quick pleasantry. More experimental professors often challenge students to face the other direction (with face toward the back of the car) the next time they get on an elevator to gauge the reaction of other riders. We learn these informal norms throughout our lives or throughout our tenure in a certain social space. Not everyone grew up around elevators but these behaviors are quickly, and often subconsciously, learned in a new context. The elevator example is trivial but highlights this point: without even thinking about it, our behavior in social settings is influenced by social norms.

Like an elevator, a classroom has norms. Imagine sitting down in a classroom and the professor spends the class period performing standup. With the clothes, the language, the mannerisms, and the act-outs you would expect to go along with it. That would be confusing, right? We have shared expectations for what behavior fits where. You would not expect to see standup in a college classroom, nor would you expect to see a college lecture at a comedy club (although allegations that their comedy is a TED Talk or a lecture have been lodged at many postmodern comics, including like Hannah Gadsby, who will be discussed later in this book).

As such, if your professor broke into absurdist, whimsical, hyperbolic, or comedic diatribes in the classroom, this behavior would deviate from ascribed norms and could possibly result in professional censure. This is especially true for professors from marginalized communities who are asked to fit within a narrower window of professionalism. Social scientific research has continually found bias in student evaluations, wherein faculty from marginalized groups receive lower marks due to features of their identity, such as sex, race, national origin, and intersections therein.[5,6] For example, MacNell et al. (2014) found that assistant instructors for an online course received higher marks when they presented with a traditionally male name, and lower marks when they presented with a traditionally female name.[7] This is for the same instructors, switching their names for different student sections. Awareness of such bias places additional binds on faculty members from marginalized groups to adhere to expected norms, lest they be professionally penalized.

Utilizing media like standup clips in the classroom enables circumvention of these norms and standards (within reason, of course). Professors can bring fresh perspectives into the classroom, blown up in absurdist and comedic ways which resonate with students, while still adhering to ascribed classroom etiquette. We have discussed briefly, in this section, how comedy is an effective sociological tool for seeing the world through a new lens. But in the next section, we will dig more explicitly into a sociological theory of humor called incongruity theory to explain how laughter helps us identify oddities or contradictions in our own behaviors, beliefs, and traditions.

Incongruity Theory

Sociologists have three classical theories of humor used to understand why we laugh (remember "dissecting the frog"). One common joke form effectively demonstrates comedy's parallels to sociology: the disruption of logic. Humor scholars classify jokes that "disrupt logic" as ones that juxtapose two ideas that usually do not agree with one another.[8] **Incongruity theory** posits that jokes put forth a disagreement in logic that must then be resolved. Essentially, humor stems from contradictions in subject matter or in the form by which the joke is delivered.[9] This can come from the comedian doing or saying something the audience does not expect, or from incongruity in the person delivering the message and the content.

The book *What's So Funny? The Comic Conception of Culture and Society* (1993), by Murray S. David, posits that the work of comedy and sociology has the same goal: bringing *disorder* to social norms and expectations. Both comics and sociologists use outsider lenses to challenge social expectations, rules, and taboos; flip the script to show a phenomenon in a new light; challenge hypocrisy; and highlight how social norms, rules, and perspectives change across time and space.[10]

The existence of incongruity supports the sociological notion that society is made up of sets of norms that guide social interaction. Norms must exist for them to be broken. Through jokes, our sense of some phenomenon is shaken up in a way that challenges our sense of reality.[11] This causes surprise and confusion. The laugh comes when we can place and contextualize that incongruity within our own reality and identify that maybe it is our reality that is wrong. Simply put, we laugh because we question our own reality. We envisioned one version of reality and the punchline hands us another.

The disruption of logic starts with a shared understanding of our world that we strive to discuss, interpret, and understand in sociology classrooms. Then, a joke hands us a punchline that shocks us. Two modern comics interested in understanding and describing the role of logic disruption in joke structure are

Kenny and Keith Lucas, a comedy duo (and set of twins) most well-known by their stage name: the Lucas Brothers (born in Newark, New Jersey, 1985). An idea held by the Lucas Brothers, attributed to a quote from Austrian philosopher Ludwig Wittgenstein, is that a sound philosophical text could be composed entirely of jokes.[12] In an interview on *Vulture*'s *Good One* podcast, they discussed the strong, overlapping relationship between philosophy and comedy – both of which came to life in ancient Greece.

As the Lucas Brothers explain, jokes and syllogisms follow the same basic structure. A syllogism is a logical argument in which two premises are given (e.g., "Cobras are snakes." and "All snakes are reptiles.") which share one common conclusion (e.g., "Cobras are reptiles."). The difference between a joke and syllogism, however, is that the conclusion – the punchline – will be a little off. It will deviate from expectations and invalidate the logical argument.[13]

A trained comedian can use their skills to set up a shared reality between themselves and their audience, then sharply pivot into a new reality that breaks their audience's chain of logic. Indeed, there needs to be a shared understanding between the comedian and the audience for the comedian to disrupt it. You set up an agreed upon premise but then deviate in the conclusion. (*Cue laughter!*) That is the incongruity theory of humor in a nutshell.

If we really want to really "dissect a frog" to exemplify the incongruity theory of humor, we can put a joke into a logical diagram (sociologists love diagrams!). In this book, we use Greg Dean's joke structure diagram, as seen in Figure 3.1.[14] We will practice filling out this diagram in the following chapter.

Throughout the book, we will dig into how generational, cultural, political, and geographic divides influence one's understanding of, and response to, comedic content. We will then interpret those divisions sociologically. For example, we could turn to jokes crafted by comedians from communities other than our own. For example, if a comedian from another country or one who belongs to another religion bases their content on a specific set of norms or cultural understandings, their jokes may fall flat to an outsider. Their jokes may work well in their own communities but make absolutely no

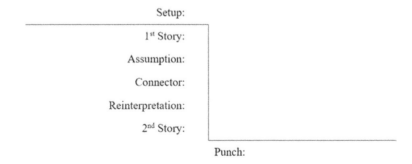

Figure 3.1 Joke Structure Diagram

sense in another. If an audience member does understand a joke's setup, they will likely not laugh at the punchline.

In addition to generational or cultural differences hampering shared understanding, there are myriad other divisions that impact whether two people understand each other. For example: country of origin or country of residence. The examples included in this book were selected for undergraduate students in the United States. As such, those examples focus heavily on the U.S.-specific phenomena and lean on the U.S.-based comedy, television, and other media to elucidate points. However, certainly not everyone reading this book will come from a U.S. background. In your classroom, I encourage you all to discuss your different experiences with one another and discuss how your different histories and backgrounds may influence your knowledge of, and response to, the various examples discussed throughout the book. This book intends to foster conversation and connection; I hope you learn more from each other than you can from a book.

While most of the examples in this book are U.S.-specific, the book also engages comedians from other geographies to highlight how social norms are not global or static entities; they differ across countries and cultures. Comedy is a great avenue to learn about different social norms across geographic and cultural boundaries.

For example, I recommend turning to standup comedian and screenwriter Zarna Garg. In her 2023 Amazon Prime Video special, *One in a Billion*, Garg's standup material covers her life and experiences as an Indian woman now living in the United States. Garg jokes about wearing a bindi, unclean drinking water, and the ways she parents her sons as compared to her daughter.[15] Garg makes her jokes accessible to mainstream audiences who may not have previous familiarity with Indian traditions or experiences.

Let us go back to discussing how laughter can occur when someone expects one conclusion but is given another. Humor scholars posit that humans create mental spaces filled with expectations. Those expectations are based on our prior understanding of, and interaction with, the outside world. So when we hear words, read words, or see physical movements, our prior experiences preemptively suppose what will happen next. This is the tough balance of standup comedy: placing jokes within contexts which audiences understand while still managing to surprise them.

An example of this in action can be seen in the body of work from Andy Kaufman. Kaufman was born in New York City in 1949 and is oft revered as one of the greatest comedians of the 1970s. However, Kaufman never referred to himself as a comedian. He considered himself an entertainer. His aim was to entertain, not to make audiences laugh. He insisted he had never "told a joke."[16] Kaufman's performances were designed to mess with the audience's head. Digging into Kauffman's style can help us understand preconceived notions about what comedic performances are expected to look, sound, and feel like. I use Kaufman as an example for how we can use the sociological imagination to interpret what is, and is not, comedy.

Audiences would roll into a comedy club with the normal expectations that come with it. We all expect a comedian to stand on stage, deliver some jokes, and for the audience to laugh. This was not Kaufman's style. In one of his most well-known bits, Kaufman would stand in front of a comedy audience and earnestly read *The Great Gatsby*. The audience would laugh at the absurdity of it but Kaufman would admonish the audience for their laugher and threaten to start over if the audience continued to interrupt him.[17] In one instance, Kaufman offered a nightclub audience the choice of listening to him read or listening to a record. The audience chose the record, and in a comedic twist, it was a recording of Kaufman reading.

While he did not describe himself as a comic, Kaufman's work was comedic in the way it disrupted people's expectations. It highlights the expectations and norms associated with different types of performances. If audiences went to a literary event, perhaps at a bookstore or library, the normal expectation is that an audience would not be inclined to laugh at someone reading from a classic novel. But when that novel is being read at a comedy club against the audience's expectations, the incongruity between content and venue sparks laughter. Kaufman's admonishing of the audience is to say, "Hey, why are you laughing at a book reading?! Stop interrupting!" which would be the expected response at a literary event. Kaufman is acting as a sociologist here. He is showing audiences that performing actions (like a book reading) not in line with venue-appropriate (like a comedy club) expectations break the chain of logic in one's head about what goes together. It reminds audiences how many subconscious expectations we carry with us. Like how to ride in an elevator, how to listen quietly and respectfully at a book event, or when it is appropriate to laugh in a comedy club.

To highlight an opposite example of this point, comedian Nate Bargatze (born in Nashville, Tennessee, 1979) provides a thought experiment for his standup audience when regaling them with a story about a time he and his father, who is a magician, performed together (which they do with some regularity). Bargatze explains that he once performed at a magician's convention in Des Moines, Iowa.[18] A magician's convention is like any other professional convention; here, magicians buy and sell trick, give lectures, and perform in a big show. The organizer of the Des Moines convention reached out to Bargatze, asking if he would come to perform as a surprise to his father, Stephen. The idea was that Stephen would perform his magic act, and Nate would secretly switch places with Stephen's female assistant, pop out of a box (the same box in which the assistant had, moments before, climbed inside), and end Stephen's set by performing five minutes of standup comedy.

Bargatze's plan succeeds, and he exits the box with performative grandeur (this was, after all, not Nate's first magic show), but the audience's reaction is medium at best. Then, it occurs to Nate that the audience has no idea who he is. The audience does not understand that he is Stephen's son, nor that he is a comedian. As Bargatze jokingly explains, the audiences think that they are just seeing a really bad magic trick, one where a pretty lady goes into a box and a middle-aged man comes out.

Then, Nate must perform his standup set. But as he just realized, the audience does know he is a comedian. Nate explains to his audience to whom he is later recounting this tale that when you perform comedy to an audience expecting to see something else, the material does not read to them as comedy. They are confused and certainly not laughing. And, in Bargatze's joke-filled retelling, they are also worried about the health and safety of the disappearing woman. Bargatze's set provides another example for understanding how socially defined signals, like place, impact our reactions to stimuli.

Compared to Kaufman, who performed non-comedy to an audience expecting comedy, Bargatze performed comedy to an audience expecting magic. In both cases, the comedians highlight that context and environment matter for how their art is received. Kaufman had audiences laughing at someone reading *The Great Gatsby*, which they would not have done if they were at a library or bookstore listening to an author. And for Bargatze, the audience did not laugh at the magician's convention even though they likely would have if they were in a comedy club.

The examples from Kaufman and Bargatze highlight two similar points. First, by using our sociological imagination, we see how our expectations for something like a performance shape our understanding of what it actually is. What we do, and how we feel about what others do, is largely contextual and socially defined. Second, I hope you understand how comedy can help us learn this. Bargatze fell into this understanding at the magic show. Then, he reevaluated what happened and shared his experience with his standup audience in his later bit. Kaufman used his sociological imagination to understand what audiences expected, then subverted it for laughs.

The disruptions of our expectations teach us something about our world and about ourselves. Comedy, like sociology, shapes our understanding of our own selves within the world. It makes us question why we laugh at a book when it is read in a comedy club but not when it is read in a bookstore. It makes us question how and why our brain makes connections between things (here: between books and bookstores, and in later chapters, we will get into meatier material around stereotypes, pertaining to race, ethnicity, sex, gender, sexuality, social class, religion, and other features of one's social identity). Asking those questions is both comedy and sociology in a nutshell.

Crowd Work

We just discussed two instances where comedians deviated from social norms (Kaufman on purpose; Bargatze on accident). But often, standup comedians want to begin their sets by identifying and mirroring the social norms of the comedy room, so their audience will feel comfortable, seen, and ready to listen to some jokes. Now is time to talk about crowd work – perhaps the most clearly sociological single element of standup comedy!

Crowd work is when a comedian engages in conversation directly with the audience or a specific member of the audience. The most basic form of crowd work, which we will discuss in this section, is jokes which allow the comedian to learn about their audience and build a personal connection with them. For example, a comedian may ask, "Who in here is married?" Based on the audience reaction (via a show of hands, round of applause, or hoots-and-hollers), the comedian may alter their material to better suit an audience of predominantly single versus predominantly married individuals. If a comedian has a full set of "married" jokes and everyone in the audience is single, the jokes may not land. They may not land because, as we just discussed, comedy rests on shared understanding. If the comedians' premises are all based on the nuances of marriage, someone who has never entered into marriage may not identify with or understand the setup, and therefore, not laugh at the punchline.

Another example of a classic piece of crowd work is asking audience members where they are from. A comedian playing a room in New York City, for example, may be playing to all New Yorkers (which may be one set of jokes) or all to tourists (which may be another). Only the greats can masterfully tell niche city jokes to a national or international audience (we will discuss Katt Williams' 2018 Netflix standup special *Great America* later in this book). For audiences, identifying with your comedian is a big part of enjoying comedy. Throughout the book, we will discuss examples of comedians who were long excluded from professional comedy breaking into the scene and finding their audience.

Another form of crowd work is a self-deprecating joke. Whenever we see someone, we make assumptions about them. These assumptions may be based on race, sex, physical shape, and may include assumptions about their sexual identity or social class, based on cues such as how they are dressed or groomed. Comedians *know* the audience is making assumptions about them. Comedians can presume what the audience is thinking. By making a self-deprecating joke, the comedian lets the audience know it is okay to laugh at them. Or, self-deprecation seemingly puts comedians "in their place," making an audience more receptive to a performance by someone to whom they may otherwise not listen.

To dig more into the idea that comedians *know* the audience is making assumptions about them, let us introduce identity contingencies. **Identity contingencies** are the circumstances you must handle or overcome in society that are due to your social identity – such as your age, race, sex, gender, sexuality, or intersections therein. They constrain your behavior in both physical ways (such as which bathroom you may legally use based on your biological sex and/or gender identity) and psychological ways (such as through the threat of retribution). One form of identity contingency is stereotype threat. **Stereotype threat** stems from how we all hold "knowledge" of stereotypes that may apply and we navigate the world with this awareness in our heads. Specifically, stereotype threat refers to the ways we change our behavior out of fear of confirming a negative stereotype others may hold about us.[19]

As written by Claude M. Steele in his book *Whistling Vivaldi* (2010): "This means that whenever we're in a situation where a bad stereotype about one of our own identities could be applied to us – such as those about being old, poor, rich, or female – we know it. We know what 'people could think.'" We will further discuss stereotype threat later in this book when we discuss experiments conducted by Steele and colleagues finding evidence that women underperform on math exams and Black students underperform on verbal reasoning exams, when – and only when – stereotype threat is present. Stereotype threat is usually a silent or internal process, which is why researchers like Steele must conduct experiments in laboratory settings to identify and isolate its impact. But outside of the lab, we can turn to comedians to see what it looks like when people express awareness of stereotype threat out loud. This may allow us to get a sense of how omnipresent stereotype threat may be for folks in our society.

In the next chapter, we will dive into the work of two comedians – Moms Mabley and Phillis Diller – and discuss what their material teaches us about the social expectations placed on women and women of color in society. Informed by the scholarship of Dr. Stephanie Brown, we will discuss what their crowd work teaches us about the expectations placed on women for their physical appearance.

Gender and Performance

In our discussion of crowd work, we discussed how comedians tailor their performance to better align with expectations from the audience. But this process is not reserved for "performers" (e.g., comedians or actors), and it is not reserved for only when they are on a stage. According to sociologist Erving Goffman, we are *all* performers and "all the world's a stage."[20] To elucidate this point, let us turn to gender. Sociologists and symbolic interactionists understand we perform our gender. To review, symbolic interactionists study how people interact with another other based on shared meanings and particularly shared norms. Symbolic interactionists assert pieces of our identities are created and maintained via our interaction with others. Specifically, we perform aspects of our identity to align with the norms and values of the individuals or groups with whom we are interacting.

Charles Horton Cooley – who, along with Mead, developed the concept of symbolic interactionism – put forward the concept of the looking-glass self.[21] The **looking-glass self** refers to the idea that our own self-perception is not innate but instead reflects how others see us. We understand how others see us – our parents, our friends, our coworkers, etc. – and we take on those views. There are three components to the looking-glass self: (1) we consider how others view us in different social situations. For example, we may consider if we seem "cool" as we walk into a party. (2) We consider how others may judge us based upon their views of us. For example, we imagine if and how they will judge us for being "uncool" – perhaps they mock our outfit. We may then choose to *change* our outfit before leaving the house, out of fear of it being mocked. (3) We form our self-perceptions based upon components 1 and 2. Taken together, our behaviors and our sense of self are informed by how we *think* others view us and how they may judge us. The most important thing to take away from the looking-glass self is that our self-perception is a response to how others see us and respond to us. Our self is social.

Now, let's define **gender**. Sociologists tend to discuss sex, gender, and sexuality as distinct phenomena. According to most sociologists, sex is biologically based (but is, nevertheless, categorized and defined according to cultural factors). Gender, however, is socially constructed. Tethered to the concepts of femininity and masculinity, gender is performed through clothing, mannerisms, behaviors, and roles.[22] For example, modern American individuals may perform femininity by wearing dresses, providing care for others, and expressing emotions. Behaviors classified as "feminine" are not fixed; they vary over time and across place.

Dr. Judith Butler (born in Cleveland, Ohio, 1956) coined the term **gender performativity** in 1990 to describe the ways in which gender is learned, performed, and imposed upon individuals by heteronormative societal norms. **Heteronormativity** refers to a specific worldview which upholds heterosexuality as normal, natural, or preferred. Butler's theory of gender performativity contrasts with the heteronormative notion that genders are innate features of one's biology and identity. It is worth noting Butler did not invent the idea of gender-as-performance but they did help unpack and codify the theories with their book *Gender Trouble: Feminism and the Subversion of Identity*. Butler expanded on the theory of gender performance by positing adherence to performing one's gender is a survival strategy in the "compulsory system" of heteronormativity. Not all people feel the threat of this compulsory system equally. People in more marginalized positions in society – women of color or LGBTQ+ folks, for example – face greater threats for non-adherence to gender norms than do people with more status.

A related concept in sociology is that of "doing gender," which was a concept first devised by sociologists Candace West and Don Zimmerman in their 1987 article published in the peer-reviewed journal, *Gender and Society*.[23] **Doing gender** refers to the idea that gender is not an innate or biological construct but one that is socially constructed and must be performed through wearing specific clothes (like dresses for women and suits for men), behaving in certain ways (like being demure as a woman and assertive as a man), and taking on specific occupational or personal roles (like being a family caretaker as a women and the "breadwinner" as a man). This is an extension of symbolic interactionism. Recall, **symbolic interactionism** asserts understanding and communication between people are based upon shared understanding of symbols. Someone's clothes are symbols; their hairstyles are symbols; their mannerisms are symbols.

None of the categorizations described above – for clothing, behavior, or roles – are hard-and-fast rules. For example, men are family caretakers and women are "breadwinners," just as trans and non-binary people can inhabit either of those roles. But the examples are meant to show that when taken together, the social meaning placed on modes of dress, behavior, and roles can intersect to form one's gender performance.

The core concept here is that there is nothing inherently natural or biological about a two-gender system; it is our performances of "being a woman" or "being a man" in line with social expectations that create and maintain the existence of gender.[24] Femininity and masculinity, then, are social constructs. Dressing and acting in accordance with these gender constructs constitutes social norms. To give two examples of traditional femininity and masculinity in the United States, it is often considered (1) feminine to wear dresses and masculine to wear suits and (2) feminine to present as quiet or reserved and masculine to present as confident, loud, or brash.

Before we go forward, I want to discuss how the term "women comedians" is used throughout this book. I refer to "women comedians" as a broad category of comedians who have historically been marginalized or excluded from mainstream avenues for success. I do not use the term "woman" to tie folks to a specific understanding of biological sex or gender identity. Instead, this term attempts to capture the "otherness" of women as a social or political category. Following Dr. Stephanie Brown's lead, my use of the term "women comedian" attempts to broadly categorize folks whose contributions or potential have been minimized by beliefs like "women aren't funny."[25]

Similarly, I refer to Black comedians and Brown comedians throughout the book as broad categories, which as general terms minimize the nuance of people's backgrounds, identities, and experiences. Race is a social construct, but for reasons which will be described throughout the book, a very socially and politically meaningful one. I do not use the terms "Black" or "Brown" to tie folks to specific phenotypic presentations. Instead, these terms are used (arguably, far too simply) to refer to groups of people who have been racialized as Black and Brown.

Summary

This chapter defines core sociological concepts, which we will call back to throughout the book. I briefly introduced two comedians who performed non-comedy in comedy spaces and comedy in non-comedy spaces (Andy Kaufman and Nate Bargatze, respectively) to discuss how social norms and context influence our expectations and interpretations of phenomena. A book reading in a comedy club is: comedy. Comedy during a magic show is: confusing. Our sense of what is "normal" or "expected" is influenced by social norms which we learn through socialization. The comedic concept of incongruity theory highlights these sociological principles. We took these same principles and applied them to our personal identities. Our identities are formed through our interactions with others. We do not exist in a vacuum. Throughout the book, we will delve deeper into this idea.

Discussion Questions

3-1: With a classmate, share and discuss a symbol that you know has a certain meaning in one country or culture but a different meaning (or no meaning) in another.

3-2: With a classmate, share and discuss examples of one <u>formal norm</u> and one <u>informal norm</u>.

3-3: Consider your own <u>socialization</u> process. Who were your <u>agents of socialization</u>? How did you learn <u>formal norms</u> and <u>informal norms</u> for different settings?

3-4: With a classmate, discuss ways in which you change your own behavior based upon <u>norms</u> of the setting. Consider this in various areas of your life, such as school, work, religious services, family functions, or social media.

3-5: Think of a time you experienced <u>stereotype threat</u>. How did it impact your behaviors, self-perception, or performance?

3-6: Consider Charles Horton Cooley's concept of the <u>looking-glass self</u> in the social media era. How do you think the looking-glass self operates similarly, or differently, on social media relative to life offline?

3-7: How does Cooley's concept of the <u>looking-glass self</u> reinforce <u>traditional gender norms</u>? Consider what would happen to a person's self-perception if they are primarily praised for their physical appearance or the way they provide care for others, compared to another person that is primarily praised for being smart and strong?

3-8: Do you agree with Erving Goffman's assertion that "<u>all the world's a stage</u>"?

3-9: Describe how Candace West and Don Zimmerman's concept of <u>doing gender</u> relates to <u>symbolic interactionism</u>.

3-10: Think about how your own ways of dressing and behaving hold symbolic meaning. Do they make you who you are (e.g., are tied to your identity)? Why or why not?

Notes

1 Mills, C. W. (2000). *The Sociological Imagination*. Oxford University Press.
2 Blumer, H. (1986). *Symbolic Interactionism: Perspective and Method*. University of California Press.
3 For anyone unfamiliar, in Western culture, showing one's middle finger – or, "the bird" – to another person is an obscene hand gesture which signifies anger or disdain.
4 *"Seinfeld" The Robbery*. (1990). NBC. https://www.imdb.com/title/tt0697768/
5 Russ, T., Simonds, C., & Hunt, S. (2002). Coming out in the classroom … An occupational hazard?: The influence of sexual orientation on teacher credibility and perceived student learning. *Communication Education*, *51*(3), 311–324. https://doi.org/10.1080/03634520216516
6 Thomas, N. (2019). In the service of social equity: Leveraging the experiences of African American women professors. *Journal of Public Affairs Education*, *25*(2), 185–206. https://doi.org/10.1080/15236803.2018.1565041

7 MacNell, L., Driscoll, A., & Hunt. (2014, December 5). *What's in a Name: Exposing Gender Bias in Student Ratings of Teaching | SpringerLink.* https://link.springer.com/article/10.1007/s10755-014-9313-4

8 Hurley, M. M., Dennett, D. C., & Adams, R. B. (2011). *Inside Jokes: Using Humor to Reverse-Engineer the Mind.* MIT Press.

9 Morreall, J. (2020). Philosophy of Humor. In E. N. Zalta (Ed.), *The Stanford Encyclopedia of Philosophy* (Fall 2020). Metaphysics Research Lab, Stanford University. https://plato.stanford.edu/archives/fall2020/entries/humor/

10 Granato, A. (2016). *"Yeah, But You Rape Women": Hannibal Buress and the Comedy Community's Role in Shaping Public Opinion of the Bill Cosby Sexual Assault Allegations* [College of William and Mary]. https://scholarworks.wm.edu/honorstheses/930/

11 Hurley, Dennett, & Adams, 2011.

12 Madigan, T. (1999). *Philosophy and Humor.* Philosophy Now. https://philosophynow.org/issues/25/Philosophy_and_Humor

13 *Good One: The Lucas Brothers' History of Western Philosophy.* (2019, February 24). https://podcasts.apple.com/ie/podcast/the-lucas-brothers-history-of-western-philosophy/id1203393721?i=1000430481890

14 Dean, G. (2016). *Free Funny the eBook: Writing Comedy, Jokes, and Humor for Business, Public Speaking, or Just for Laughs.* https://www.free-ebooks.net/business/Free-Funny-the-eBook-Writing-Comedy-Jokes-and-Humor-for-Business-Public-Speaking-or-Just-for-Laughs

15 Volk-Weiss, B. (Director). (2023). *Zarna Garg: One in a Billion* [Documentary, Comedy]. Amazon Studios, Comedy Dynamics.

16 Dessau, B. (2012). *Beyond a Joke: Inside the Dark Minds of Stand-Up Comedians.* Random House UK.

17 Jones, J. (2018, December 6). *Andy Kaufman Reads Earnestly from The Great Gatsby and Enrages His Audience.* Open Culture. https://www.openculture.com/2018/12/andy-kaufman-reads-earnestly-great-gatsby-enrages-audience.html

18 *8 Minutes of Dad Jokes With Nate Bargatze—YouTube.* (2021). https://www.youtube.com/watch?v=et2O5fdK8DY

19 Steele, C. M. (2010). *Whistling Vivaldi: How Stereotypes Affect Us and What We Can Do.* W. W. Norton & Company.

20 Goffman, E. (1959). *The Presentation of Self in Everyday Life.* Doubleday.

21 Cooley, C. H. (1922). *Human Nature and the Social Order* (Revised edition). Charles Scribner's Son.

22 Butler, J. (1999). *Gender Trouble: Feminism and the Subversion of Identity.* Routledge.

23 West, C., & Zimmerman, D. H. (1987). Doing gender. *Gender and Society, 1*(2), 125–151. https://www.jstor.org/stable/189945

24 Butler, 1999.

25 Brown, S. (2018). Open Mic? Gender and the Meritocratic Myth of Authenticity in the Cultural Production of Stand-Up Comedy (Dissertation). *University of Illinois at Urbana-Champaign.*

4 Presentation of Self

This chapter explores the complicated act of presenting oneself in life and in comedy. This chapter explores the identity of the outsider and describes how one's outsider status relates to social constructions of "deviance." This chapter reviews examples that highlight the way deviance evolves over time alongside changing social norms. For example, we may consider a joke that was historically obscene as now tame, and we may recognize a joke that was once considered appropriate as offensive today. Using historic examples of stereotypic tropes employed in comedy, character comedians, and other displays of impression management, this chapter examines the ways comedy has evolved over time and varies with place. This chapter uses more recent comedic examples of impression management to highlight how this still operates today.

This chapter discusses the role and effectiveness of satire and parodic news programs in social criticism and introduces the concept of "clapter" to explain how the lack of a comedic perspective in satirical content can feed the status quo. This chapter draws on the work of Erving Goffman, Amber Day, Rebecca Krefting, Pierre Bourdieu, James E. Caron, Jean Baudrillard, and Thorstein Veblen. Sociological concepts include impression management, the dramaturgical theory of the self, parrhēsia, feminist theory, stereotypes, deviance, simulations, social scripts, equality, equity, repressiveness, constraints, falseness, and role overload. The concepts of superiority theory and the comedic perspective are used to elucidate sociological principles.

History of Presenting Oneself

In the following sections, we will discuss examples of comedic performances that show how comedians present themselves on a comedy stage in relation to social norms and expectations. Starting with a description of character comedy exemplified by Moms Mabley and Phyllis Diller, this chapter will discuss how and why comedians present themselves in certain ways and why they perform where they perform, including the Chitlin' Circuit and discovery clubs. We'll then compare Diller's comedy to jokes by a male comedian from her same era, Rodney Dangerfield, to highlight how identity, social stratification, and social norms intersect to shape one's comedic perspective.

DOI: 10.4324/9781003469537-5

Character Comedy with Moms Mabley and Phyllis Diller

Figure 4.1 highlights the "Borscht Belt, Chitlin' Circuit, & Theaters" era of comedy, roughly spanning 1948–1960. This era provides rich sociological information about the way "outsiders" were excluded, marginalized, and/or forced to assimilate to gain acceptance. This section highlights how social norms dictate behaviors and opportunities, and how social norms evolve over time.

Jackie "Moms" Mabley, born in Brevard, North Carolina, in 1894, began her comedy career in the 1920s. She debuted as a performer at a club called Connie's Inn in Harlem, New York City. Connie's Inn featured Black performers but restricted its audiences to only White patrons.[1] This was common at the time. The most well-known club of this style was the Cotton Club (also in Harlem), but there was at least a half-dozen others in Harlem alone. Mabley was one of the first openly gay comedians in the United States after coming out to the public in 1921.

Because of discrimination and institutional racism, Mabley spent most of her career making rounds through in the Chitlin' Circuit.[2] The **Chitlin' Circuit** was a collection of nightclubs, theaters, and music venues throughout the United States that showcased Black performers and catered to Black audiences. The Chitlin' Circuit was born out of necessity, as Mabley and other Black performers were barred from performing at most White clubs. The Apollo Theater in Harlem was the crown jewel of the Chitlin' Circuit. Mabley became a "cross-over" success shortly after the racial integration of clubs in the 1960s, finding mainstream appeal across the United States and even performing on nationally televised programs like *The Ed Sullivan Show*.

Mabley was what is known as a character comedian. A **character comedian** is someone who takes on the persona of a fabricated character. They usually lean into this character by using an alias name, presenting a specific aesthetic achieved through clothing, makeup, or wigs, and employing an accent or different vernacular. Mabley's character, Moms, was a toothless old lady who wore frumpy house dresses and floppy hats.[3] The old-lady persona was nonthreatening to audiences. As such, it allowed Mabley to deliver brash material that may have been "over the line" if delivered by Mabley as herself. For example, Mabley often joked about her penchant for younger men.[4] Mabley paved the way for comedians who came later to speak about sex and sexual desire openly in their material.[5]

Mabley's material also tackled racism, sexism, and the civil rights movement. Her character allowed for a greater breadth of material that otherwise may have been too edgy for audiences coming from a woman, especially a Black woman, at the time. Moms could express herself more freely than the real Mabley because of her character's looks, dress, and demeanor.

White women had more opportunities than did Black women at this time, although White women comedians still had trouble getting stage time in mainstream comedy clubs. Comedian Phyllis Diller (born in Lima, Ohio, 1917) came up in the late 1950s and early 1960s. Diller entered comedy

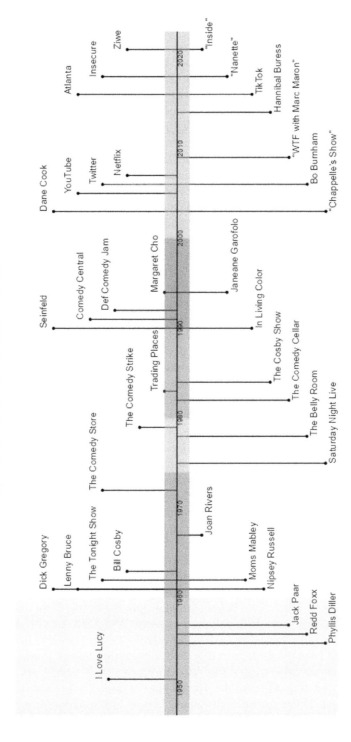

Figure 4.1 The Borscht Belt, Chitlin' Circuit, and Theaters Timeline

when popular culture put pressure on White women to be housewives and nothing else. Diller was a housewife, but she hated it. Her husband was lazy and emotionally and sexually abusive. They suffered from poverty. Their house was always dirty because housekeeping simply did not interest Diller. She later worked that sentiment into her act.

Early in her career, Diller primarily performed in venues called "discovery clubs." As a term, a discovery club is where talent can get "discovered." Notable discovery clubs frequented by Diller included Mister Kelly's in Chicago, the Purple Onion and the *hungry i* in San Francisco, the Blue Angel in New York, and the Crescendo in Los Angeles.[6] In Diller's case, the clubs where she found accepting audiences were those which had gay bars.[7] Bars and clubs being welcoming of gay patrons was not as common or as accepted in the 1960s as they are today. These audiences welcomed Diller and her contemporaries. Diller has spoken in interviews about how gay audiences were her first fans. Diller was given the freedom to be bold and loud in these spaces. In the discovery clubs, Diller could get stage time, work out her material, and slowly build a bigger name for herself.[8] Once she got on television, her fanbase expanded to include women. As her fame rose, men and children came next.[9]

As Diller would get on stage, she would use the classic standup introduction ("Yes, this is who I am") then blow it up into tightly packed jokes that made herself and her audience erupt into laugher. Diller's jokes included rags on her own cooking and cleaning, such as: "I don't like to cook; I can make a TV dinner taste like radio." Diller's comedy was based upon breaking expectations placed upon women to be good cooks and keep a clean home at that time. Indeed, her comedic persona stood in direct opposition to how wives and mothers were "supposed" to behave.[10] She was messy and loud. She had a big personality.

Recall that **feminist** thinkers – like Mary Wollstonecraft – understand that the observed differences between women and men in society are due to differential trajectories of socialization and unequal access to resources. Women are not innately destined to be homemakers. That is a social norm imposed upon women. Being "bad" at housekeeping is not a failure of what it means to "be a woman." Diller's comedy highlights this point.

Similarly, there are social norms expected of women to be "put together" and take care of their appearance for the sake of men. As such, Diller was also "supposed" to be beautiful. Diller commented on this by extending her jokes to her personal appearance. Diller employed jokes like, "I will never give up. I'm in my 14th year of a ten-day beauty plan" (Phyllis Diller, *Ed Sullivan Show*, 1969), or, "When you play spin the bottle, if they don't want to kiss you they have to give you a quarter. Well, hell, by the time I was twelve years old I owned my own home" (Diller, n.d.).[11] Diller's comedic style was indeed largely self-deprecating. **Self-deprecating humor** points out one's "flaws" before others can. The self-deprecating comic attempts to deflect ridicule by beating others to the punch. But the targets of her self-deprecation were an act. Diller intentionally made herself look unconventional for the sake of her routine and wore baggy clothes to hide her figure. She made her hair and makeup wild. She knew picking her image apart and playing as ugly and as a bad housewife would get big laughs.

Recall Judith Butler's discussion of **gender performativity**. Audiences placed certain expectations on Diller because she was a woman. They expected her to take care of physical appearance, home, husband, and children in ways that align with social norms. Diller's comedy was based on subverting those norms. Think about how Diller's comedy relates to our discussion of crowd work. Diller *knew* expectations her audience would have of her as a woman comedian.

Phyllis Diller was a pioneer in the intentional presentation of the self. Human beings have the tendency to be aware of how other people see them. This is the **looking-glass self**. Diller understood how she was perceived and played with that image. This created her comedy persona. To sum up Diller's comedy: she identified social norms about the role of a wife and mother, then, aided by her frumpy, bad-housewife character, intentionally broke them for laughs.

For her doctoral dissertation titled *Open Mic? Gender and the Meritocratic Myth of Authenticity in the Cultural Production of Stand-Up Comedy* (2018), Dr. Stephanie Brown analyzed the complex social norms regarding physical appearance women comedian must navigate onstage. Brown conducted ethnographic research studying comedians in Chicago and central Illinois.[12] Through interviews, surveys, and participant observation, Brown explored how social norms shape women's experiences in standup comedy.

Brown's findings highlight a paradox. Comedy is a craft which allows for the skewering of social norms, yet comedians may still feel bound by those social norms on stage. Their audiences still hold certain expectations from the performer based on who they are and what they look like, and the performer knows that. For women comedians, Brown finds they feel pressured to perform their gender in line with social norms. This places a burden on comedians coming from marginalized groups. These comedians do not just need to be "funny." They need to be funny in a very specific way, fitting into a narrow window of what the audience considers socially acceptable appearance and behavior for the performer.

The way social expectations placed on women's physical appearance have impacted comedy has evolved over time. In her book *Pretty/funny: Women Comedians and Body Politics (2014)*, Dr. Linda Mizejewski, distinguished professor in the Department of Women's, Gender, and Sexuality Studies at The Ohio State University, discusses how women have historically been viewed as either pretty or funny.[13] Women comedians of the past – such as Moms Mabley and Phyllis Diller – had to choose to either be pretty *or* be funny. These were the socially accepted options available to them. Moms Mabley and Phyllis Diller chose the latter. They made successful careers in comedy through their willingness to *look funny*. The social norms changed over time. In later eras and today, women comedians must be both pretty *and* funny.

Brown draws on Mizejewski's work in her dissertation. Results from Brown's ethnographic research confirm that women comedians face pressure to be both pretty and funny. Brown refers to this as a paradox of comedy. Comedy is a platform which allows for the subversion of social norms, yet, women must adhere to social norms of physical appearance to be taken seriously by their audiences.

Stereotypes with Rodney Dangerfield

Diller's comedic character was sociological in the way that it challenged the expectations placed upon women by men (from a White woman's perspective). Let us compare this to character comedy of the same era that didn't strive to challenge the status quo. A few jokes from Rodney Dangerfield will set the scene. Dangerfield was born as Jacob Rodney Cohen in Deer Park, New York in 1921. As the son of a vaudeville performer, Dangerfield started comedy at age fifteen but struggled to break through. Dangerfield ultimately quit comedy in the 1950s, becoming an aluminum siding salesman to provide for himself and his family.

But Dangerfield started rebuilding his comedy career in the 1960s and began performing at the Catskill Mountains under his real name, Jacob Cohen. Catskill audiences were only moderately interested in his comedy. This is when Dangerfield realized he would need a comedy character to act as his distinguishing identifier. He anglicized his name (becoming Rodney Dangerfield) and designed his character, which was quickly successful with audiences, as a man for which nothing ever went right. His catchphrase "I get no respect!" was his character's identifying feature. By using this character in his standup, Dangerfield made his way through nightclubs in New York City and later became a regular on late night talk shows. His breakout movie role came in 1980 when he played Al Czervik in *Caddyshack*.

Dangerfield was one of the many Jewish comedians during this era who anglicized their stage names (to name a few: Celine Zeigman became Jean Carroll, Leonard Schneider became Lenny Bruce, Melvin Kaminsky became Mel Brooks, Jerome Levitch became Jerry Lewis, Yakov Mosher Maza became Jackie Mason, and Sheldon Greenfield became Shecky Greene).[14] Anglicizing stage names opened doors for comedians in nightclubs and other venues that otherwise may have shut them out because of their ethnicity and religious heritage.

One of the primary ways for Jewish comedians to get stage time during this era was to perform in the Catskill Mountains outside of New York City, New York. The Catskill Mountains were a popular summer vacation destination during the decades surrounding the 1960s. Due to its many Jewish vacationers, the area came to be known as the "Borscht Belt," named for the Eastern European sweet-and-sour soup which was popularized in the United States by Jewish immigrants.[15] The Borscht Belt covered a relatively small area (reports vary between 30 and 50 square miles) but comprised 130 hotels.

In the Catskills Mountains, Jewish patrons had access to Kosher meals, socializing (or dating) with other Jewish people, entertainment, and vacation without fear of ethnic discrimination.[16] It is important to note here that comedy was not the main attraction for these vacationers. Catskill crowds could be difficult for comedians. The comedians called it "working the mountains," and it was not necessarily a desirable gig for comedians.

New York City offered many more desirable gigs with potentially greater exposure and greater pay. Nevertheless, the Borscht Belt holds a place in comedic history because of the number of legendary comedians who played there and nods to the Jewish roots of comedy. While many Jewish people anglicized their names to perform in mainstream clubs due to ethnic discrimination against Jewish people, the Borscht Belt celebrated their Jewish identity. Perhaps more than it celebrated their comedy.

While Jewish people were accepted and celebrated in the Catskills – unlike other areas – women still faced being the butt of the joke. Back to Dangerfield. Dangerfield's jokes were in line with the style of humor at the time wherein men's wives were a common target of their jokes. He would commonly joke about how his wife was a bad cook or a bad driver. In one joke, for example, Dangerfield describes a day in which his wife came home and told Dangerfield there was water in their car's carburetor. Dangerfield asks her, "Where's the car?" His wife responds, "In a lake."[17]

Recall that comedy rests on socially shared understandings of the world. Comedians may employ stereotypes about a particular group to take advantage of the universality of those social understandings. A **stereotype** is an oversimplified and often exaggerated idea about an entire group of people. Let's use Dangerfield's joke as an example, in which he employs the common stereotype that women are bad drivers. Let's take a look at this joke using the trusty joke structure diagram in Figure 4.2[18]:

The disruption of logic in this joke is that, normally, when someone says there is water in the carburetor, we would assume the carburetor was flooded due to mechanical issues, and thus the first story we tell ourselves is it

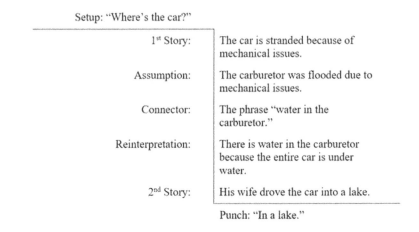

Setup: "Where's the car?"	
1st Story:	The car is stranded because of mechanical issues.
Assumption:	The carburetor was flooded due to mechanical issues.
Connector:	The phrase "water in the carburetor."
Reinterpretation:	There is water in the carburetor because the entire car is under water.
2nd Story:	His wife drove the car into a lake.
Punch: "In a lake."	

Figure 4.2 Dangerfield's Joke in a Joke Structure Diagram

stranded somewhere because of mechanical issues. The punchline breaks that chain of logic. It provokes us to realize that the carburetor is not wet because of mechanical issues but because his wife drove the car into a lake.

But, recall, for a syllogism to work, there needs to be a shared understanding of *each element* embedded in the joke. By employing the stereotype that women are bad drivers, audiences could immediately understand the punchline. The punchline caused audiences to laugh because there was a twist; it did not follow the chain of logic about a car's carburetor. But the punchline only works because it was in line with audience's shared understanding of the world and a shared understanding of stereotypes about women drivers.

Think about how this shared understanding – exemplified by this comedic example – relates to stereotype threat. Notice that Dangerfield's comedic character is one who gets no respect and one for whom nothing goes right, yet it is his wife who is the butt of the joke here. We will come back to this idea later when we discuss appropriation of the underdog identity, but Dangerfield's comedy paints him as a victim of his wife's bad cooking and bad driving. His wife has no voice and, as far as audiences can see, seemingly no redemptive quality. There is no nuance to women's identity or role in these jokes.

Let us now compare Dangerfield's and Diller's comedic characters. Diller leaned into the same norms and stereotypes as did Dangerfield regarding social expectations for women at the time, but she showed audiences she was *more* than a wife and mother. She was a whole person; a loud, funny, wild, and entertaining one. Dangerfield's comedy makes fun of a *person*. His wife is failing at the one thing she is supposed to do; and Dangerfield, as a result, is forced to eat bad food and deal with the consequences of her bad driving. Meanwhile, Diller's comedy makes fun of *norms*. Her comedic performances make audiences ask: why *should* she be at home cleaning when she hates it, is bad at it, and clearly belongs on stage? The way Diller and Dangerfield use stereotypes in their act, with Diller challenging, and Dangerfield reinforcing, is linked to how their social position and identity influence their lens.

Comedy Roasts, Superiority Theory, and the Evolution of Humor

Comedic styles evolve alongside changing norms in society. Certain stereotypes or tropes are employed for a while, then go out of style when those stereotypes or no longer valid or novel – like jokes about nagging girlfriends or jokes about women being bad drivers. This is most evident through the historical progression of the comedy roast. **Comedy roasts** refer to comedy performances wherein a comedian (or a lineup of comedians) dumps insults on one particular individual; the evening's guest of honor. They are often insult-laden, brash, and/or raunchy performances. Roasts are a long-standing comedic tradition dating back to the early 1950s, when they were hosted by the Friars Club. The Friars Club, a New York City establishment since 1904, is a private club composed primarily of comedians and performers.

The Friars Club would host roasts inside the club, and would either keep the evening's event private, or broadcast a "cleaned up" recording on television (broadcasting began in the 1960s).[19]

In the early roast era, the norms of society were narrower and more restrictive than they are today. The Friars Club has historically been a "boy's club." Liza Minelli became the first female member in 1988, and even today only a small share of members are women (20 percent in 2019).[20] Phyllis Diller famously attended a male-only Friar's Club roast dressed in male-drag in 1983. Journalist Rachel Abrams wrote of the club's narrow culture for the *New York Times*. Abrams detailed how they had a large and powerful influence in the world of entertainment, and its membership and events were managed by White male actors and comedians – including Jerry Lewis, Frank Sinatra, and Ed Sullivan. The club's roster and schedule looked a lot like mass entertainment in the United States at the time. In this era, there were only a small number of television channels and a similarly small number of major stars who graced the stage and the screen. The norms were set by a specific and powerful segment of society primarily composed of men were overwhelmingly rich, powerful, older, and White.

With the makeup of the Friar's Club in mind, let us go back to one of their most popular exports – the comedy roast. Comedy Central picked up the tradition in 1998 and began airing roasts of celebrities.[21] Some of the celebrities who have sat in the hot-seat include Bob Saget (2008), Larry the Cable Guy (2009), Joan Rivers (2009), Donald Trump (2011), Roseanne Barr (2012), James Franco (2013), Justin Bieber (2015), and Alec Baldwin (2019). Comedy Central's Roasts have multiple comics on the stage all roasting the primary roastee and each other.

Why was the comedy roast so popular? Superiority theory philosophizes about why people may laugh at the expense of others. **Superiority theory,** which traces back to early works of philosophy, posits that humor comes from an audience's understanding that we (the collective "we" of the audience) have some form of superiority over the target of derision; the person or group who is the butt of the joke.[22] Perhaps we have less money or power, but we have more moral fortitude. Or better hair. Whatever. It boosts our collective agency, self-esteem, or feelings of worth by identifying and validating areas where we feel superior to the target.[23] Jokes reaffirm differences and feelings of superiority.

Punching Up and Punching Down

Scholars have long theorized how it is acceptable for individuals, specifically comedians and court jesters, to criticize those with more power than them using comedy as a shield. Comedy allows social taboos to be temporarily suspended so we can explore the causes and consequences of specific feelings. Before we go forward with this point, let us discuss the concepts of "punching up" and "punching down" in comedy.

Punching up is when someone lobs jokes at a person or group of people who have more power than they do.[24] Jokes that punch up generally do not strip people of their power. The court jester does not take power away from the king. Comedians "speaking truth to power" tends to fall under the umbrella of punching up.

Compare that to **punching down**. When someone punches down, they lob jokes at people who have less power than they do. Punching down may be intentional, like the jokes we saw from Rodney Dangerfield about women. Or, punching down can result from being unaware of appropriate language or cultural norms. For example, take language which did not properly recognize the identity of transgender or non-binary people.[25]

Let us use an example from comedian, actress, and podcaster Cameron Esposito (born in Western Springs, Illinois, 1981). Esposito has a joke about periods. She used to say "women," but an audience member asked her to change the joke to say "people with periods," because some people who have periods are trans men and not all women have periods. Esposito changed the joke. She did not want to punch down. She knows that the people most impacted by her word choice – specifically, trans folks – are incredibly marginalized in our society. A simple wording change can prevent making them feel further excluded or marginalized.[26]

Recall our discussion of symbolic interactionism. Words carry meaning. Referring to people by their desired pronouns, for example, are important ways we can show respect for each other.[27] Words also change. Over time, cultural awareness around individuals' identities, physical or mental abilities, occupations, and a whole host of other factors shift, and language shifts with it. Comedians can adapt their jokes and their language in line to be more reflective of accepted language and cultural norms. Esposito's agreement to change the language in her joke reflects a postmodern perspective. Esposito lets the community to which she is referring define themselves, versus letting anyone else (including her) define it for them.

Evolution of "Pregnant" as Deviant with Lucille Ball and Joan Rivers

The evolution of language to describe people and bodies is nothing new. To see a historical example – and see how today, and tomorrow, are along a long continuum from the past – let us look to how pregnant bodies were discussed (or not) on screen. First, let us turn to the hit sitcom *I Love Lucy*, which aired on CBS from 1951 to 1957. The show centered around a married couple; Lucy Arnaz (played by Lucille Ball) and Desi Arnaz (played by Desi Arnaz), and their two best friends, Ethel and Fred Mertz (played by Vivian Vance and William Frawley, respectively). Ball got her start in show business by guest appearing on popular radio programs in the 1940s. Executives at CBS were captivated by Ball's radio performances and quickly cast her in a half-hour radio sitcom titled *My Favorite Husband*.[28] In the show, Ball portrayed a zany housewife named Liz who was always getting into trouble. Her husband,

George, was the straight-man who stepped up to solve her problems (played by Richard Denning, who took over from Lee Bowman after the series pilot). Each episode ended with Liz saying to George: "Thanks, George. You're my *favorite* husband." Ball's performance in the show made it a hit.

CBS pitched Ball the idea to transition the radio show *My Favorite Husband* to television alongside Richard Denning. However, Ball wanted her real husband, Desi Arnaz, to play her husband on the television series. CBS refused to cast Arnaz because he was Cuban. The network did not believe audiences would be comfortable with an interracial relationship between a White woman and a Latin man. So Ball and Arnaz set out to prove CBS wrong. To prove audiences would love them, they began performing together as a vaudeville act alongside Arnaz's orchestra at the Ritz Theater in Newburgh, New York. Ball and Arnaz were right: audiences did love them. CBS signed the duo and *I Love Lucy* went on to become the most popular show on American television for many years.[29]

During the show's second season, Lucille Ball became pregnant with her son, Desi Arnaz Jr. They worked Ball's pregnancy into the current storyline of the series at the time (something the network discouraged Desi Arnaz from doing while Ball was pregnant with their first child, Lucie, during the first season of the show). In the show, Ball's character (Lucy Arnaz) was also pregnant with a son (Little Ricky). The 1953 episode in which Lucy gives birth, titled "Lucy Goes to the Hospital," was played by 71.7 percent of all television sets in the United States. This was more popular than any other television episode that came before, and even had higher ratings than Dwight D. Eisenhower's presidential inauguration, which aired one day later.[30] Despite the popularity of Lucy's pregnancy and Little Ricky's delivery as an *I Love Lucy* storyline, "pregnant" was a forbidden word. CBS only allowed characters on the show to say Lucy was "expecting."[31] Ball was a powerful, socially disruptive figure, but she was still limited by restrictive and gendered social norms.

Second, let us turn to comedian Joan Rivers. Rivers was born as Joan Molinsky in Brooklyn, New York, 1933, and much of her comedic material tackled what it meant to be a woman in the United States: to be harassed, demeaned, and to struggle with expectations of beauty or love. During the time Rivers was coming up in comedy, Johnny Carson was the ultimate comedic gatekeeper. He ruled late night television with his show, *The Tonight Show Starring Johnny Carson*. Carson liked essentially no women comedians. When men see themselves as judge and jury of who is funny, prejudice against comedy written and performed by women inhibits an unbiased review of its humor. Carson excluded most women comedians from performing on his show.

But Carson liked Rivers. She had moxy. She joked about men being intimidated by funny women.[32] And her appearances on *The Tonight Show* were a catalyst for her career. What set Rivers apart at the time and stuck with her throughout her career was her courage to call others out on their hypocrisy or impropriety. Rivers pushed the boundaries of her era.

Yet, Rivers still had to play by the institution's rules – which were largely dictated by men – to be allowed on stage. The best example of how this relates to changing norms comes from a 1967 appearance by Rivers on *The Ed Sullivan Show*. Rivers performed on the show while eight months pregnant with her daughter, Melissa. Performing on television as a pregnant comedian was groundbreaking. This was an era when pregnant people were rarely shown on screen. It was so rare, in fact, that while audiences could see her pregnant belly, CBS would not allow Rivers to say the word "pregnant." The network considered it indecent.[33] The official language approved by CBS (which, according to Rivers, took much consideration) to air on the show was she "would soon be hearing the pitter patter of little feet." She said this line wearing a poofy dress Rivers compared to a tent to obscure her pregnant belly.[34] If Lucille Ball or Joan Rivers had performed pregnant on television today, they would be able to say "pregnant." Hearing this word on television was considered indecent and deviant then but would be considered normal now. Norms change, and therefore, so does deviance.

Evolution of "Deviance" with Lenny Bruce

Consider comedian Lenny Bruce (born in Mineola, New York, 1925). Bruce's comedic legacy is oft regarded as that of a "free-speech martyr."[35] Why? He got arrested and blacklisted many times for what he said on stage. Indeed, Bruce was arrested fifteen times for obscenity (including being sentenced to four-months of hard labor for obscenity in New York), and because of his arrest rate, he had an understudy follow him around to gigs just in case he got into trouble with the cops. He was ultimately blacklisted by so many nightclubs that it effectively ended his career. Based on his arrest and blacklisting record, we can assume lawmakers, police officers, nightclub owners, and audience members considered Bruce's comedy deviant.

But if you listened to Bruce's comedy today, you would not think of him as a particularly edgy or "rabble-rousing" comedian. His jokes which broke social norms in the 1950s seem relatively tame by today's standards. Humor, like language, changes alongside social and cultural norms. What is considered humorous, shocking, or surprising evolves alongside social norms. What constitutes *breaking* social norms, then, evolves too. Bruce would certainly not be arrested for obscenity if he performed his same acts today. Bruce's legacy helps us understand that deviance cannot be an innate quality (someone is a deviant or they are not), since what constitutes deviance itself changes over time.

Dr. Stephanie Brown notes how the rebel comedians of the 1950s and 1960s – most notably Lenny Bruce and Mort Sahl – deviated from comedians before them by using their own lives and experiences for material, giving audiences shows that felt personal, individual, and authentic.[36] This was a drastic deviation from prior comedy eras. During the vaudeville era, for example, comedy acts were not designed around the individuality of the performer.

They were designed to simply be entertaining. Writer and comedy historian Kliph Nesteroff describes this transition – from impersonal to personal comedy – as "stand-up's great change."[37]

The evolution of comedy provides a window through which we can discuss evolutions in social norms and how social hierarchies are maintained. This book began with an introduction to the foundational concept of the sociological imagination to invite the reader to see the world in a new way. By seeing how social norms change over time, we can use our sociological imagination to understand that social norms are not static or innate. Definitions of "deviance" are socially constructed and are used as a tool by those in power to maintain their hegemony.

Thus far, we have discussed how social conceptions of "deviance" change over *time*. But they also vary by *place*. We can see how what is considered "deviant" varies by place through a comedic example. Let us turn to Vir Das (born in Dehradun, India, 1979). Das is an Indian comedian, actor, writer, and musician who was raised and educated in India, Niger, and the United States. Das is a cross-culture comedian. His multinational upbringing allowed him to view the world through a unique lens. He can understand multiple cultures while still having the ability to view them as an outsider.

Das made international headlines in 2021 following the performance of a comedic poem titled "Two Indias," which Das delivered at The John F. Kennedy Center for the Performing Arts in Washington, DC. The comedic poem highlighted hypocrisies Das identified in Indian policies and cultural norms, including the treatment of women (speaking specifically about sexual violence) and the working class.[38] Seven separate legal charges were filed against Das following the speech on charges of defamation and sedition.[39] Das was labeled by some as a "terrorist" for insulting India. Aditya Jha, a vice president of the Bharatiya Janata Party under Prime Minister Narendra Modi's administration, called for an investigation into Das and expressed desire for his arrest.[40] Das described the comedic poem as satire intended to point out hypocrisies which exist within India. But, as Das notes, the comedic poem was not intended to vilify India as a country; a country he loves. He notes that similar hypocrisies exist within all countries and cultures.[41]

James E. Caron, professor emeritus of English at the University of Hawai'i at Mānoa, asserts that satire is a comedic parallel to the Greek concept of parrhēsia. **Parrhēsia** refers to speaking truth to power, even at a risk of personal consequence, out of obligation to the greater good.[42] Das' comedy is an example of parrhēsia. Das knows the humanity of those for whom he spoke up – women and the working class, among others – was worth the backlash. However, Das notes that he performed his work on U.S. soil, versus Indian soil, due to the risk of legal consequence.[43] Das' experience provides an example of how labeling someone a "deviant" serves to maintain the status quo. Laws which prohibit speaking out against hypocrisy or injustice maintain hegemonic power through conflict and coercion.

Satire and Comedic Perspective

Before moving forward, let us review this book's definition of comedy. This book defines comedy as any written, oral, or visual display which presents the world in a way which shines light on an issue, speaks truth to power, and aims to disrupt the status quo. Inherent in this definition is that comedy is respectful and not derogatory or traumatizing. When done well, I believe comedy can bring connection and instill hope. In the following sections, we will discuss satire. **Satire** is the comedic use of hyperbole or irony to criticize an issue.[44] We will discuss if and how it can be used as an effective tool to fight against oppression.

The Purpose of Satire

Journalist and author Lindy West (born in Seattle, Washington, 1982) provides a helpful description of satire's function in comedy and society. West is perhaps best known for her book, *Shrill: Notes from a Loud Woman*, which was adapted as television series on Hulu, also called *Shrill*, that premiered in 2019. West describes the approach and goal of satirical writing as the ability to use hyperbole. Traditional journalism is supposed to report the facts. Satirical writing can take those same facts then highlight their absurdity.[45] West makes the distinction that a straight description of facts often cannot uncover the underlying emotional truth of a situation or story. It is satire that allows a storyteller to take facts and add emotional weight to them. The idea that satire, and comedy writ large, can be "truer than true" is an idea that we will return to throughout this book. It is for this reason that I believe comedy adds so much to a sociological classroom. By spinning up absurdity or injustice, comedy puts a magnifying glass on social troubles.

I will add an addendum to West's quote. When using satire to spin up facts and add emotional weight to them, the satirist often aims to highlight injustice and foster social change. The goal is to open people's minds and get them to see the world differently than they did before. Refer to Moms Mabley's and Phyllis Diller's character comedy and how these comedians used satire to challenge the social norms of their era.

However, satire's definition does not require the satirist to change people's perspectives. In execution, satire often serves to reinforce a certain way of thinking. Our own biases inform how we consume information, which is a challenge also present in teaching sociology. Satire's limitations in challenging people's perspectives and fostering social change can be called "the Archie Bunker problem." For readers unfamiliar with the reference, Archie Bunker was a character from the 1970s sitcom *All in the Family* (CBS, 1971–1979). Archie was a war veteran and blue-collar worker. One of his defining characteristics was how he was unafraid to share his racist, misogynistic, and bigoted beliefs.

The "Archie Bunker problem" reflects how the creators of *All in the Family* attempt to satirize "American rednecks" through the character of Archie. They thought Archie would highlight flaws like bigotry, which the creators believed to be too common among the people Archie represented. The satirical problem, however, was the audiences who identified with Archie loved him genuinely, with no irony. The way people respond to characters who reinforce their preexisting beliefs is generally positive, as we can see by how audiences responded to Archie's character. The creators of *All in the Family* did not effectively criticize the social norms of racism, misogyny, and bigotry through Archie's performance. The creators did not take an appropriate sociological or comedic lens to what they saw as Archie's flaws because they assumed those flaws were obvious.

Assuming something is "obvious" is a limitation of one's own lens. This is why sociology professors often teach students about the sociological imagination at the very beginning of their sociological training. We must see things from outside our own perspective to understand each other, understand the world, or challenge someone on why they believe the things they do or behave the way they do. Things we assume are universally understood or universally normal are based upon our own biases and experiences. Things that are deviant or unusual to us may be normal to someone else. If we want to challenge a belief, we need to highlight *why* we think it is problematic. We cannot simply showcase its existence and assume others will see things the way we see them. This is the challenge in both comedy and sociology.

When satire is used effectively, it can identify the causes and consequences of injustice in society from a systemic perspective. In *All in the Family*, the goal was to satirize racist, misogynistic, and bigoted beliefs. However, the show used a personal lens, not a systemic one. They asked audiences to ponder "Is Archie Bunker bad?" versus "Is systemic and persistent racism bad?" This approach allowed those who agreed with Archie to see him positively and those who disagreed with Archie to see him negatively. The "Archie Bunker problem" shows us how our own biases shape our consumption of information and our understanding of the world.

The Satirist's Point-of-View with The Onion

Effective satirists must consider how their work will be interpreted and what story it will tell. For an episode of the podcast *This American Life*, host Ira Glass spent a week at the offices of the satirical newspaper *The Onion*. His goal was to understand their process of coming up with satirical headlines and subsequently writing the articles to go with them. Glass describes their writer's room, where writers pitch over 600 headlines per week. Six hundred! They have a well-honed process for dissecting jokes and identifying if, and why, they are funny. Glass explained the underlying assumptions of this process are not something he was privy to as an outsider to the writer's room. Glass, specifically, details an example of a standout headline,

"Local girlfriend always wants to do stuff" (*This American Life*, "Tough Room," 2008).[46]

> It's sometimes hard to figure out why, for instance, 'Local girlfriend always wants to do stuff' was a good enough headline to make it into the paper, while a headline that seems nearly identical, 'Nation's girlfriends call for more quality time,' literally gets jeers. Jeers.

While Glass was lost to the difference between these two headlines, *The Onion* editors Todd Hanson and Dan Guterman explained. They told Glass that the story following the "Local girlfriend always wants to do stuff" headline was written to make fun of the boyfriend's lack of motivation to get out of the house and engage in activities with his girlfriend. It is making fun of the guy for deriding the girlfriend for wanting to go outside and be around people, friends, and new environments. The story that would have gone along with the headline "Nation's girlfriends call for more quality time" would have been about nagging girlfriends. The former, which made it into the paper, helps you understand the girlfriend's point, while the latter, which received jeers, vilifiers her. The former indicates we should step up in our relationships with the ones we love, and the latter says our loved ones should shut up and stop asking so much from us. Put more succinctly: one questions misogyny and the other does not.

Think back to the different ways that character comedians Phyllis Diller and Rodney Dangerfield both played with the same social norms about women as housewives and mothers. While their material was based on the same social expectations and stereotypes, one presentation served to challenge the status quo, and one presentation served to reinforce it. Comedy is a game of perspective. The distinction between "Local girlfriend always wants to do stuff" and "Nation's girlfriends call for more quality time" takes a real understanding of how individual experiences fit within social norms. In the episode of *This American Life*, *The Onion* writer Megan Ganz explained that headlines which are initially funny may not actually have a deeper meaning. In selecting their headlines, *The Onion* writers need to ask what story follows the headline. The answer to that question is their comedic perspective.

There is no one way to inject magic into something and make it funny. Audiences are drawn to comedians for their comedic perspective. Two comedians can take the same setup and arrive at different punchlines. The lens they use to uncover what is funny about something is their comedic point of view. This is the comedy equivalent of a sociological imagination. By having unique comedic perspectives, this is how different comedians identify particular phenomena to discuss on stage, and how they unpack those phenomena differently than another comedian would.

The way comedians think sociologically is not as simple as reading the news or writing funny standalone headlines. The way comedians think sociologically is by taking stock of why something is funny and spinning that up to absurdity. When done effectively, it brings issues to life and helps audiences understand an issue's social impact. This can drive new ways of thinking, compel action, create more connection, and cause social change. That is the true function of satire. Satire takes something simple, like an observation or an interaction, and makes it bigger, more meaningful, and more universal. We can think of satirical joke writing in the same way a caricature-artist would sketch out their art; find the absurd and amplify it. It makes the issues hard to not see.

Parodic News Programs

We just discussed print news with *The Onion*, now let us discuss satirical news programs on television. Satiric news programs rose to prominence over the past several decades. In her book, *Satire and Dissent: Interventions in Contemporary Political Debate* (2012), Dr. Amber Day defines three of the most common and high-profile forms of satiric news: parodic news shows, satiric documentaries, and ironic activism.[47] We will focus on the parodic news show here.

Parodic news shows generally feature fewer scripted sections, such as impersonations or sketches – which were markers of the variety shows which preceded them – and instead lean on deconstructions of the news and shocking "gotcha moments" achieved by "ambushing" public figures.

This type of news program became extremely popular. One of the most popular programs was *The Daily Show with Jon Stewart* (Comedy Central, 1999–2015). *The Daily Show* was a very popular late night talk show series which aired on Comedy Central from 1996 to 2022. It was the longest-running program on the network. The series had three distinct eras marked by its different hosts: Craig Kilborn (1996–1998), Jon Stewart (1999–2015), and Trevor Noah (2015–2022). When it first launched in 1996, the show was primarily focused on popular culture. When Stewart took the helm from Kilborn, the show was revamped to become more focused on satirizing politics and the mainstream news.

Stephen Colbert (born in Washington, DC, 1964) was a correspondent on the series from 1997 to 2015. Colbert played a character (bearing his same name) that was a parody of television political pundits. The Colbert character was meant to appear high-status and politically ill-informed. Jon Stewart wanted the Colbert character to have a political point of view. This, already, was a departure from what news programs purported themselves to be at the time, which was to be objective. By leaning into a specific viewpoint, Colbert (in his role as correspondent on *The Daily Show*) could deconstruct it.

Day notes such deconstruction is central to the format of a parodic news program. The structure of the program is meant to challenge standard media frameworks used in more traditional news programs. The parodic nature of *The Daily Show with Jon Stewart*, through its "ambush" interviews and caricature-like correspondents, gave them more leverage to highlight political hypocrisies, absurdities, and injustices. According to Day, parodic news shows can "poke holes" in the more mainstream political or news narratives. Part of their effectiveness was their entertainment value. Tuning in was *fun;* not a chore. Fans and critics alike loved *The Daily Show with Jon Stewart.* It earned twenty-three Primetime Emmy Awards and two Peabody Awards for its coverage of the 2000 and 2004 Presidential elections.[48–50]

Threats to Satirical Integrity

We just talked about the format, style, and comedic effectiveness of parodic news programs. Let us now discuss their effectiveness of delivering the news. For this discussion, we will use the Stephen Colbert-spinoff of *The Daily Show with Jon Stewart,* which aired on Comedy Central 2005–2014, titled *The Colbert Report.* On *The Colbert Report,* Stephen Colbert plays his same caricature character that he did on *The Daily Show with Jon Stewart.* Colbert (the person) is politically progressive but his character is designed to satirize right-leaning political beliefs. Colbert reports on political news and interviews guests on politics, the economy, and global events without ever breaking character.

A group of researchers studied the role of humor in media. In one study, they focused on the use of satire in *The Colbert Report* and how ambiguity within Colbert's satirical performance (such as ambiguity regarding whether or not audiences understood that Colbert is not actually a conservative) impacts their reaction to the show. The research group showed clips of *The Colbert Report* to their research participants and asked questions about their perceived intent of Colbert's representation of politics in his monologues and his guest interviews.

The researchers found that the more liberal a viewer was, the more likely they saw Colbert as a liberal persona taking aim at conservative viewpoints. The more conservative a viewer was, the more likely they saw Colbert as a conservative persona taking aim at liberal viewpoints.[51] As Dr. Heather LaMarre, one of the researchers of this project and associate professor and chair of the Department of Communication and Social Influence at Temple University, described audiences as seeing their own views reflected on the screen. Like *All in the Family,* *The Colbert Report* is an example of how our own biases shape our perceptions of statements or events.[52] A threat to satirical integrity occurs when it reaffirms biases instead of challenging them.

In her book, *All Joking Aside* (2014), Dr. Rebecca Krefting, associate professor of American Studies at Skidmore College, discusses this type of comedic work. She explains that the comedic performances delivered by late night talk show hosts can best be described as "pseudo-satirical." Pseudo-satire refers to humor which caricatures public figures like celebrities and politicians without making any critical assessments or taking political stances on them or their issues.[53] They at first may appear to be based in satire because of their use of caricature and humorous delivery, but they lack a political stance.

There is a term for comedy which reaffirms beliefs rather than challenges them to gain audience approval: clapter. **Clapter** is an industry term for a joke or statement intended to make the audience applaud rather than to make them laugh. Clapter, by definition, is void of the thoughtful and reflective perspectives that form this book's definition of comedy. This book defines comedy as a mechanism for audiences to view the world through a new perspective. Clapter, however, is a way of reinforcing a particular perspective. The term was first coined by comedian, actor, and late night host Seth Meyers (born in Evanston, Illinois, 1973) in the mid-2000s to lament the phenomenon of comedians prioritizing pandering to audience's political beliefs over creating thoughtful and reflective comedic material.[54]

To understand why audiences want their beliefs reinforced, we can think about this sociologically. This idea relates to how sociologists think about **distinction** in consumption. Sociologists have observed that people strive to use their consumption behaviors to distinguish themselves from others. As described by Pierre Bourdieu, a famous sociologist born in Denguin, France, 1930, people strive to distinguish themselves from others through the material goods and the culture they consume.[55] This is also a central concept in Thorstein Veblen's *Theory of the Leisure Class* (1899).[56]

Of particular interest to Bourdieu was how elites often try to distinguish themselves from people of lower class status through their language, dress, or consumer behavior. Picture someone carrying an NPR tote bag. This tote bag acts as a signal of a certain social grouping, that of a supporter of public radio who likely leans progressive in their political ideology. For another, picture someone wearing a "Make America Great Again" hat; the material centerpiece of Donald Trump's 2016 presidential campaign. This hat is widely understood as a signal of a particular political ideology aligning with Donald Trump's platform. This idea of distinction is not just about material consumption, but also relates to cultural consumption. Examples of cultural consumption may be attending the opera or reading the *New York Times* (*NYT*). These consumption behaviors are shaped by cultural understandings of what the opera, or reading the *NYT*, signal about taste or social standing. Clapter is an extension of this idea. What you watch and what you clap at signal something about your taste and your ideology. These work to distinguish you from others. In this way, watching *Last Week Tonight with John Oliver*, an HBO satirical news show with a liberal slant hosted by John Oliver, or watching *The Colbert Report* (if you identify as a liberal) are the comedic news equivalents of stuffing your *NYT: Sunday edition* into your NPR tote bag.

Dr. James E. Caron, in his book *Satire as the Comic Public Sphere: Postmodern "Truthiness" and Civic Engagement* (2021), defines this genre of satirical news program as "truthiness satire."[57] Caron notes that these satirical news anchors lean on the shared norms and values of their viewers to play with the news format. This shared lens allows the shows to use more postmodern techniques for reporting the news – less rational and linear, and more abstract and absurd. This also creates a sense of community for the audience with the creators and other viewers of the show. It feels good and meaningful to be in on the joke. Knowing why and when to laugh is a form of distinction.

However, there is a downside to this community. If a news program aims for consensus, that may stifle more nuanced descriptions of complicated topics. As Caron explains, steering away from such nuance and stickiness in reporting the news can serve to maintain the status quo. It can stoke division and stifle compromise or progress. It can result in an underinformed public. Caron describes how leaning into one specific viewpoint can turn into reporting of "alternative facts" – loosely defined as information, which is misleading or inaccurate, reported in service of validating one's own viewpoint. Caron connects the reporting of alternative facts to sociologist Jean Baudrillard's concept of the **simulation**. Recall that a simulation is a false narrative or reality – presented as "real" – crafted by editing or curating images or information.

Impression Management

Now let us consider how we craft our own image. **Impression management** refers to techniques and behaviors that influence how others view you. In sociology courses, we talk about classical and contemporary theories for human behavior. These theories attempt to bring rationality and order to the question, "Why do people behave the way they do?" using social, cultural, and structural lenses. Theories put forth by sociologist Erving Goffman (born in Alberta, Canada, 1922) attempt to address this question. Goffman was responsible for the creation of a new area of sociology focused on understanding "everyday life." His book, *The Presentation of Self in Everyday Life* (1959), utilizes theater references to explain how people perform and act in the presence of others to manage their social image compared to when they are alone.[58]

Goffman's theater-based description of human interaction is the **dramaturgical theory of the self**. The core components of Goffman's dramaturgical theory center on what he refers to as the **front stage** and **back stage**. The front stage and back stage theories of behavior provide important context for understanding differences in how people behave and present themselves in differing contexts. The following sections will review these theories individually.

Front Stage Behavior

If you think about your own behavior, you may agree with the sociological notion that individuals shape their behavior according to where they are and who else is occupying that space. People do this consciously or unconsciously based on internalized norms and expectations. Imagine you are in a theatrical play. You walk out onto a stage wearing a costume, speaking with a particular tone, and staging your interactions with your fellow actors. All these cues and actions serve to tell your audience something about your character and the world they inhabit. Is the character rich or poor? Are they hypermasculine or hyperfeminine? Are they confident or shy? By using audio, visual, and behavioral cues, you can signal your answers to the audience without ever speaking to them directly. One of the skills of acting is to communicate through action rather than announcement.

Exit the theatrical stage and think about how you operate in daily life. Is it really that different? According to Goffman, "all the world is a stage." The **front stage** refers to the set of behaviors we don when we know or feel we are being watched by someone else, and the set of behaviors that we consider normal and expected in a given space based on what we have learned by observing others.

An example of impression management is what I would do in front of the classroom when seeking to establish myself as a professional scholar worthy of trust and respect. I would do this in the way I dress (donning professional attire in lieu of casual clothing), the way I hold myself (good posture, no slouching), and the way I speak (formally, by using sociological and statistical jargon largely reserved for classroom discussions or peer-reviewed journals). There is room for deviations in these behaviors, like engaging jokes to break tension or foster connection in the classroom. But those must be noticeable deviations, not the norm, if I am to keep my air of authority.

In the classroom, I use professional signals to impress on my students that "I am the authority here." These patterns of dress, posture, and modes of conversation certainly differ from the way I conduct myself around my friends, which is much more relaxed, informal, and perhaps crasser (although I am sure my students and friends would agree that my puns are equally terrible irrespective of audience). As a young woman, I relied more heavily on these outward signals than some of my older male peers, whose authority was more likely to be presumed.[59] This presumed authority could let them wear jeans, deliver lectures sitting on a desk, or use slang or curse words (basically, things cool professors do in movies). And certainly, my colleagues of color and colleagues for whom English is not their first language face greater hurdles than I did when it came to battling expectations of who is or is not an assumed person of authority.

Comedian John Mulaney's style is a contemporary example of impression management in comedy. Mulaney was born in Chicago, Illinois, 1982 and is known for his observational standup comedy. Some of Mulaney's best-known comedic contributions are from his time as a writer for *Saturday Night Live* (2008–2012) and his myriad specials including, *The Top Part* (2009), *New in Town* (2012), *The Comeback Kid* (2015), *Kid Gorgeous* (2018), and *Baby J* (2023). Mulaney is known for almost exclusively wearing suits for his standup performances and other appearances. When asked why he is always suit-clad, Mulaney told *The Ringer* in 2018 that he made the decision after performing a show in Atlanta where he was dressed just like everyone else. He realized there was nothing signaling why he should be the one on stage. After that, he started wearing suits. To Mulaney, he saw being the most dressed-up person in the comedy club as proper signal that he was the performer. That the audience was there to see him.[60] Just as a professor dons professional attire in a classroom to set themselves apart from the students, Mulaney uses wearing a suit to separate himself from the audience. Mulaney uses his clothing to justify why he has the microphone the same way I use my clothing to justify why I have the lectern.

Back Stage Behavior

You may feel more comfortable being your authentic self in what Goffman deems as **back stage** behavior, or "what you do when no one is looking."[61] The back stage in this context refers to times when you are alone or in the company of trusted family or close friends. You may dress more comfortably (hello, sweatpants!), or literally and metaphorically let your hair down.

The back stage is also where you prepare yourself for the front stage or decompress after a front stage experience. You may rehearse a presentation in front of the mirror or change your outfit several times before deeming one appropriate for an upcoming event. Even in the back stage, you are aware of front stage expectations.

Front Stage versus Back Stage Behavior

To explore the distinction between front stage and back stage behaviors, we can discuss the political satire comedy series *Veep*, which ran for six seasons (2012–2019) on HBO. The show centers around Selina Meyer (played by Julia Louis-Dreyfus) as the vice president of the United States, who later becomes President. Meyer and her staff are foul-mouthed, brash, self-serving queens and kings of political gaming. The show is absurdist, though many DC insiders claim that it is a shockingly realistic portrayal of the U.S. political system.[62]

Its institutional legitimacy aside, *Veep* can help us unpack front and back stage behavior on a collective and individual level. In *Veep*, we get a peek into what's happening with each character as soon as they leave the lectern. *Veep* shows us how Meyer and her staff talk about their political opponents, the general public of the United States, and each other in one way when they are in front of an audience and another way when they are behind closed doors.

In season 4, *Veep* audiences watched Meyer court potential voters on the campaign trail for her presidential bid. She spoke about patriotism and democracy; she shook hands, attended pancake brunch fundraisers, and figuratively kissed babies. This is Meyer in the front stage. The results of the presidential election are shown in the season finale episode "Election Night." Most of the episode takes place in a hotel suite where we see Meyer and her staff anxiously watching the results of the election roll in, celebrating when Meyer takes a state and political game-planning when she loses one.[63]

Late in the evening, Meyer and her opponent are projected to be tied for Electoral College votes. Panicked by the unprecedented tie, everyone immediately pulls out their smartphones to figure out what happens next. The idea that potential leaders would behind closed doors typing "What happens if there's a tie in a presidential election?" into an Internet search engine is certainly a lack of knowledge those candidates would not want to showcase to the public. While her staff is busy searching the Internet for answers, Meyer grows frustrated. She screams to her staff, ranting about how she tries to serve people but is stymied by them being too "ignorant" and "dumb." Here, Meyer is speaking with back stage confidentiality about her desire for power (which is immense) and how she views the American public (which is very negatively).

Veep provides myriad examples of what switching between the front stage and the back stage looks like. Louis-Dreyfus' performance as Meyer shows fast-paced delivery and incredible comedic timing. Her rants are iconic. Indeed, Louis-Dreyfus surpassed female comedy legends, including Mary Tyler Moore and Lucille Ball in Emmys for best actress in a comedy series with six consecutive wins for her performance as Meyer.[64] *Veep*, itself, won the best comedy series Emmy three times.

In celebration and recognition of her stellar career performances as the United States' favorite foul-mouthed and endlessly talented comedic actress, Louis-Dreyfus was awarded the Mark Twain Prize for American Humor in 2018. Since 1998, the prize has been presented by the John F. Kennedy Center for the Performing Arts to humorists recognized as having had "an impact on American society in ways similar to the distinguished nineteenth-century novelist and essayist Samuel Clemens, best known as Mark Twain."[65] Specifically, Twain's qualities highlighted by the Kennedy Center as important for this award include his role as a social commentator, satirist, observer of society, and one with an "unpromising perspective on social injustice and personal folly" (Kennedy Center, 2021). That sounds like sociology! It is fitting for this book that the highest prize for comedy is a sociology award.

Grooming Gap with *Crazy Ex-Girlfriend*

Veep effectively showed us the front stage and back stage as it relates to politics and power. We will now use another comedic example, from *Crazy Ex-Girlfriend*, to highlight the front stage and back stage as it relates to gender norms and grooming expectations. *Crazy Ex-Girlfriend* was a musical comedy sitcom which ran on the CW for four seasons (2015–2019). The show follows real estate attorney Rebecca Bunch (played by Rachel Bloom) as she quits her high-powered and high-paying job in New York City to follow her high school camp boyfriend, Josh Chan (played by Vincent Rodriguez III), to the not-so-glamorous town of West Covina, California, after she bumps into him on the street.

Created by Rachel Bloom and Aline Brosh McKenna, *Crazy Ex-Girlfriend* relies heavily on cut-aways to musical numbers which take place entirely in the protagonist's head. Before *Crazy Ex-Girlfriend*, Bloom got her start creating original comedy songs and videos and posting them on YouTube. *Crazy Ex-Girlfriend*'s songbook is filled with brashly titled songs; ones you might not recite for family dinner. With 157 songs in their songbook by the end of the series, the musical numbers develop the characters as the plot moves forward.[66]

The show depicts how gender norms influence every facet of life, including the way we suffer from and attempt to cope with mental illness (we will return to this point later in the book). It does so by breaking the fourth wall between how we live our lives publicly and privately. The musical numbers reveal hidden features of the human condition associated with one's mental health, like depression, anxiety, and sadness, but also features of the human condition associated with one's physical form. Like the discomfort of having heavy breasts, getting a UTI, and having (and removing) body hair.

Feminist theorists have outlined the social norms which dictate expectations for women. Women are supposed to "put together"; to have their minds, bodies, and homes in pristine condition without breaking a sweat. In "The Sexy Getting Ready Song," in *Crazy Ex-Girlfriend*, the hidden work of maintaining a woman's body to adhere to such social expectations is put out into the open. Starring the character Rebecca and featuring rapper Nipsey Hussle (as himself), the lyrics of the song and visuals of the performance show Rebecca getting ready for a date. Unlike most shows, which portray women waking up with perfectly curled hair and a fully touched-up face of makeup, this song highlights the reality of the common beauty regimen before going out on a date or out into the world.

The visuals of the performance include Rebecca plucking nose hairs, grating dead skin off the bottom of her feet, waxing her anus (with blood squirting across the room for dramatic effect), accepting assistance from a friend to help her jump into tight shapeware, and, of course, a few tears. The comedy comes from the juxtaposition of these images to Rebecca's sexy-sultry vocals and cut-aways to beautifully styled stage performances (think: cabaret) by Rebecca and beautiful back-up dancers in lingerie and heels (albeit, with wax strips on their upper lips and curlers in their hair, among other beauty items).

The number includes multiple cut-away shots to her date, Greg, asleep on his couch in jeans and a tee shirt, implying he is not expected to engage in hours of prep time before their evening date. The next and most on-the-nose portion of comedy comes from Nipsey Hussle's performance in the music video. He begins rapping in the bathroom where Rebecca is getting ready.

Rebecca is dancing along to Hussle's performance from the edge of her bathtub. Hussle then takes stock of what is really happening in Rebecca's beauty routine. He stops rapping, turns around and addresses Rebecca directly, expressing his shock.[67] Hussle tells Rebecca how horrified he is by what the patriarchy requires her to do. He leaves, saying that he must apologize to some women.

The scene ends with Greg picking Rebecca up for their date, and he compliments the way she looks (she *does* look great, after all!). Rebecca responds with a casual shrug "Oh, I totally just woke up from a nap." In less than three minutes, the video demonstrates the painful, time-consuming, and expensive beauty routines women are expected to undergo to achieve a look that is "natural" or "effortless," and how men are largely spared from this grueling reality. I encourage you to seek out this clip on the Internet to get the full experience.

The way you behave in social situations – like dates – including what you wear, what activities you engage in, and who is expected to pay, are what are known as social scripts.[68] A **social script** is a set of behaviors and actions that are expected of a particular situation or within a particular context. What you do when you get on an elevator is performing a social script for proper elevator etiquette. I have used the topic of social norms on dates in my sociology courses to illustrate this concept. It is also a great tool for reframing social exchange to make distinctions between the concepts of equality and equity.

To get into this discussion topic, let us first define equality. **Equality** is the state of ensuring two or more things are identical in measure or having identical access to resources and opportunities. So, if we have equal views about gender roles in a heterosexual, cisgender dating relationship, who should pay for dinner on a first date? The man? Or is that antiquated? The bill should be split down the middle, right? Well, let us think about the cost of the date holistically. The cost of the meal (or the coffee or movie tickets) is not the only expense associated with showing up for the date. Each person had to get ready. And in a heterosexual cisgender couple adhering to social grooming standards, it is likely the woman spent additional time, energy, and money to show up for the date in line with socially acceptable norms of appearance.

Consider shots of Rebecca getting ready for the date stitched against shots of Greg taking a nap. Rebecca's time is worth money. Her wax strips, her curlers, and her makeup all cost money, too. Rebecca is required to spend more in time, energy, money, and *blood* than Greg before the date even begins. Returning to the hypothetical example: if the couple splits the cost of dinner equally, we should now have a better understanding of how the woman spent more on the entire date experience than the man. Partner this with unequal wages, and the woman spent a much greater share of her income on the date experience than the man. Suddenly, splitting the check does not seem so fair.

Equity, however, is the state of operating fairly based on a holistic assessment on all factors. It may be more equitable to have the man pick up the check, considering the investment the woman has made to prepare for the date. The definition of equity is certainly less specific than is the definition of equality. It is easier to measure if two things are identical in number (like splitting a dinner check exactly down the middle) than it is to assess if an overall exchange is fair (determining if the overall cost of time, energy, and money for two people having a date experience is holistically fair). It makes the calculation of fair even *more* difficult when much of women's cost and labor is behind closed (bathroom) doors. "The Sexy Getting Ready Song" opens that door wide open for audiences (and Nipsey Hussle) to see the bloody reality of dating inequity. We can consider it deviant to reveal what it really looks like for women to prepare for a date both in real life and in television. Recall that social constructions of deviance serve to maintain a status quo which underpays and overcharges women relative to men.

This song highlights the phenomenon known by sociologists as the **grooming gap**.[69] The grooming gap refers to unequal social norms placed on women (with intersections by race, ethnicity, sexuality, urbanity, and socioeconomic status therein) to maintain a manicured appearance. The grooming necessitated by these social norms requires women to spend more time, energy, and money than is required of men. This unequal expenditure of time, energy, and money is the grooming gap.

Women's products, from hygiene products like deodorant and razors, to services like haircuts and dry cleaning, tend to cost more than the comparable "men's version" of the same product or service. Women pay more for the very same things. This is what is referred to as the pink tax. The **pink tax** is the difference in price between comparable men's and women's products, such as the higher markup for women's razors, shaving cream, deodorant, and hair care products.

Editor-in-chief of the personal finance website *The Balance*, Kristin Myers, conducted a price comparison study of personal care products listed on the websites for large national stores like CVS, RiteAid, Walgreens, and Walmart, and noted price differences in products marketed for men versus those marketed for women.[70] Myers found that products marketed for women cost, on average, 13 percent more than products marketed for men. This varied by product type, with the largest price disparity being for razor cartridges. For this product type, razor cartridges marketed for women were 25 percent more expensive than those marketed for men. California became the first state to outlaw gender-based pricing for comparable products, and noted that women paid an additional $1,315 dollars annually compared to men due to the pink tax.[71] While efforts, like those enacted in California (like the pink tax ban enacted in New York in 2020), attempt to limit gender-based pricing, studies indicate that 42 percent of products still carry differential pricing for products marketed toward women and men.[72]

In addition to the price differences observed for the same products men and women buy, there are also more types of products women buy. For example, women buy most of the makeup sold in the United States. A 2015 survey commissioned by Stowaway Cosmetics, which was sent to 4,000 women, found that the women respondents own an average of forty makeup products.[73] While anyone not identifying as a woman was not included in the survey, other studies suggest men own and use markedly fewer makeup products than do women. Indeed, a poll conducted by *The Huffington Post* found that 54 percent of men do not use a single personal care or beauty product as part of their morning routine. This does not just pertain to makeup, but to any product such as face wash or face lotion.[74] Meanwhile, women often do not just use one product, but many products. In fact, 17 percent of women polled used three to four products and 7 percent used over six products in their morning routine. Those products do not just cost women more money but also more time. Women spend an average of 55 minutes on personal grooming every day.[75]

These expenses compose a larger share of women's incomes. Women, on average, are paid 83 cents to men's dollar, and this difference is starker when you break it down by race.[76] When all of these elements combine, women are required to spend a greater share of their time, energy, and money to meet social norms. Recall our discussion of how we collectively enforce societal norms. How are grooming standards enforced in the United States? Money is one big factor. Women who meet standards of conventional attractiveness are paid more than are less conventionally attractive women.[77] For women, there are monetary penalties to not adhering to these social appearance and grooming standards.

An important point here is the way "conventionally" attractive has long been based on White standards in the United States. The example I use here is based on a White woman's experience personified by the character Rebecca. The time, energy, and money it takes to live up to White standards are heightened for Black women and women of color. There are long histories of Black women's hair being both informally and formally regulated in schools, workplaces, and social engagements. Both the costs and the penalties of not adhering to these White appearance and grooming standards are higher for Black women and women of color.

It can be hard for a show that breaks social norms to be appealing to mainstream audiences. *Crazy Ex-Girlfriend's* low audience ratings may be reflective of a trend in television and movies in which women exist as physically and mentally flawless beings, unlike the protagonist Rebecca; whose flaws, anxieties, and body hair were all laid bare. Mainstream audiences did not understand how they were supposed to like her.

But *Crazy Ex-Girlfriend* had a strong cult following and received praise from critics who considered it one of the best shows on television.[78] That went a long way for toward keeping *Crazy Ex-Girlfriend* on the air for four seasons. In fact, *Crazy Ex-Girlfriend* was the lowest rated television series *ever* to be renewed by a major broadcast network when it was renewed for season three.[79] Timing was everything. The CW renewed *Crazy Ex-Girlfriend*, again and again, in part because executives knew the show would thrive on streaming. The CW was one of the first major broadcast networks to identify how streaming platforms transform low-rated shows into hits by helping them find their audience. On streaming, *Crazy Ex-Girlfriend* found a younger, more devoted following than was accessible on broadcast television. Broadcast ratings mean less and less in a streaming world.

Role Conflict with Ali Wong and Amy Schumer

Finding mainstream success through traditional platforms has long been hard for women and people of color. Consider the incredibly successful standup comedian, writer, and actress Ali Wong (born in San Francisco, California, 1982). Wong was not a popular nightclub comic; she faced hostile crowds who were not interested in her or her comedy.[80] But Netflix gave her an opening to a broader set of people, including people who do not regularly go out to comedy clubs. The people who connected with Wong's comedy *really* connected to it.

Earlier in her standup career, Wong was hesitant about getting married and having kids because she was concerned it would detract from her career as a comedian (a profession which requires a lot of travel and late nights). However, friend and fellow comic Chris Rock (born in Andrews, South Carolina, 1965) advised Wong that the United States is full of married people and parents; and those folks are itching for content that speaks to their experiences.[81] By getting married, having kids, and weaving those experiences into her standup material, Rock knew she could become a comedy star. And that is exactly what happened.

Let us expand on some of the themes we saw in *Crazy Ex-Girlfriend* and extend them to pregnant, birthing, and post-partum bodies. Wong's first two specials – *Baby Cobra* (2016) and *Hard Knock Wife* (2018) – are notable in the comedy special landscape because Wong performs visibly pregnant. She openly discusses pregnancy, motherhood, and marriages in ways that many women experience, yet it remains shocking to hear women speak about openly. In the sociology classroom, there are lessons for students to learn about the experiences of pregnant people, birthing people, and parents. These stories are often hidden or silenced in the United States. For example, in her 2018 Netflix special, *Hard Knock Wife*, she describes her experience having a baby while living in the United States – which includes feelings of isolation, healing one's "demolished" body, and no guaranteed workplace benefits.[82]

Wong describes in her specials what sociologists call role conflict. **Role conflict** refers to the incompatible or untenable expectations coming from multiple roles, such as the roles of being an employee and of being a parent.

The expectations of each are at odds with one another when you cannot give your full time or attention to both simultaneously.

Wong's experiences are real to her and to countless other new parents. There are entire sociology courses on the topic of maternity leave policies (or lack thereof). What Wong touches on in her joke is the exceptionalism of the United States in its lack of support to birthing people and new parents.[83] There are zero guarantees of paid maternity leave.[84] According to a 2018 report from the U.S. Bureau of Labor Statistics, only 17 percent of workers in the United States get paid family leave benefits through their employer.[85] This figure drops even lower when looking specifically at low-wage workers.

Like Wong, comedian and actress Amy Schumer (born in New York City, New York, 1981) has mined her pregnancy, childbirth, and early motherhood experiences for material. Schumer's comedy juxtaposes the cultural expectations placed on women during pregnancy (that of being happy and excited for their impending motherhood) with the reality of how it felt for her to be pregnant. This is evident in one of her jokes from her 2019 Netflix special, *Growing*, which Schumer performed while visibility pregnant. Mimicking people joyously asking about the sex of her baby, Schumer retorts – in a sing-songy voice – that she is having "hemorrhoids" (Schumer, 2019).[86] Schumer had a particularly difficult pregnancy which included suffering from hyperemesis; a condition that causes severe and persistent vomiting. Baring the realities of what it feels like to be pregnant is something the form of comedy affords that polite conversation often does not.

At one point in the special, Schumer lifts her satin blue dress to reveal multiple bandages over her bellybutton, which were placed there to stop her raised pregnancy bellybutton from showing through her dress. In doing so, Schumer reveals an element of her back stage preparation for this special; wherein she covered her belly in bandages to minimize the evidence of what pregnancy has done to her body.

We have come a long way (recall that neither Lucille Ball nor Joan Rivers could say the word "pregnant" when performing while pregnant on television in the 1950s and 1960s, respectively); yet, the way people are supposed to talk, act, and feel during pregnancy and after childbirth is still largely regulated by social norms.

As an example of this regulation, sociologists note the pressure placed on women, particularly by the media, to be supermoms. A **supermom** is as a "domestic goddess" who fulfills all her children's needs and desires and does so with a smile on her face. Mothers are bombarded with images on social media of celebrity domestic goddesses. Take the media presence of mom and mogul Jessica Alba. Alba, in addition to being successful actress, founded The Honest Company in 2011. The Honest Company sells myriad natural home-goods products, including diapers made with plant-based materials and synthetic-fragrance-free baby lotions. Alba started the company, which has been valued at nearly $1 billion dollars, after her baby daughter experienced welt rashes from mainstream laundry detergent in 2008. The media and social media images from the company show happy smiling babies and their happy smiling parents. Even though they sell diapers, there is no mess in sight.

Recall that Jean Baudrillard developed the conception of **hyperconsumption**; we live in a state of consumption which exceeds our needs or means. Hyperconsumption results, in part, from advertising and social media selling us lifestyles which are not realistic or entirely false. Baudrillard calls these unrealistic or false realities **simulations**. Products, and anxieties, are sold to us based on these simulations.

Falseness is a term used by critical theorists to define how **mass culture**, such as through advertising, "false reality." Consider the images that are omnipresent on social media. Mommy bloggers and influencers take over social media feeds. It can be hard for parents to see themselves reflected in those images of clean, smiling babies, or calm, sunlit images of babies effortlessly breastfeeding.

Repressiveness, also used by critical theorists, refers to how mass culture's false messages work to maintain status quo. Mass culture represses by selling individuals false promises which serve capitalism. Commercials on television or on social media, for example, may sell you a product on the promise of a better life – through improved health, sleep, or energy, for example. What those commercials do *not* tell you how current social structures – like those related to patriarchy or capitalism – may be depriving you of the health, sleep, or energy you desire.

This may create for parents the feeling of **role overload**, a term sociologists use to explain situations in which the expectations placed on people in a given role (such as their role as a student, employee, or parent) are too great and far exceed their ability to handle them. Like an employee being assigned far too many tasks, the pressure placed on moms to be "supermoms" can create feelings of perpetual failure. Comedians can help alleviate feelings of role overload for their audiences by playing with taboos. They can talk about their "demolished" bodies and hemorrhoids. They likely still feel the pressure of being "supermoms" but they can laugh at their own expense.

Although the role of mother is often lauded in society (we frequently hear messages implying mothers are performing "the most important job in the world"), in reality, mothers are often treated as outsiders to their own experiences. Think of the male producers who have told pregnant people like Lucille Ball or Joan Rivers that they cannot even say the world "pregnant" on television. We have come a long way since then, but in many ways, pregnant bodies are still considered deviant. Society expects pregnant people to hide or not share any details of physical pains, complicated emotions, or any other deviant behavior that results from pregnancy. Wong and Schumer attack this reality through their comedy. Not only do they say the word "pregnant" on television; they put their experiences with pregnancy at the very center of their work. Comedy allows outsiders – and yes, pregnant people are often treated as outsiders – to tell their own stories.

Identity and Broad City

Our discussion of pregnancy and women's bodies, as performed by Ali Wong and Amy Schumer, or grooming habits, such as the removal of body hair in *Crazy Ex-Girlfriend*, showcase how social norms inhibit women's abilities to talk about their bodies and how their experiences as women change throughout their lives. Indeed, women's bodies have long been covered up, misunderstood, put behind closed (bathroom) doors, or turned into punchlines. Comedians highlight these social norms by playing with the front stage and back stage. By showing back stage behavior on the front stage – and that being brash and surprising – these examples showcase the social norms which, usually, push these behaviors or bodily functions behind closed doors.

In this section, we use the television series *Broad City* (Comedy Central, 2014–2019) to discuss how seeing these characters live authentically resonated with audiences. The series was created by, written by, and starred Ilana Glazer (born in New York City, New York, 1987) and Abbi Jacobson (born in Wayne, Pennsylvania, 1984). Based on Jacobson and Glazer's real lives and dynamic friendship, the show follows the duo as they navigate their twenties in New York City. Jacobson and Glazer originally started *Broad City* as an independent web series (2009–2011). They have spoken in interviews about how they never expected much fame or success to come from the series. They just had fun stories they wanted to tell. But the series was a hit. People all over the Internet loved it.

Comedian, writer, and producer Amy Poehler (of *SNL* and *Parks & Rec* fame) loved it, too. Poehler signed on to be an executive producer of *Broad City* to help transition it from the Internet to television. Under Poehler's guidance, Glazer and Jacobson spent a year working on a script to bring *Broad City* to FX. Once the script was sent up the chain, however, FX passed; they called it "too girly" (Jacobson, 2018).[87] Jacobson later explained that they were "devastated" when FX passed on their script, but it was ultimately a blessing in disguise. They were then able to move over Comedy Central, where their script was better understood and they were given much greater creative freedom.

One edit Comedy Central requested was to change the characters' names back to Ilana and Abbi as they were on the web series (the original script given to Comedy Central called the characters Evelyn and Carly, respectively). Jacobson and Glazer changed the names back, as they agreed the edit made the show feel more authentic. For *Broad City*, it was central to the show's realness that the characters Ilana and Abbi are Glazer and Jacobson.

Something that made the series stand out as unusual in the modern television landscape while also making it feel authentic and true to life was how gross and real Glazer and Jacobson portray their characters. The character's bathrooms were common set pieces. Audiences see them live their lives in the bathroom; they relieve themselves, use a plunger, groom their pubic hair, and kiss a negative pregnancy test with joy and relief.[88] There was seemingly nothing personal that the women considered "off-limits" for the show. Nothing was off-limits because Glazer and Jacobson know that being truthful sometimes means being gross. Women do not have it together all the time, nor should they have to. Based on the acclaimed reactions to *Broad City*,[89] honest portrayals of women's messy bodies and lives on television is something audiences have long craved. It is not just making "crass" accessible to women in ways that were once only available to men. It creates space for new storylines only women could pitch.

These images did not just resonate with audiences because they felt crass or daring, but because they felt *real*. Another aspect of the show that felt real was how it portrayed young, millennial aspirations and not-yet success. Many prior network television shows set in New York City – take *Friends* (NBC, 1994–2004), for example – placed their characters in spacious apartments, the funding for which was never really known or shown. Not on *Broad City*. They showed their cramped apartments, with no air conditioning and plumbing that does not always work. They showed the terrible jobs and the side hustles the helped make ends meet.

Thinking about this sociologically, let us return to Thorstein Veblen. Recall that Veblen was a foundational theorist describing how individuals signal their social status. Veblen described in his book, *The Theory of the Leisure Class* (1899), that high-status individuals flaunt their wealth primarily through two mechanisms: conspicuous leisure and conspicuous consumption. **Conspicuous leisure** includes engaging in expensive and/or indulgent activities (e.g., playing golf or enjoying long vacations) which signal an individual has a resource reserve large enough that they do not need to constantly be working. They can afford leisure.

However, such leisure was not always observable (note: Veblen's life was pre-social media). As such, high-status individuals began signaling their wealth through more material and observable means. Large houses, expensive furniture, luxury cars, and designer clothing are just a handful of examples of such **conspicuous consumption**. Veblen noted that conspicuous consumption was easy to falsify. People could buy fake versions of an expensive handbag, for example.

In media representations, the lifestyles of high-status individuals are easy to imprint on characters who have regular jobs. For viewers, it can be disappointing to compare their own lives to the ones they see on the screen. *Broad City* did not participate in that façade. Take the season one finale, "The Last Supper," as an example. In this episode, Ilana and Abbi dine at an upscale seafood restaurant for Abbi's birthday. Ilana is seriously allergic to shellfish; a fact she does not disclose to the waiter because she wants the full decadent experience. This was a real treat for the young women (Abbi's father was paying), so Ilana was willing to risk her health and safety to enjoy the special occasion. But as duo enjoys their meal, we see Ilana's face turn red and swell. She continues to enjoy the meal without a care in the world aside from quietly scratching away at her itchy skin.[90]

Meanwhile, Abbi visits the restroom to pee. While seated on the toilet, she hears a "kerplunk," and is dismayed to see a condom has fallen out of her body. She realizes the condom must have been from the sex she had four days prior. Abbi is disgusted at herself. The audience understands Abbi feels some shame and embarrassment associated with not realizing this condom was inside her body for so many days.

Abbi returns to the table. We see Ilana's face has swollen to the size of a catcher's mitt. Abbi cannot handle seeing Ilana in her allergic state anymore and grabs Ilana's EpiPen. However, she misses Ilana entirely and accidentally jabs her own thigh. Abbi jumps atop the table in the fancy, white tablecloth restaurant, shouting and crushing a wine glass with her bare hands thanks to the adrenaline she just pumped directly into her bloodstream. Ilana collapses on the ground.

The scene next becomes an epic portrayal befitting of an Oscar-worthy movie. It is shot in slow motion and without audio, save the loud and glorious soundtrack of "Ave Maria." Abbi picks Ilana up and carries her out of the restaurant, grunting, dragging Ilana's hair through guest's meals and knocking over their wine glasses. At the end of the episode, we see the women finish out the day in the hospital and emerge onto the streets of New York City as dawn breaks the following day, still wearing their dresses and heels (and still having fun together).

What makes this episode comedically powerful is the juxtaposition between the upscale restaurant and the messiness of Abbi and Ilana's lives and bodies. For many of us watching at home, the mess (and the desire to be fancier than we really are) is what makes it relatable and funny. The episode is truly a delight for anyone who has wanted to be fancier than they are, more together than they are, more mature than they are, or less allergic to shellfish than they are. We try, we fail, we laugh, and we cry.

Ilana and Abbi's relatability also reflects a shift in generational experiences and financial stability. People are getting married later, having kids later (if at all), and have more debt and fewer assets than previous generations.[91-93] But with social media, there is a heightened expectation to feel like we need to live lavish lifestyles. *Broad City* represents the honesty of trying, failing, and laughing at new experiences.

Jacobson and Glazer made their identities and their messy lives central to their comedic work. As review, Sociologists define one's **identity** as their sense of who they are (i.e., the "self") and where they belong (i.e., group membership(s)). Our sense of who we are includes features of our personality and core beliefs, and how we present ourselves and behave. Identities are developed through interactions with other people, institutions, and the consumption of media. Our identities incorporate our understandings of how other people and institutions may perceive, label, or stigmatize us.

They focused their comedy on their identities rather than making the focus a set of neatly crafted jokes (although, those are plentiful). It was *them* – Glazer and Jacobson – that brought viewers to YouTube, and later, to Comedy Central. The *Broad City* duo used an alternative platform, YouTube, to tell their own story. They made their own space. Even with the series already a success, FX still thought it was "too girly" for mainstream television. Without proving themselves first, we may assume they never would have gotten the Comedy Central opportunity. They paved their own way by using an independent, alternative platform and the duo ultimately found success.

Summary

In this chapter, we discussed character comedians to exemplify how norms differ depending upon *where* we are (referring both to physical space and to historical, cultural, or generational context) and *who* we are (referring to the intersecting features of one's identity such as race, ethnicity, sex, sexuality, and more). Taken together, these comedians exemplify how social norms, expectations, and stereotypes differ based upon one's sex, race, and interactions therein.

This chapter then moved to more contemporary comedic examples to discuss the presentation of self. We all perform parts of our identities. We are socialized to act in accordance with social norms tied to a particular venue, like a college classroom or a comedy club, or features of our group membership. Embedded within the presentation of self and identification of social structures that shape our lives is the notion that social norms, expectations, and systems are not static. They change with place and time.

The history of the comedy roast provides an example of how social norms evolve in terms of who gets a seat (Diller famously needed to dress in drag to be welcomed inside. *Gender performance!*) and the content of the roaster's jokes. This is related to the evolution of language and the superiority theory of humor. *The Onion* writer's room shows us that how one engages with those social norms, expectations, and stereotypes constitute one's comedic perspective. Taken all together, these examples of the presentation of self in comedy and the evolution of comedy help us understand how social stratification operates and sustains itself through stereotypes and gatekeepers. This chapter discussed the role of satire and parodic news programs in social criticism, and how "clapter" may feed the status quo. The next chapter will walk through the concept of social stratification sociologically and provide comedic observations of how social stratification impacts opportunity.

Discussion Questions

4-1: What does the decision to hide a part of one's identity indicate about how different social groups are treated in society? Think about how many Jewish comedians anglicized their names, or the ways women comedians may or may not have had to fit into a "male mold."

4-2: Think about Erving Goffman's description of <u>front stage</u> behavior. Describe how the ordering in a restaurant is considered front stage behavior. Consider your own behavior in different places. If you were to visit a fancy restaurant, imagine how you would dress, speak, and eat, compared to if you were to visit a more casual restaurant. Discuss your own expectation about what a "fancy" or "casual" restaurant may look like depending upon your cultural or social background, and how customs or behaviors may differ therein.

4-3: Consider which parts of your daily life are in the <u>front stage</u> and which are in the <u>back stage</u>. How do you act differently in the front stage versus the back stage?

4-4: Think about how the "Archie Bunker problem" relates to <u>symbolic interactionism</u>. What happens when audiences have different backgrounds and viewpoints? Does this example counter the claim, argued previously in this book, that comedy requires shared understanding? Why or why not?

4-5: How does the sociological concept of <u>distinction</u> relate to Erving Goffman's <u>dramaturgical theory of the self</u> and to <u>symbolic interactionism</u>?

4-6: Describe how definitions of "<u>deviance</u>" change over time. Can you think of an example of something which was once "taboo" that has since become normalized?

4-7: Analyze Vir Das' comedic career through the lens of <u>globalization</u>. How do you think Das' experience of speaking up against hypocrisies he observed in one country, while standing in another country, relates to the concept of globalization. Consider how Karl Marx viewed the role of globalization in the alienation and exploitation of proletariat in your answer.

4-8: Do you think parodic news programs create <u>simulations</u>, as defined by Jean Baudrillard? Or do you think they serve to break us free from simulations put forward by other news sources?

4-9: Discuss how the <u>grooming gap</u> relates to <u>doing gender</u>.

4-10: If you were conducting a sociological research study on television preferences over the past forty years, how would you measure "preferences"? Consider the lessening importance of broadcast television ratings as a marker of success in a streaming world (refer to the *Crazy Ex-Girlfriend* example).

Notes

1 Brown, L. (2006). *The Encyclopedia of the Harlem Literary Renaissance*. Facts On File.
2 Nesteroff, K. (2015). *The Comedians: Drunks, Thieves, Scoundrels, and the History of American Comedy* (1st edition). Grove Press.
3 Harris. (2013, April 24). *I Got Somethin' to Tell You: Moms Mabley movie by Whoopi Goldberg revives a comic legend*. https://slate.com/culture/2013/04/

i-got-somethin-to-tell-you-moms-mabley-movie-by-whoopi-goldberg-revives-a-comic-legend.html

4 Bennetts, L. (1987, August 9). *THEATER; The Pain Behind The Laughter of Moms Mabley—The New York Times.* https://www.nytimes.com/1987/08/09/theater/theater-the-pain-behind-the-laughter-of-moms-mabley.html?sec=&spon=&pagewanted=all

5 Chibbaro, Jr, L. (2017, August 8). *Meet the legendary queer comedian 'Moms' Mabley.* LGBTQ Nation. https://www.lgbtqnation.com/2017/08/meet-legendary-queer-comedian-moms-mabley/

6 Diller, P., & Buskin, R. (2005). *Like a Lampshade in a Whorehouse: My Life in Comedy.* J.P. Tarcher/Penguin.

7 Horowitz, S. (1997). *Queens of Comedy: Lucille Ball, Phyllis Diller, Carol Burnett, Joan Rivers, and the New Generation of Funny Women* (1st edition). Routledge.

8 Diller & Buskin, 2005.

9 Horowitz, 1997.

10 Nachman, G. (2003). *Seriously Funny: The Rebel Comedians of the 1950s and 1960s.* Pantheon Books.

11 Diller & Buskin, 2005.

12 Brown, S. (2018). Open Mic? Gender and the Meritocratic Myth of Authenticity in the Cultural Production of Stand-Up Comedy (Dissertation). *University of Illinois at Urbana-Champaign.*

13 Mizejewski, L. (2014). *Pretty/Funny: Women Comedians and Body Politics.* University of Texas Press.

14 Federman, W. (2021). *The History of Stand-Up: From Mark Twain to Dave Chappelle.* Independent Artists Media.

15 Karnow, S. (1990, January 18). Goodbye to the Borscht Belt. *The Washington Post.* https://www.washingtonpost.com/archive/lifestyle/1990/01/18/goodbye-to-the-borscht-belt/bc36b764-156d-4387-b038-c6644f90c904/

16 Nesteroff, 2015.

17 Dangerfield, R. (2005). *It's Not Easy Bein' Me: A Lifetime of No Respect but Plenty of Sex and Drugs* (Reprint edition). It Books.

18 Dean, G. (2016). *Free Funny the eBook: Writing Comedy, Jokes, and Humor for Business, Public Speaking, or Just for Laughs.* https://www.free-ebooks.net/business/Free-Funny-the-eBook-Writing-Comedy-Jokes-and-Humor-for-Business-Public-Speaking-or-Just-for-Laughs

19 Federman, 2021.

20 Abrams, R. (2019, April 10). *At the Friars Club, When the Laughter Stopped—The New York Times.* https://www.nytimes.com/2019/04/10/arts/television/friars-club-nyc.html

21 Federman, 2021.

22 Morreall, J. (2020). Philosophy of Humor. In E. N. Zalta (Ed.), *The Stanford Encyclopedia of Philosophy* (Fall 2020). Metaphysics Research Lab, Stanford University. https://plato.stanford.edu/archives/fall2020/entries/humor/

23 Hurley, M. M., Dennett, D. C., & Adams, R. B. (2011). *Inside Jokes: Using Humor to Reverse-Engineer the Mind.* MIT Press.

24 Crist, A. (2019, April 12). *Female Comics on Kevin Hart, Louis C.K. and Comedy in the Age of Trump – The Hollywood Reporter.* https://www.hollywoodreporter.com/lifestyle/lifestyle-news/female-comics-kevin-hart-louis-ck-comedy-age-trump-1201578/

25 Ramirez, M. (2022, June 13). *Many young adults now identify as transgender or nonbinary as social media helps more people come out.* USA TODAY. https://www.usatoday.com/story/news/nation/2022/06/10/transgender-nonbinary-more-young-adults-come-out-awareness-grows/7535217001/

26 Crist, 2019.
27 *GLAAD Media Reference Guide—Transgender People.* (2022, February 22). GLAAD. https://www.glaad.org/reference/transgender
28 Monush, B. (2011). *Lucille Ball FAQ: Everything Left to Know about America's Favorite Redhead.* Applause.
29 Dostis, M. (2015, October 15). *Looking back at 'I Love Lucy' 64 years later.* New York Daily News. https://www.nydailynews.com/entertainment/tv/10-love-lucy-article-1.2397434
30 Sargent, R. (2021, September 23). *The Pregnancy Episode of 'I Love Lucy' Was So Controversial, It Was Almost Banned.* Ranker. https://www.ranker.com/list/pregnancy-episode-of-i-love-lucy/ryan-sargent
31 Bianco, R. (2004, February 9). *USATODAY.com—10 turning points for television.* https://usatoday30.usatoday.com/life/television/news/2004-02-09-turning-points_x.htm
32 Stanley, A. (2008, March 3). *Who Says Women Aren't Funny?* Vanity Fair. https://www.vanityfair.com/news/2008/04/funnygirls200804
33 Rivers, J., & Meryman, R. (1986). *Enter Talking.* Delacorte Press.
34 Harris, E. A. (2019, April 19). Amy Schumer, Ali Wong and the Rise of Pregnant Stand-Up. *The New York Times.* https://www.nytimes.com/2019/04/19/arts/pregnant-comedians-amy-schumer-ali-wong.html
35 Jennings, K. (2018). *Planet Funny: How Comedy Took Over Our Culture* (First Scribner hardcover edition). Scribner.
36 S. Brown, 2018.
37 Nesteroff, 2015.
38 Bhuyan, & Das, V. (Directors). (2020). *Vir Das: For India.* https://www.imdb.com/title/tt11611314/
39 Duggal, D. (2022, December 27). Vir Das: Landing: A reminder of the price we pay for speaking the truth. *Firstpost.* https://www.firstpost.com/entertainment/vir-das-landing-a-deep-dive-into-indian-cancel-culture-outrage-and-stepping-into-adulthood-11879351.html
40 Frayer, L. (2021, November 18). Comedian Vir Das called out sexual violence in India. Now he faces lawsuits. *NPR.* https://www.npr.org/2021/11/18/1056888306/comedian-vir-das-called-out-sexual-violence-in-india-now-he-faces-lawsuits
41 Ellis-Petersen, H. (2021, November 18). Indian comedian Vir Das accused of 'vilifying nation.' *The Guardian.* https://www.theguardian.com/world/2021/nov/18/indian-comedian-vir-das-accused-of-vilifying-nation
42 Caron, J. E. (2021). *Satire as the Comic Public Sphere: Postmodern "Truthiness" and Civic Engagement.* Penn State University Press. https://www.psupress.org/books/titles/978-0-271-08986-7.html
43 Duggal, 2022.
44 Voorhees, R. (2013, October 16). *Portlandia's Social Satire.* Rob's Rhetoric and Civic Life. https://sites.psu.edu/rclvoorhees/2013/10/16/portlandias-social-satire/
45 Jennings, 2018.
46 *Tough Room.* (2008, February 8). This American Life. https://www.thisamericanlife.org/348/tough-room
47 Day, A. (2011). *Satire and Dissent: Interventions in Contemporary Political Debate.* Indiana University Press. https://iupress.org/9780253222817/satire-and-dissent/
48 *The Daily Show with Jon Stewart.* (n.d.). Television Academy. Retrieved September 14, 2023, from https://www.emmys.com/shows/daily-show-jon-stewart
49 *The Daily Show with Jon Stewart: Indecision 2000.* (n.d.-a). *The Peabody Awards.* Retrieved September 14, 2023, from https://peabodyawards.com/award-profile/the-daily-show-with-jon-stewart-indecision-2000/

50 *The Daily Show with Jon Stewart: Indecision 2004.* (n.d.-b). *The Peabody Awards.* Retrieved September 14, 2023, from https://peabodyawards.com/award-profile/the-daily-show-with-jon-stewart-indecision-2004/

51 LaMarre, H. L., Landreville, K. D., & Beam, M. A. (2009). The irony of satire: Political ideology and the motivation to see what you want to see in The Colbert Report. *The International Journal of Press/Politics, 14*(2), 212–231. https://doi.org/10.1177/1940161208330904

52 *The Satire Paradox—Pushkin.* (2020, August 26). https://www.pushkin.fm/episode/the-satire-paradox/

53 Krefting, R. (2014). *All Joking Aside: American Humor and Its Discontents.* Johns Hopkins University Press.

54 Pandya, H. (2018, January 10). *The Rise of "Clapter" Comedy.* https://www.vulture.com/2018/01/the-rise-of-clapter-comedy.html

55 Bourdieu, P. (1979). *Distinction: A Social Critique of the Judgement of Taste.* Routledge. https://www.routledge.com/Distinction-A-Social-Critique-of-the-Judgement-of-Taste/Bourdieu/p/book/9780415567886

56 Veblen, T. (2001). *The Theory of the Leisure Class* (Modern library pbk. edition). Modern Library.

57 Caron, 2021.

58 Goffman, E. (1990). *The Presentation of Self in Everyday Life* (1. Anchor Books edition, revised edition). Anchor Books.

59 MacNell, L., Driscoll, A., & Hunt. (2014, December 5). *What's in a Name: Exposing Gender Bias in Student Ratings of Teaching | SpringerLink.* https://link.springer.com/article/10.1007/s10755-014-9313-4

60 Herman, A. (2018, May 1). *John Mulaney Is Happy to Be Here.* The Ringer. https://www.theringer.com/tv/2018/5/1/17305160/john-mulaney-kid-gorgeous-profile

61 Goffman, 1990.

62 Ricard, S. (2014, March 29). *D.C. Insiders Call Veep the Most Realistic Show about Politics.* https://editorial.rottentomatoes.com/article/dc-insiders-call-veep-the-most-realistic-show-about-politics/

63 Addison, C. (Director). (2015). *Veep: "Election Night."* HBO. https://www.imdb.com/title/tt3682534/

64 Louis-Dreyfus vows "Veep" character true to self until the end. (2019, February 8). *Reuters.* https://www.reuters.com/article/us-television-veep-idUSKCN1PX2FC

65 *Mark Twain Prize for American Humor.* (2021). Kennedy Center. https://www.kennedy-center.org/whats-on/marktwain/

66 A musical collaborator on *Crazy Ex-Girlfriend* was Adam Schlesinger, who died at age fifty-two of complications from COVID-19 in April 2020. At the time of his death, Schlesinger was working on Sarah Silverman's comedic musical *Bedwetter.* Like *Crazy Ex-Girlfriend, Bedwetter* also married musical comedy with themes of mental illness and complicated family dynamics.

67 *The Sexy Getting Ready Song—"Crazy Ex-Girlfriend" (feat. Rachel Bloom).* (2015, October 5). https://www.youtube.com/watch?v=ky-BYK-f154

68 Rudman, L. A., & Glick, P. S. (2021). *The Social Psychology of Gender: How Power and Intimacy Shape Gender Relations* (2nd edition). The Guilford Press.

69 Isser, M. (2020, January 5). *The Grooming Gap: What "Looking the Part" Costs Women | Salon.com.* https://www.salon.com/2020/01/05/the-grooming-gap-what-looking-the-part-costs-women_partner/

70 Myers, K. (2022, March 15). *'Pink Tax' Pushes Prices Up Nearly 13%, Study Shows.* The Balance. https://www.thebalance.com/pink-tax-pushes-prices-up-nearly-13-percent-study-finds-5222209

71 Goldman, L. (2012, March 15). *Why Women Pay More | Marie Claire.* https://www.marieclaire.com/career-advice/news/a6999/why-do-women-pay-more/

72 Elliott, C. (2015, March 29). *The Pink Tax: What's the Cost of Being a Female Consumer in 2022?* Listen Money Matters. https://www.listenmoneymatters.com/the-pink-tax/; *Former Governor Cuomo Reminds New Yorkers "Pink Tax" Ban Goes into Effect Today.* (2020, September 30). Department of State. https://dos.ny.gov/news/former-governor-cuomo-reminds-new-yorkers-pink-tax-ban-goes-effect-today

73 Stowaway Cosmetics. (2015, September 28). *Women's Beauty Habits Exposed by NEW Stowaway Cosmetics Survey.* https://www.prnewswire.com/news-releases/womens-beauty-habits-exposed-by-new-stowaway-cosmetics-survey-300149858.html

74 Mazzone, D. (2013, September 26). *Are the Prices of Beauty Products Gendered?* https://www.refinery29.com/en-us/women-outspend-men-beauty

75 Mazzone, D. (2014, February 28). *Time Women Spend on Appearance—Beauty Survey.* https://www.refinery29.com/en-us/2014/02/63501/women-beauty-routines-time-survey

76 Bleiweis, R., Frye, J., & Khattar, R. (2021, November 17). *Women of Color and the Wage Gap—Center for American Progress.* https://www.americanprogress.org/article/women-of-color-and-the-wage-gap/

77 Jæger, M. M. (2011). "A thing of beauty is a joy forever"? Returns to physical attractiveness over the life course. *Social Forces*, 89(3), 983–1003. https://doi.org/10.1093/sf/89.3.983

78 Jordan, L. (2022, January 27). *TV Rewind: The Miraculous Existence of Crazy Ex-Girlfriend.* Paste Magazine. https://www.pastemagazine.com/tv/crazy-ex-girlfriend/crazy-ex-girlfriend-streaming-legacy; Seitz, M. Z. (2016, June 29). *The Best Show on TV Is Crazy Ex-Girlfriend.* Vulture. https://www.vulture.com/2016/06/best-show-crazy-ex-girlfriend-c-v-r.html

79 St. James, E. (2017, January 10). Crazy Ex-Girlfriend's unexpected season 3 renewal shows how TV's rules are changing. *Vox.* https://www.vox.com/culture/2017/1/10/14206016/crazy-ex-girlfriend-season-3-renewal

80 *The Specials: Hannah Gadsby's "Nanette."* (2022, January 20). https://www.patreon.com/posts/1-year-ep-hannah-61430355

81 *The Specials: Ali Wong's "Don Wong."* (2022, February 24). https://www.patreon.com/posts/ali-wongs-don-63000297

82 Karas, J. (Director). (2018). *Ali Wong: Hard Knock Wife.* Netflix. https://www.netflix.com/title/80186940

83 Francis, E., Cheung, H., & Berger, M. (2021, November 11). *How does the U.S. compare to other countries on paid parental leave? Americans get 0 weeks. Estonians get more than 80.* The Washington Post. https://www.washingtonpost.com/world/2021/11/11/global-paid-parental-leave-us/

84 Arneson, K. (2021, June 28). *Why doesn't the US have mandated paid maternity leave?* https://www.bbc.com/worklife/article/20210624-why-doesnt-the-us-have-mandated-paid-maternity-leave; Francis, Cheung, & Berger, 2021.

85 *National Compensation Survey: Employee Benefits in the United States* (March 2018 (Tables 16 and 32)). (2018). U.S. Bureau of Labor Statistics and U.S. Department of Labor. https://www.bls.gov/ncs/ebs/benefits/2018/employee-benefits-in-the-united-states-march-2018.pdf

86 Schumer, A. (Director). (2019, March 19). *Amy Schumer: "Growing"* [Comedy]. It's So Easy Productions, Netflix.

87 Ivie, D. (2018, October 30). *FX Passed on Broad City Because It Was Deemed Too 'Girly.'* Vulture. https://www.vulture.com/2018/10/fx-passed-on-broad-city-because-it-was-deemed-too-girly.html

88 Wolper, C. (2019, March 28). *How Broad City Encouraged Women to Be Their Grossest, Truest Selves.* Vulture. https://www.vulture.com/2019/03/broad-city-gross-humor-women.html

89 *Vanity Fair* and *Rolling Stone* both named *Broad City* as one of the best shows of the decade.

90 Poehler, A. (Director). (2014). *"Broad City" The Last Supper*. Comedy Central. https://www.imdb.com/title/tt3342620/

91 *Census Bureau Releases New Estimates on America's Families and Living Arrangements*. (2021, November 29). Census.Gov. https://www.census.gov/newsroom/press-releases/2021/families-and-living-arrangements.html

92 Kent, A. H., & Ricketts, L. (2021, March 29). *Millennials Are Catching Up in Terms of Generational Wealth*. https://www.stlouisfed.org/on-the-economy/2021/march/millennials-catching-up-earlier-generational-wealth

93 OECD. (2018). *SF2.3 Age of mothers at childbirth and age-specific fertility*. OECD Family Database. https://www.oecd.org/els/soc/SF_2_3_Age_mothers_childbirth.pdf

5   Social Stratification

This chapter explores a foundational concept in sociology known as social stratification. This chapter draws on the work of Karl Marx, Émile Durkheim, Max Weber, Friedrich Engels, Georg Simmel, and Robert K. Merton. This chapter defines the concepts of social class, social status, inequality, strain theory, explanatory theories of deviance, the myth of meritocracy, forms and types of social interaction, dysfunctions, rational choice theory, rationalization, the iron cage, the glass ceiling, pink collar, sexual harassment, identity, and social integration.

The comedic concepts of relief theory, self-deprecating humor, and crowd work are discussed to expand on these sociological principles. This chapter describes the concepts of false consciousness, class consciousness, labor unions, and collective bargaining. It highlights them using a historical comedy labor strike. The chapter follows with a discussion of how outsider comedians used "alternative spaces" out of necessity, as they were not welcome anywhere else.

Examples from comedy's history show how marginalized comedians created unconventional spaces for their comedy to create their own avenues for their success. This chapter discusses how social status is tied to perceptions of authenticity. The goal is for you to leave this chapter with a thorough understanding of what social stratification means and what influences it has on individuals' access to opportunities and success.

Comedy's progression over the past decades, as detailed in the prior chapter, highlights how comedians were and still are afforded different opportunities and freedoms based on who they are. This highlights an important sociological concept: social stratification. **Social stratification** refers to the hierarchical categorization of people in society based on socioeconomic indicators such as wealth, income, occupational prestige, educational attainment, race, ethnicity, sex, gender, sexual identity, and religious affiliation. For example, people are categorized into different social groups such as "upper class," "middle class," and "lower class," which have an implied and impactful hierarchy.

A primary categorization scheme for social stratification is social class. **Social class** refers to one's economic position in society. This often comprises myriad economic factors, including occupational and educational prestige, financial and material wealth, and income. As an example of social class stemming from one's educational background, a person who attains a college

DOI: 10.4324/9781003469537-6

degree may be held in higher esteem than someone without a high school diploma. There is further differentiation even among people with the same level of education. A person who earned a college degree from an ivy league institution (like Harvard or Princeton) may be held in higher esteem than someone who earned a college degree from a less prestigious institution. The prestige assigned to a person's social position is referred to as one's **social status.**

Social status affords people more or less power in society. In sociological understandings of social stratification, **social power** refers to a person's influence over others. Examples of people who hold power in society are politicians, religious leaders, employers, landlords, and police officers. The people who hold these powerful positions can compel coercion from people they rule over.[1] Examples of people with very limited power, conversely, are low-wage workers (especially those who are nonunionized), undocumented immigrants, and sex workers.[2] The people in these low-power positions may lose out in confrontations with more powerful actors. For example, if a boss wants an employee to work an extra shift, the employee may not have the power to say no, even if they want to, out of fear of being fired. This fear may increase among people who live paycheck to paycheck relative to people with greater financial security, or among people of undocumented legal status (out of fear their boss may report them to Immigration and Customs Enforcement (ICE) in retribution[3]) relative to people with legal residency in the United States.

Class distinctions are based on social norms and values as determined by the **ruling class**; those with the most power and resources and the ability to dictate the rules and opportunities for others. In this chapter, we will use concepts such as the idea of social power, superiority theories, stereotype threat, and discrimination to understand social stratification and its applications to comedy. We will review how social classification schema are socially constructed, not innate; yet, they have a meaningful impact on the treatment of, and opportunities afforded to, individuals based upon their social standing.

Capitalism, Karl Marx, and *Trading Places*

The 1983 film *Trading Places* is a fictionalized sociology experiment on the social structure of capitalism. Before getting into the film, let us review Karl Marx's theories on capitalism. **Capitalism** is an economic system based on the private ownership of the means of production. When the **bourgeois** (capitalists) own the means of production, the **proletariat** (workers) have only their labor to sell. Increasing revenue is a goal under a capitalist system. Capitalists, thus, have incentive to **exploit** workers for their labor. There is an incentive to pay workers as little as possible for capitalists to maximize their own profit. Capitalism prioritizes speed and efficiency, and thus, workers are often assigned one specific task along a production line. This leads to workers experiencing **alienation** between themselves and the finished product and other workers. Such alienation separates workers from what it means to be human; to think, create, and connect.

Marx understood that capitalism survives through **false consciousness** of workers. Capitalists propagate false ideologies to workers about how capitalism *benefits* workers. When capitalists create false ideologies, it allows them to decrease wages, increase job demands, and further exploit and alienate workers. Only when these false ideologies are broken, a phenomenon Marx called **class consciousness**, can workers revolt against their exploitation.

There are two key points I want to highlight before moving forward. First, a capitalist social structure concentrates power in a small set of hands. Second, false consciousness hides the unjustness of the social system. Let us discuss these points using *Trading Places* as an example.

Trading Places explores how two men of different social statuses would fare if their life circumstances were reversed.[4] Dan Aykroyd (born in Ottawa, Ontario, Canada, 1952) plays the rich, educated, and posh commodities broker Louis Winthorpe III. Eddie Murphy (born in New York City, New York, 1961) plays down-and-out street hustler, Billy Ray Valentine. The two men's paths cross early in the film when Winthorpe accuses Valentine of attempting to steal his briefcase on the sidewalk (he was not). Winthorpe immediately starts screaming for help. Cops arrive, and based solely on Winthorpe's word, they arrest Valentine on the spot.

The incident proves exciting for two very rich brothers, Randolph and Mortimer Duke, who own the Duke & Duke Commodity Brokers firm where Winthorpe is managing director. Pleased with Winthorpe's performance at work (and at home; Winthorpe is, to their delight, engaged to their niece), the Duke brothers had previously chatted about how Winthorpe's bloodline was deterministic for his success. But upon the introduction of Valentine into their lives through his arrest, the brothers decide to test this thesis. Mortimer believes Valentine's current circumstances simply speak to his surroundings and lack of opportunities (in his words: Valentine was a "product of a poor environment").

Randolph, however, holds prejudicial views toward Valentine due to his race. He believes Valentine, a Black man, is naturally "deviant." Mortimer proposes a wager: if they set up Valentine with the proper resources and environment, he might be able to perform just as well as Winthorpe at their commodities brokerage. They set the wager to test if Winthorpe's current success and Valentine's current lack thereof was due to innate qualities of the men (like work ethic or smarts), or if the men's life courses were determined by environment. The idea that life courses are largely determined by environment is a core tenet of sociology. There are countless real-life sociology experiments which get at the heart of what *Trading Places* is asking us to consider: What would happen if one's environment was altered?

For Valentine to prove his chops as a commodities broker, he must first get hired by a brokerage firm. A seminal sociological experiment conducted by Dr. Devah Pager (2003) speaks to how racial bias – and to a lesser, but significant, extent, prejudice against individuals with a criminal conviction – influences hiring decisions. Pager conducted this experiment in Milwaukee, Wisconsin, by employing four college students (two Black men and two White) to act as job-seekers for entry-level positions.[5] As a part of their selection, the testers matched on general self-presentation and physical appearance.

Pager provided the testers with resumes showing matching educational attainment, job experience, and requisite skills. Working in same-race pairs during the first week of the study, one of each pair was randomly assigned to disclose to the potential employers that he had a criminal record for a non-violent drug offense. In the next week of the study, the men switched. Those who previously reported no criminal record began reporting a criminal record, and vice versa. This switch went back-and-forth weekly for the remainder of the study. The pairs applied to fifteen randomly assigned job postings each week. The study's outcome of interest was whether the men received an offer for a job interview by the prospective employer.

Pager's study assessed whether the number of job interview offers extended to the testers differed by the applicant's race, criminal record, or by the intersection of those two features. Results showed that both features mattered for the applicant's likelihood of being offered an interview from the prospective employers. But it was the applicant's race more than their criminal record that made a larger individual impact. In fact, White men *with* a criminal record were more likely to be offered an interview than Black men *without* a criminal record (17 percent versus 14 percent, respectively). White men without a criminal record received the most offers for interviews (34 percent), while Black men with a criminal record received the fewest offers (5 percent).

Consider how Pager's study relates to the work of Marx. Under a capitalist system, people are rewarded for their effort and merit. If you are smart enough, talented enough, or work hard enough, you will get a good job, a good income, and rise to the top. But, power is concentrated and opportunities are not afforded equally. Yet, one's economic status – high wages, low wages, or unemployed – is seen as a personal effort.

To bring this back to *Trading Places*, the results from Pager's experiment indicate that Black men like Valentine have a harder time even getting an interview, let alone a job offer, because of racial discrimination. This impact is doubly damaging when paired with the fact that Black men are over-policed and over-criminalized compared to their White counterparts (see this book's later discussion of the **war on drugs**). Black men are therefore more likely to also have a criminal record compared to White men with similar behavioral histories, which negatively impacts their job prospects even further.

Eventually, the Duke brothers frame Winthorpe for stealing money and dealing drugs. Then, they fire him, lock him out of his opulent home (which is owned by the Dukes), and cut him off from his money by freezing his bank accounts. Meanwhile, the brothers set up Valentine in Winthorpe's former home (complete with a butler) and his former job. Winthorpe proves successful in commodities trading by showing his immense logic which is bolstered by his knowledge of the everyman. In the end, Mortimer wins the bet: both Valentine and Winthorpe were shown to be products of their respective environments.[6]

Trading Places is a type of film that can effectively illustrate the impact of social stratification and social environment on life chances. The medium allows us to visualize the literal trading of places. Switching environments is something we cannot replicate easily in life; there is no alternate reality where I can ask readers to go back in time, be born to a different family, and see how their own lives change. Instead, I cite studies like Pager's to highlight the consequences of discrimination by race, ethnicity, or other features of one's identity or life experiences. But for those who may not have experienced identity-based discrimination, citing these studies alone may not be enough to disrupt their reality.

Trading Places lets us visualize how environment and institutions influences one's life chances beyond individual choices and behaviors. Winthorpe's life becomes much harder once he is cut off from his resources, and Valentine achieves success once he has security, comfort, and is no longer vilified as a criminal. For those on the fence about these concepts, the comedic tone of the movie cuts the tension of these tough topics. It allows us to break down our own defenses and really pay attention.

Through the film, people learn about inequality in a way that can really resonate because they are laughing while they are learning. **Inequality** results when different social positions afford unequal levels of economic opportunity, social status, and power to individuals. *Trading Places* is not simply a good example based on its own merit but also because it showcases the mechanisms of inequality in such a visible way.

Explanatory Theory of Deviance

We just discussed how social stratification relies on understanding social sorting mechanisms. A core focus of social sorting in sociology is the definition of *insiders* and *outsiders*, and how those definitions relate to conceptualizations of deviance. A core tenant of sociology is the notion that deviance is socially constructed rather than innate. In this section, we will first define deviance. Second, using explanatory theories of deviance, we will link deviance to the operation of social stratification and describe how definitions of "deviant" behavior seek to maintain the status quo and existing social hierarchies.

Let us first define deviant behavior as understood and defined by sociologists. First, sociology does not define deviance only in relation to crime, which can be a common conflation among general audiences. To a sociologist, **deviance** refers to departing from expected norms, values, and behaviors.[7] This not only includes crime but also includes other types of behaviors that may not be generally accepted by a specific community. For example, some communities and faiths consider homosexuality deviant behavior, though same-sex marriage is fully legal in the United States.

There are two primary theories of deviance we will cover in this book: explanatory theories and constructionist theories. **Explanatory theories of deviance** explain *why* deviance occurs in a society. The unit of focus of analysis for explanatory theories is on the "deviants" themselves. Central to explanatory theories of deviance is the notion that deviant behaviors are real and observable. So the theories simply seek to explain *why* people engage in these behaviors.

According to explanatory theorists, factors driving deviance could be biological urges or conditions of the social structure. Sociologists tend to focus on the conditions of the social structure. For example: if someone is living in poverty in a social system without universal access to necessary resources (such as food, shelter, or healthcare), they may choose to steal food to survive. Later in this book, we will dig into examples of people not having resources to meet their daily needs. We will also discuss work restrictions placed on asylum-seekers which prohibit them from legally working in the United States without proper authorization, which can be a very lengthy process.

A set of theories that fall under the explanatory umbrella are the **structural/ functional** theories. Recall, Durkheim argued that deviance is functional for society.[8] Recall this book's discussion of values and norms. Durkheim asserts that were it not for deviance, there would be no way for a society to define and maintain its values. For example, social groups which want to promote the idea that heterosexuality is the "norm" must then define homosexuality, bisexuality, or other sexual orientations as "deviant."

A more modern update to the structural and functional study of deviance focuses on the *strain* social systems produce. This approach is called **strain theory,** and it acknowledges that rifts exist between social ideals and how individuals can achieve them. Thus, individuals will engage in deviance to close that divide. For example, material success is highly coveted in the United States. Money and expensive material goods are held in high regard, but extreme economic inequality, unequal access to opportunities, and outright discrimination inhibit the ability of huge swaths of people to ever achieve material success through traditional means.[9] Most impoverished people may never have access to the pathways necessary for achieving economic success, but they are still being sold the idea of the rags-to-riches American dream. These people are experiencing **strain.** They may resort to non-sanctioned pathways to achieve the material success that society holds up as a value, like committing crime.

Strain is a central focus of Moses Storms' 2022 HBO special, *Trash White.* Much of Storm's material in the special focuses on what it was like to grow up experiencing extreme poverty. Storm was one of the six children raised by a single mom with no child support. They were on food stamps, and when those ran dry, the family dove into dumpsters to search for food. Storm jokes about the experience in his special, including being the lookout in his siblings' dumpster-diving operation and speed-eating ice cream after a grocery store's freezer broke (followed by Storm and all his siblings throwing it all up into a crowded pool they had just snuck into with their mom).[10]

But Storm frames his jokes with the message that upward mobility in the United States is a myth. This myth propagates because stories like Storm's – moving up the social ladder from dumpster-driver to celebrity – are championed as what happens if you just work hard enough. Storm explains that these myths make people feel like the status quo is working. Make people feel like we do not need to take any action to make our system any less oppressive to the folks on the bottom. Storm's material in his special attempts to **debunk** the myth of meritocracy.

Sociologists define **meritocracy** as an ideology in which individuals have opportunity for success, regardless of their background, circumstances, or features of their identities. Therefore, the professional success they achieve (or fail to achieve) is directly tied to their effort and abilities. If the United States was a true meritocracy, the number of children who grow up to make it to the top of the income distribution as adults would be equal across income tiers at birth. Your chances of growing up to be rich would be equal whether you were born into a low-income, middle-income, or high-income family. In reality, that is just not the case. About 8 percent of children born in the lowest quintile of the income distribution (bottom 20 percent) grow up to make it to the highest quintile of the income distribution (top 20 percent) as adults. That number is lower than what is observed in countries with more equitable policies (e.g., in Denmark, about 15 percent of children achieve the same marker of mobility).[11] Indeed, there are series of news articles with titles like: "The American Dream is Alive in Canada."[12]

There is ample evidence suggesting it is a myth that the United States is a meritocracy. The **myth of meritocracy** refers to the notion that upward social mobility based on one's own merits, skill, or hard work – regardless of one's own social class – is not achievable because of the limitations imposed on people in a capitalist society. These limitations include unequal access to education and job opportunities, low wages, and limited access or affordability of healthcare and childcare.[13] Representation of people's stories and journeys matter because they keep us grounded. To a critical theorist, inaccurate portrayals of information are meant to pacify and repress. The goal is to keep us thinking the American dream is alive in America lest we revolt (or move to Denmark or Canada).

Recall, Robert K. Merton defined a social structure's **functions** through a structuralist/functionalist lens. Functions are the observable, positive impacts of a social structure. Functions are adaptable and allow the social structure to survive over time. However, social structures also have **dysfunctions**. Dysfunctions are the observable, negative impacts of a social structure. Dysfunctions harm the social structure; limiting its ability to survive over time. An example of a social structure is the visa process for foreign-born individuals to live and work in the United States. The application process can be seen as a positive function. The United States can screen out individuals it deems as unfit or dangerous. However, a dysfunction is the process is slow and harms individuals from living a productive and healthy life in the United States.[14]

To better understand a social structure's functions and dysfunctions, Merton defined **manifest functions** and **latent functions**. Manifest functions are the positive *intended* impacts of a social structure, while latent functions are its positive *unintended* impacts. As sociologists, we understand that what may be positive for one group may be detrimental for another.

For an example of unequal protections, let us turn to the Netflix show, *Mo*, which began airing in 2022. The show was created by and stars Mohammed "Mo" Amer. Amer is of Palestinian descent and was born in Kuwait in 1981. With his mom and siblings, Amer immigrated to Houston, Texas when he was nine years old to flee the Gulf War.[15] Amer plays a semi-autobiographical character, Mo, on the show. Like Amer (the person), Mo (the character) is an undocumented, Palestinian, Muslim man in Houston, Texas. In the show, Mo has been waiting for his asylum case for twenty-two years.[16] Indeed, it took Amer nearly twenty years to get asylum and citizenship in the United States.[17] The series documents what it is like living in legal limbo for such a long time.

For example, to be allowed to work in the United States, you need a Social Security Number or Employee Identification Number (also known as a Federal Tax Identification Number). For refugees, like Mo, the primary way to work legally is to win your asylum case. However, due to backlogs in applications, the average wait time for asylum cases in 2021 was 1,621 days.[18] That is nearly four-and-a-half years.

To work before a decision on their asylum case has been reached, asylum applicants can apply for an Employment Authorization Document (EAD). They must wait for a minimum of 150 days on the initial decision of their asylum application before they can apply for an EAD.[19,20] United States Citizenship and Immigration Services (USCIS) then has 30 days to respond to EAD applications. In this case, the soonest someone could be eligible to work is roughly 180 days after applying for asylum in the United States. That is a long time to wait for someone who likely has few resources available to them. There are also resources needed just to submit the EAD application form (USCIS Form I-765). Forms must be submitted in English, or if submitted in another language, a full English translation – accompanied by a signed certificate by the translator – must be submitted, as well.

In the *Mo* series pilot, titled "Hamoodi" (which is a nickname for Mohammed), an early scene opens with Mo arriving for work at a mobile phone store in Houston. He fixes a cell phone for a happy customer, who marvels at his speed and efficiency, while Mo simultaneously helps one of his co-workers find a product. Then his boss, speaking Arabic, calls Mo to the back of the store. Mo immediately knows something is wrong, noting that his boss never speaks Arabic in front of the customers.

His boss explains to Mo that U.S. ICE raided their other store location. If they receive another infraction, the boss explains, the business will get shut down. Mo does not have a work permit, so it is illegal for his boss to be employing him. Mo begs for his job, assuring his boss that his asylum case is coming up soon. To which his boss reminds him, Mo has been waiting for his asylum hearing for over twenty years. On his way out the door, Mo notes this is not the first time he has lost a job due to interactions with ICE. The camera closes in on Mo's face, and audiences can feel Mo's pain. Without words, Mo's face expresses the weight of losing his ability to provide for himself. The lack of control. The lack of means. The confusion. The fear. Mo was good at his job, and as he reminded his boss – he basically ran the place, but because of a piece of paper for which he has been waiting for over twenty years, Mo just has to walk out the door with no sense of where his next paycheck will come from.

Recall, Georg Simmel defined two key elements of social interaction: forms and types. **Forms** refer to how social structure determines how two or more people of different social positions (e.g., boss and employee) interact with one another. **Types** refers to features of one's social identity (e.g., whether someone is undocumented) which also influence social interaction between two or more people. Recall, there is a power imbalance between a boss and an employee stemming from the *form* of their interaction. If that employee is undocumented and the boss is not, that will heighten the power imbalance based on the *types* of individuals involved in that interaction.

Let us continue with this episode of *Mo* to discuss **rational choice theory**. Later in the episode, after Mo loses his job at the mobile phone store due to his undocumented status, you see Mo loading merchandise into the back of his car. It is counterfeit merchandise. Counterfeit versions of luxury-branded watches, handbags, and sunglasses, unlicensed sports gear and other clothing and footwear items. Mo parks his car in front of the mobile store from which he earlier lost his job. Mo chats up people as they pass by on the sidewalk. When he finally catches the attention of a potential customer, audiences see that Mo is a fantastic salesman. Playing up a Texas twang in his voice, Mo sells a fake pair of Yeezys to a middle-aged Texas cowboy, closing the sale with the gift of a counterfeit Chanel handbag for the customer's wife.

Rational choice theorists understand that people act rationally to achieve their goals. By **rational**, rational choice theorists posit that how people achieve their goals is a logical decision based upon the set of choices a person has in front of them. Resources are not afforded equally. Therefore, how people achieve their goals will differ. People face constraints. The two primary constraints people face in trying to reach their goals are (1) limited access to resources and (2) restrictions imposed by social structures.[21]

Mo's way of supporting himself is now via an illegal profession. Is it "rational" to engage in criminal activity to earn a living? Unless a business is willing to take a risk (and they have their own sets of "rational" choices), no one can hire Mo without a work permit. He is excluded from the legal labor market. The "rational" choice for how to make a living looks different for Mo than someone who is legally allowed to work in the United States.

Rationalization

Let us return to Max Weber's discussion of **rationalization**. According to Weber, social structures are *rational* in that they attempt to find most efficient means of achieving their goals. A comedic example highlighting the concept of rationalization can be found in the season two premiere of the television show *I Love Lucy*, in an episode titled "Job Switching" (1952).[22] In the episode, the two main female characters, Lucy and Ethel, and the two main male characters, Desi and Fred, get into an argument about whether the "women's work" of keeping up the home or the "men's work" of earning income outside the home is harder. They agree to "switch jobs" to find out.

Lucy and Ethel get a job at a candy factory where they are tasked with performing quality control over chocolates coming across a conveyer belt. Things start out fine, but as time goes on, the conveyer belt goes *faster, faster, and faster* – to the point that it was not humanly possible for the women to keep up. The comedic relief comes from Lucy and Ethel shoving chocolates into their mouths as quickly as they can to prevent the candies from going down the line unchecked. Using our sociological lenses to interpret this scene, we can see that speeding up the assembly line without more workers to monitor it is a cost-saving mechanism used to increase production without additional labor costs. And, as we can also see, it harms the worker. Lucy and Ethel were frazzled, stressed, and unable to perform the duties asked of them. But hey, at least they got to eat some chocolate! (As an aside: Desi and Fred had a similarly difficult day at home.)

Let us connect this to Weber's concept of the "iron cage."[23] The **iron cage** describes that, because of capitalist social structures' emphasis on rationality and efficiency, individuals are caged into certain ways of thinking and behaving. There is little to no room for creativity or artistic expression. There is immense pressure placed on individuals to perform in ways which meet the ever-increasing demands of the capitalist social structure. Rationality and efficiency are considered beneficial to everyone in society; effectively trapping individuals inside the iron cage. Think about what would happen next if Lucy and Ethel wanted to keep their jobs, or even seek advancement within those jobs. Work harder and faster? To what end? How would their personal, familial, and creative lives suffer?

Labor Unions and the 1979 Comedy Store Strike

We just discussed how people with limited power under a capitalist system have limited protections and face greater exploitation. Now, let us talk about how workers can gain power through collective action, using the 1979 Comedy Store strike as an example.

To set the scene: The Comedy Store is an iconic comedy club opened by Sammy Shore in West Hollywood, California in 1972. Sammy ran The Comedy Store as a place where his comedian guy friends could hang out. The comics could go back and pour their own drinks, he let comics do long sets of varying lengths, and the club happily made no money. When Sammy needed to leave town for a yearlong contract in Las Vegas, his then-wife Mitzi Shore volunteered to take over. Mitzi changed The Comedy Store's operation from those of Sammy's laissez-faire model. In doing so, she made a lasting mark on standup comedy in the United States. Mitzi changed the physical space by adding plants and painting a black backdrop behind the stage. She gave comics fifteen-minute sets and ran two shows per night. These changes gave her comedy shows a structure, which was eventually replicated by clubs across the country. Other clubs looked to The Comedy Store for the way Mitzi's shows gave customers a good time and left them wanting more.

Mitzi was a savvy businessperson who knew how to make a profit in the comedy club business. But, much of Mitzi's financial success came from *not paying* the comedians. Mitzi's justification for the lack of pay was that she considered the comedians to be apprentices. She saw the stage time as a free opportunity for them to practice their craft and gain exposure for bigger opportunities. But the comedians began to see their role at The Comedy Store differently; they knew their labor made Mitzi money. Audiences came to see the comics and had to pay a cover charge and follow a two-drink minimum to do it.

Mitzi had the power in this dynamic; she dictated the rules and the pay. Recall that conflict theorists believe society operates through the coercive forces of more powerful positions and groups, like employers who have the power to coerce compliance from employees (excuse me, "apprentices"). At The Comedy Store, the conflict between the comedians and Mitzi came to a head when Mitzi started putting "Original Room" comedians on stage in the "Main Room." The Original Room was more of a workshop room, while the Main Room was a professional room which also showcased national headliners. As Mitzi argued she did not need to pay the comedians because they were apprentices being given the opportunity to learn and grow, by moving comedians up to the Main Room without pay, the comedians saw that Mitzi's argument did not hold water. They were trained, professional comedians whose labor was invaluable to The Comedy Store's success.

Karl Marx describes how a capitalist social system **exploits** workers for their labor. The means of production (i.e., comedy clubs) are owned by one group of with people, while everyone else (e.g., the comedians) can only make money by selling their labor. The capitalists can then exploit their workers by only paying a small share of the money earned and keeping the rest for themselves. To make more money under a capitalist social system, there is incentive for capitalists to keep growing their business *and* to pay workers less and less.

A hidden component of capitalism, as described by Marx, is the false narratives put forward by capitalists to trick workers into thinking the capitalist system benefits them. This creates a **false consciousness** in workers which keeps them in a cycle of exploitation. Feeding workers false stories about how the capitalist social structure "benefits" them gives capitalists opportunity to further exploit workers by further increasing job demands and decreasing wages. Marx saw the antidote to capitalism as **class consciousness**. Class consciousness occurs when workers become wise to the exploitation they face, driving them to fight back against the system.

Referring to the comedians as "apprentices" created a false consciousness. Realizing they were worth more is an example of class consciousness. It was the catalyst for them banding together to call for change. Conversations about pay between the comedians and Mitzi began. In those initial conversations, the thirty comics who made the leap to the mainstage were effectively able to negotiate their pay.[24] But when it came to paying the comics still working the Original Room, the Belly Room, or The Comedy Store's Westwood location, Mitzi did not budge. So, in 1979, the comedians who played regularly at The Comedy Store had had enough of their labor being taken for free, and began the 1979 Comedy Store strike.

Some recognizable names from the comedy strike effort included David Letterman (born in Indianapolis, Indiana, 1947) and Jay Leno (born in New Rochelle, New York, 1950). The comedians attempted to form a union but an issue they ran into was that they were not technically employees. They were apprentices. To understand why the comedians wanted to unionize, let us discuss the roles of labor unions. A **labor union** is an organization that acts as an intermediary between employees and employers (e.g., factory workers and company owners) to advocate and fight for the interest of workers.[25] Labor unions can serve to provide protections against unfair compensation and unsafe working conditions, or to advocate for additional benefits. A labor union is one example of what a conflict theorist would call a **conflict group**.[26] Conflict groups form based on consensus of their beliefs which stand in contrast to those of the ruling powers. They may use protest or other forms of rebellion – such as labor strikes – to fight for social change.

Labor unions drive improvements for employees through **collective bargaining**; the process of negotiating for better contracts, wages, benefits, and protections for the employees.[27] Collective bargaining can be effective because there is power in numbers through unionizing. While one individual employee may not have the power or influence to make in their contract, a union represents all or most of workers. There is power in numbers.

If the employer does not come to the bargaining table with an offer that is satisfactory to the union, they can strike. A **labor strike** is when company employees collectively stop working until an agreement is reached. This can bring companies to a halt. So a strike, or even the threat of a strike, can give employees immense bargaining power.[28] Even though The Comedy Store comedians did not have a labor union backing them, they still had the ability to collectively withhold their labor. And that is exactly what they did. They refused to get on stage at The Comedy Store, picketed out front, and talked to media. They used their collective voices to put pressure on Mitzi to make changes and to rebalance the power dynamic.

How did this pan out for The Comedy Store comedians? First, receiving national attention aided the movement. The strike was in national headlines daily for the duration of the strike (particularly following the death of comic Steve Lubetkin who died quite publicly by suicide during the strike, allegedly hoping his death would aid the comics in their labor dispute efforts). This national attention put pressure on Mitzi. During the third week of the strike, Mitzi agreed to pay the comics.[29] Eventually, other comedy clubs around the country began paying comics for their sets, too.

It was a win for the comedians. The pay offered to comedians at The Comedy Store was nominal, but getting paid even very little for their work made a big difference for a lot of comedians. Many of them were young and had limited financial resources. Getting paid for their comedy spots made all the difference for them. It meant they could continue working as a standup and (potentially) not need a second or third job to make ends meet. They could use that time, instead, to write and work out new material. It takes time and money to produce art.[30] The 1979 Comedy Store strike made real, lasting change for comedians across the country and made comedy more accessible for people who could not afford to give their labor away for free. This is the power of collective bargaining.

Stereotype Threat

The comedy strike of 1979 highlights how opportunity is not always afforded equally and talent is not always valued equally – particularly without class consciousness. Other areas of social life operate similarly. We can use postsecondary education as another example before bringing the discussion back to media. A 2021 *New York Times* article titled "A College Program for Disadvantaged Teens Could Shake Up Elite Admissions" details the success of the National Education Equity Lab initiative in providing elite educational opportunities for students in underserved communities. Funded by a New York-based nonprofit organization, the Equity Lab enrolls high school juniors and seniors from high-poverty schools in selected cities across the United States in an online Harvard course taught by Dr. Elisa New, titled *"Poetry in America: The City From Whitman to Hip-Hop."* The students were held to the same standards as Harvard undergraduates.[31] The students fared exceptionally well. The success of the students showed there is indeed talent and aptitude across communities and socioeconomic and demographic backgrounds in the United States. However, the ability to attend Harvard as an undergraduate is an opportunity not afforded equally.

This, of course, was a pilot test. But the results indicate opening up traditionally closed-off opportunities into an online environment can both (1) make opportunity more equitable and (2) give the world a chance to find some of its best and brightest in areas often overlooked. There is a representation problem in postsecondary education in the United States.[32–35] Students who grow up in families and in areas with resources are more likely to attend college than students coming from areas with poorly funded schools and whose families cannot afford tutoring, extracurricular activities, or tuition; or whose own education or language prohibits them from helping their children with homework or applications, or who do not have the necessary networking or legacy status to give their students an advantage toward college admissions.[36]

Attending college or university in the United States is also not just a binary (did you, or did you not, attend) indicator. Colleges and universities have different levels of status and prestige associated with them. Attending an ivy league university, for example, holds a level of sway that perhaps a public university does not. Refer to this book's earlier discussion on **social status**. But access to ivy league universities is not afforded equally. For example, consider **legacy admissions**. An applicant at a university has "legacy status" if a member of their family attended that university. For universities which consider legacy status in review of their applications, legacy applicants get a "bump." In other words, if there were two similarly eligible applicants – based upon factors such as standardized test scores and GPA – the legacy student would have an advantage over the non-legacy student.[37] *The Guardian* reported in 2019 that legacy applicants are admitted at approximately four times the rate of overall applicants at Princeton University, and at approximately twice the rate at Georgetown University and the University of Notre Dame.[38] These practices are more common at prestigious and selective universities, like Princeton University and Harvard University.

Legacy admissions policies stand in opposition to efforts to increase diversity and representation in university acceptance. Consider how many of the prestigious universities which consider legacy status do not have a long history of accepting Black or Brown students in large numbers.[39] These universities' alumni are predominantly White, and the children of their alumni who are accepted with legacy status are predominantly White.[40]

The policies have an intentionally racist history. Ivy league universities began implementing them in the 1920s when they saw a rise in the number of Jewish students being admitted to their university through their merit-based admissions processes.[41] Admissions policies were adapted to consider more individual and familiar factors. Today, the rationale for maintaining legacy admissions is less explicitly racist and more explicitly capitalist. Universities benefit from admitting legacy students for financial reasons. Legacy students tend to require less financial aid and contribute to greater donations relative to their non-legacy peers – personally, or via their alumni family members.[42]

There are policies in place to change legacy admissions. Bills have been put forward to end, or charge universities for, considering legacy status in university admissions in Connecticut, Massachusetts, and New York.[43] In June 2023, President Biden directed the Department of Education to investigate legacy admissions and similar practices which unequally benefit those with greater privilege.[44]

Consider legacy admissions through the lens of a structuralist/functionalist – including its manifest functions, latent functions, and dysfunctions. Recall that **manifest functions** are the positive *intended* impacts of a social structure, and **latent functions** are its positive *unintended* impacts. Recall, what is positive for one group may be negative for another group. These unanticipated consequences can threaten the ability of a social structure to survive if contested by an outside group. **Dysfunctions** are the observable negative impacts of a social structure which limit its ability to survive. Bills to end legacy admissions policies are examples of threats to the survival of the social structure which benefits students with legacy status.

We just discussed inequality in how people get accepted into universities, now let us discuss cost. Postsecondary education at most universities (but especially selective universities) has become prohibitively expensive in the United States. This can be seen partly through the shrinking population of students attending university who come from middle-income families relative to students from low-income families (who are eligible from need-based scholarships and grants), and students from high-income families.[45] Without financial assistance or real assets, the ability to afford attending college is shut off to a large share of people in the United States. Opportunity Insights conducted a study measuring what would happen if students with equal test scores attended selective universities at the same rates, irrespective of family income (note: there are myriad reasons why students of higher incomes get higher test scores irrespective of knowledge or ability, such as access to tutoring services). They found that the share of students at selective universities coming from lower-income and middle-income families would raise significantly (rising from 7.3 to 8.6 percent and 28 percent to 38 percent, respectively).[46]

Mainstream media – like university admissions – has and largely remains inequitable in opportunity. In both cases, it can be hard just to get in the door. Of the top 100 grossing films in 2020, only 21 percent of those behind the scenes were women (measured as writers, directors, cinematographers, editors, producers, and executive producers).[47] Various initiatives have funneled much attention and money to increase diversity in media to little avail. In 1979, a group of female directors formed the Women's Steering Committee within the Director's Guild.[48] They filed a lawsuit to pressure studios to increase opportunity and diversity, specifically focusing on women in television and film.

In an opinion piece published in the *New York Times* in 2016 by writer and producer Nell Scovell, she argues that studio executives often state they are looking to hire female directors; yet, that is not what happens. Scovell likens it to looking for sunglasses on your head. The talented women directors are *right there*, but the studio executives just do not see them. Scovell goes on to discuss findings from much sociological research that reveal decisions for men's hiring, promotion, and funding are based upon their assumed *potential*, whereas the same decisions for women are based upon their past *experience*. The reasons for this relate to socially normative expectations for men and women's behavior.

Think about the traits that we consider socially normative masculine and feminine behaviors. For whom is it considered more in line with social expectations to be loud and brash, versus quiet and demure? For whom is it considered more in line with social expectations to take charge, versus offer care or support? Now, think about how those same traits and behaviors align with socially normative "leadership qualities." After this exercise, you may wonder if men are more natural leaders. Turn on your sociological imagination for a moment. Is a "leadership quality" something innate and universal, or something socially defined?

In a 2019 study published in *Frontiers in Psychology*, Player et al. conducted two hiring simulation experiments for leadership positions.[49] These experiments allowed the researchers to analyze how respondents valued a candidate's leadership potential and leadership performance and to measure differences in respondents' value ratings by candidates' sex. The researchers found that respondents valued leadership potential more than leadership performance for the male candidates, and valued leadership performance more than leadership potential for the female candidates. These experiments imply, in short, that men are more likely to be hired or promoted based on potential, and women on experience.

The motivations for Player et al.'s study are sociological. The researchers note that women in the workplace are often penalized for exhibiting leadership qualities as they deviate from socially acceptable gender norms. A woman who is brash, who interrupts, has agency, or takes charge rubs people the wrong way and is less likable. They are considered "less hirable" than women whose behaviors more closely align with gender expectations.[50] Women who want to be leaders need to fit into a men's mold defining what makes a strong leader, but then are penalized for doing just that.

Structural/functionalists believe a meritocratic system is beneficial in society by enabling firms to identify and hire the best and brightest.[51] If this were true, then, certainly, a meritocracy would result in the best CEOs for a Fortune 500 company; or in major production studios picking up the best-written film or television projects for production; and the best directors, showrunners, and actors being selected and cast. However, only 8.2 percent of CEOs of Fortune 500 companies are women (while this is low relative to women's share of the population and of the workforce, I will note this is an improvement over prior years).[52] If we believe the United States is a meritocracy, then we would have to believe men are almost universally better and more deserving leaders. We would have to believe professional success women achieve (or fail to achieve) is directly tied to their effort and abilities.

Conflict theorists, however, do not see the world as a meritocracy. Instead, conflict theorists see that more powerful groups can provide better opportunities for people connected to them, such as providing legacy status to their children in university admissions, leveraging alumni or other networks for professional recruitment opportunities, or valuing leadership qualities that match their own in hiring or promotion decisions. Indeed, research shows women are discriminated against in hiring and promotion, as hiring managers may hold prejudicial feelings against women candidates and make hiring decisions that favor men.[53]

Consider the glass ceiling. The **glass ceiling** is a term used to describe the often-invisible barriers that prevent women and other members of marginalized groups from reaching managerial and leadership positions in the workplace.[54] These invisible barriers may include factors such as bias, discrimination, and stereotype threat, as well as features of the work environment like flexibility for working parents and access to safe and affordable childcare services.

In her book, *Just the Funny Parts* (2018), Nell Scovell shares her experiences as a television comedy writer (among other forms of screenwriting, directing, and all-around media magic). Scovell got her start in television writing in the late 1980s, with a couple of her first notable writing gigs being on *It's Garry Shandling's Show* (1987) and *The Smother Brother's Comedy Hour* (1988). She was often the only woman in the room. And the male writers made sure to remind her of this.[55]

Scovell's first gig as a television writer was a freelance position on *It's Garry Shandling's Show,* after the show bought a script she wrote on spec ("spec" refers to *speculative,* meaning an unsolicited script a screenwriter submits hoping it will be purchased for an existing show or picked up for a new production). When Scovell was introduced to Shandling (a comedy legend), he "complimented" her by telling her that she wrote like a man. Scovell details in her book about how she initially radiated with delight for being acknowledged and complimented by one of her comedy idols. Upon reflection, however, she understood the negation that came with this "praise." The implication of Shandling's comment is that if writing like a man is a compliment, then writing like a woman is an insult.

This interaction was certainly not the only time in Scovell's career wherein her first day was marked with comments about her sex. She had a similar experience while working in the writer's room of *Late Night with David Letterman.* During her first day of work, her new *Late Night* colleagues popped by her office throughout the morning to introduce themselves. One new male colleague casually foreshadowed on his way out the door that, sometime during Scovell's tenure on the show, he would see her drop a tampon. Scovell interpreted the comment from the male writer as a way to "remind" of her gender because of the long-held myth that "women aren't funny." He was reaffirming the idea that idea that women do not belong in writer's room. Scovell's experience provides additional examples of stereotype threat. **Stereotype threat** is when people worry about adhering to stereotypic behaviors about their social group (like being too "girly").

Let us expand on the consequences of stereotype threat using the work of Claude M. Steele. In his book, *Whistling Vivaldi* (2010), Steele et al. conducted experiments testing the theory that women underperform in advanced math classes, relative to men, due to stigma (not due to limited math abilities). The researchers posited that women experience stigma in advanced math classes as stereotypes exist stating that women are "not good at math." Their control case was advanced English classes. The researchers posited that, as similar stereotypes about women's English skills are not a part of the dominant culture, women will not experience the same stigma in English class. Therefore, the researchers hypothesized there would be less (or no) gap between women's and men's grades in the advanced English classes.

The researchers conducted their experiment on University of Michigan freshman and sophomores with high math ability and interest. This was measured by a student achieving a high quantitative SAT score (in 85th percentile of entering class), earning a B or higher in two calculus courses, and stating math was valuable to them personally and professionally.[56] After selecting their sample of students, the researchers brought them into the lab and gave half the participants a math test and the other half an English test. Both tests were thirty-minute sections from the GRE (math and English literature, respectively). The researchers found that women did, indeed, underperform relative to men on the math test, but English test results were similar between the women and men.

Now that researchers have their baseline, it was time to test the mechanism. With the next set of participants, the researchers told half of them women *usually* earn lower grades on math tests, however, that is *not* the case with this test. The researchers used this message to rid women of the idea that they would inevitably score lower on this test than their male peers so they could be more confident going into the test. The results are compelling. The women who did *not* hear that instruction, just like the group of participants before them, underperformed relative to the men. However, the women who heard the instruction (which was intended to be confidence-boosting) earned scores equal to the men. The researchers conclude that women's underperformance relative to men in math courses is due, then, to stigma.

Steele et al. later conducted a similar study at Stanford University looking at the impact of racial stigma on Black student's verbal reasoning scores. They found the same results. In the baseline study, Black students underperformed relative to White students on the verbal reasoning section of the GRE. Half the participants were then given the instruction that the test did *not* measure intellectual ability. It was simply a "task" designed to see how people solve problems. The Black participants who heard that instruction earned higher scores than the Black participants who did *not* hear the instruction, and earned scores equal to that of the White participants. Again, the researchers conclude that underperformance is due to stigma, not ability.

The impact of stereotype threat is usually not observable. It is largely an internalized process. An instance of stereotype threat might be personal and overt – like the examples Nell Scovell provided earlier in this chapter. But usually, stereotypes are baked into the very fabric of a society. Notice how Steele et al. did not need to *introduce* a stereotype in the baseline studies. The stereotype was already present. But their experiments offer hope. We can counter stigma pressure through new messaging and new norms. The relative underperformance of women students and Black students is a social problem (i.e., not a personal problem), and it is fixable if we combat our social norms.

It is important to note that these studies did not look at intersections between sex and race.

These baseline theory of these experiments is that – were it not for stereotypes – women can perform *as well as* men and Black people can perform *as well as* White people. I generally believe that we should all aim to view each other as equals without that idea that any group of people is "better" than another. But I also think it is important to celebrate the unique contributions we all bring to the table, without trying to "match" the performance of another group on indicators selected by the dominant group (e.g., standardized test scores). So let us first return to Nell Scovell's experiences, then carry this idea into the next section.

Faced with stereotype threat, Scovell was treated like an outsider. Yet, Scovell understood that her "outsider status" as a woman was beneficial in the writer's room. When Scovell wrote for *Warehouse 13*, a beloved show on the Syfy channel where Scovell was co-executive producer (2010–2012), she wrote an episode in which the female lead of the show (Myka, played by Joanne Kelly) becomes pregnant and experiences a heightened sense of smell. As the writing team discussed notes on the script, a male executive was confused about the smelling plot point. He asked if it was a real phenomenon that can occur during pregnancy.[57] Scovell responded "Yes" before realizing that she was the only person (of the seven) on the notes call who had been pregnant. More experiences (such as cultural, physical, geographic, and religious) allow for more material. You cannot write a story about how pregnancy affects sense of smell if you do not even know that phenomenon exists.

Even fictional stories are grounded in real emotions and experiences taken from the world around us. Science fiction, fantasies, and even teenage werewolf dramas are all based on real human emotions. That is what allows people to connect to them. Comedy is no different. Representation in media matters because there are more experiences to draw from and more stories to tell. An irony of comedy is that while there is vast inequality in access to opportunity for writing or performance gigs, comedy is an artform that is often employed to confront inequality. In comedy rooms, the best jokes and the toughest lessons often come from comedians *leaning into* specific injustices or speaking truth to power.

Flipping Stereotypes with Margaret Cho

Comedian Margaret Cho has spoken extensively in interviews about how representation matters in media because it humanizes the experiences of people who are too often excluded, ignored, or misunderstood. She believes media should be a mirror-image of society; allowing audiences to see themselves and their stories on screen, and enabling everyone to have a fuller understanding of, and appreciation for, one other.[58]

In a 2018 episode of *Comedians in Cars Getting Coffee*, Margaret Cho talked about her time coming up as a young standup comedian – including how her intersectional perspective was an advantage in her comedy. Recall, Kimberlé Crenshaw coined the term **intersectionality** to define how we cannot separate out individual features of our identities, such as race, ethnicity, sex, gender, sexuality, or social status.[59] These features *intersect* and shape our social experiences. Cho noted that when she was coming up in comedy, comedy clubs were dominated by White male comics. She always felt like she did not belong. But she knew that by being a young, queer, Asian woman, she experienced the world differently than everyone else getting up in comedy clubs. She has something new to offer.[60] Here, Cho touches on a core element of what a comedian must be able to do: see things as an outsider. While anyone is capable of developing this skill (hello, sociological imagination!), Cho acknowledges that her intersectional identity already gives her a leg up. She sees the world as an outsider because that's how the world sees her. She can use her outsider lens to take aim at the racism, sexism, and homophobia lobbed against her.

As an example, we can use a joke Cho used to perform when doing standup in San Francisco in the 1980s. Cho discussed the joke on a 2021 episode the *Good One* podcast.[61] Cho told host Matt Wilstein that there was a large Asian American population in San Francisco, and it was common for (White) standup comedians to "punch down" and make fun of the Asian Americans community in their act. Many comedians, for example, worked negative stereotypes about Asian Americans being bad drivers into their material. Cho wrote a joke in response. She would get on stage, say her name, then tell the crowd she was a good driver. The crowd was immediately confronted with their own implicit assumptions about her. Recall how Rodney Dangerfield joked about women being bad drivers. In his jokes, Dangerfield made women (specifically, his wife) the butts of his jokes. In Cho's joke, she plays with a similar stereotype that Asian people are bad drivers, but she makes the *audience* of the butt of the joke instead of herself.

Being able to find humor in one's circumstances speaks to the relief theory of humor. **Relief theory** holds that laugher is a mechanism for maintaining physical and mental homeostasis in times of distress.[62] Laugher is a stress relief valve. In this way, relief theory aligns with the adage that "laugher is the best medicine." Humor and laughter protect our bodies, minds, and social relationships.[63] Comedy takes the edge off and allows one to cope with their struggles. For outsiders or those who are not members of the dominant class, relief comes from laughing at oneself, not from being the butt of the joke.

Something implicit in this joke is the way marginalized people can never escape from the stereotypes, bias, or discrimination others hold against them. Cho walks into that comedy club and *knows* members of the audience likely think something untrue about her based on her race, sex, or sexuality. Cho has routinely spoken about the way comedy is "about the perspective of the outsider" and tends to speak positively about the way her outsider perspective makes her a stronger comedian (Cho, 2021).[64] Instead of regurgitating racist tropes, Cho thinks creatively about ways to engage with racist stereotypes in ways that surprise audiences and challenge the status quo.

While Cho's Asian driver joke is nearly forty years old, the comedic landscape is certainly still filled with comedians who lean into racist stereotypes. Cho was interviewed about racist and bigoted comics on *The Last Laugh* podcast. Cho believes it is important for comedians to take risks; however, it is pretty sad if someone's definition of "being risky or edgy" is "being racist."[65] Cho describes how all comedians are trying to push boundaries and push the status quo. But an important distinction Cho makes here is the conflation made by many comedians between being edgy and being offensive. This point is particularly important when we acknowledge that racism is, and has long been, the status quo in the United States. Falling back on racist tropes is lazy, boring, and serves to reinforce structural boundaries, not challenge them.

Comedians using their intersectional perspectives, as Cho does, can provide an antidote for the kind of comedy that reinforces structural boundaries and systems of oppression. Cho is an important case study in this section for the ways she was both bound by and deviated from traditional norms. Examining Cho's television series, *All-American Girl* (ABC, 1994–1995), will help us understand how structural barriers inhibited her art. In the late 1980s and early 1990s, many women comedians transformed into television sitcom stars, including Roseanne Barr (*Roseanne*, ABC, 1988–1997), Ellen DeGeneres (*Ellen*, ABC, 1994–1998), and Margaret Cho.[66] *All-American Girl*, which aired on ABC, was the first sitcom about an Asian American family in the United States. However, unlike Barr, DeGeneres, and their contemporaries, Cho was the only Asian woman and the only one without creative authority over the show. While *All-American Girl* was loosely based on Cho's life as a young Korean American woman, none of the writers, directors, or producers for the show were Korean American (two of the eleven writers were Chinese American).[67] The show failed to find its voice and ran for only one season (1994–1995) before it was cancelled by the network.[68]

Cho has explained in interviews over the years that *All-American Girl* received simultaneous criticism for being "too Asian" and for being not "Asian enough." Actor BD Wong (born in San Francisco, California, 1960), who played Cho's father on the show, described how the network took a talented young Cho and "sanded her down." Wong understood the poor reception to *All-American Girl* was not because Cho was Asian American, but because the show did not allow her to authentically showcase her Asian American identity and experience.[69,70] Criticisms of the show's representation of Asian American people note the way Koreans were mispresented. For example, giving the character of Cho's mother a stereotypically Asian (but, not Korean) accent or inaccurately portraying dinner table customs.[71]

As a Korean American woman, Cho has spoken about the way she never felt fully accepted either as a "Korean" or as an "American." Cho described a visit to her family's home country of Korea wherein she experienced resentment from others for being an American. With this experience, Cho felt she had no real home.[72] In this feeling, Cho describes how being Korean American feels as though one is always an outsider. That outsider experience is shared by many in the United States. In 1994, there were 12.2 million children in the United States who were first-generation or second-generation immigrants. By 2017, that figure was 19.6 million.[73] For *All-American Girl,* leaning into Cho's experiences as a Korean American woman would have strengthened what the show could do, and certainly would have resonated with audiences.

Even within the Korean American community, Cho is an outsider. An additional facet of Cho's identity is her sexuality; she is an openly bisexual woman and she discusses sex and her sexuality on stage. Cho experienced biphobic pushback throughout her career, and this sometimes came from the Korean American community. For example, there was a strong backlash from the Korean American community in Los Angeles around the time of the LA riots. The LA riots are marked by the 1991 arrest and beating of Rodney King, a Black man, by LAPD officers. The officers were acquitted in 1992, sparking protests and riots across the city. But in 1991, before all of this, the resentment and violence between the African American and Korean American communities in LA had reached a boiling point. Tensions stemmed from racism, economic inequality, and a lack of shared understanding between the communities. As a result of this context, Cho explained that the Korean American community in LA was taking careful steps to protect their public image.[74] To authorities in the LA Korean American community, including church ministers, Cho was not the representative they wanted. These churches threatened to protest against *All-American Girl.*

Why did churches threaten to protest against Cho's television series? As Cho explains, she was not the representative the community wanted because, (1) she was a woman and (2) she was "raunchy." Facing backlash from her own community was hard for Cho, but she did not take it lying down. She called ministers from Korean churches that had threatened to protest from her landline and spoke to them directly. Advocating for herself and for others in similar situations has been a guiding principle for Cho throughout her career, both off and on the stage. It certainly was a big part of her stage routine.

To see the form this advocacy took in her comedy routines, let us look at a bit from her 2002 show, *The Notorious C.H.O.* The title of the show is a nod to the late rapper, The Notorious B.I.G., who was killed in 1997. In the show, Cho says many sociological things. Cho speaks directly to folks who are treated as minorities in the United States, including women, people of color, LGBTQ+ people, and people who do not fit into socially normative body size standards. While not using this term directly, Cho employs the lens of critical theory to explain how one's status as a minority member restricts full participation in society and offers words of hope and positive change. In her show, she explains that limiting folks' self-esteem and self-confidence through marginalization and belittlement keeps folks trapped. It makes folks hesitant to dream big, to seek a promotion or a raise, or to report crimes committed against them. Cho explains that, as such, having self-esteem is "an act of revolution."[75]

Cho has always been a proud and vocal advocate for marginalized.[76] She uses her platform to bring messages of hope and positive change to the stage and the screen. This is the power of what comedy can do. Cho understands comedy can help us connect with one another, especially in response to trauma. Cho leverages her outsider perspective to share her story and provide a platform for change. What is remarkable about Cho, and countless other comedians, is that her motivation to share her story has always been grounded in hope.

During an interview on the *Good One* podcast, host Jesse David Fox asked Cho how she currently feels about comedians doing "Asian" jokes. Cho explains that there are ways to joke about race – such as her own experiences navigating the world as an Asian American woman – which do not play into stereotypic tropes. They can provide a window into one's life and culture which are generally not included in American media.[77] Such a comedic approach can increase representation and understanding of one's community to a wider audience. Such an approach can also serve as an avenue for connection, healing, and relief for one's own community in times of need.

The interview was recorded shortly after the deadly mass shootings that took place at spas and massage parlors in Atlanta, Georgia on March 16, 2021. Eight people died, six of whom were Asian American women. Cho discussed in the interview how close-to-home this mass shooting was for her. She lived in Atlanta for seven years and is a former sex worker. Paired with her discussion of this tragedy, Cho explains that comedy helps her grieve during times of extreme tragedy, sadness, and loss. Comedy helps her process her emotions. Laughter forces her to breathe, and to breathe is to reaffirm being alive. In this description, Cho summarizes the power of comedy to connect and heal. Great comedians are those who can elevate important issues and provide a bit of light in times of darkness. When done properly, comedy can offer community and shared understanding for folks who may really need it.

Self-Deprecating Humor

Members of marginalized groups have long been shut out from the opportunities afforded to more privileged groups. Comedians with outsider status – whether that is based on their race, ethnicity, sex, gender, sexuality, physical abilities, or other facets and intersections of their identities – have used **self-deprecating humor** to fit into spaces that otherwise would not accept them. Recall, self-deprecating humor deflects derision by joking about one's own "flaws" before others can.

This is seen frequently in comedy. Comics get on stage and immediately start making fun of, say, their physical appearance. They may play off a common stereotype of their race or a trope about their sex or sexuality.

These jokes are grounded in **social norms**. The comedian acknowledges the assumptions or stereotypes the audience may hold about them based upon their physical appearance or presentation. The comedian knows the audience assumes certain things about them. Self-deprecating jokes are, therefore, a conversation with the audience. It lets the audience know they understand the world in the same way.

Self-deprecation also allows comics – on the stage or on the screen – to make their audiences feel comfortable; to make their audiences feel they are in on the joke. This has been true in comedy for generations. Women comedians long needed to present as "frazzled or frumpy," regardless of how they looked and behaved offstage.[78] For generations, it was the norm in comedy that women and members of other marginalized groups could only be funny if the laughs they generated were at their own expense. Think back to Phyllis Diller, who in addition to making jokes about her talents (or lack thereof) as a housewife and mother, Diller made herself less attractive so she could make fun of her appearance. She did this to gain acceptance and to make jokes about herself before others could.

Sexual Harassment and Comedy with *Hacks*

For a fictionalized version of what the world looks like for women comedians who have to beat others to the punchline, let us turn to the show *Hacks*, which premiered on HBO in 2021. While set in modern time, one of the main characters, Deborah, is an older female comedian who came up in comedy from working clubs like much like The Comedy Store in the 1970s. The character (played by Jean Smart) is a legendary comedian with a long-running residency at the Palmetto in Las Vegas whose act is starting to stale. Opposite Deborah is Ava (played by Hannah Einbinder), a twenty-five-year-old comedy writer who is down on her luck after getting canceled for an insensitive tweet and subsequently losing her television writing gig. Ava's agent, Jimmy (played by Paul W. Downs), sends her out to Las Vegas to write for Deborah to freshen up her act.[79] The core humor of the show comes from Deborah and Ava's generational rift in their views of the world and their views of comedy.

Ava pitches macabre, Internet-savvy, identity-driven, off-kilter jokes, which are almost (but not always) shot down by Deborah in favor of tightly packaged observational humor or wordplay. Deborah has the power and the money in the relationship, but central to the show is the fact that Deborah's (and her entire generation's) grasp on the reigns of comedy and celebrity is loosening. Generational divides play heavily into the characters' relationship. In an episode from the show's first season, Deborah mistakenly refers to Ava as a "millennial." Ava (a member of Gen-Z) is shocked and outraged to be mistaken for a member of such an "old" generation, noting – with disgust – that some millennials are forty years old.[80] While the characters themselves clash in *Hacks*, something I like about the series is it does not pit the generations against each other with a clear winner or loser. We see both Deborah and Ava (and thereby, the generations their characters represent) as equally funny, interesting, lovable, and at times loathsome, but ultimately as people. These are people with different histories, experiences, and ways of seeing the world. Their different perspectives are what make their relationship better, richer, and funnier.

There is perhaps no better example of this rich generational divide in *Hacks* than in the episode titled "1.69 million" (season 1, episode 8). After learning her residency contract at the Palmetto is being prematurely ended and her celebratory 2500th show will be her last, Deborah is desperate to hold on to her fame and stage time. She decides to do something wild for her 2500th show to create buzz in the hopes of getting picked up by another casino or showcase. The wild thing she decides to try is what Ava pitched all along: identity-driven comedy that weaves jokes into Deborah's personal narrative and life story.

The two immediately get to work writing the hour-long set. They fly to a comedy club in Sacramento, California called the HaHa, where Deborah got her start, to work out some of the new material before the Palmetto show. At the HaHa, Deborah and Ava have drinks with an old friend, Francine (played by Anna Maria Horsford), who is another female comic with whom Deborah came up in the clubs. The friend tells Deborah the old owner of the club, Ira, died. The women celebrate the death of a man who sexually harassed, groped, and required sexual favors for payment of the young female comics. **Sexual harassment** is a form of harassment with a sexual nature. Sexual harassment may include unwelcome comments about one's body, the verbal expression or implication of one's sexual actions or desires, or unwanted physical engagement – ranging from unwanted touching to assault.

When Ava asks who Ira was, Francine and Deborah explain through their laughter that they would enter the stage with their backsides pressed against the wall so he could not grope them from behind. Ava is aghast. Later, in the greenroom, Ava asks Deborah why she did not report Ira. Deborah tells Ava that Ira owned half the clubs on the West Coast and reporting him would have ended her career. Ava accuses her of prioritizing her own fame and career over the welfare of other women. The scene showcases a generational rift in two ways. Deborah is there to try out new material which Ava suggested and helped write. Ava sees reporting as the braver, more selfless way to have handled being sexually harassed and groped by Ira. Deborah knows the system was very different for women in comedy when she was coming up. There was no protection for young comics. The only thing that would have happened was Deborah burned all her bridges in town and would have needed another career. There was no way to win when there was no power.

Recall, conflict theorists hold society is held together by **conflict** and **coercion**. Individuals are kept "in line" through coercive forces – such as threats or experiences of harassment – from individuals in positions of power. An example is comedy club owners or emcees who have the power to decide who gets on stage. Up-and-coming comedians who need stage time to practice their craft or earn some money have little choice but to obey.

In an *LA Times* interview with *Hacks* co-creator, writer, and producer Jen Statsky, she details how this episode was written based on real experiences for women at comedy clubs. The article is aptly titled "How HBO Max's hot new comedy took down the toxic man in 'every single standup club.'"[81] In the article, Statsky explains there was a lot of back-and-forth in the writer's room around how much Ava should challenge Deborah in his scene. The writers want to be truthful to Ava's character as a young yet emotionally intelligent person who truly understands that Deborah experienced immense levels of sexism everywhere she went. Ava understands that. It is exactly because Ava understands the pervasiveness of sexism in Deborah's time that she wished Deborah had taken action. Ava sees it as a duty to others.

As Statsky explained in the article, Ava is simultaneously right and wrong. Ava is *right* in that it would have been powerful for Deborah to have stood up for herself and other women comedians, versus letting Ira continue to objectify them. However, Ava is *wrong* in thinking that stopping Ira would be easy, possible, or free of consequences. Statsky notes this dance between rightness and wrongness was at the core of their writing for *Hacks*. When Deborah and Ava are at odds with one another, it is often because they are both right in some ways and wrong in others.[82] Getting the balance right between how the audience understands and agrees with Ava's and Deborah's respective worldviews is integral to the core message of the show.

Things are changing today. Women and other marginalized comedians are speaking up and ushering in real change. Indeed, change can happen one gatekeeper at a time. The apex of the "1.69 million" episode is when Deborah sees there is a new "Ira" in the same position of the one who died. The HaHa's emcee, Drew (played by Adam Ray), is Ira 2.0. Deborah sees him sexually harass a young female comic as she comes back to the greenroom after getting off stage. Deborah realizes nothing has changed. Nothing except her own power. When Drew introduces Deborah to the crowd as she later gets on stage for her set, he does so by commenting about her breasts and implying that – because she is a woman – she is "crazy." This time, Deborah does not let it slide. When she gets up on stage, Deborah starts roasting Drew. Drew tries to play along, which ends with him "jokingly" offering her drugs which may be used in drug-facilitated sexual assault. This threat is enough for Deborah to stop joking around. She turns to the audience and begins explaining what is happening in this interaction. She lays out in very clear words what the audience does and does not see.

Deborah explains to the audience that Drew's heckles and pretend-flirting give Deborah only two options. Option one: she shuts him down by refusing to play along. But, as Deborah explains, the audience would see her as "cold" or as a bad sport with no sense of humor. If she takes this option, she then has a big uphill battle to win the audience back as she continues her set. Option two: she plays along. Which, as Deborah notes, is easier. But then she objectifies herself on Drew's terms. Her set becomes all about him – someone she detests and barely knows. He effectively steals her set from her; something she has worked hard to develop, practice, and identifies her as a performer and a person. Summing up, Deborah tells the crowd – through an exasperated sigh – there is always someone who will objectify you when you walk onstage. Ira may be dead but Drew is very much alive.

Deborah's need to swim upstream in her interaction with Drew and conduct counter-misogynist prework before she can be taken seriously is one example of an emotional tax. An **emotional tax** is the heightened burden members of marginalized groups, including women and people of color, experience in everyday interactions.[83] It is akin to always needing to be "on guard" and it is detrimental to one's physical, emotional, and professional health. The emotional tax is one which impacts the health and professional lives of Black women and women of color to a greater extent than to that of White women, due to increased experiences of harassment and required vigilance in everyday life.

Deborah continues to walk the audience through how Drew's sexist introduction stripped her of her chance to perform her set the way she planned. Deborah is effectively stripped of her ability to try out new material because now she is playing defense. Now she has to grapple with how to rebound from being the butt of the joke, while she is also angry, exhausted, and beat down. So Deborah decides to take action this time. She asks Drew what it will take for him to just stop. His answer: "$69 million" (said with a smirk, as Drew clearly finds the "69" clever and hilarious). Deborah counters, saying she will cut him a check for $1.69 million if he agrees to stay away from comedy clubs for the rest of his life. Deborah tells the crowd she cannot rid the comedy world of all the "Drews" but she can start with one.

After Drew agrees and they shake on the deal, the biggest applause from the crowd yet comes when Deborah, fully embracing her newfound power, fully roasts Drew as he heads out the door. The whole exchange is fictionalized and hyperbolic (as most television is), and there certainly can be questions raised, such as should *Drew* be the one getting the 1.69 million? Versus the women he harassed? Would he have settled for less, like maybe $690,000 or $69,000? Regardless, the point is the same: trailblazers like Deborah put up with a lot of discrimination to make it where they are now. There is power and beauty in turning around to help others onto the stage, and sometimes you need to push (or pay) off a Drew to do it.

Deborah did what she perhaps always wanted to do but never had the power (or the money) to accomplish. She spoke truthfully to her audience about the harassment she experienced as a woman in comedy. She effectively conveyed that harassment against women comics does not only come from individual bad actors. It is systemic. The comedy they see on stage is a direct reflection of the harassment she experiences. She walked the audience through how her comedic performance is impacted by harassment. When she plays along to "be a good sport," that is not her authentic self. The audience is left to question their own complicit behavior. When they laugh at jokes by people playing along to avoid harassment, what exactly are they laughing at?

Consider how Deborah's experiences may be linked to the work of structural theorist Friedrich Engels. Engels understood capitalism and patriarchy were the social structures responsible for the subjugation of women in society. Engels posited that the desire to own property drove the subjugation. Men's desires for more property provided a catalyst for prohibiting women from doing the same. Without women as competition for the same finite resources, there was more property available for men. Engels' theories were built upon the experiences of White women and men, but the capitalist desire to own more property and subsequent subjugation of other people can be extended to treatment of Black, Brown, and Indigenous people in the United States, as well as land and resource disputes across the globe.

Engels saw the abolishment of **private property** ownership as the remedy to the patriarchal subjugation of women. Eliminating the "goal" of patriarchal and capitalist social orders (i.e., private property) would, in Engel's view, remove incentive for the means (i.e., subjugation of women). While Engels' focus was on property, the idea of competition over a finite resource can be extended to other assets – including stage time. Under this framework, if men desire more stage time (and by extension, more success and notoriety as comedians), it benefits them to deny it to women. Denial of stage time can be through the explicit exclusion of women on stage, or, through heckling, interjection, and harassment.

The Belly Room as a Pink Ghetto

Figure 5.1 highlights the "SNL & Richard Pryor" era of comedy, roughly spanning 1974–1980. In the next section, we will dive into the ways women and other marginalized comedians were excluded from mainstream performance stages using the Belly Room, housed within The Comedy Store, as a prominent example.

Comedy clubs were boy's clubs for a long time and sometimes still are. Because men often ran the clubs and appreciated a male-centric sense of humor, women were considered not funny and thus undeserving of stage time.[84] To ensure women have a dedicated space to perform without the judgmental eye of male comedians or anti-women audiences, what about separate comedy rooms for women comedians? Let us use our sociological toolkit to discuss the promise and pitfalls of such spaces. We will talk specifically about the Belly Room, which was a stage opened for women comedians inside The Comedy Store in 1978.

Recall our introduction to The Comedy Store and Mitzi Shore. Mitzi wanted women comedians to get stage time and to have a safe space to try out new material, but she was also a savvy businessperson. As much as she wanted women to have stage time, she knew bumping men (and the handful of women who found success) off The Comedy Store's Original Room or

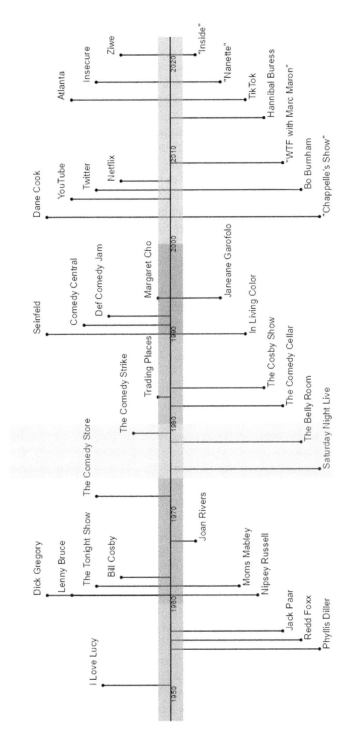

Figure 5.1 SNL and Richard Pryor Timeline

Main Room stages was not going to make her money. The Original Room and Main Room shows were lucrative exactly as they were, and Mitzi did not want to mess with that. So Mitzi opened the Belly Room in The Comedy Store in 1978 as a stage for women comedians to get stage time without needing to bump any male comedians from the Main Room.

The Belly Room was housed in a small room upstairs in The Comedy Store.[85] The opening of the Belly Room was divisive. Some women comedians, like Emily Levin and Sandra Bernhard, liked that you could consistently get time for longer sets and on weekend nights, which were hard for women to get on other stages. Some women also felt the safer environment gave them more freedom to experiment with their material without being heckled, having to follow a male comic's sexist act, or fear of never getting on that stage again as the woman who "bombed." Bombing is a privilege women comedians and comedians from other marginalized groups are not afforded.

Other comedians recognized the Belly Room's flaws. Elayne Boosler and Marsha Warfield refused to play the Belly Room. Merrill Markoe described her experience in the Belly Room in *We Killed* (2013). She explains that Mitzi touted the Belly Room as place where women comedians could shine. But, in Markoe's view, it was a place where all the women comedians were pushed to the side and the only folks in the audience were those waiting for space to open up in one of the other rooms downstairs. Her argument attempts to **debunk** the claim that the Belly Room was designed to further women comedians' careers.

For the reasons Markoe describes, the Belly Room is a pink ghetto. The term **pink ghetto** was coined in 1983 to describe occupations primarily filled by women.[86] It was used to define the occupational segregation women experienced when they were shut out from more prestigious occupations primarily filled by men.

Before we go further in this section, let us dive into a bit of important history regarding the term **ghetto**. The term ghetto dates to the year 1516 when Jewish people were cast out of Venice and relegated to a small island on the end of the city. The island was dubbed "New Ghetto" ("Ghetto Nuovo" in Italian) and formerly served as a copper foundry.[87] The word ghetto likely stems from the Venetian word meaning to pour or cast (*gettare*), a nod to the island's foundry roots. In the following centuries, Jewish people were expelled from cities all over Italy and were forcefully segregated into small, enclosed areas. The term ghetto stuck through the late 1800s and early 1900s as Jewish people immigrated to the United States and often lived in ethnic enclaves inside American cities (e.g., Manhattan's Lower East Side was formerly called the New York Ghetto).

An **ethnic enclave** is a geographic area comprising a high concentration of a particular ethnic group. Take New York City, for example. There are potentially hundreds of ethnic enclaves in the city, represented as neighborhoods with high concentrations of a particular ethnic group. In addition to the historical legacy of Manhattan's Lower East Side as an ethnic enclave for

Jewish people, a few examples of enclaves in New York City today are Chinatown in Lower Manhattan, the Haitian community in Flatbush, and the Pakistani community in Queens.[88-90] Ethnic enclaves are often born of necessity. With waves of migration, landing in a community with shared language, food, customs, and social or professional networks allows new migrants to find familiarity, security, or to get established with housing or a job.[91]

"Ghetto" eventually morphed in meaning and became a disparaging term lodged against Black communities. In the early 20th century, cities were passing zoning ordinances that blocked Black residents from living in White neighborhoods. While these zoning ordinances were declared illegal in 1917, informal systems driving residential segregation remained.[92] Black folks in the United States began using ghetto as political shorthand to describe the residential segregation to which they were being subjected. The term was particularly politically salient during the civil rights movement of the 1960s. As Jewish people were forcefully segregated into ghettos, so too were Black people forcefully segregated in their cities.

However, people from the dominant majority (White people) began using ghetto as a pejorative label to suggest Black communities are undeserving of equal respect or opportunity. When ghetto is lodged as a pejorative term against a group of people, it serves to make that systemic oppression invisible. That label serves to blame Black and Brown people for their own oppression, giving others permission to treat them as if they are underserving of anything better.

It is important to acknowledge the negative racial and socioeconomic connotations associated with the term ghetto before moving forward. The pink ghetto is a predetermined concept name that I use in this section. Knowing the history of the term ghetto aids understanding for how forced segregation based on one's group serves to maintain inequality, and how this applies to women in professional spaces. The Comedy Store's Belly Room is considered a pink ghetto because of its limited respect, audience size, and mainstream exposure relative to the club's other stages – and it was the stage to which most women comedians were relegated.

There were landmark attempts to extend equal opportunity and equal pay for women in the workplace in the decades leading into the Belly Room's opening in 1978. The Equal Pay Act of 1963 and Civil Rights Act of 1964 were important ones. The Equal Pay Act of 1963 outlaws unequal pay for substantially equal work based on sex (the Act does not regulate pay discrimination based on other identities, including race, religion, national origin, sexuality, or physical ability).[93] The Civil Rights Act expanded this work. The Act outlawed discrimination in the workplace based upon sex, race, religion, and national origin in the realms of hiring, firing, and promotions.[94] However, businesses still found ways around the laws.

To skirt equal pay for equal work requirements (which were outlined in the equal pay chapter of the Civil Rights Act of 1964), the Wheaton Glass Company of Millville, New Jersey, gave men the job title of "selector-packer-stackers" and women the job title of "selector-packers."[95] Different job, different pay. It didn't take long for someone to file a lawsuit: Shultz v. Wheaton Glass Company. In 1970, the U.S. Court of Appeals for the Third Circuit ruled in the plaintiff's favor. The new ruling strengthened understandings of what was outlined in the Civil Rights Act by deeming it illegal for employers to use different job titles for women and men performing comparable job functions.

In 1977, the term **pink collar** work gained recognition upon the publication of Louise Kapp How's book *Pink Collar Workers: Inside the World of Women's Work*. The term is used to describe sex segregation in the workplace. It is another categorization like "white collar" (referring to professional or managerial work, like law or engineering) or "blue collar" work (referring to manual work like construction or transit operating). Pink collar work refers to professions dominated by women such as teaching, nursing, childcare, and secretarial work. An important element of pink collar work is that these professions often pay relatively little and receive relatively minimal respect and prestige compared to positions which require similar levels of training and difficulty but are primarily dominated by men.

Even when women are in male-dominated spaces, their work is not recognized or compensated equally. Another example of a 1970s lawsuit that served to secure more equal rights for women in the workplace comes from the *New York Times*. Women employed at the *NYT* uncovered large pay gaps between themselves and their male counterparts. The initial gap they discovered was an average of $59 per week, which ballooned to nearly $99 per week by 1977. The latter figure translates to roughly $472 per week in 2022 dollars. The women of *NYT* slapped the newspaper with a class action lawsuit. *Ms. Magazine* dubbed it "the world series of sex-discrimination suits."[96] The women won.

This was the political landscape at the time. Women were making strides and gaining equal footing in the workplace, but had to do so one class action lawsuit at a time. They were still getting harassed. That is what the women at The Comedy Store experienced. Getting heckled and harassed for your sex or for other features of your identity is damaging, unfair, and certainly not funny (but it was legal! Workplace sexual harassment did not become illegal until 1986). Guaranteed gender-based harassment makes it undesirable for women comedians to get up night after night, knowing what is coming your way. This is a hurdle the White men at The Comedy Store did not need to overcome.

Janeane Garofolo and the Alternative Comedy Movement

Figure 5.2 highlights the "Alternative, Def Comedy Jam, & Sitcoms" era of comedy, roughly spanning 1990–2000. In the next section, we will dive specifically into the sociological significance of the alternative comedy movement in comedy's history.

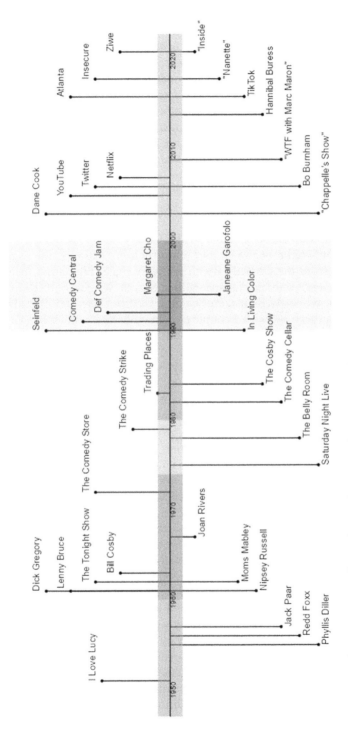

Figure 5.2 Alternative Comedy, *Def Comedy Jam*, and Sitcoms Timeline

In the 1980s, there was a new wave of comedians who broke out of main-stream clubs to express their comedic perspectives in places they were cel-ebrated. Comedian historians refer to the 1980s as the "Comedy Boom."[97] Comedy was hot. Hundreds of new comedy clubs popped up all over the country throughout the decade. Comedy clubs were carved out of old night-clubs, restaurants, bars, live music venues, and bowling alleys. According to comedian, actor, author, and historian Wayne Federman, these spaces needed four elements to be reborn into a comedy club: (1) a liquor license, (2) access to comedic talent, (3) a microphone system, and (4) tables and chairs. Clubs overwhelmingly followed a standard ninety-minute show for-mat which comprised an emcee or opener, an opening comedian, and a head-lining comedian. Openers and headliners toured clubs around the country, enabled by cheap airline travel and vast interstate highway systems (paired with cheap gasoline).

Popular comedic styles during the Comedy Boom included observational comedy and tight one-liner joke construction. Most of the biggest com-edy stars from the Comedy Boom era were male. Big names include Eddie Murphy, Jerry Seinfeld, Dennis Miller, Steven Wright, Sam Kinison, Louie Anderson, Robin Williams, and George Carlin. Character comedy was also big during this time, with a couple popular character comics like Gilbert Got-tfried and Andrew Dice Clay trying out alternative personas on stage.

During the standup comedy boom of the 1970s and 1980s, when standup clubs popped up all across the country, women entered in the field in droves.[98] A handful of popular women comics broke through, including Roseanne Barr, Ellen DeGeneres, and Whoopi Goldberg. Though at this time, women comedians and experimental comedians still had trouble getting stage time in mainstream clubs. The women who did make it up were often expected to fit nicely into a "male mold" – the "standard" or "ideal" set of mascu-line styles and mannerisms to which all comedians were expected to adhere. Women who were deemed unpretty, unfeminine, too explicit about women's personal or bodily troubles were denied stage time and, effectively, shut out from comedic opportunities.

Comedy clubs made sexist and seemingly arbitrary rules about their line-ups. Such rules included only one woman on the lineup per night, or no two women could perform in succession. These rules made the number of slots available to women minuscule compared to men. To get time on stage, women were largely limited to performing at "all-woman comedy nights." Like the discovery clubs Diller played in the 1960s, the audiences who at-tended these women's comedy nights were overwhelmingly women and gay men. Straight men were just not that interested.

Eventually, these women and experimental comedians began to carve out their own opportunities in a movement that came to be known as the "alter-native comedy" (alt comedy) movement.[99] Alt comedy first referred to any comedy performed outside of a traditional comedy club. Comedians set up comedy shows in any space that would have them, like coffeehouses, theaters, and laundromats. These spaces allowed for greater freedom of material and were more welcoming environments for stage (or, washing machine) time. While the original identification of alt comedy was largely tied to space, there were certain features of the performers and their comedic perspectives that further united this movement.

The alt comedy movement was spearheaded by comedian Janeane Garofolo (born in Newton, New Jersey, 1964). Garofolo believed comedy was more about sharing your identity and being a truth-teller than it was about telling a neatly packaged joke. While there had previously been "alternative" comedians, whose style broke from the norm, the alt comedy movement marked the first time there was an entire category of comedians and spaces that followed this path. This distinction is important because audiences learned to expect these alternative styles, which tended to be less "jokey," more personal, and sometimes resembled stream of consciousness in their delivery (a deviation from the tight one-liner style popular in mainstream clubs). Alt comedians had a "wide latitude" and felt encouraged to break from mainstream styles and comedic expectations by audiences in these spaces. Women especially thrived in alt comedy spaces. Here, women finally had the freedom to be loud, crass, and messy – a luxury which (most) men in comedy always had.

Garofolo rose to prominence during the early 1990s as she began her long-lasting and prolific career in film and television alongside her standup comedy work. Two of her biggest roles during this era were on *The Larry Sanders Show*, a revered comedy on HBO which ran from 1992 to 1998, and in an iconic movie-of-the-generation, 1994's *Reality Bites*.[100] In 1994, *Saturday Night Live* decided to hire Garofolo as part of their plan to rebuild the show following its terribly rated 1993–1994 season. Garofolo was funny, cool, and importantly, a woman (which *SNL* desperately lacked). Garofolo was a big get. Part of Garofolo's appeal was that she was a fierce, sarcastic, take-no-flack performer for a generation that idolized those qualities.

Unfortunately, it did not take long before the Garofolo-*SNL* partnership turned sour. Garofolo was not happy about the sexism she experienced at *SNL*. *SNL* was originally groundbreaking for the (relative) gender equality in its cast. In fact, the first cast member ever hired was Gilda Radner. In its first season (1975), the cast included three women and four men and three female writers.[101] But bias was explicitly baked into the process. The high ratio of male-to-female writers resulted in fewer acting parts written for the women. Male writers rarely wrote sketches for the women performers, and when women wrote scenes, some of the male actors refused to act in them.[102]

In the first few months Garofolo was on *SNL*, the roles she played were largely those of waitress, girlfriend, and wife; supporting roles with few lines and a limited opportunity to be funny.[103] Garofolo felt pigeonholed into those roles and thus left partway through her first season.[104] Garofolo remained an outsider even inside the *SNL* studio walls. But instead of pulling away from that outsider identity, Garofolo leaned into it. Garofolo believed that the outsiders and deviants of the world had unique perspectives to lend their audiences. To Garofolo, an outsider's personal story *is* their comedic material. They do not need clever punchlines to make comedy; their stories lend the edge, surprise, and a countering of the status quo that defines comedy. Garofolo's comedic point of view focused on the belief that comedy requires you to get to know the identity of the comic.[105]

Identity-based comedy relates to the presentation of self in that it does not fall back on stereotypic, normative views of who someone is. Think about the era in which Phyllis Diller was coming up, which was one that required her to use self-deprecating humor to adhere to social views of women at the time. She was breaking the rules by being boisterous and independent woman, but she still had to lean into stereotypes about her flaws (or at least, her character's flaws) as a woman to gain acceptance.

Garofolo, however, was not trying to become an insider. Instead, Garofolo's status as an outsider brought its advantages: she was free to perform comedy in her own style without feeling bound to more traditional comedic forms or stereotypic tropes. She was not trying to be girly or proper. She told jokes about being a mess or being bad in relationships, but not in a way that implied she was failing at being a proper woman. The alt comedy movement gave her and other comedians the space to speak about themselves authentically. Their real strengths and their real flaws. Its authenticity was the alt comedy scene's edge and that was exciting to audiences.

Earlier, women comedians often felt pigeonholed into a male-dominated model of comedy.[106] By creating their own spaces, the alt comedy movement, shepherded by Garofolo, gave women more space to express and define their own identities. They had more latitude to be loud, crass, and messy. Their creative expression could be more closely tied to their comedic sensibility when the fear of heckling, harassment, or labeling was removed.

Consider how having ownership over *space* allowed Garofolo and her comedic colleagues to be more themselves. Consider how the alternative comedy movement provides a counterexample to the fictionalized example of Deborah in *Hacks* in the earlier section. Consider if and how removing the competition for property – whether that be physical property, stage time, or screen time – can reduce or eliminate the subjugation of women and members of oppressed groups.

Trends in comedy reflect social structures and social norms. Women and marginalized comedians were denied stage time, heckled, or demeaned in mainstream clubs. Their identity-based comedy was not accepted by mainstream audiences. They had to make their own spaces where they did not need to fit into a White, male comedic mold.

Identity-based, truth-telling comedy did not grab hold of mainstreams audiences when Janeane Garofolo, Margaret Cho, and their contemporaries were doing it. They needed to make their own spaces for their comedy to be accepted by audiences. What happens when that style of comedy is appropriated? *Enter: Louis C.K.*

The Louis C.K.-ification of Truth in Comedy

Comedian Louis C.K. (Louis Székely born in Washington, DC, 1967) got his start playing in both alternative venues and mainstream comedy clubs on his way to finding massive mainstream success. He went on to define a new generation of comedy in which comedians were lauded as truth-tellers and (per Charlie Rose) described as "philospher-kings."[107] His show *Louie*, which premiered on FX in 2010 and ran for five seasons, was instantly lauded as a groundbreaking show and hailed by many as one of the best shows ever on television.[108] The same year *Louie* ended in 2015, C.K. sold out Madison Square Garden three times during a single comedy tour. He was the first comedian to ever do that.[109]

C.K. achieved as much mainstream success as is possible for a comedian. But to understand how he got there, let us go back to where he got his start. Alternative spaces allowed comedians who were generally excluded from, or unwelcome in, traditional comedy clubs to try out new, innovative material in venues that were welcoming and generally non-hostile. Women comedians gravitated toward these spaces because they were often excluded, demeaned, or harassed in traditional comedy clubs. But male comedians played to these spaces too; men whose comedic perspectives were more alternative than the traditional standup comedy format. They had a choice, and they chose alt comedy.

There were also male comedians who played to both spaces to get more stage time and more chances to work out their material to a variety of audiences. C.K. played to both spaces to work out material that had universal appeal. What C.K. found is that the truth-telling comedy that worked in alternative clubs also worked in mainstream comedy clubs.

This, of course, is the exact comedy style that the women who spearheaded the alternative comedy movement, like Janeane Garofolo and Margaret Cho, did not fit into and thus were laughed out of comedy clubs. Then C.K. did it. He brought truth-telling comedy to mainstream clubs, but with a more masculine and aggressive tone.[110] C.K. did not hold back from sharing the dark, aggressive voices in his head.

We can use some examples from his closing bit, referred to as "Of Course … But Maybe," from his 2013 HBO special, *Oh My God*. In the bit, C.K. explains to the audience that everyone has "good thoughts" and "bad thoughts" which are in constant competition in our brains. We hope the good thoughts win out, yet the bad thoughts are always there.[111] C.K. then explains to the crowd that those bad thoughts compose a category in his brain which he dubbed "Of Course … But Maybe." He then lists examples of these thoughts. For example, children who have nut allergies should be protected (that is the good thought), but maybe if we let all children with nut allergies die, then we would as a species be done with nut allergies forever (that is the bad thought).[112,113]

With bits like "Of Course … But Maybe," C.K. was declared revolutionary for sharing his inner truth, including things about which people normally feel ashamed or things they feel the need to hide. This was revolutionary for a time when most mainstream comedy club comedians were performing neatly packaged jokes (think: Jerry Seinfeld). There was such a swift and dramatic turn in the universally understood "job" of the comedian from entertainer to truth-teller that some audiences and critics began to turn against comedians like Seinfeld for their "hacky," over-rehearsed material. Comedians were not there to entertain; they were there to tell the truth.

But as it turns out, C.K. was not telling the truth. His material was not confessional in the ways audiences assumed for two primary reasons. First, C.K. worked it out heavily. Just like Seinfeld did, and (spoiler alert) almost every single comedian. By the time audiences saw C.K.'s specials or shows, his material had been worked, reworked, tweaked, and refined to get the most laughs. And for C.K., he often found that the darkest material is what resonated most strongly with audiences. The darkness that was his brand was not necessarily because that is who he was, but because that is what audiences wanted.

Second, C.K.'s material was not what it appeared to be. Remember those bad thoughts he dared not act on? Well, sometimes he did. C.K. had a lot of material about women, sex, and masturbation, including dark thoughts about his sexual desires and voracious need to masturbate. While the material was usually dark, C.K. painted himself as a good guy; able to separate his dark desires from the way he actually treated women.

We can take another example from C.K.'s 2013 special to get a sense of this. In one bit, C.K. rhetorically asks the audience why women continue to go on dates with men, considering men are their greatest threat. He likens it to men going on dates with wild animals (giving the imagery of a mythical amalgam of a bear and a lion). He jokes the men would need to be pretty optimistic, or delusional, to assume *this one* will go against their wild nature and treat their date with safety and respect. In this bit (while, admittedly, placing blame on women for choosing to go out with men), C.K. acknowledges the danger and fear women face at the hands of men. In the special, C.K. presents himself here as an advocate for women by using his platform to speak out against the violence and sexual predation women experience at the hands of men (speaking specifically about women who date men). He built a career out of calling out male hypocrisy and was lauded as an advocate for women.[114]

The problem is that C.K. is an actual sexual predator. Rumors swirled for years that C.K. would masturbate in front of women associates without consent or with coerced consent. Such allegations came to public light in 2017. This was during an era in which many prominent male figures were being taken to task for their past (or present) sexual harassment or assault lodged against women as a result of the #MeToo movement. Finding out the truth about C.K. did not just feel like a betrayal against women, it felt like a betrayal against his audience and against truth-telling comedy as an artform.

Dr. Stephanie Brown describes how audiences' assumptions about a performer's "authenticity" are tied to who a performer is or what they look like. "Authenticity, though, is arbitrary, and the uncritical usage of the term to define *good* comedy and *talented* comedians has become a means through which to police the boundaries of standup and to 'foreclose possibilities,' often validating certain racial and gendered performances over others" (Brown, 2018).[115] As Brown describes, the uncritical usage of the term "authentic" in comedy is based on, and magnifies, existing social hierarchies. "Authenticity" is not assigned based on the validity of the performance or the performer, but instead, based upon social hierarchies valuing and the words and experiences of White men over others.

C.K. took advantage of that assumed credibility. Critics noted that C.K.'s material about his *dark thoughts* about women – which C.K. told audiences he rose above and treated women with respect – was more than just untruthful. It was self-serving. He dangled false threads in front of audiences while walking away as a rich and powerful man.[116] The intent here matters in comedy. A point we further explore later in this book is that comedy does not need to be factually true, but it does need to be emotionally true. It is one thing to hype something up to aid audiences' understanding of an experience or emotion. It is quite another to use lies and half-truths to hold onto your image and further gain status, money, and power. Especially when amassing status, power, and money allows you further control over women and over your own narrative.

C.K.'s impact on comedy in this era was long-lasting. Young comedians tend to emulate their heroes. For years and years, that meant you would see young (generally, male) comedians at comedy clubs "confessing" their dark thoughts. Often, those thoughts were sexually aggressive toward women or disparaging against marginalized groups. Sharing darkness or hateful thoughts was, then, equated to being confessional. This has defined most of the past fifteen years of comedy. The general idea of sharing your truth on stage was appropriated from people trying to share their stories to audiences who were receptive, welcoming, and interested in connecting on a deeper level. The Louis C.K.-ification of that style was to make it aggressive, exclusionary, and appeal primarily to mainstream comedy audiences dominated by straight, White, male sensibilities. But the evolution of comedy is perpetual. In remaining chapters in this book, we will see how young comedians are changing the narrative today.

Summary

Social stratification defines an organization of society that affords people different treatment and opportunities based upon social class and identity-based group membership. This chapter paired comedic examples, like *Trading*

Places and *Mo,* with sociological studies to teach concepts about how social stratification operates and sustains itself. Understanding social stratification as a social sorting mechanism provides the scaffolding for interpreting what identities and behaviors define "outsiders" and "deviants," and how social hierarchies are reinforced in the face of evolving social and cultural norms. The 1979 Comedy Store strike showed sociological concepts in action – such as those put forward by Karl Marx. Discussions of women in comedy highlighted sociological concepts, including stereotype threat, sexual harassment, and the glass ceiling.

Outsider status in comedy has exclusionary effects which impact hopeful comedians' professional opportunities and personal experiences. Comedians who fell under outsider status and out of mainstream comedy sought alternative spaces that would cultivate their creative expression. This chapter used Louis C.K.'s rise to prominence as an example of the way truth in comedy can be appropriated for the mainstream and discussed how the Louis C.K.-ification of truth impacted a generation of comedians. Readers should leave this chapter with an understanding of what social stratification means and what influences it has on individuals' access to opportunities and success.

Discussion Questions

5-1: Does Nell Scovell's description of how women directors and showrunners are hired lend support for the structural/functionalist or conflict theory perspective of meritocracy?

5-2: How do explanatory theories of deviance relate to rational choice theory?

5-3: Describe the (a) manifest functions and (b) latent functions of the Immigration and Customs Enforcement (ICE) restrictions imposed upon the character Mo in the Netflix series *Mo.*

5-4: Consider the constraints placed on Mo, as defined by rational choice theorists. What were his constraints in finding and maintaining steady and legal employment? Were his subsequent (and illegal) means of making money rational, or irrational, in your view?

5-5: How does the myth of meritocracy relate to Max Weber's concept of the iron cage? Consider if elements of false mythology encourage or maintain the iron cage.

5-6: Describe the stages of the 1979 Comedy Store strike using the language of Karl Marx.

5-7: Do you agree with Friedrich Engels' belief that private property ownership was the core driver of patriarchal social structures? Why or why not? Do you think Engels is missing anything in this view?

5-8: Do you think the Belly Room was beneficial or detrimental to the success of women comedians at the time? Use sociological theories to justify your answer.

5-9: How do social stratification and social power influence who is seen as capable and trustworthy in society? Consider the sociological concepts of impression management, social stratification, representation, and intersectionality in your answer.

5-10: What did you learn about the concept of privilege from thinking about comedians who have mainstream appeal versus comedians who inhabit alternative spaces.

Notes

1 Jacobs, D. (1979). Inequality and police strength: Conflict theory and coercive control in metropolitan areas. *American Sociological Review, 44*(6), 913–925. https://doi.org/10.2307/2094716
2 Clark, E. M. (2014). Sociological theories of low-wage work. *Journal of Human Behavior in the Social Environment, 24*(1), 38–50. https://doi.org/10.1080/1091 1359.2014.844601
3 Khouri, A. (2018, January 2). More workers say their bosses are threatening to have them deported. *Los Angeles Times*. https://www.latimes.com/business/la-fi-immigration-retaliation-20180102-story.html
4 Peisner, D. (2018). *Homey don't play that!: The story of In Living Color and the black comedy revolution.*
5 Pager, D. (2003). The mark of a criminal record. *American Journal of Sociology, 108*(5), 937–975.
6 A lot more happens in *Trading Places*, including detailed representations of the commodities trading market and insider trading, which were later referenced in a 2010 Congressional testimony on commodities trading reform. These plot points are important and interesting but not relevant here.
7 Franzese, R. J. (2015). *The Sociology of Deviance: 2nd Ed*. Charles C Thomas Publisher.
8 Durkheim, É. (1893). *The Division of Labor in Society.*
9 Merton, R. K. (1938). Social structure and anomie. *American Sociological Review, 3*(5), 672. https://doi.org/10.2307/2084686
10 Bangs, L., & Storm, M. (Directors). (2022). *Moses Storm: "Trash White."* https://www.imdb.com/title/tt17048424/
11 Rank, M. R., & Eppard, L. M. (2021, March 13). The "American Dream" of upward mobility is broken. Look at the numbers. *The Guardian*. https://www.theguardian.com/commentisfree/2021/mar/13/american-dream-broken-upward-mobility-us
12 Klein, E. (2019, August 15). *You have a better chance of achieving "the American dream" in Canada than in America*. Vox. https://www.vox.com/2019/8/15/20801907/raj-chetty-ezra-klein-social-mobility-opportunity
13 Kinsley, M. (1990, January 18). The myth of meritocracy. *The Washington Post*. https://www.washingtonpost.com/archive/opinions/1990/01/18/the-myth-of-meritocracy/ff68b614-f5bd-44e3-9c66-f1f0957a3a49/
14 McNeely, A. (2022, March 4). How USCIS visa processing time delays are hurting immigrant workers and jobs—Bloomberg. *Bloomberg*. https://www.bloomberg.com/news/features/2022-03-04/how-uscis-visa-processing-time-delays-are-hurting-immigrant-workers-and-jobs

15 Langer, A. (2018). *Mo Amer on Growing Up as a Muslim Refugee in Houston – Texas Monthly.* https://www.texasmonthly.com/the-culture/mo-amer-on-growing-up-as-a-muslim-refugee-in-houston/

16 Naim, S. (Director). (2022, August 24). Hamoodi. In *Mo.*

17 Vognar, C. (2022, August 19). Mohammed Amer is a salad bowl. *The New York Times.* https://www.nytimes.com/2022/08/19/arts/television/mohammed-amer-mo-netflix.html

18 *A Mounting Asylum Backlog and Growing Wait Times.* (2021). TRAC, Syracuse University. https://trac.syr.edu/immigration/reports/672/

19 The 150 days is not a constant; it changes with political tides. For example, it went up to 365 days under the Trump Administration, a change which was reversed under the Biden Administration. Cary, B. (n.d.). *When Can Asylum Applicants Get a Work Permit (EAD Card)?* NOLO. Retrieved September 14, 2023, from https://www.nolo.com/legal-encyclopedia/asylum-applicants-work-permit-timing-32297.html

20 Cary, n.d.

21 Friedman, D., & Hechter, M. (1988). The contribution of rational choice theory to macrosociological research. *Sociological Theory,* 6(2), 201–218.

22 Asher, W. (Director). (1952). *"I Love Lucy" Job Switching.* CBS. https://www.imdb.com/title/tt0609243/

23 Weber, M. (1904). *The Protestant Ethic and the Spirit of Capitalism* (Abridged edition). Merchant Books.

24 Knoedelseder, W. (2009). *I'm Dying Up Here: Heartbreak and High Times in Stand-Up Comedy's Golden Era* (1st edition). PublicAffairs.

25 Ahlquist, J. S., & Review, A. (2017). Labor unions, political representation, and economic inequality. *Annual Review of Political Science,* 20(1), 409–432. https://doi.org/10.1146/annurev-polisci-051215-023225

26 Lewis, C. A. (1956). *The Functions of Social Conflict.* Routledge & Kegan Paul PLC. https://www.abebooks.com/9780710033598/Functions-Social-Conflict-Coser-Lewis-0710033591/plp

27 Ahlquist & Review, 2017.

28 Rosenfeld, J. (2011). Little Labor: How Union Decline Is Changing the American Landscape. In *The Inequality Reader* (2nd edition). Routledge.

29 *The Strike of '79.* (2022). The Comedy Store. https://comedystorela.wpengine.com/the-strike/

30 Knoedelseder, 2009.

31 Green, E. L. (2021, February 18). A college program for disadvantaged teens could shake up elite Admissions. *The New York Times.* https://www.nytimes.com/2021/02/18/us/politics/college-admissions-poor-students.html

32 Amour, M. S. (2020, February 21). *The 'Missing Middle' at Ivy-Plus Colleges.* Inside Higher Ed. https://www.insidehighered.com/news/2020/02/21/middle-class-heavily-underrepresented-top-private-colleges-report-finds

33 Chetty, R., Friedman, J., Saez, E., Turner, N., & Yagan, D. (2020, February 12). Income Segregation and Intergenerational Mobility Across Colleges in the United States. *Opportunity Insights.* https://opportunityinsights.org/paper/undermatching/

34 Gross, D. (2019, January 23). *How elite US schools give preference to wealthy and white "legacy" applicants | US universities | The Guardian.* https://www.theguardian.com/us-news/2019/jan/23/elite-schools-ivy-league-legacy-admissions-harvard-wealthier-whiter

35 Sandel, M. (2020, November 19). *High family income, not SAT scores, is your real ticket to Harvard, Yale, and Princeton.* https://theprint.in/pageturner/excerpt/high-family-income-not-sat-scores-ticket-to-harvard-yale-princeton/547180/

36 Gross, 2019; Sandel, 2020.

37 LaGesse, S. (2023, July 21). Legacy Admissions: What It Is and Why Colleges Are Reconsidering It. *U.S. News.* https://www.usnews.com/higher-education/articles/legacy-admissions-what-it-is-and-why-colleges-are-reconsidering-it

38 Gross, 2019.

39 Suk Gersen, J. (2023, August 8). The End of Legacy Admissions Could Transform College Access | The New Yorker. *The New Yorker.* https://www.newyorker.com/news/daily-comment/the-end-of-legacy-admissions-could-transform-college-access

40 LaGesse, 2023.

41 Suk Gersen, 2023.

42 LaGesse, 2023.

43 de Visé, D., & Lonas, L. (2023, September 4). Are legacy admissions on the way out? *The Hill.* https://thehill.com/homenews/education/4183749-are-legacy-admissions-on-the-way-out/

44 House, T. W. (2023, June 29). *Remarks by President Biden on the Supreme Court's Decision on Affirmative Action.* The White House. https://www.whitehouse.gov/briefing-room/statements-releases/2023/06/29/remarks-by-president-biden-on-the-supreme-courts-decision-on-affirmative-action/

45 Amour, 2020.

46 Chetty, Friedman, Saez, Turner, & Yagan, 2020.

47 Lauzen, M. M. (2020). *The Celluloid Ceiling: Behind-the-Scenes Employment of Women on the Top U.S. Films of 2020.* https://womenintvfilm.sdsu.edu/wp-content/uploads/2021/01/2020_Celluloid_Ceiling_Report.pdf

48 Scovell, N. (2016, July 16). Opinion | How to get more women into the director's chair. *The New York Times.* https://www.nytimes.com/2016/07/17/opinion/sunday/how-to-get-more-women-into-the-directors-chair.html

49 Player, A., Randsley de Moura, G., Leite, A. C., Abrams, D., & Tresh, F. (2019). Overlooked leadership potential: The preference for leadership potential in job candidates who are men vs. women. *Frontiers in Psychology, 10.* https://www.frontiersin.org/articles/10.3389/fpsyg.2019.00755

50 Williams, M. J., & Tiedens, L. Z. (2016). The subtle suspension of backlash: A meta-analysis of penalties for women's implicit and explicit dominance behavior. *Psychological Bulletin, 142*(2), 165–197. https://doi.org/10.1037/bul0000039

51 Collins, R. (1979). *The Credential Society: An Historical Sociology of Education and Stratification.* Academic Press.

52 *Women CEOs in America: Changing the Face of Business Leadership* (p. 99). (2021). Women Business Collaborative (WBC). https://www.wbcollaborative.org/wp-content/uploads/2021/10/Women-CEOS-in-America_2021_1013-2.pdf

53 Player, Randsley de Moura, Leite, Abrams, & Tresh, 2019; Williams & Tiedens, 2016.

54 Lockert, M. (2022, March 10). *Understanding what the glass ceiling is and how it affects women in the workplace.* Business Insider. https://www.businessinsider.com/personal-finance/glass-ceiling

55 Scovell, N. (2018). *Just the funny parts: And a few hard truths about sneaking into the Hollywood boys' club* (First edition). Dey Street, an imprint of William Morrow.

56 Steele, C. M. (2010). *Whistling Vivaldi: How Stereotypes Affect Us and What We Can Do.* W. W. Norton & Company.

57 Scovell, 2018.

58 *Good One: Margaret Cho's Asian Chicken Salad.* (2021, March 25). https://podcasts.apple.com/us/podcast/margaret-chos-asian-chicken-salad/id1203393721?i=1000514347434

59 Crenshaw, K. (n.d.). *Demarginalizing the Intersection of Race and Sex: A Black Feminist Critique of Antidiscrimination Doctrine, Feminist Theory and Antiracist Politics. 1989*(1), 31.

60 *Comedians İn Cars Getting Coffee S08 E02 Margaret Cho You Can Go Cho Again—Dailymotion Video*. (2018, April 24). Dailymotion. https://www.dailymotion.com/video/x6ica5l

61 *Good One: Margaret Cho's Asian Chicken Salad*, 2021.

62 Morreall, J. (2020). Philosophy of Humor. In E. N. Zalta (Ed.), *The Stanford Encyclopedia of Philosophy* (Fall 2020). Metaphysics Research Lab, Stanford University. https://plato.stanford.edu/archives/fall2020/entries/humor/

63 Campisano, F. (2016). *A Case Study of Comedian Hannibal Buress and Humor as an Agent for Change*. 11.

64 *Good One: Margaret Cho's Asian Chicken Salad* (2021).

65 *The Last Laugh: Margaret Cho on Chappelle, Tarantino and Alt-Comedy*. (2022, May 5). https://podcasts.apple.com/us/podcast/margaret-cho-on-chappelle-tarantino-and-alt-comedy/id1456474041?i=1000559795753

66 This era also saw many men (as in many *more* men than women) comedians become network stars, such as Tim Allen, Drew Carey, Ray Romano, Jerry Seinfeld, and Garry Shandling.

67 Jung, E. A. (2014, November 9). *Los Angeles Review of Books*. Los Angeles Review of Books. https://lareviewofbooks.org/article/american-girl-20-evolution-asian-americans-tv/

68 1994–1995 was the same television season Garofolo was a cast member on *SNL*.

69 And sand her down, they did. The network told Cho that she needed to lose weight for the show and she ultimately landed in the hospital from renal failure following her restrictive eating patterns. Higgins, B. (2015, February 2). *Throwback Thursday: Margaret Cho Was First to Spotlight an Asian-American Family on TV – The Hollywood Reporter*. https://www.hollywoodreporter.com/tv/tv-news/throwback-thursday-margaret-cho-was-769078/

70 Higgins, 2015.

71 Vorrasi, A. (2019, March 19). *Margaret Cho's 'All American Girl' Sent Me on an Unexpected Emotional Rollercoaster 20 Years Later*. https://www.romper.com/p/margaret-chos-all-american-girl-sent-me-on-unexpected-emotional-rollercoaster-20-years-later-16961456

72 Jung, 2014.

73 *Immigrant Children*. (2018). Child Trends. https://www.childtrends.org/indicators/immigrant-children

74 *The Last Laugh: Margaret Cho on Chappelle, Tarantino and Alt-Comedy* (2022).

75 *Margaret Cho: "Notorious C.H.O."* (2022). https://www.imdb.com/title/tt0300274/

76 Schelle, A. N. (2016). Cho-feminism: What's so feminist about Margaret Cho? *New Views on Gender*, 17, 130–147. https://scholarworks.iu.edu/journals/index.php/iusbgender/article/view/21426

77 *Good One: Margaret Cho's Asian Chicken Salad* (2021).

78 Jennings, K. (2018). *Planet Funny: How Comedy Took Over Our Culture* (First Scribner hardcover edition). Scribner.

79 This book discusses the Internet in social media as avenues for success in comedy. In the spirit of that discussion, I will note that one of the breakout stars of *Hacks* is Megan Stalter (born in Cleveland, Ohio, 1990), who plays Jimmy's assistant, Kayla. Stalter landed an agent after garnering a large and passionate social media audience for her oft-viral Twitter and Instagram posts and comedy videos.

80 *Hacks: "1.69 Million."* (2021). HBO. https://www.imdb.com/title/tt14180266/, p. 69.

81 *How "Hacks" took down the toxic man in "every single stand-up club."* (2021, June 4). Los Angeles Times. https://www.latimes.com/entertainment-arts/tv/story/2021-06-04/hacks-hbo-max-episode-8-jean-smart-hannah-einbinder

82 *How "Hacks" took down the toxic man in "every single stand-up club"* (2021).

83 Khosroshahi, H. (2021, May 10). *The Concrete Ceiling (SSIR)*. https://ssir.org/articles/entry/the_concrete_ceiling

84 Feeney, N. (2013, July 11). *Why Aren't There More Women On The Top-Earning Comedians List?* Forbes. https://www.forbes.com/sites/nolanfeeney/2013/07/11/why-arent-there-more-women-on-the-top-earning-comedians-list/

85 Kohen, Y. (2013). *We Killed: The Rise of Women in American Comedy*. Picador.

86 *Pink-collar workers fight to leave "ghetto" | The Seattle Times*. (2006, January 8). https://www.seattletimes.com/business/pink-collar-workers-fight-to-leave-ghetto/

87 Schwartz, D. (2019, September 24). *How American Segregation Changed the Meaning of "Ghetto" | Time*. https://time.com/5684505/ghetto-word-history/

88 Hughes, C. J. (2015, May 20). Jackson Heights, Queens: Diverse and Evolving. *The New York Times*. https://www.nytimes.com/2015/05/24/realestate/jackson-heights-queens-diverse-and-evolving.html

89 Semple, K. (2013, June 8). New York City's Newest Immigrant Enclaves. *The New York Times*. https://www.nytimes.com/interactive/2013/06/09/nyregion/new-york-citys-newest-immigrant-enclaves.html

90 Weichselbaum, S. (2012, June 26). Nearly one in four Brooklyn residents are Jews, new study finds. *New York Daily News*. https://www.nydailynews.com/new-york/brooklyn/brooklyn-residents-jews-new-study-finds-article-1.1100080

91 University of Auckland, & Maani, S. (2016). Ethnic networks and location choice of immigrants. *IZA World of Labor*. https://doi.org/10.15185/izawol.284

92 While these ordinances were found to be illegal, racially restrictive language was not necessarily removed from neighborhood covenants. To show what these covenants looked like and how long many stayed on the books, refer the Seattle Civil Rights & Labor History Project at the University of Washington, which is an archive of racial restrictive covenants in the Seattle area. https://depts.washington.edu/civilr/covenants.htm

93 *The Equal Pay Act of 1963*. (1963). US EEOC. https://www.eeoc.gov/statutes/equal-pay-act-1963

94 *The Civil Rights Act of 1964*. (1964). U.S. Department of Labor. https://www.dol.gov/agencies/oasam/civil-rights-center/statutes/civil-rights-act-of-1964#

95 *Schultz v. Wheaton Glass Company | New Jersey Women's History*. (2022). https://njwomenshistory.org/discover/topics/schultz-v-wheaton-glass-company/

96 Whyte, M. (2018, January 14). *How women in media won some pay equality in the 1970s, and why they're still fighting today*. The Conversation. http://theconversation.com/how-women-in-media-won-some-pay-equality-in-the-1970s-and-why-theyre-still-fighting-today-89914

97 Federman, W. (2021). *The History of Stand-Up: From Mark Twain to Dave Chappelle*. Independent Artists Media.

98 Kohen, Y. (2016, February 5). *How Comedy Finally Caught Up to Female Comedians*. Vulture. https://www.vulture.com/2016/01/how-comedy-finally-caught-up-to-female-comedians.html

99 Federman, 2021.

100 Smith, C. (2008, June 5). *How "Saturday Night Live" Became a Grim Joke*. New York Magazine. https://nymag.com/arts/tv/features/47548/

101 Scovell, 2018.

102 *The History of Comedy*. (2017). CNN. https://www.cnn.com/shows/history-of-comedy

103 Smith, 2008.

104 Robinson, M. (2014, January 17). *23 Times Women Made History On "Saturday Night Live."* Business Insider. https://www.businessinsider.com/history-of-women-on-saturday-night-live-2014-1

105 Kohen, 2013.

106 Federman, 2021.

107 *Louis C.K. Charlie Rose interview: Louie talks parenting, comedy, and more.* (2014). http://www.slate.com/blogs/browbeat/2014/05/09/louis_c_k_charlie_rose_interview_louie_talks_parenting_comedy_and_more_video.html

108 Powers, J. (2014, May 6). *"Louie" is one of the best shows on TV.* https://www.businessinsider.com/louie-is-one-of-the-best-shows-on-tv-2014-5

109 C.K., L., & Rose, L. (2015, April 8). *Louis C.K.'s Crabby, Epic Love Letter to NYC: "Everyone's Dealing with the Same S— ... Elbow to Elbow" – The Hollywood Reporter.* https://www.hollywoodreporter.com/news/general-news/louis-cks-crabby-epic-love-786746/

110 Fox, J. D. (2017, November 10). *Louis C.K. Influenced a Generation of Comedians. What Happens Now?* Vulture. https://www.vulture.com/2017/11/louis-ck-influenced-generation-of-comedy-what-now.html

111 C.K., L. (Director). (2013). *Louis C.K. "Oh My God."* https://www.imdb.com/title/tt2510998/

112 Nut allergies are not entirely determined by genetics – so this example is not necessarily logically sound. Zhang, Q., Zhang, C., Zhang, Y., Liu, Y., Wang, J., Gao, Z., Sun, J., Li, Q., Sun, J., Cui, X., Wang, Y., & Fu, L. (2023). Early life risk factors for food allergy: Dietary and environmental factors revisited. *Comprehensive Reviews in Food Science and Food Safety*, n/a(n/a). https://doi.org/10.1111/1541-4337.13226

113 C.K., 2013.

114 Ryzik, M., Buckley, C., & Kantor, J. (2017, November 9). Louis C.K. is accused by 5 women of sexual misconduct. *The New York Times.* https://www.nytimes.com/2017/11/09/arts/television/louis-ck-sexual-misconduct.html

115 Brown, S. (2018). Open Mic? Gender and the Meritocratic Myth of Authenticity in the Cultural Production of Stand-Up Comedy (Dissertation). *University of Illinois at Urbana-Champaign.*

116 Seitz, M. Z. (2017, November 9). *Louis C.K. Is Done.* Vulture. https://www.vulture.com/2017/11/louis-ck-is-done.html

6 Subcultures and the Fracturing of Comedy

This chapter discusses sociological concepts related to group membership. We discuss the work of Émile Durkheim – including anomie, deviance, social integration, and mechanical and organic solidarity – and Camara Phyllis Jones – with her allegory "The Gardener's Tale." Additional sociological concepts discussed in this chapter include subcultures, xenophobia, pluralism, assimilation, ethnocentrism, cultural relativism, prejudice, discrimination, representation, and diversity. This chapter expands upon these concepts by discussing how the "fracturing of comedy" allows performers to create more authentic and personal material that resonates with their audiences and why representation in media matters for both its creators and its consumers.

Subcultures with Joel Kim Booster

In this section, we will describe the sociological concept of subcultures. A **subculture** refers to a group of people with a shared sense of identity or community who are not fully accepted by – or choose to remove themselves from – the dominant culture due to their lifestyle or beliefs.[1] For example, when a dominant culture holds a heteronormative social structure, LGBTQ+ folks may form a subculture of people with whom they can live more free and celebrated lives. Subculture affiliations form organically. People find one another throughout the course of their life and choose these bonds. This differs from, for example, family groupings into which one is born. In this section, we will discuss the role and importance of subcultures in society using an example from comedian Joel Kim Booster (born in Jeju Island, South Korea, 1988 and raised in Plainfield, Illinois).

In Booster's 2022 Netflix special *Psychosexual*, he plays with the idea that his comedic content – as a gay, Asian male – is seen as "niche" and does not appeal to White, straight, male audiences.[2] Booster does this through asking for a White, straight, male audience member to volunteer (that volunteer was named Ben). Booster regularly checked in with Ben (who was given a microphone) throughout the special to ask if Ben feels alienated by the material. The bit is certainly done for laughs but it signals something important. Booster says explicitly that he has always had to find ways to connect to people like Ben but people like Ben have rarely had to find ways to connect with people

DOI: 10.4324/9781003469537-7

like Booster. Booster's material is considered niche, while material from people who look like Ben is considered universal. Here, Booster turned the tables.

Booster understands that his material is strengthened by his outsider status as someone who grew up as a child adopted into a family and community that does not look like him. In an episode of *The Last Laugh* podcast, Booster explains the importance of providing audiences with a window into your origin story. For him, growing up as a gay and Asian man in a White Evangelical Christian family afforded him a unique lens with which to view the world. Booster explains how always feeling like an outsider gave him an outsider's point of view. This is the core of the comedic lens and the sociological imagination. Seeing things as both an insider and an outsider gives insight and understanding while still allowing for recognition of the absurd. Booster describes his particular point of view as "skewed" and "goofy," making for great comedy when he flips common experiences like dating on their heads.[3]

Booster also explains in *The Last Laugh* podcast how his unique identity and perspective inhibit his act from ever reaching the mainstream. In Booster's view, there used to be one main audience from which all comedians were drawing. Only comedians with broad and mainstream appeal effectively catered to these audiences and found mainstream success. Appealing to the mainstream would require Booster to cater his material to every person, from every age, background, and region coast-to-coast. Such material would not be true to who he is as a person. But, as Booster argues, the Internet fractured audiences into a greater and more niche set of people from which comedians can draw their fan base. Booster can focus on his audience, instead of generalizing his material to suit all audiences

Consider how Booster's desire to *not* cater to the social norms of the mainstream relates to the work of Émile Durkheim. Durkheim held a positive view of how social structures impose norms on values on individuals in society. Durkheim believed norms and values keep people in check. Otherwise, he posits, people would submit to their sins and passions in ways which harm society. Norms regulating behavior are what Durkheim called **social facts** and society's shared beliefs about good and evil form its **collective conscience**. The collective conscience is the most important social fact for maintaining a functional society.

Durkheim's most well-known work was *Suicide* (1897), which was a notable shift from prior works on suicide.[4] Unlike prior works, which focused on the individual factors associated with suicide, Durkheim focused on the social factors. Durkheim noted the most prominent form of suicide was *anomic suicide*, stemming from individuals experiencing anomie. **Anomie** is the lost feeling which results from individuals not being sure of their purpose and direction in life. Durkheim saw anomie as a social problem, one which was increasing over time as there was a loosening of shared social norms and expectations. The remedy to anomie, in Durkheim's view, was social integration. **Social integration** is the bond between individuals with their social groups.

Durkheim viewed social integration in relation to one collective conscience. Booster, here, demonstrates how one can feel more strongly integrated into a subgroup. Booster views his nicheness as his strength. He is not a comic who strives to be a Stephen Colbert who emphasizes clapter (he calls this out in his 2022 special *Psychosocial*) or a John Mulaney who garners broad appeal. Booster's comedic philosophy is more aligned with that of alternative comics and those with unique points of view or identities. Similar to Janeane Garofolo and Margaret Cho before him, Booster leans away from audiences that view him as an "outsider" and finds his space where he is an "insider."

We previously discussed insiders versus outsiders as they relate to the dominant culture. Those who are "outsiders" in the dominant space are "insiders" within their subculture. Insider status is marked by shared traits such as language, style of dress, knowledge, or behaviors.

Outside of comedy, an Internet subculture may include video gamers, anime fans, sports fans, beekeepers, or other interests; or LGBTQ+ folks, religious groups, or other features of one's life and identities. Online, people who share these interests or traits can find one another – even if geographically separated – and can share information or offer support. Myriad online platforms exist for such subcultures, including Discord, Facebook, Instagram, Reddit, TikTok, Twitch, Twitter, and YouTube, among countless others. There is a handful of subcultures which exist on just one platform, TikTok, a short-form video sharing app. On TikTok, there is "Christian Tok," "Fashion Tok," "Kink Tok," and "Mom Tok," to name a few.

Internet subcultures exist specifically within the field of comedy as well, and overlap with these other topical subcultures. Comedians who are part of the LGBTQ+ community, for example, can find fellow comedians and audience members within online spaces and can dig deeper into the subculture to find others they connect with. I use LGBTQ+ as a broad category here but it is composed of myriad groups of people. Lesbian women can find each other, gay men can find each other, trans people can find each other. And they can dig further. Gay men who love *Lord of the Rings* can find each other. Folks can niche-ify themselves and their comedy as much as they desire. Niche comedy is an intangible "space" for the marginalized to feel safe, comfortable, and express themselves on their own terms. In this way, consider if and how subcultures may serve to fight against anomie.

Mechanical and Organic Solidarity with Danny McBride

Comedian, actor and writer, Danny McBride (born in Statesboro, Georgia, 1976) understands the difficulty of creating good comedy when one is trying to be too "universal." In a 2019 episode of the *Good One* podcast, McBride noted that specificity is necessary in good comedy; yet, specificity can be antithetical to universal appeal.[5] In other words, good comedy is specific, but specific comedy is niche. Consider how this statement fits within our earlier discussions of shared understanding and social norms. Something specific may not be widely understood by the masses.

McBride was on the podcast discussing his show *The Righteous Gemstones*. Premiering on HBO in 2019, The Righteous Gemstones follows a family of conniving, greedy, and crass megachurch televangelists headed by patriarch Eli Gemstone (played by John Goodman). McBride explained why it was important to him that the show be set in his home state of South Carolina – versus a more common television setting like New York City or Los Angeles.

McBride explains that he does not see many stories coming out of the American South. He compares the lack of regional representation in movies and television, which almost entirely comes out of New York City and Los Angeles, to music. He asks folks to imagine how boring it would be if music only came out of New York City and Los Angeles. Imagine, for example, there are no scenes for Motown, jazz, or country music like Austin, Detroit, or Nashville. (These being U.S.-specific examples; this argument is made even more powerful on a global scale.) We need stories from different creators, histories, and places to have a true mosaic in movies and television. Like with music, imagine how boring it would be if we only had one style or perspective.

Consider how McBride's perspective links to Émile Durkheim's descriptions of mechanical and organic solidarity. Durkheim defined **mechanical solidarity** as the solidarity of people based upon having similar experiences and sharing a collective conscience.[6] As work became less concentrated in factories and expanded into new and different avenues, people started having more diverse experiences. Thus, their daily lives began to look very different from one another. They faced new challenges and experienced new joys. The solidarity between individuals in society became less mechanical and more organic.

Organic solidarity occurs when individuals with diverse jobs, resources, and expertise rely on one another more to meet their needs, forming interdependent bonds. Durkheim's views relate more to individual interdependencies – such as how individuals rely on people from different professions, such as farmers, accountants, and childcare workers to operate their lives. But it can be helpful to pull back and look at these ideas with a more macro lens. Consider, for example, the interdependence of people from different regions within the United States. Each region contributes economically and culturally to the fabric of the nation. Think about how you may rely on goods, services, and cultural productions from the American South.

As people's experiences, norms, and values became more varied, Durkheim saw a decline in the collective conscience of society. Durkheim viewed this decline of the collective conscience negatively. He believed less collective conscience results in more deviance, as there is less collective agreement on the "rules" of society *and* less ability to enforce them. Consider how and why varied experience result in less agreement on the "rules" of society. Consider regional differences in norms and behaviors. Do you think regional differences make the United States stronger or weaker?

For McBride, he sees it as his and our responsibility to tell stories that represent our region, background, and culture. He believes we *should* be highlighting our uniqueness – and not striving to create content with one, monolithic viewpoint. If media is supposed to hold a mirror to society, in McBride's view, we need lots more mirrors. Our society is marked by a diversity of experiences – based on regional, cultural, and economic factors, among others. Consider how having a limited window into the experiences of others relates to the collective conscience. To have only one image represented on screen serves to erase our differences, limit understanding of one another, and is generally less interesting.

Cultural Relativism and Critical Theory with Ramy Youssef

Comedian, actor, and writer, Ramy Youssef (born in Queens, New York, 1991), shares McBride's view. Youssef describes comedy as a place to "explore the subconscious."[7] Comedy allows for a messy, uncomfortable, inappropriate, or reductive exploration of oneself and one's view of the world. The subconscious is all those things, and therefore, so is comedy.

Youssef explained in an interview on *The Last Laugh* podcast that the goal of comedy is not to be "correct" in a factual sense.[8] Instead, comedy is about being "correct" in an emotional sense. The goal is to get the emotions right. If you need to tweak some details here or there to reach that goal, that is okay. If you are true to how you felt, that is emotional correctness.

A sociology lecture tends to lean more toward the factually correct way of presenting information, such as citing statistics or aggregated qualitative observations. A sociology professor leverages those statistics to bolster a student's historical or political knowledge and enables them to broaden their understanding of social reality by adding context outside of their singular experience. A comedian may come at this same goal from another angle. Instead of citing statistics providing broader context, a comedian may deploy an absurdist, heightened version of a singular experience to shock the audience into realizing it is absurd they thought that was the only reality. This hyperbolic version of reality is *emotionally correct* in the sense that emotional correctness means that it is connected to a true feeling or experience of the creator. It is a parable or an allegory. The events may not have played out beat-for-beat as described in the story but the story was specifically relayed to the audience in a way that accurately conveys the underlying feelings the story represents.

Comedians use their comedic perspective to break sociological concepts down (whether they realize they are doing it or not). Youssef can teach us about concepts such as xenophobia and ethnocentrism by focusing on the emotional correctness of his personal experiences versus retelling incidents beat-by-beat as they occurred. He leans into the emotions.

Let us look at this using an example from Youssef's 2019 HBO standup special, *Feelings*. Youssef is a young, Egyptian American, Muslim man. He describes in his special what it is like to live in the intersection of these identities. He starts out a particular bit by saying that when people find out he is Muslim, they ask him absurd questions. He specifically mentions a woman who, after learning Youssef is Muslim, tells him that she was in the Middle East experiencing a day that got up to 100 degrees in temperature and saw a woman sweating in the heat while wearing her headscarf. The woman asks Youssef why his religion requires women to wear a headscarf.[9] This woman's statement exhibits xenophobia. **Xenophobia** refers to prejudicial or discriminatory actions or beliefs that vilify groups that are part of the majority.

The implication of her question is that Muslim men force Muslim women to wear headscarves, even in hot weather. This was the focus of the woman's experience while she was in the Middle East. Compared to her own singular experience as a non-Muslim American woman, she identified something different (and something she found problematic) about Muslim traditions. In his special, Youssef begins his response to this woman's question by saying something incredibly sociological. He says that just because someone else's culture is different from your own, that does not inherently mean that it is strange, wrong, or oppressive. He encourages people to view their own culture as an outsider. It may then seem strange, too.

We can tie this idea to the sociological definition of **pluralism**. Pluralistic societies are those in which a diversity of groups can coexist and thrive while maintaining their unique qualities. Pluralism assumes minimal need for **assimilation**, which refers to the process wherein a **minority group** assumes features of the **majority group** to fit in, gain opportunities, or be successful. For example, folks may give up their traditional language, clothes, foods, and customs to gain acceptance by the more mainstream group(s) in society.

Youssef uses his comedic perspective to uncover the second unspoken implication of the woman's question. He describes a date he was on with a woman on a cold day in January in New York City. The temperature was below freezing but Youssef's date wanted to look nice. In this case, "nice" is proscribed by American fashion trends that dictate what a young, cool woman wears on a date: a short dress and high heels. Even in the winter and even when it is seven degrees outside.

Youssef describes them getting out of a cab two blocks away from their date-spot. His date is shivering cold but she cannot hurry down the block because she is slowed by her heels. There is a look of panic in her eyes. She was cold. Her feet hurt. Her hair was blowing in the wind. Youssef tells the crowd he began to wonder why American culture made the woman dress like that. He jokes that, had she worn a scarf, her hair would be saved from the wind.

Youssef flips the script on the original woman's question. Instead of responding to why Muslims or why people in the Middle East have their traditions, he asks the woman to respond to why Americans have their traditions. Perhaps by seeing her own culture through the same lens she is applying to another culture, there is a chance for two different people to begin to understand each other. Through this bit, Youssef is hoping to make the audience see the woman's **ethnocentrism** – the assumption that the norms and values of one's own social group are superior to the norms and values of other social groups – and perhaps question their own ethnocentrism.

To embed Youssef's comedy within a sociological theoretical landscape, we can employ **critical theory**. Critical theory asserts that society operates through coercion and focuses on the coercive power of culture and media.[10] A century ago, critical theorists focused on the influence of radio, film, and magazine publications. Today, the focus has shifted to television, social media, and the Internet.

Recall from our discussion of Max Weber, critical theorists refer to **culture industry** as a dominant social structure which sells products and lifestyles and homogenizes people. In other words, culture makes us more like each other when popular culture sells us a set of idealized ways of looking and being. This is the hallmark of **mass culture**. Think about social media influencers as an example of how this operates. Companies pay influencers to pitch their products to droves of followers who, in turn, buy those products to follow the lead of the influencer's lifestyle. The same occurs when celebrities pitch products. Culture acts as a mechanism for capitalism.

Sociologists critique the narrow lens of the culture. Culture applies itself to the way we consume products and to the way we consume information. Critical theorists understand there is still immense consolidation of power in media. For example, there are potential catastrophic consequences of tight control over the news that is disseminated on television and major news websites, tight control over the stories that are told, and even more control over the people who get to tell them.

In recent years, major media companies have just embarked on a spree of buying up small, local news channels.[11] According to a Pew Research Center report, in 2016, 37 percent of news stations nationwide were owned by only five companies.[12] Media consolidation impacts the focus and political slant of local news coverage. First, after being bought by a major media conglomerate, local news stations tend to begin covering more national news and less local news. In one before-and-after study evaluating the changes in broadcasted content from stations acquired by Sinclair Broadcast Group, stations began airing 25 percent more national news following acquisition. National news costs less to produce, as research, footage, and stories can be shared by stations all over the country.[13]

Second, news coverage tends to slant more toward the conservative side of the political spectrum than they did prior to acquisition. In the same study of Sinclair Broadcast Group acquirees, the researchers quantified the number of times news coverage used certain terms – such as "illegal aliens" versus "undocumented immigrants," which tend to be used more frequently among conservative-leaning versus progressive-leaning people, respectively. Results indicate that Sinclair stations tend to use more conservative-leaning phrases than non-Sinclair stations overall, and stations began using more conservative-leaning phrases after acquisition by Sinclair than they did before acquisition.

While focusing on national news may not sound like a bad thing at first, the problem is that there is little opportunity left for local news coverage, if at all. There are already national news broadcasts specifically for people who are looking to tune in to the national news. But local news tends to be only covered by, well, the local news. So if the local news turns national, there is no local left.

Similarly, when a media conglomerate with a particular political viewpoint has the power and opportunity to snap up local news stations and influence the political tone of coverage, that is the political viewpoint which becomes widely disseminated across the country. Sinclair Broadcast Group, for example, reaches nearly 40 percent off the U.S. population through their 191 stations as of 2018. A study by Dr. Gregory Martin of the Stanford Graduate School of Business and Joshua McCrain of Emory University found that stations newly acquired by Sinclair tend to lose about 600 viewers per month following acquisition and rival stations tend to be more popular than Sinclair stations in the same viewership markets, with an average of 7,000 more households tuning into the rival's coverage.[14]

What are the consequences of the consolidation of information? Critical theorists see the consequence and the goal of **mass culture** as that of pacifying and repressing the masses. To **pacify** is to keep people satisfied with the status quo or ignorant to alternatives. To **repress** is to inhibit acts of protest or rebellion aimed at disrupting the existing social power dynamics. One example of how mass culture pacifies the masses is by focusing on America's strengths and other countries' weaknesses around a particular issue. For example: healthcare. There are news stories about long waiting periods in countries with socialized medicine, forcing people to wait for (and die while waiting for) necessary appointments, medicines, or procedures. Meanwhile, less coverage is dedicated to the wins of socialized healthcare or the pitfalls of the United States' healthcare system. Such coverage is intended to keep the masses satisfied with the status quo and repress any requests or actions for change.

Now let us apply our new understanding of critical theory to Ramy Youssef's work. Specifically, let us dive into the way Youssef's bit highlights cultural relativism. **Cultural relativism** asserts that there are no universally accepted norms, values, or traditions. Instead, the relative value or acceptability of a set of norms must be assessed within one's own culture.[15] If the woman who asked Youssef "Why do you make her wear that?" had instead asked that same question of her own culture, she would be engaging in a cultural relativist approach.

Recall our earlier discussion of gender performance. I ask you to question your own gender performance to get you thinking about you may, or may not, impose your own social beliefs on yourself. Now, I want you to consider how you may, or may not, impose your own social beliefs onto others. It is human to engage in this behavior at times. We judge others' decisions when they do not align with what we think we would do in the same situation. We form judgments based on our own beliefs about right and wrong. And what Youssef does in his comedy is get audiences to reconsider their own barometer for right and wrong.

Youssef's comedy is based on the emotional experiences of fielding questions like: "Why do you make them wear that?" when he knows the foundation of such questions is hypocrisy. Youssef can easily see the hypocrisy of expectations for women's clothing for some Muslim cultures and for the broader United States because he is a member of both of those worlds. He can use his insider knowledge of one world to critically examine the other.

In an interview on *The Last Laugh* podcast, host Matt Wilstein questions Youssef about his approach and motivation for representing Muslims on television, especially following events in American history like the 9/11 attack on the World Trade Center in New York City and President Trump's "Muslim ban" (Executive order 13769, officially titled Protecting the Nation from Foreign Terrorist Entry into the United States, and colloquially known as the "Trump travel ban" or the "Muslim ban," was an executive order issued by President Donald Trump in January 2017 that banned entry into the United States for people from a list of several Muslim-majority countries, among other restrictions on travel and refugees).[16] Youssef explained that his goal is to bring light and humanity to the people too-often pushed to the edges of society.[17] Representation provides opportunities for understanding and connection.

Media and Stereotypes with Mo Amer and Hari Kondabolu

Many folks may have never seen someone who looks like them, talks like them, or prays like them on stage, on screen, or in positions of elected office. If they do see someone who looks like them, that person or character may not represent their beliefs or values. **Representation** refers to the how – and the extent to which – different people and groups are seen and presented in society by image-makers like the media.

Before defining the causes and consequences of the unequal social treatment of people based on their group membership, we must first understand how group membership evolves over time.

Groups, like social groupings based upon race, ethnicity, sex, or gender, are continually redefined in tandem with more inclusive and expansive understandings of identities and intersections therein. This book includes examples from comedians who employ an intersectional lens to showcase the way group membership evolves and group identities intersect and to showcase why representation matters in comedy and media.

While reading this book an important thing to remember is that limited representation of who makes it on the screen narrows the ability of people to tell their own nuanced stories. That results in skewed or limited portrayals of entire groups of people in media, which, in turn, can cause misunderstanding and eventual othering of those groups by society. In more sociological terms: lead to prejudice and discrimination. **Prejudice** refers to negative feelings held about minority groups. **Discrimination** is the unequal or unfair treatment of minority groups based upon prejudicial feelings. Representation has a real, on-the-ground impact on how entire groups of people are understood, and accepted, by others in their community.

To continue discussing representation, let us return to standup comedian and actor Mohammed "Mo" Amer. Amer discusses his experiences as a Muslim person in the United States and abroad through his comedic work. In his 2021 Netflix comedy special, *Mohammed in Texas*, which was filmed during the COVID-19 pandemic, Amer jokes early in his set that he thought his career as a standup comedian was over when COVID-19 hit. Live performances, comedy clubs, and nightclubs all took a major hit as public health officials recommended against indoor gatherings. But as live performances resumed, including the filming of Amer's Netflix special, Amer expressed gratitude for the salvation of his career. He joked that COVID-19 was the second time he thought his career as a standup comedian had come to a premature end. The first time was 9/11. Amer jokes, "My own brother looked me dead in my eyes and goes, 'Your career is over ... Look how they're talking about us on the news ... Nobody wants to see a 'Mohammed' on stage telling jokes. Your career is over.' I said, 'Omar, you're a pilot'" (Amer, 2021).[18] The punchline of this joke refers to how there was much hostility, racism, and xenophobia lodged against Muslim people on airplanes after 9/11 – whether they be passengers or crew. It was, and remains, difficult for Muslim people in the United States to separate themselves from 9/11 in the public eye.

There is a lack of understanding of Muslim communities in America which leads to undeserved distrust. In a 2017 Pew Research Center survey of Muslims in the United States, researchers report that 75 percent of respondents agree there is "a lot of discrimination against Muslims in the U.S.," and 62 percent of respondents do not believe "American people see Islam as part of mainstream society." Further, 50 percent of respondents said that, in recent years, being Muslim in the United States has "gotten harder" with only 3 percent of respondents said that it has "gotten easier."[19]

In the joke detailed above, Amer effectively demonstrates how stereotypes and prejudice can crush dreams and careers. Amer's brother, Omar, is indeed a pilot – a career which takes many, many years of training and great levels of expertise – and the audience can easily see how his career may have been negatively impacted by anti-Muslim bias and discrimination. It can be helpful to understand the real-world impact of concepts such as stereotypes, discrimination, and Islamophobia. It puts a face (or at least, a name; Omar) to what people unfairly fear.

For more examples from Amer, viewers can turn to his semi-autobiographical Netflix show, *Mo* (introduced earlier in this book). Recall, through Amer's character Mo, Amer details highlights how his life is shaped by his undocumented status and his identity as a Muslim Palestinian man living in Texas. For example, we see Mo's difficulty holding and finding legal employment due to his undocumented status and his creative – but, illegal – hustles to make ends meet (discussed previously), his constant fear of U.S. Immigration and Customs Enforcement (ICE) officers, and his juggling of the familial and social consequences of his interracial and interfaith relationship with his Mexican American girlfriend, Maria (played by Teresa Ruiz).

Audiences also see Mo's identity constantly being misidentified based on his skin color, faith, and Palestinian origin. In season 1 episode 1 (titled "Hamoodi"), we see Mo telling some Texan olive farmers that he is Palestinian, to which one of the farmers responds "Shalom" ("shalom" roughly translating to "peace" in Hebrew), implying the farmer believes Mo to be Jewish and/or Israeli. Mo retorts to the farmer that his confusion was due to Palestinians having a "branding issue," a reference to the limited understanding of the differences between Israelis and Palestinians – including religious differences – held by many folks in the United States.[20]

Amer is not the only comedian to talk about being misidentified based on skin color, faith, or country of origin. For example, Muslim comedians, Arab comedians, and Central Asian comedians, among others, grapple with what it means to be "Muslim-looking." There is a conflation of being brown and being Muslim-looking among some in the United States, perhaps attributable to narrow (and largely negative) media representations of segments of the Muslim world. In a 2020 opinion piece for *The Huffington Post*, comedian Dean Obeidallah, who was born in Lodi, New Jersey, 1969 and is of Palestinian and Italian descent, wrote about what he calls "the Muslim double standard."[21] In the piece, Obeidallah discusses how terrorism executed by a handful of Muslim men gets presented in the media as "All terrorists are Muslims" (as stated on air by *Fox News* anchor and radio host by Brian Kilmeade). Kilmeade's declaration, as Obeidallah notes, ignores the terrorist acts executed by White men, including Timothy McVey, who was responsible for the Oklahoma City bombing in 1995, and Ted Kaczynski (known as the "Unabomber"), among countless others. Indeed, most domestic terrorists in the United States are White men. According to the Anti-Defamation League's 2018 Murder & Extremism report, most domestic terrorist murders were committed by right-wing extremists, with 78 percent of domestic terrorist murders being tied to White nationalism.[22]

Obeidallah attributes the ability of mainstream news anchors to spout xenophobic and Islamophobic mistruths with impunity is tied to the fact that there is limited positive media representation of Muslim people. Obeidallah argues that one day, Muslims may have a popular sitcom that will showcase the myriad positive elements of Muslim communities (this hypothetical sitcom is sarcastically titled by Obeidallah as *Everybody Loves Ramadan*, a riff on comedian Ray Romano's successful sitcom *Everybody Loves Raymond*, which ran on CBS from 1996 to 2005). Obeidallah feels that a sitcom will be able to do what narrow representations of Muslim folks in the mainstream news media cannot; add depth, humanity, and perhaps levity to situations where folks may be uninformed about the diversity of Muslim people and kindness of Muslim communities.

Muslim comedians have used the standup stage to provide context and information about their lives using their comedic lens. This includes breaking down the conflation between being Arab-looking and being Muslim (which is not a direct link; there are many non-Arab Muslims and many Arab non-Muslims), and the conflation between being Muslim and being a terrorist (which is also not a direct link; most Muslims are not terrorists and most domestic terrorists in the United States are not Muslim).[23] I agree with Obeidallah's argument that there are too few positive and nuanced media representations of Muslim folks. And certainly one show, like *Everybody Loves Ramadan*, would not be sufficient. Muslim communities are so diverse that a show about one family (if going with the *Everybody Loves Raymond* parallel, which focused on one Italian American family, the Romanos, living in Long Island, New York) would not be able to capture that diversity. Muslim people are those who adhere to Islam but they come in all different races, genders, backgrounds, and places.[24]

To see another example of why better representation of the diversity of all people, cultures, and religions in media is important, consider a joke told by comedian Hari Kondabolu (born in Queens, New York, 1982). Kondabolu, a Hindu man, has had to contend with misunderstandings around his religious background. Much of Kondabolu's material centers on racism, xenophobia, and colonialism, among other lighter topics. In a 2011 bit from Kondabolu, he tells his audience a story about interacting with a xenophobic person at a party. Kondabolu overheard a man at a party lamenting that an Islamic community center was being constructed at Ground Zero (the former site of the World Trade Center buildings in New York City, which were destroyed during the 9/11 terrorist attacks). The man mistakenly thought that it was a mosque, not a community center, and that it was being constructed to "terrorize Americans."[25]

Kondabolu first corrects the man by stating it is a community center, not a mosque, then adds the commentary that even if it were a mosque, that would be just fine. The man retorts, saying Kondabolu only holds that opinion because he is Muslim. However, Kondabolu is Hindu. Not Muslim. The man does not understand there are any differences between the two religions. Kondabolu kindly explains the difference and the man apologizes, but as the man reiterates, Kondabolu certainly *looks* like a Muslim.

Kondabolu jokes to his audience, "Fair enough. I was wearing a Weezer t-shirt and Converse sneakers … which is what all Muslims wear at all times regardless of our context." Kondabolu continues telling the audience what he said to the man: "Islam is perhaps one of the most racially diverse religions in the world. So technically, White man, you also look like a Muslim" (Kondabolu, 2011).[26] In this exchange, Kondabolu attempts to teach both his audience and the man at the party about the diversity of Islam. What Kondabolu does here is recenter Islam less as "the other" and more as a faith and set of communities that may overlap with your own. Muslim people, like Hindu people, are multidimensional in many facets, including race, origin, and political beliefs, but the lack of representation of Muslim people and Hindu people in media has limited people's understanding of both the religions and the people who practice them.

Let us link Kondabolu's point back to a television example, diving into Ramy Youssef's self-titled series, *Ramy*, which premiered on Hulu in 2019.

Ramy follows the main character Ramy Hassan, played by Youssef, as he explores his identity as a young, Egyptian American man living in New Jersey while navigating relationships and faith alongside his family and friends. The show adds representation and a unique perspective to the comedic landscape specifically because it is so detailed and narrowly focused. Even while being reflective of large and important issues in society like racism, xenophobia, and Islamophobia, Youssef's comedic point of view is uniquely his own.

Youssef once described himself as feeling like "the 'hyphen' in Muslim American" (Youssef, 2020).[27] Youssef pitched it as a show about integrating his dual identities – basically, about feeling like the hyphen in his Muslim American identity. Representation of Muslim Americans and Egyptian Americans on television in a real, nuanced way is at the forefront of how he and his team wrote and produced the show.

In a 2019 interview on *The Last Laugh* podcast, Youssef was clear that he could not depict "the Muslim experience" because there is no such thing as *one* Muslim experience. He can only depict his own experience coming from an Arab-Muslim family in New Jersey.[28] Indeed, *Ramy* is not meant to be a monolith or to depict all Muslims or all Egyptian American families. For example, most Muslims in the United States are Black, not Arab. His show does not depict what life looks like for Black Muslim Americans. As such, Youssef has noted that he did not originally desire to name the show after himself but he knew he could not have used a more generic name like *"Muslims"* because the show does not represent all Muslims.

Representation is not just about who is on screen but also how well their depictions match their reality. Youssef sees bringing his own, unique perspective to his creations as fundamental to his work. When discussing writing or his show, Youssef explains the "filter" he uses when deciding what makes it onto the show. He notes that any good writer could successfully write a show about a family that looks like his. In Youssef's example, he talks about a hypothetical White guy who lives in Sherman Oaks and has been writing in Hollywood for ten to fifteen years. This guy could most likely write a good, funny show about a Mexican family or Muslim family from his basic understanding of their cultural traditions paired with more universal ways of writing about family dynamics and individual character arcs. But Youssef strives to always go beyond standard tropes and universal understandings of human dynamics, and chooses to only write material that could be written by someone from his community. Youssef's filter for each scene, then, is if that hypothetical White guy in Sherman Oaks could write the scene based on his limited outsider knowledge of Youssef's community, the scene is cut. The show simply does not need it.

Think about how this relates to the sociological imagination. We talked about how a comedic perspective is one of an outsider. In this case, Youssef (an insider to his own community) is using his comedic perspective to share his experiences to broad audiences (many of whom are outsiders to his community). By elevating what is authentic to his own experiences in a relatable way, he is still seeing his own experiences like an outsider. He can see what about his culture's traditions are universal. That is the sociological imagination in action.

Let us walk through Youssef's point using a scene from the show, from an episode titled "Do the Ramadan" (season 1, episode 5). The episode takes place in a diner just before dawn *(fajr)* during Ramadan. Ramy and two friends, Mo (who runs the diner and is played by Mo Amer) and Ahmed (played by Dave Merheje), discuss philosophies around identifying the exact moment of sunrise – the marker of the day's fast during the holy month of Ramadan. Ramy is waiting on Mo to serve him a plate of food as he anxiously stares at an app on his phone which will chime at dawn, ending Ramy's opportunity to eat until dusk.

The scene centers on the three men's differing interpretations of how they can tell the timing of sunset and sunrise, which mark the start and stop times they are allowed to eat during the Ramadan fast. Ramy is worried that he will not be able to eat the food if his wait goes on for much longer. He anxiously refreshes the sunrise app on his phone, counting down the remaining time for his opportunity to eat. Ramy's eating must strictly adhere to sunset and sunrise as determined by a tech-based app.

For Mo, it is about intention. Since Ramy placed his order before sunrise, Mo thinks that intention aligns with the principles of the fast, even if the food arrives after the sun peaks above the horizon. After all, there were no sunrise apps during the time of the Prophet. Meanwhile, their friend Ahmed is standing outside, looking at the horizon, trying to figure out if he sees the sun or just ambient light from a new Target department store.[29] The conversation shows the nuanced beliefs on what it means to be a practicing Muslim during Ramadan in the times of iPhones and cityscapes aglow from neon signs. It shows what it means to have different religious interpretations and approaches from your friends. At least, what it means for these three men. Consider if you think a White guy in Sherman Oaks could have written that. It is a very specific experience. But it is also a relatable one. How do we observe and respect long-standing traditions in today's modern world? That question is universal.

Summary

This chapter discussed group membership and how the "fracturing of comedy" allows performers to create more personal material which resonates with their audiences. Breaking free from mainstream taste allows non-mainstream comedians to be more freely themselves. This chapter discussed the concept of subcultures and spoke to their role in providing a sense of community and acceptance for people of different backgrounds and identities. This chapter discussed sociological concepts related to cultural relativism and xenophobia, and uses comedic examples to bring things concepts to life. This chapter used these examples to highlight why representation in matters in media – for both creators and consumers of content. In the next chapter, we will discuss comedians using intersectional lenses to explain why representation matters in comedy and media. We will use examples from comedians who use intersectional lenses to show not just how group membership evolves, but how group memberships intersect.

Discussion Questions

6-1: Émile Durkheim posited there is one collective conscience which guides norms and values, and the decline of the collective conscious results in anomie. If and how does Joel Kim Booster's experience fit into Durkheim's theories related to social facts, collective conscious, anomie, and social integration?

6-2: Durkheim believed the transition from mechanical solidarity to organic solidarity was detrimental to society as people's experiences, beliefs, and social norms became more varied and there was a decline in the shared collective conscience. If and how do Danny McBride's views of varied experience fit into Durkheim's theories related to collective conscience, mechanical solidarity, and organic solidarity?

6-3: How does the concept of privilege relate to comedians who have mainstream appeal versus comedians who have more niche audiences?

6-4: Consider how media and news organizations shape our understanding of the "truth"? Do you believe direct-entry platforms like YouTube disrupt some (or all) of this power? Why or why not? Use sociological theories or comedic examples to justify your answer.

6-5: Define pluralism. Do you think the United States is a pluralistic society? Why or why not?

6-6: With a classmate, discuss if and why you believe representation matters in media.

6-7: Which contemporary sociological theory does the prioritization of "emotional correctness" over hard facts best fit into?

6-8: Explain what critical theorists mean in saying that the goal of mass culture is to pacify and repress the masses. Explain the *why* and *how* of this statement.

6-9: What would Max Weber and other critical theorists say about the consolidation of news outlets and slanted media?

6-10: With a classmate, discuss the sociological concepts Mo Amer's and Hari Kondabolu's jokes touch on, including stereotypes, xenophobia, prejudice, and discrimination. Do you think their comedy effectively teaches their audiences about these sociological phenomena? Why or why not?

Notes

1 Ritzer, G. (2013). *Introduction to Sociology*. SAGE.
2 Hagay, D. M. (Director). (2022). *Joel Kim Booster: Psychosexual*. https://www. netflix.com/title/81311995
3 *The Last Laugh: Could Joel Kim Booster Be the First Gay Male Stand-Up Superstar?* (2021, May 31). https://podcasts.apple.com/ca/podcast/could-joel-kim-booster-be-the-first-gay-male-stand-up/id1456474041?i=1000523735793
4 Durkheim, É. (1897). *Suicide*. Routledge & Kegan Paul.
5 *Good One: Danny McBride's The Righteous Gemstones's Opening Scene*. (2019, August 19). https://podcasts.apple.com/us/podcast/danny-mcbrides-the-righteous-gemstoness-opening-scene/id1203393721?i=1000447224514
6 Durkheim, É. (1893). *The Division of Labor in Society*.
7 Marchese, D. (2020, May 12). Ramy Youssef is not using comedy to teach you about Muslims. *The New York Times*. https://www.nytimes.com/interactive/2020/05/12/magazine/ramy-youssef-interview.html
8 *The Last Laugh: Ramy Youssef Discovers Himself*. (2019, April 16). https://podcasts.apple.com/my/podcast/ramy-youssef-discovers-himself/id1456474041?i=1000435045626
9 *Ramy Youssef "Feelings."* (2019). HBO. https://www.imdb.com/title/tt10432620/
10 Adorno, T. W., & Bernstein, J. M. (2020). *The Culture Industry: Selected Essays on Mass Culture* (2nd edition). Routledge. https://doi.org/10.4324/9781003071297
11 Andrews, E. (2019, July 30). *Media Consolidation Means Less Local News, More Right Wing Slant | Stanford Graduate School of Business*. https://www.gsb.stanford.edu/insights/media-consolidation-means-less-local-news-more-right-wing-slant
12 Matsa, K. E. (2017, May 11). Buying spree brings more local TV stations to fewer big companies. *Pew Research Center*. https://www.pewresearch.org/fact-tank/2017/05/11/buying-spree-brings-more-local-tv-stations-to-fewer-big-companies/
13 Andrews, 2019.
14 Andrews, 2019; Martin, G. J., & McCrain, J. (2019, February 19). *Local News and National Politics | American Political Science Review | Cambridge Core*. https://www.cambridge.org/core/journals/american-political-science-review/article/local-news-and-national-politics/C8EEA488A777C37C7987964F8F85AEB5
15 Nickerson, C. (2022). *Cultural Relativism | Definition & Examples—Simply Psychology*. https://www.simplypsychology.org/cultural-relativism.html
16 Dennis, B., & Markon, J. (2017, January 29). *Amid protests and confusion, Trump defends executive order: 'This is not a Muslim ban.'* The Washington Post. https://www.washingtonpost.com/national/health-science/trump-gives-no-sign-of-backing-down-from-travel-ban/2017/01/29/4ffe900a-e620-11e6-b82f-687d6e6a3e7c_story.html
17 *The Last Laugh: Ramy Youssef Discovers Himself* (2019).
18 *Mohammed in Texas-2021 Netflix Special*. (2021). https://www.netflix.com/title/81435608
19 *U.S. Muslims Concerned about Their Place in Society, but Continue to Believe in the American Dream | Pew Research Center*. (2017, July 26). https://www.pewresearch.org/religion/2017/07/26/findings-from-pew-research-centers-2017-survey-of-us-muslims/
20 Naim, S. (Director). (2022, August 24). Hamoodi. In *Mo*.
21 Obeidallah, D. (2010, October 19). *The Muslim Double Standard | HuffPost Latest News*. https://www.huffpost.com/entry/the-muslim-double-standar_b_767951
22 *Murder and Extremism in the United States in 2018*. (2022, May 3). https://www.adl.org/resources/report/murder-and-extremism-united-states-2018
23 Chambers, S. (2021, January 21). *Islamophobia in Western media is based on false premises*. The Conversation. http://theconversation.com/islamophobia-in-western-media-is-based-on-false-premises-151443

24 *The World's Muslims: Unity and Diversity.* (2012, August 9). *Pew Research Center's Religion & Public Life Project.* https://www.pewresearch.org/religion/2012/08/09/the-worlds-muslims-unity-and-diversity-executive-summary/.

25 *Hari Kondabolu on Russell Howard's Good News.* (2011, April 4). https://www.youtube.com/watch?v=W-KSI5Z0I90

26 Mogahed, D., & Mahmood, A. (2019, May 1). *American Muslim Poll 2019: Predicting and Preventing Islamophobia | ISPU.* https://www.ispu.org/american-muslim-poll-2019-predicting-and-preventing-islamophobia/

27 *Ask Me Another: Ramy Youssef.* (2020, May 29). NPR. https://www.npr.org/programs/ask-me-another/864841201/quarantv-ramy-space-force-and-lady-dynamite

28 *The Last Laugh: Ramy Youssef Discovers Himself* (2019).

29 *"Ramy" Do the Ramadan.* (2019). Hulu. https://www.imdb.com/title/tt9082310/

7 Race and Racism

This chapter expands on concepts discussed in the prior chapter. This chapter uses data to detail the current state of representation in media and explores the effects and necessity of representation. This chapter discusses the work of W.E.B. Du Bois, Kimberlé Crenshaw, Rebecca Krefting, and Darnell Hunt. Sociological concepts include White privilege, double consciousness, intersectionality, code switching, cultural appropriation, residential segregation, internalized racism, personally mediated racism, and institutional racism. To bring these concepts to life, this chapter draws on examples from comedians who tell their own stories using an intersectional lens.

White Privilege

Representation, including simply seeing a comedian who looks like you or has a background similar to yours, is important for audiences to feel seen, heard, and understood. Comedians who straddle multiple worlds can teach important sociological lessons about what it means to see the world through an intersectional perspective. A cultural shift toward greater representation, however, can feel threatening to people who have never had to share the spotlight or consider experiences outside their own.

White privilege refers to the relative advantages for White people compared to Black people and people of color that stems from the historical exclusion from economic, educational, and residential opportunities.[1] White audiences who see diverse creators representing themselves in media can sometimes interpret that representation as an attack against White people. Feelings of unease may set in when *what was seen as* a fair system begins to fall apart due to new understanding. And if it tilts in a direction not in your favor, that suddenly feels very unfair. This is White privilege.

Take an example from the University of Texas, wherein a student sued for "reverse racism" in her application. She claimed she was not accepted to the university simply because she was White. She claimed students of minority racial and ethnic groups with similar grades and test scores were given preference over her. Her lawsuit was a part of a larger legal scheme (this student was hand-picked to be the face of the movement), and the case ultimately lost in the Texas Supreme Court.

DOI: 10.4324/9781003469537-8

We see this in comedy and media too. When the television screen no longer has the same White, male faces on it, some viewers see this as a personal attack. The reason is that White audiences are "new" to paying attention to perspectives and experiences outside of their own. Being "forced" to pay attention to a new face or a new voice is a disruption to the status quo. This is revealing about how well (or, not) White audiences understand their privilege and power and how comfortable they have gotten being the only people represented in influential media for so long.

White Male Bias in Media

Hollywood has a long history of producers, directors, creators, and writers being largely White and male, which severely narrows the lens of focus. A 2017 study titled, "Race in the Writers' Room," written by Dr. Darnell Hunt, dean of Social Sciences at UCLA, examined episodes from the total universe of all scripted series airing on eighteen broadcast, cable, and streaming platforms during the 2016–2017 season.[2] That census included over 1,600 episodes from 234 shows. Hunt's study found vast inequities in race- and sex-based representation among television showrunners and writers, with the series' showrunners being 91 percent White and 80 percent male. Only 14 percent of the series' writers were members of a minority racial or ethnic group, and only five percent of writers were Black. Nearly 67 percent of shows had zero Black writers, with an additional 17 percent of shows having just one Black writer.

The report discusses how the exclusion of Black creators results in stereotypic or dehumanizing representation of Black characters on screen. To the extent that Black characters are even present, they are often unkind, inaccurate, or "cardboard" characters (an industry term for characters that lack substance or emotion; simply clichés or there to fill space). This, according to Hunt, "whitewashes" the narratives displayed on television. Thinking about viewers at home, not everyone has opportunities to engage with folks unlike themselves. All they may know about members of another group is what they see on television or in film. This is why accurate and humanizing representation in media matters.

The study found that writers' rooms that were White-dominated were more likely than rooms with Black writers to produce stereotypic Black characters (like a flat Black "sidekick" to the show's White protagonist). In White-dominated writers' rooms, writers of a minority racial and/or ethnic group may be treated as a **token**, a person who is viewed as a symbol of representation of diversity without actually allowing the person's voice to be heard or respected, or viewed without acknowledgment of their individuality separate from their role representing their racial or ethnic group. The experience of being tokenized is described by screenwriter and producer Felicia D. Henderson, who worked on *Family Matters, The Fresh Prince of Bel-Air, Soul Food,* and *Empire*.[3] The CBS show *Family Matters* (running 1989–1997) centered around a Black family called the Winslows living in Chicago, Illinois. Plus, of course, their quirky and nerdy neighbor, Steve Urkel (played by Jaleel White).

The father of the house, Carl (played by Reginald VelJohnson), worked as a police officer. Henderson described tension in the writer's room during the writing of the 1994 episode of *Family Matters* called "Good Cop, Bad Cop." In the episode, Carl's teenage son, Eddie (played by Darius McCrary), comes home very upset about being harassed by the Chicago police, wherein they forced Eddie to the ground. Carl does not believe Eddie's version of the events and states that Eddie must have provoked the cops' response. Carl thereby implies his son was not unjustly harassed, but that he must have behaved in a way that justified the police officers' actions. Henderson did not agree with the dialogue. She strongly believed there was no way a Black father would say this to his Black son. But that is the line that aired on the show.

So how did that line still make it to air? Henderson describes that there are hierarchies in writers' rooms. Junior writers are underneath senior writers, and they are all underneath the showrunner. Henderson explains that such a hierarchy became apparent when she attempted to advocate for her perspective. She was one of only a handful of Black staffers on *Family Matters* and she was a junior writer (this was her first season on the show). Henderson thus lacked the sway that additional seniority affords. As the writers' room work-shopped Carl's line, Henderson knew it felt disingenuous to her. She shared her view with the room. The room fell eerily silent. According to Henderson, the showrunner defended Carl's line and took Henderson's pushback with offense. The line aired, despite Henderson's warning that it felt unrealistic.

What are the consequences of this line making it to air? First, it is a potentially unrealistic portrayal of conversations that happen within Black families. Instead, it is a White version of conversations that happen within Black families. For people who identify with the Winslow family, there is a lack of connection on screen with their own experiences. For people coming into the Winslow's home from the outside, there is a misrepresentation and a misunderstanding of what those homes look and sound like.

What can happen when writers are tasked with writing for someone outside their own viewpoint? Certainly, it happens all the time. A writer may write lines for anyone in the script – men, women, children, aliens, you name it. That is fine and not the point of this critique. The point here is the consequences of writing for a group you do not understand can result in inaccuracies in how that group is represented. There are consequences if you misunderstand what it means to Muslim or to be Black, or to be both, and that misrepresentation ends up on screen.

When *Saturday Night Live* debuted in 1975, Garrett Morris (born in New Orleans, Louisiana, 1937) was the show's only Black writer. As explained by David Peisner in his 2018 book, *Homey Don't Play That*, the reason there was only one Black writer was that racism was baked into the hiring process. It was structural. The writer's room was predominantly White because of unequal opportunity stemming back decades or centuries in the past.[4] Peisner explains that Lorne Michaels and his colleagues hired people for the original *SNL* cast and crew based on the people they knew from their time in the improv and standup scenes. Those comedy scenes were largely White; therefore, so were the people they hired from them. This example shows how opportunity was, and largely still is, not afforded equally. To get hired on *SNL*'s first season, you essentially had to know Lorne Michaels. And most people who knew Lorne Michael were White.

Having only one Black writer in the room limited if and how Black characters were written for *SNL* and for other shows with a similar lack of diversity. Peisner's book details many accounts from Black actors discussing Black characters they played or auditioned to play that, because they were written by White writers, did not resonate with their personal experience. Keenen Ivory Wayans (born in Harlem, New York, 1958) read a script for a role as a "street thug" on the television series *The Renegades* (which aired just six episodes in 1983). According to Wayans, the script contained a lot of street jargon that neither he nor his Black colleagues had heard before. They asked the writers who crafted the lines. The writers told Wayans that they had made up the street slang. Without representation behind the camera, there are inaccuracies in front of it.

Racism and Privilege with W.E.B. Du Bois

One of the foundational sociological scholars for the concept of privilege is W.E.B. Du Bois. Du Bois was born in Great Barrington, Massachusetts, 1868. One of the Du Bois' seminal works (which is regarded as a foundational sociological text) is his 1903 book, *The Souls of Black Folk*. *The Souls of Black Folk* is a collection of essays about race, racism, and the Black experience in the United States.

One of the many major sociological contributions to come out of *The Souls of Black Folk* is the concept of the double consciousness as it relates to Black people's experiences in society. **Double consciousness** refers to the internal conflict experienced by members of marginalized and oppressed groups within a socially stratified society. The double consciousness explains the internal conflict between one's own sense of self (such as who they are, including their strengths, values, and desires) and how others may view them (as sub-human and must be controlled, dominated, and owned like property). Du Bois explains this internal conflict in *The Souls of Black Folk* (1903):

This sense of always looking at one's self through the eyes of others, of measuring one's soul by the tape of a world that looks on in amused contempt and pity. One ever feels his two-ness—an American, a Negro; two souls, two thoughts, two unreconciled strivings; two warring ideals in one dark body, whose dogged strength alone keeps it from being torn asunder. The history of the American Negro is the history of this strife—this longing to attain self-conscious manhood, to merge his double self into a better and truer self. In this merging he wishes neither of the older selves to be lost ... He simply wishes to make it possible for a man to be both a Negro and an American without being cursed and spit upon by his fellows, without having the doors of opportunity closed roughly in his face.[5]

Within Du Bois' words is an explanation of the social, psychological, and physical impacts of the ways Black people experience social stratification when they are viewed as lesser, oppressed, and shut out from opportunities and full and equal participation in society. What does it mean to move through the world as someone who holds a marginalized identity? In more recent years, scholars have expanded Du Bois' work to include additional layers of intersectionality. For example, the term **triple consciousness** was coined to describe the internal conflict experienced by Black women.[6] Scholars have further expanded the concept of **multiple consciousnesses** to include the internal conflict experienced by other marginalized groups, such as members of the LGBTQ+ community, particularly Black and Brown members of the LGBTQ+ community.[7] The degree to which LGBTQ+ people may need to "police" their own behaviors in different spaces and social settings depends upon other features of their identity – including race and ethnicity.

While not expressly written in this quote, the other side of the coin is apparent through Du Bois' words. There are myriad privileges that come with belonging to the ruling class. For White people, for example, there is extreme privilege in moving through the world in White skin. White people have the freedom to be whoever they want to be without sacrificing, or merging, pieces of oneself and ones' culture (although, it should be noted that who classifies as "White" in the United States has evolved over time, and people who may now be considered "White," such people of Irish or Italian descent, where long treated with derision). Being White comes with great privilege and affords someone positive social assumptions about their value and potential simply for the color of their skin.

Intersectionality and the Expectation to Represent

Actor, writer, and director Issa Rae (born in Los Angeles, California, 1985) has long known the importance of representation on television and in comedy. Rae grew up watching and loving television in the 1990s. The 1990s were a particularly golden era of sitcoms featuring Black characters and families. Particularly, sitcoms in the 1990s – such as *The Fresh Prince of Bel-Air* (NBC, 1990–1996), *Living Single* (Fox, 1993–1998), and *Moesha* (UPN, 1996–2001) – featured Black characters who had their own stories, relationships, personality, and were relatable to mainstream audiences.[8] This was influential for Rae. From a young age, she knew she wanted to create content that was both relatable and reflective of her own experience as a young Black woman.

Rae developed her own web series called *Awkward Black Girl* that streamed on YouTube. The show followed the character J as she navigated life, love, and career as an awkward and insecure young woman. People *loved* it. Rae and her co-producer, Tracy Oliver – a former classmate of Rae's who later wrote *Girls Trip* and other major comedic films – started a Kickstarter campaign hoping to raise $30,000 for the show. Their fans nearly doubled that.

The success of *Awkward Black Girl* afforded Rae and Oliver the opportunity to develop and shoot a pilot (called *I Hate LA Dudes*) produced by television superstar Shonda Rhimes. However, the pilot never aired. As Rae describes of the experience, she paid too much attention to what the network wanted for her show, and she paid too little attention to her own story and own voice. Rae knew she needed to tap into her specific viewpoint that was first made *Awkward Black Girl* such a success. Consider how Rae's experience here relates to **White privilege**; the advantages afforded to White people, relative to Black people and people of color, which stem from the historical exclusion of Black and Brown people from opportunities.[9] Consider how fitting into a network mold pulled Rae too far away from her own voice and vision as a Black woman.

After *I Hate LA Dudes* failed to launch, Rae joined forces with comedian, writer, producer, actor, and *Daily Show* correspondent at the time, Larry Wilmore (born in Los Angeles County, California, 1961). Together, they developed *Insecure*, which ran for six critically acclaimed seasons on HBO. *Insecure* focuses on race and sex without being reductive in of their individual aspects.[10] The stories are told using an intersectional perspective. Recall, Kimberlé Crenshaw coined the term **intersectionality** to refer to the idea that we cannot separate someone's experiences based on features of their identity – such as race, ethnicity, sex, gender, sexuality, or social status separately – as these features intersect.[11] Issa is not simply a woman; she is a Black woman.

Insecure effectively demonstrates how racism shapes the lives of Black people – specifically Black women. It shows the harsh realities of what that means; the racism, the microaggressions, the struggle to "make it" when the deck is stacked against you. But *Insecure* also shows the joy of being a Black woman. It shows the celebration, pride, and kinship that bonds Issa and her friends. *Insecure* celebrates and normalizes the lives of Black women. The characters laugh, hang out, go on dates, fall in love, experience heartbreak, and experience joy. In these everyday moments, audiences see how the characters are just like "everyone else."

As the creator and star of *Insecure*, Rae regularly fields questions about being a monolithic example for the entire Black community. As Rae makes clear, there is often expectation by networks, journalists, and (White) audiences that a Black creator and actor is somehow expected to represent what it means to be Black in the industry. This experience, unfortunately, is all too common for Black creators.

White people are not asked during interviews what it is like being a White star. The media institution understands that there are many ways to be White. But experiences of minority groups are often assumed to be monolithic. In her book, *All Joking Aside*, Dr. Rebecca Krefting, associate professor of American Studies at Skidmore College, writes about how male comedians are viewed as neutral. Material about their struggles, then, is considered material about human struggles. That is not the case for women. Material about women's struggles is considered niche comedy and is considered only relatable and funny to women.[12] As such, women are trained to identify with men early on, while men are not given the same task.

In her book, *Laughing to Keep From Dying: African American Satire in the Twenty-First Century* (2020), Dr. Danielle Fuentes Morgan, assistant professor in the Department of English at Santa Clara University, expands upon Krefting's argument. Specifically, Morgan notes the importance of understanding intersectionality in discussions of what is considered "neutral." It is not simply maleness, but White maleness, that represents the norm. As Morgan explains, it is White male struggles which are deemed human struggles and struggles of other folks – specifically those of Black or Brown women – are viewed as special interest or niche struggles.[13] This point acknowledges the reality that many creative projects created by women of color are set up to fail. If a story is thought of as "too niche" or "not relatable," it is less likely to be picked up for production. The perception that Black women's stories are "niche" results in Black creators facing an additional burden which is not placed on White creators.

In an interview with *Vox*, Rae describes some of her comedic influences as *Seinfeld* (NBC, 1989–1998), *Curb Your Enthusiasm* (HBO, 2000–Pres), and the UK's original version of *The Office* (BBC, 2001–2003).[14] She loved these shows because they depict normal, everyday experiences and interactions. They show the humor in everyday life. Indeed, *Insecure*'s strongest comedic moments happen inside of normal and awkward social interactions.[15] This was seen as revolutionary for a show centered around Black characters. All of these popular shows (*Seinfeld*, *Curb Your Enthusiasm*, the UK's *The Office*) – which have been praised for their comedic takes of everyday life – are told through the lens of White male main characters. These shows are additional examples of what Krefting and Morgan describe as White male stories being considered "neutral." Shows like *Insecure* widen the net; showing what everyday life looks like for folks not represented by those other shows.

When Black and Brown creators can tell their stories, audiences can see those experiences play out on the stage or on the screen. They can celebrate their own experiences, identities, and humanity. Celebration of Black cultures, traditions, and identities are crucial for breaking free of the psychological barriers imposed by the White dominant society which stall revolution.[16] In *Insecure*, the show includes the parts of life which have long been displayed in media; friendships, relationships, and going out with friends. The show also includes the parts of life often ignored in media, like the multifaceted ways Issa and her friends experience racism throughout their daily lives. In the following sections, we will discuss examples of Issa at work which exemplify the constant need to code switch for Black and Brown folks in countless professional and social situations, and the mental, physical, and emotional toll of doing so.

Code Switching with Insecure

Code switching is the process of adjusting one's speech, behavior, or appearance in difference situations to make others feel more comfortable with their presence. People engage in code switching behaviors all the time. It can include changing your tone of voice between talking on the phone with your friends and talking on the phone with a parent or your boss. Consider what code switching may say about the "acceptability" of certain language or behaviors in different spaces. If you refer to Erving Goffman's discussion of **impression management**, code switching is a good example of how features of personality – like how you speak or dress – are products of social interaction.

First entering the lexicon in 1954, code switching gained broader understanding in 2012 after a video of President Barack Obama went viral (which here refers to content that spreads widely and rapidly over the Internet). The video shows President Obama in the locker room of the U.S. Men's Olympic basketball team greeting the players and coaching staff. The video went viral for the way it shows President Obama greeting the White assistant coach with a handshake, then greeting star forward Kevin Durant, who is Black, with a *bro hug* (a combination of a handshake and a one-armed hug, often seen occurring between two men).

The video was spoofed in the satirical sketch comedy series *Key & Peele*, which ran for five seasons on Comedy Central (2011–2015). In the sketch, as President Obama (played by Jordan Peele) moves down a long line of people at a political meet-and-greet, he vacillates between cold and robotic handshakes for the White people and dances, hugs, belly bumps, and elaborate high-five routines for the Black people. Even President Obama, the leader of the United States at this time, adapted his behavior to fit expectations from person to person. The discussion of how minority groups are often pressured to code switch to gain acceptance by elites or by social institutions is important and frequent in the field of sociology. Research indicates code switching if often utilized in environments where language, dress, or behaviors commonly associated with Black people are not considered "acceptable" or "appropriate" by other folks in that setting.[17]

We can see code switching behaviors similar to President Obama's locker room example in Boots Riley's 2018 surrealist comedy *Sorry to Bother You*.[18] The movie follows Cassius, nicknamed Cash (played by Lakeith Stanfield), as he gets a new job as a telemarketer after struggling to pay his bills. Cash has a lot of trouble making sales until a more senior coworker shares a tip with him: he needs to use his "White voice" (as in, he needs to sound White in terms of vernacular and tone). Cash creates an alternate White persona, voiced by comedic actor David Cross. Cash begins to make sale after sale and quickly rises in the company while making the money to match but it also leads him into the surreal underworld of the telemarketing corporate industry.

Code switching happens in numerous small moments throughout *Insecure*, but it is a primary focus of the season one episode titled "Racist As F**k."[19] Molly (played by Yvonne Orji), is the only Black woman associate at a predominantly White law firm. In the episode, a young Black woman named Rasheeda, nicknamed DaDa (played by Gail Bean), joins the office as a new intern. Rasheeda is unapologetically herself; she is loud, ends her sentences with *girl,* and jokes around with her White coworkers telling racy jokes and stories.

Molly, as the only other Black woman at this firm, is approached by one of the partners at the firm (a White woman) and is asked to speak with Rasheeda about her demeanor. The partner believes Rasheeda does not fit the firm's culture. The implication is that Rasheeda is "too Black." Immediately, two things happen. First, the audience sees the policing of stereotypical Black language or behaviors in professional environments (all-too-often White environments). Second, the audience sees the additional burdens placed on Black employees for mentoring or monitoring other Black employees (if there *are* other Black employees). In addition to Molly's job as a lawyer, she is now tasked with having behavior management conversations with Rasheeda. These conversations not only take time, but they also take a heavy toll on emotional health and social relationships.

As one of the two Black women at a predominantly White firm, Molly understands Rasheeda's actions reflect back on her.[20] What one of them does impacts the other. This is a burden the White staff members do not bear. Molly has the conversation with Rasheeda where she tells the young intern that success at the law firm requires knowing "when to switch it up" (meaning: when to code switch). Rasheeda is taken aback by Molly's advice, noting she did not switch it up during law school (where she was editor of the school's law review) or during her interview for the firm's internship. The conversation is difficult, tense, and ultimately forces the two women to stand on opposite sides of an incredibly difficult issue: what does it mean to be a Black woman in a White professional space? Should you be yourself? Or adapt to survive? In the end, the difficult interaction serves to divide the only two Black women at the firm. *Insecure* centers the ways Black women talk to *each other* about race; something not prominently featured in Whiter, more mainstream shows. This allows for real conversations on tough subjects in a space that is safe and understanding.[21]

Triple Consciousness with Insecure

Insecure did not shy away from issues not commonly portrayed on television. In addition to seeing them play out in people's daily lives, *Insecure* also gave audiences a window into the mental and emotional toll taken on the character of Issa when experiencing prejudice, discrimination, and her triple consciousness.

Let us first review and expand upon the work of W.E.B. Du Bois. Recall, the unjust social structure of the United States systemically benefits White people at the detriment and exclusion of Black and Brown people. In his work, Du Bois detailed the resultant social, psychological, and physical consequences experienced by Black people due to this oppression. Du Bois notes that Black people have to hold their identities as "Black" and as "American" separately yet simultaneously, which results in what he calls **double consciousness**. Double consciousness can pressure Black people to separate themselves from their history and culture in efforts to fit in, or assimilate, with "American" life. Du Bois argues that we need to widen the definition of what it means to be "American." Being "Black" and "American" should not be not exclusive identities.

More recent scholarship has expanded on this idea. **Triple consciousness theory** (TCT), an extension of Du Bois' double consciousness, is a framework which explains the juggling act of being a Black woman in America.[22] TCT is also informed by work by Alice Walker, Bonnie Thornton, and Frances Beale – all of whom wrote about the perilous situations Black women face due to their intersecting race and sex. Black women exist within social structures which prioritize White patriarchy, White feminism, and Black hypermasculinity over the interests and experiences of Black women. TCT explains that the "American" lens prioritizes White patriarchy, the "Black" lens prioritizes Black hypermasculinity, and the "woman" lens prioritizes White womanhood. Black women must simultaneously see themselves as "American," as "Black," and as "a woman." Look for these in the examples from *Insecure* below.

Earlier in this chapter, we discussed how *Insecure* thoughtfully presented how Black women talk to each other. Other thoughtful and unique elements of the show are the ways it presents Issa talking to herself. These elements bolster sociological analysis of Issa's experiences by showing her back stage – revealing for audiences how she navigates, experiences, and performs in the social world. Using two distinct styles, *Insecure* shows Issa's back stage (refer to Goffman's dramaturgical theory of the self). First, as we will discuss using the pilot episode, we hear Issa's inner monologue as voiceover, and second, as we will discuss later in this section, we see Issa talking and rapping to her self-conscious in her backroom mirror.

Voiceover

In the first season, much of *Insecure*'s beloved awkwardness and messiness of the show comes from Issa's interactions with her coworkers at an inner-city youth outreach program called We Got Y'all. Early in *Insecure*'s pilot episode (titled: "Insecure as F**k"), we see Issa giving a presentation about We Got Y'all alongside her White coworker, Freida, to a classroom of mostly Black and Brown middle school students. Standing in front of the classroom, Issa details in a very upbeat voice the details of We Got Y'all's services, such as after school tutoring and standardized test coaching. She asks the students if they have any questions, and an awkward interaction follows. A student asks a question about Issa's manner of speech – saying she sounds "White" and not Black. Caught off-guard, Issa chuckles and jokingly retorts that she is a White girl in blackface. Her joke is followed by a long, awkward pause, and no one else laughs. In a whisper, Freida tells Issa her joke was racist.[23]

The interaction between Issa, the students, and her White colleague efficiently sets up a key element of the show as it relates to Issa's job. White women compose 75 percent of workers in the nonprofit sector.[24] In her role, Issa is repeatedly confronted with awkward and challenging questions about what it means to be a professional Black woman working for a nonprofit with White savior vibes (more on that in a moment) which serves primarily Black and Brown students.

Audiences see this further as the show transitions to the We Got Y'all office. Guided by Issa's voiceover, the camera first pans around the office showing images of the We Got Y'all logo (which is a White hand lifting Black children), Africana art, a Beyonce poster, a photo of Martin Luther King Jr., and another photo of Issa's White boss shaking hands with President Obama. The camera then holds on Issa and her boss in a meeting. The audience hears Issa's inner monologue as voiceover, explaining that her boss founded We Got Y'all to serve children "from the 'hood'" but did not actually hire anyone with a background similar to that of the children they serve.[25] In the following section, consider how this scene fits with our discussion of cultural appropriation.

The camera continues to pan around the office, showing an almost entirely White staff. The camera stops in the We Got Y'all breakroom as a group of people are mid-conversation while Issa walks into the room. Her White coworkers asked her to explain the meaning of "on fleek" to them. Issa, clearly frustrated and exhausted, throws her hands up in the air and, in a soft and casual tone, tells them she does not know. Audience then hear Issa's inner monologue as voiceover, and, in a serious tone, notes that she *does* know what that means. Issa is clearly exhausted with these types of questions and is not going to answer this one.

As seen in this exchange, much like the scene showing Issa giving the school presentation, the shots around the We Got Y'all office details for viewers how exhausting a day in Issa's professional life is. She is treated by her coworkers as We Got Y'all's token Black person in every interaction. From the very beginning, *Insecure* sets up the notion that this show is about the little daily interactions which compose Issa's life.

Bathroom Mirror

Let us now pivot to *Insecure*'s second signature element of Issa talking and rapping to herself in her bathroom mirror. This is where audiences see Issa process her emotions. For example, audiences see Issa rap about her anger while going through a breakup or about how it feels to date new people while she is still thinking about her ex. Throughout the show, Issa's bathroom mirror scenes give audiences a window into her self-conscious. This is sociologically powerful. It gives us a window into Issa's back stage.[26]

Recall, the **front stage** refers to our behaviors when we know we are being watched by someone else. Through socialization, we learn what behaviors are considered "appropriate" in various settings.[27] The **back stage**, according to Goffman, is where you can live as if no one is watching and you can be more of your authentic self.[28]

Now, consider how *Insecure* shows us the interplay between Issa's front and back stages. We see Issa giving herself pep talks before a big event, pumping herself up before going out for the evening, or reckoning with herself when she is struggling. We see how Issa, as a Black woman, is pressured to adapt behaviors as she moves through different spaces more so than would be expected of White women. Indeed, *Insecure* allows for deep sociological analysis of how we are always performing, how expectations differ by intersections of one's race, sex, and other features of identity, and how performance can be emotionally, mentally, and physically taxing. Consider how and why expressions of the burden of triple consciousness experienced by Black women may be reserved for the back stage. Consider if you think that hearing Issa's inner monologue as voiceover or seeing how Issa speaks or raps to herself in the bathroom mirror could help audiences understand her triple consciousness.

Cultural Appropriation with *Atlanta*

The We Got Y'all office, which is a predominantly White-staffed organization yet is decorated with Black icons and imagery, is a great jumping off point for discussions of cultural appropriation. **Cultural appropriation** refers to the unacknowledged adoption (really, theft) of the practices, behaviors, and forms of one group by another usually more powerful group.[29] This can include music, art, clothing, hairstyles, vernacular, and other elements of culture.

A question that can comes up frequently upon learning about cultural appropriation is: what is the difference between appropriation and appreciation? One way to spot appropriation is to understand that appropriation is selective. When a White person appropriates Black culture, for example, they appropriate "everything but the burden."[30] Elements of Black culture are vilified when expressed by Black people, but allowed (and even lauded) when expressed by White people. Let us start with hair.

First, hairstyles common among Black people have long been restricted in many workplaces and schools across the United States for being so-called "unprofessional," "messy," or "unclean."[31] These hair discrimination policies are an example of systemic racism.[32] Racist hair policies have removed Black adults from the workplace and Black children from school. These policies have danced around overt racial discrimination laws by claiming the laws apply equally to all and that they are about professional appearance; yet, they specifically and disproportionately target features of Black bodies.

In March 2022, the U.S. House of Representatives passed the CROWN (Creating a Respectful and Open World for Natural Hair) Act, outlawing race-based hair discrimination in the workplace when receiving benefits from federally funded programs or when securing public accommodations.[33] Many states had already passed their own versions of the CROWN Act. During the voting, Representative Ayanna Pressley (D-MA) spoke about how Black girls have long faced discrimination and penalties for wearing their hair as it naturally grows said. Hair discrimination policies provide another example of how deviance (like wearing braids to work) is socially constructed. In other words, deviance is not a natural or objective set of bad behaviors but is instead based on a set of rules established by the ruling class, which serves to preserve White privilege.

For those unfamiliar, it is important to acknowledge the physical and cultural elements of Black hairstyles. Black hair tends to express as tight, elastic coils that lend themselves to breakage. Straightening the hair, for example, can be quite damaging. As such, Black folks may wear protective hairstyles to preserve hair health. These may include braids, twists, or locs.[34] Wearing durags (alternative spelling: do-rags) can help maintain natural hair oils, prevent hair breakage, and maintain hair pattern.[35] Second, Black hairstyles, like cornrows, afros, and bantu knots, have strong ties to culture, identity, and Black pride.[36] The requirement to change one's hair to fit within White views of professional appearance serves to ignore and erase Black identity and culture.

When White people appropriate Black hairstyles, they have the *choice* of where and when to wear that hair. An example is Kim Kardashian wearing her hair in Fulani braids to the 2018 MTV Movie & TV Awards.[37] In examples like this, the choice to appropriate Black hairstyles is made in opposition to the long history of oppression which Black people have been subjected to in the United States. This is the burden White people do not take on when appropriating Black hairstyles. Appropriating Black hairstyles ignores the generations of trauma and immense resilience of Black people and communities.[38] After considering this context, it becomes clear that appropriation is *not* synonymous with appreciation.

Let us walk through an example of cultural appropriation using the television series *Atlanta*. *Atlanta* was created by, written by, and starring the talented multi-hyphenate (actor-comedian-musician-writer-producer-director-etc.) Donald Glover (born in Edwards Air Force Base, California, 1983). *Atlanta* premiered on FX in 2016, quickly receiving praise from critics and fans (including Chris Rock, who allegedly told Glover "*Atlanta* is the best show on TV, period") and winning two Emmys and two Golden Globes after its first season.

Atlanta follows the life of Earnest "Earn" Marks (played by Glover), a Princeton dropout who manages the budding music career of his cousin, Alfred, who goes by Paper Boi (played by Brian Tyree Henry). In addition to personal and professional struggles, the show tackles issues of racism, inequality, and depictions of how Earn navigates life as a Black man in the United States. We will return to more examples from *Atlanta* shortly, but let us begin with the episode "Juneteenth" to provide additional distinction between appropriation and appreciation.[39]

In "Juneteenth," Earn and his ex-girlfriend Vanessa attend a Juneteenth party thrown by a wealthy interracial couple. (Juneteenth is a holiday commemorating June 19, 1865, when enslaved African Americans in Texas were notified they had been freed – a full two years after the emancipation proclamation.) The husband of the host couple is a White man obsessed with Africa and African American culture to a degree that instantly comes off as objectifying and creepy. The audience feels the extreme discomfort and outrage felt by Earn as his own heritage is explained to him by a "woke" White man. This man collects and amasses value from his collection of art, music, and stories from Black and African people without taking on any of the discrimination or historical trauma they have experienced. The man only benefits from his appropriation. That is different from *appreciation*, which can include admiring or respecting the cultural productions of other groups without taking it in a way that benefits you. Meanwhile, the audience feels the pain and anguish of Earn biting his tongue in these moments, as he is there to support Vanessa as she attempts to secure a job through networking at events like these.

Watching the episode, audiences can see that the way the wealthy couple's home is adorned with the collection of Africana artwork and mementos feels more obsessive than it does honorific. A sociologist would refer to this man as a **cultural omnivore**. This term refers to the theory that "elites" prefer to distinguish themselves from individuals with lower status by choosing (and being able to afford) to have wide and diverse tastes. The vastness of their knowledge and taste is what enables elites to distinguish themselves from lower class individuals who may have fewer resources and less leisure time to dedicate to a multitude of hobbies or sets of knowledge.

Postmodern Hyperreality with Atlanta

Atlanta consistently shows the multitude of ways Earn and his friends navigate being Black in the United States. The viewer sees Earn and his friends achieve successes and experience failures, feel confidence and fear, and experience proud moments and insecure ones. Audiences see Earn, Paper Boi, and their inner circle interact with White people and White institutions as they engage in the code switching and tongue-biting that is oft required of Black people to make White people feel comfortable.

Glover was very intentional about all the character choices and storylines that made it into *Atlanta*. He was not catering to a White audience. In a 2016 interview, Glover outlines instances where he needed to explain, and advocate for, the inclusion of specific pieces of Black culture or Atlanta culture to *FX*. For example, Glover wanted to include a character that speaks patois (a creole language that is part of the Jamaican diaspora). First, the studio did not understand what those elements were, and second, they did not understand why patois needed to be included.[40] The lack of understanding and appreciation for cultural nuance (and the studio's subsequent decision that those elements should not be included in the show) is exactly what Glover hoped to disrupt when creating *Atlanta*. By being culturally specific and including a character that speaks patois, Glover was making a point. Representation matters in media, and what representation of Black characters on television looks like should not be determined by predominantly White studio executives.

Atlanta is a **high-concept** show. There is more than one way the term "high-concept" can be used in media. For our purposes here, we use the definition of a high-concept show as a production more tethered to its central concept than to its characters.[41] Conversely, **low-concept** shows are those more tethered to the relationships between characters than to its central concept. While *Atlanta* does focus on a set of primary characters – Earn and his friends – one of the core elements that makes *Atlanta* a high-concept show is its interweaving of the normal and the bizarre as means to highlight the absurdity-of-the-normal and challenge the status quo (here is the sociological imagination again).

Compare this description of *Atlanta* to a low-concept show. A low-concept version of *Atlanta* would likely rely more heavily on the relationships between characters and their dialogue to explain (i.e., translate) cultural concepts or realities for primarily White audiences. *Atlanta* does not rely on characters explaining their experiences to each other (and therefore, to the audience). Instead, audiences see characters as they navigate their world. The storylines and cinematography feel very surreal. Audiences are tasked with thinking about how they would feel and behave if placed in the same surroundings.

Let us walk through an example from the season 2 episode "Helen." In the episode, Earn and Vanessa attend a German Fasnacht festival in Vanessa's hometown of Helen, Georgia.[42] Vanessa grew up celebrating Fasnacht, so she feels comfortable and joyful with the celebration's games, dances, and garb (which includes lederhosen, dirndls, and masks). But for Earn, the festival is confusing and borderline scary. Directorial and tonal choices make these feelings clear to the audience, especially as the episodes transitions between Earn's and Vanessa's points of view (POV). In Earn's POV, there are no subtitles when Vanessa speaks to another man in German. Like Earn, the audience (at least, the non-German speaking members of the audience) have no idea what is happening in this conversation. It is confusing and isolating. When the episode later transitions to Vanessa's POV, there are subtitles for the conversation. The audience feels like a part of the interaction and thus, a part of the in-group. Using a postmodern motif, the episode effectively demonstrates what it *feels* like to be treated as an outsider. In *Atlanta*, the high-concept approach of the show routinely allows non-Black audiences to get a small glimpse into how it *feels* like to be Black in the United States.

Let us compare the high-concept approach to how some low-concept sit-coms have approached topics of race and racism. The first example is in the 2013 episode titled "The Cabin" on the Fox sitcom *New Girl,* running from 2011 to 2018. The B plot of this episode focuses on the relationship between friends and roommates Schmidt, who is a White Jewish man played by Max Greenfield, and Winston, a Black man played by Lamorne Morris. In the episode, Schmidt wants to "be the best Black friend [Winston] ever had" after seeing Winston interact with his Black friends with ease and charm (*New Girl*, Fox, 2013).[43] Schmidt acts out a series of escalating stereotypic behaviors to get closer to Winston, including eating soul food, wearing a Rastafarian hat, and attempting to buy crack. Winston is upset by Schmidt's behavior, but at the end of the episode the friends reconcile. In their con-versation, Winston explains to Schmidt that being Black "means whatever I want it to mean," including his choice to live with three White friends. The two then go out for frozen yogurt, with Schmidt initially vowing to order a vanilla-chocolate swirl. The episode focuses on the relationship between Schmidt and Winston, not Winston's personal thoughts or feelings associated with the situation.

A second example can be seen in the 2011 episode titled "Blax, Snake, Home" from the ABC sitcom *Happy Endings*, running from 2011 to 2013.[44] In the episode, Max, who is a gay, White, Jewish man played by Adam Pally, sees his friend Brad, a Black man played by Damon Wayans, Jr., sneaking around to hang out with a group of his Black friends. Brad refers to his clos-est friend in the group as *Black Max* (the character's name is really Darryl), and conversely, Brad refers to Max as *White Darryl*.[45] Feeling left out and motivated by spite, Max befriends a group of gay men and dubs one of them *Gay Brad*. The end of the episode shows Brad and Max reconciling, with Brad comparing their friendship to that of Murtaugh and Riggs from the buddy comedy movie *Lethal Weapon* (starring Danny Glover, who is Black, and Mel Gibson, who is White).

Both the *New Girl* and *Happy Endings* episodes seemingly strive to walk audiences through Winston's and Brad's motivations for wanting to be around friends of their same race, but only do so through the lens of their friendships with White characters. Both episodes end with happy conversations about the strong relationships between the individual characters (including comparisons to famous Black and White duos like chocolate and vanilla ice cream and Murtaugh and Riggs from *Lethal Weapon*), ignoring larger discussions of how the friends' lives may differ because of their race or how their interracial friendships may differ from their other intra-racial friendships. When sitcoms are character based, it can be beneficial for the characters to reconcile. This is not the approach taken by high-concept shows like *Atlanta*. *Atlanta* does not view Black characters through the lens of their relationships to White characters, nor does it resolve each episode with light and easy discussion between two friends.

To discuss one more episode of *Atlanta* which uses high-concept storytelling techniques to cover heavy social and political topics, we can refer to season 1, episode 7 ("B.A.N.").[46] The episode focuses on Paper Boi and is entirely shot as though audiences are watching an episode of the fictional talk show *Montague* on the (also fictional) Black American Network (B.A.N.). In the episode, the catalyst for Paper Boi's appearance on "Montague" was him tweeting he would not have sex with Caitlyn Jenner (a trans woman). Paper Boi debates his controversial beliefs on trans people, gender, and race with his fellow guest, Dr. Deborah Holt (a trans activist played by Mary Kraft).

The dynamic is thrown for a loop when a third roundtable guest joins the show; Antoine Smalls (played by Niles Stewart). Smalls is visibly a Black man, but identifies as White (picture a reverse Rachel Dolezal[47]). The talk show is intermixed with "commercials," each more absurdist than the last. A car commercial is an excuse for a man to revel in his divorce. A cereal commercial doubles as a commentary on police brutality. The episode of "B.A.N." is both absurdist and authentic, a seeming oxymoron that good comedy can afford.

The result of this mashup is that audiences are exposed to heavy discussions regarding serious topics of race, gender, identity, and politics. Through the talk show format, audience sees where people can come together and where others fail to align. While the experience of watching the episode feels incredibly surreal, the after-effect is that audiences begin to question their own reality using their sociological imagination. The episode is a simulation, but one which becomes indistinguishable from reality. It is an example of **hyperreality**. Audiences may ask themselves: are these seemingly bizarre and surrealist situations representative of my life? Consider how engaging hyperreality, like Glover did with this episode of *Atlanta*, is an example of the sociological imagination. Glover won a Primetime Emmy Award and was nominated for a Directors Guild of America Award for his direction of the episode "B.A.N."

Residential Segregation with Katt Williams

An underlying element of the show *Atlanta* is race and racism in the city of Atlanta. As we discussed previously, context matters. The lives of Earn and his friends in Atlanta will differ from White people in Atlanta or from Black people in another city (or from people who are of different identities and circumstances in Atlanta or elsewhere). Since the concept of place is a central tenet of the show, I want to take this opportunity to pivot and discuss how someone's physical place shapes their daily lives and their life trajectories. Specifically, let us talk about residential segregation.

Segregation refers to social or physical separation (such as in schools, churches, clubs, or residential neighborhoods) between groups in society based upon factors such as race, ethnicity, sex, gender, or economic class. Black performers restricted to the Chitlin' Circuit is an example of segregation. Prior to 1964, the legal segregation of people based on race or ethnicity was legal in the United States. Under Jim Crow laws, it was perfectly legal to bar entry or designate separate entry on buses or in restaurants, hotels, schools, churches, libraries, hospitals … the list goes on.

Residential segregation refers to the geographic separation of groups. As of 2021, Atlanta's population is 49.8 percent Black, 40.4 percent White, 4.8 percent Asian, 0.4 percent Alaska Native or American Indian, 3.2 percent two or more races, and 4.9 percent Hispanic or Latino.[48] These numbers tell us about the overall racial and ethnic composition of Atlanta, but not anything about how people reside in the city. Do people tend to live in single-race predominant neighborhoods, or are neighborhoods racially diverse?

To answer this question, sociologists use the **index of dissimilarity** to measure the segregation of two groups within a geographic area.[49] For example, a sociologist might use the index of dissimilarity to measure the residential segregation between Black and White residents in Atlanta. The index is calculated by measuring the percent of each racial group who would need to relocate for their representation in each neighborhood to match their total share of the total population in the city. To break this down, the index of dissimilarity between Black and White residents of Atlanta would ask: What percent of Black Atlantans would need to move so *each neighborhood* comprised 49.8 percent Black residents?

This is a hypothetical exercise in which we can imagine many residents of primarily Black neighborhoods suddenly needing to move out of their neighborhood and move into predominantly White neighborhoods. The same is true in reverse; with a need to reshuffle White residents so each neighborhood comprised 40.4 percent White residents. The index ranges from 0 (complete integration; 0 percent of the people in the subpopulation need to move) to 100 (complete segregation; 100 percent of people in the subpopulation need to move). The scale is broken into ranges of 0–30 (low segregation), 31–60 (moderate segregation), and 61–100 (high segregation).

The Black/White index of dissimilarity for Atlanta is 65.[50] This number indicates 65 percent of Black people in Atlanta would need to relocate for there to be equal representation across neighborhoods in the city. At 65, the index of dissimilarity indicates there is a "high" level of residential segregation. Let us now dig into how residential segregation occurs and discuss some of its consequences.

One of the systems establishing residentially segregated cities was redlining. **Redlining** is a process wherein banks (or other institutions or service providers) withhold service from groups of people they deem "high risk."[51] Specifically, in the history of the United States, mortgage lenders regularly and systematically denied loans to Black people because banks designated primarily Black neighborhoods as risky investments.

The term redlining goes back to the 1930s, when New Deal programs began offering government-backed mortgages to drive homeownership.[52] However, the government-backed mortgages were not extended equally. The program drew color-coded maps of more than 200 cities in the United States, ranking the areas from "A" (least risky) to "D" (most risky; and marked in red). The banks considered the "D" areas to be unworthy of mortgage lending, so neighborhoods, homes, and people who fell into those zones were systematically excluded from this government-backed program. The areas these programs marked as "D" were overwhelmingly Black neighborhoods and communities of color.

Redlining is a form of institutional racism that systemically denied Black people the opportunity to own their own home. These policies have long-lasting and widespread consequences. Home ownership is one of the primary mechanisms through which people build wealth in the United States and pass wealth on to their children. The impact of these policies lasts generations. Some formal and informal mechanisms of residential segregation remain active today.

There are many examples from social research that find mortgage lenders deny home loans to Black people and people of color at higher rates than their White counterparts, or if a loan is extended, offering a higher interest rate, which results in overall higher cost of homeownership.[53] There are myriad studies indicating realtors steer people toward different communities based on perceived racial or ethnic group membership, which serves to maintain racial segregation in cities or communities. These factors are strongly tied to the persistent and pernicious state of residential segregation in the United States. When President Lyndon B. Johnson signed the Civil Rights Act of 1964, he struck down Jim Crow laws and made explicit segregation of spaces illegal under the law. But, residential segregation has hardly changed in the 60 years since.[54]

Even as the country has become more diverse, most people today live in segregated neighborhoods in the United States like they did in the middle of the 20th century. In 1960, White people represented 88.6 percent of the total U.S. population, compared to 80 percent in 1980, 69.1 percent in 2000, and 57.8 percent in 2020.[55-57] The share of the total U.S. population composed of people of other races, ethnicities, and multiple races and ethnicities has grown. The three fastest-growing populations in the past two decades in the United States have been among Hispanic or Latino, Asian, and Black populations, followed by people of two or more races and Alaska Native or American Indian populations.[58]

While the United States has become more diverse, neighborhoods have not diversified nearly as quickly. The book *Cycle of Segregation* (2017) was co-authored by Dr. Maria Krysan of the University of Illinois at Chicago and Dr. Kyle Crowder of the University of Washington. The authors note that levels of residential segregation have declined over time in the United States, but the declines have been reasonably small and slow.[59] In their book, the authors detail the many factors which contribute to residential segregation. Specifically, the history of residential segregation has resulted in differential access to education and job opportunities for different communities. This, in turn, impacts the composition of one's social network and community ties.

Think back to the example of "legacy status" in admission to selective universities. Under a legacy admissions system, if your parent went to a selective university, then you are more likely to gain admission to that university than someone of equal caliber who does not have legacy status. That parent may also have extensive alumni and professional networks that can help you land a desirable internship or a job. These are examples of the benefits of having high levels of social capital. **Social capital** refers to the ability of an individual to obtain resources or valuable assets (which may include information) from their social networks.

Now, flip the same idea around. If your parents did not attend university, they cannot help you gain entry to that university through legacy status. If your parents do not have a wide professional network because they were shut out of professional opportunities, they cannot call on their professional network to help you get a job, for example. This is an example of the detriments of having low levels of social capital. Even if legally enforced residential segregation is no longer legal, the ways social networks and community context influence one's life course opportunities remain tied to that history.

These examples are limiting because they are grounded on the assumption that folks want a certain life; a White-looking life. But we must also discuss how people like living among communities that understand and accept them. Fear of discrimination and harassment, plus limited access to culturally specific places of worship, services, food markets or restaurants, and people who speak your language are all reasons why people may prefer to reside in single-race dominant neighborhoods or ethnic enclaves. Think about how and why the absence of those protections and access to culturally specific resources may be absent in other areas. Consider that while the institutional enforcement of residential segregation is no longer legal, the social mechanisms which drive segregation are still very much alive.

An example of residential segregation's ubiquity today comes from Katt Williams's 2018 Netflix special *Great America*. Williams (born in Cincinnati, Ohio, 1971) performs his special at the Florida Theater in Jacksonville, Florida. Comedians often start sets on the road with some riffs on the city in which they are performing. It helps connect with the audience. For specials, which are intended for wide (national, and even international) audiences, however, comics tend to perform more generic material. Perhaps they will give a quick nod to their location, but that is about it. Williams, however, opened his special with twelve minutes of jokes about Jacksonville. *Twelve minutes*.[60]

Williams' Jacksonville jokes covered topics such as the names of local neighborhoods. He riffs on a concept about how neighborhoods like Washington Heights, Cleveland Arms, and Eureka Gardens all sound like they should have their own scary television shows. His jokes killed. Not just for the live Florida theater audience, but for viewers of the special across the world. The reason it was so successful was that you do not need to know the ins-and-outs of Jacksonville, specifically, to understand the context underlying Williams' jokes. Residential segregation is so pervasive in this country, no one in the streaming audiences misunderstands the references. Remember that comedy rests on shared understanding. Audiences understand the markers of residential segregation well enough to laugh at jokes centered on the neighborhoods of Jacksonville.

The segregation of people in cities, and the resultant differences in neighborhood experiences of safety and comfort, are largely universal. We just talked about the causes of residential segregation, but what about its consequences? For one, residential segregation has a significant impact on health. One of the strongest predictors of one's health in the United States is a person's zip code.[61] Even within the same city. The life expectancy for residents of Chicago, Illinois, for example, is 77.3 years overall, but varies by 30.1 years depending on residents' neighborhood.[62] *Over thirty years.* In Jacksonville, Florida, the life expectancy is 76.2 years overall but varies by 25.3 years depending on residents' neighborhood.

Cities with large variations in life expectancy across neighborhoods like Chicago or Jacksonville are cities that tend to be more racially segregated than are cities with lower life expectancy variation. Neighborhoods with lower life expectancies tend to be composed largely of racial and ethnic minority populations who have more limited access to resources which afford good health, such as educational and economic opportunities; clean air and water; safe housing; safe neighborhoods in which to exercise or play; reliable modes of transportation; and access to quality, affordable, and culturally relevant healthcare services. Further, residents of these communities tend to experience higher levels of chronic stressors resulting from financial instability, concerns of safety, and experiences with racism and discrimination. Chronic stress is an important determinant of one's mental and physical health outcomes.[63]

Social determinants of health are the social, cultural, and environmental factors that influence our mental and physical health.[64] Examples of social determinants of health include safety of housing, air quality, violence exposure, experiences of bias and discrimination, access to nutritious (and culturally appropriate) foods, and safe places to exercise, as well as well-paying, safe, and insurance-providing job opportunities.

These are often described as **upstream factors** related to health. Upstream factors come before the onset of illness. If corrected, upstream factors can help lower incident cases of illness. Think environmental pollution. Unsafe air quality can lead to negative health conditions such as emphysema.

Treating the resultant acute illness is a **downstream factor** of health. But if we prevent environmental pollution or remedy existing environmental pollution, we are treating the upstream factor. By correcting the upstream factor, we may prevent the onset of emphysema entirely.

Racism has a direct impact on physical health, mental health, and overall well-being. Direct links between racism and health exist through avenues such as racially fueled violence and the body's stress response following experiences of racism and discrimination. The experience of stress, like that which results from experiences of racism and discrimination, directly impacts physical and mental health through the body's stress response system. The stress response process includes systems such as the autonomic nervous systems and hypothalamo-pituitary-adrenal (HPA) axis, which adapt to enable individuals to respond to challenges through physiological changes.[65] The body's ability to maintain homeostasis through responding to changing environmental demands is referred to as *allostasis*.

Deregulated hormones and associated responses of excessive allostatic load, such as inflammation, cause "wear and tear" on the body.[66] Stress researchers highlight that allostatic load leads to dysregulation in several systems within the body, which can impact the brain and a wide array of bodily organs. As a result, repeated cycles of allostasis deteriorate physical and mental health,[67] and cumulative stress exposure is posited to account for a large share of the physical health disparities observed across sociodemographic groups.[68]

Indeed, racism is stressful and physically and mentally harmful. There are multiple levels through which the impact of racism operates. Racism is an important social determinant of health.[69] To understand how, let us turn to The Gardner's Tale. The Gardener's Tale is an allegory on racism grounded in a gardening metaphor. This allegory was written and taught by Dr. Camara Jones, who serves as Research Director on Social Determinants of Health and Equity within the Division of Adult and Community Health at the Centers for Disease Control and Prevention. The three levels of racism illustrated by Jones are internalized, personally mediated, and institutional.

Internalized racism occurs when an individual begins to believe the negative stereotypes and ideologies perpetuated about their race, ethnicity, or culture which are propagated by the White dominant society. Internalized racism can lead to low self-worth and feeling as though the negative treatment one experiences because of their race is "deserved." As such, internalized racism serves to maintain the status quo by forcing Black people and people of color into accepting oppression.

Personally mediated racism, also referred to as **interpersonal racism**, occurs when an individual holds negative views about a group based on stereotypes or biases and allow that to impact their perceptions or interactions with members of that group. This can manifest as avoiding members of the racial group out of fear (e.g., crossing the street to avoid someone), making unkind or uninformed comments about one's abilities or background (e.g., about whether someone speaks English based upon their race), calling them slurs, or engaging in physical violence, among others. Personally mediated is the most understood form of racism (compared to internalized and institutional racism). Despite it being commonly understood as a concept, the omnipresence and perniciousness of personally mediated racism is not easily understood by those who are not impacted by it daily.

Before I define institutional racism, I will now walk you through Jones' allegory. As you move through this section, consider parallels between The Gardener's Tale and the section you just read on residential segregation. Note the examples of internalized and personally mediated racism embedded within the example.

In The Gardener's Tale, Jones asks us to imagine a gardener. The gardener has two flowerpots. One of the pots has rich, nutrient-dense soil, while the other pot has rocky, nutrient-depleted soil. The gardener also has two packets of seeds; one that produces red flowers and one that produces pink flowers. The gardener prefers red flowers, so she plants the red seeds in the nutrient-dense soil, and plants the pink seeds in the nutrient-depleted soil. And, lo and behold, the red flowers grow tall and vibrant. The pink flowers struggle. Many of the pink seeds never sprout, and those that do survive grow to be short and weak.

The red and pink flowers propagate by dropping their seeds into the respective soils. The red flowers drop their seeds into rich soil while the pink flowers drop their seeds into depleted soil. The cycle of birth and death begins again, then again, and again. After ten years, as the gardener looks over the garden. It is full of healthy and vibrant red flowers, and weak and sad pink flowers. The gardener, seeing this scene, feels *validated* in her preference for red flowers over pink.[70]

Separating the seeds into different pots with different opportunities for growth and survival represents institutional racism. **Institutional racism** refers to the oppressive conditions placed on racial and ethnic minorities through the routine functions of social institutions and social structures.[71] This color-based segregation, which happens upstream, determines the richness of the environment in which the red and pink seeds live. Consider how this relates to our discussion of residential segregation – including differential access to opportunities, wealth accumulation, safety, and health – and how those continue to propagate across time and generations. The continuation of institutional racism survives when the pink flowers are blamed for being shorter and weaker than the red flowers. The gardener sees their lack of height and vibrancy as inherent faults, not the products of living in a deprived environment.

Summary

This chapter discussed the concept of White privilege and how the lack of diverse perspective among media executives perpetuates the same stories being told again and again. In this chapter, we used the television series *Insecure* and *Atlanta* to highlight how and why having ownership over one's own story is important for creators and audiences alike, and how these examples relate to sociological concepts including intersectionality, triple consciousness, and cultural appropriation.

This chapter used comedic examples highlighting sociological concepts, including code switching and residential segregation. These concepts help explain how the status quo is maintained over time through unequal access to opportunities. In the next chapter, we will apply similar sociological concepts to the examination of health and illness. We will discuss how health and illness are socially defined and discuss how those definitions evolve over time and use comedic examples to highlight how individuals engage in impression management (often to avoid stigma) when dealing with ill health.

Discussion Questions

7-1: From a critical theory perspective, what are the societal motivations for, and consequences of, Carl Winslow's reaction to his son Eddie's interactions with the police as it was portrayed in *Family Matters*?

7-2: Compare and contrast the structural processes which led to the first season of *SNL* being primarily staffed by White writers and actors, with the legacy admissions policies for college admissions to selective institutions.

7-3: What parallels do you see between (a) media executives defaulting to tropes, models, and creators they have relied on in the past, with (b) the long-standing continuation of residential segregation?

7-4: Explain how the television terms high-concept and/or low-concept relate to postmodernism.

7-5: How does the concept of pluralism relate to cultural appropriation and cultural omnivores?

7-6: Consider how pressure from network executives to fit into a specific mold – such as experiences noted by Issa Rae and Donald Glover – places limits on their creative freedom and higher stakes on their success or failure. How does this relate to White privilege and institutional racism?

7-7: Discuss the pilot episode of *Insecure* through the lens of symbolic interactionism. Can you interpret the interaction between Issa and her coworkers regarding the term "on fleek" using Erving Goffman's dramaturgical theory of self? What do Issa's experiences teach audiences about triple consciousness?

7-8: With a classmate, describe how code switching relates to Goffman's concept of impression management. Discuss other sociological concepts to which code switching is related. For example, consider what code switching says about social norms, symbolic interactionism, presentation of self, racism (personally mediated, internalized, and institutional), and cultural appropriation.

7-9: Discuss with a classmate the existence and/or extent of <u>residential segregation</u> in a city you have lived in or visited. Consider what, if anything, the sociological concepts discussed in this chapter taught you about your own surroundings.

7-10: With a classmate, discuss how <u>personally mediated</u>, <u>internalized</u>, and <u>institutional racism</u> work together to maintain the status quo and continue the subjugation of people of color.

Notes

1 Bonilla-Silva, E. (2001). *White Supremacy and Racism in the Post-Civil Rights Era*. Lynne Rienner Publishers.
2 Hunt, D. (2017). *Race in the Writers' Room: How Hollywood Whitewashes the Stories that Shape America*. https://hollywood.colorofchange.org/wp-content/uploads/2019/03/COC_Hollywood_Race_Report.pdf
3 Giorgis, H. (2021, September 13). *"The Unwritten Rules of Black TV."* The Atlantic. https://www.theatlantic.com/press-releases/archive/2021/09/october-2021-issue-press-release/620054/
4 Peisner, D. (2018). *Homey don't play that!: The story of In Living Color and the black comedy revolution.*
5 Du Bois, W. E. B. (1903). *The Souls of Black Folk*. A. C. McClurg & Co.
6 Welang, N. N. (2018). Triple consciousness: The reimagination of Black female identities in contemporary American culture. *Open Cultural Studies*. https://doi.org/10.1515/culture-2018-0027
7 Triple-Consciousness: The Souls of Intersectional Folx. (2017, July 31). *Young Invincibles*. https://younginvincibles.org/triple-consciousness-souls-intersectional-folx/
8 Spanos, B. (2021, April 15). Issa Rae Can't Stop, Won't Stop. *Rolling Stone*. https://www.rollingstone.com/tv/tv-features/issa-rae-insecure-hbo-1155867/
9 Bonilla-Silva, 2001.
10 Morgan, D. F. (2020). *Laughing to Keep from Dying: African American Satire in the Twenty-First Century*. University of Illinois Press.
11 Crenshaw, K. (n.d.). *Demarginalizing the Intersection of Race and Sex: A Black Feminist Critique of Antidiscrimination Doctrine, Feminist Theory and Antiracist Politics. 1989*(1), 31.
12 Krefting, R. (2014). *All Joking Aside: American Humor and Its Discontents*. Johns Hopkins University Press.
13 Morgan, 2020.
14 Framke, C. (2016, October 7). *"I just wanted it to be a regular story about black people": Issa Rae on creating and starring in HBO's Insecure*. Vox. https://www.vox.com/culture/2016/10/7/13176104/issa-rae-insecure-hbo-interview
15 Sims, D. (2016, October 8). *"Insecure" Is Quietly Revolutionary*. The Atlantic. https://www.theatlantic.com/entertainment/archive/2016/10/insecure-hbo-review/503363/
16 Du Bois, W. E. B. (1899). *The Philadelphia Negro*. University of Pennsylvania Press.
17 McCluney, C. L., Robotham, K., Lee, S., Smith, R., & Durkee, M. (2019, November 15). The Costs of Code-Switching. *Harvard Business Review*. https://hbr.org/2019/11/the-costs-of-codeswitching
18 Riley, B. (Director). (2018). *Sorry to Bother You*. https://www.imdb.com/title/tt5688932/
19 Matsoukas, M. (Director). (2016b, October 23). *Insecure: "Racist as Fuck."* https://www.imdb.com/title/tt5730706/

20 Bastién, A. J. (2016, October 24). 'Insecure' Season 1, Episode 3: Code Switching. *The New York Times*. https://www.nytimes.com/2016/10/23/arts/television/insecure-season-1-episode-3-recap.html

21 Katsha, H. (2022, January 6). *What Black Women Loved About Insecure: "I Felt Seen From The Very First Episode."* Huffington Post UK Life. https://www.huffingtonpost.co.uk/entry/insecure-documentary-why-black-women-love-the-show_uk_61d454d5e4b061afe3aaf3db; Terrell, K. (2017, July 21). *HBO's Insecure and the Importance of Black Female Friendship on Television | Vogue*. https://www.vogue.com/article/insecure-issa-rae-yvonne-orji-black-female-friendship-onscreen

22 Welang, 2018.

23 Matsoukas, M. (Director). (2016a, October 9). *Insecure: "Insecure as Fuck."* https://www.imdb.com/title/tt5038246/

24 Katz, H. (2021). The role of executive coaching in managing organizations. *Human Service Organizations: Management, Leadership & Governance*, 45(3), 177–183. https://doi.org/10.1080/23303131.2021.1915439

25 Matsoukas, 2016a.

26 Goffman, E. (1990). *The Presentation of Self in Everyday Life* (1. Anchor Books edition, revised edition). Anchor Books.

27 Matsoukas, 2016b.

28 Goffman, 1990.

29 Papallo, J., & DeWald, M. (2016, December 13). Addressing Cultural Appropriation in the Classroom: Tools and Resources. *Education Week*. https://www.edweek.org/teaching-learning/opinion-addressing-cultural-appropriation-in-the-classroom-tools-and-resources/2016/12

30 Collins, P. H. (1990). *Black Feminist Thought: Knowledge, Consciousness, and the Politics of Empowerment*. Hyman; Ritzer, G. (2013). *Introduction to Sociology*. SAGE.

31 Young, D. (2020, December 6). *Black Hair Is Called 'Ghetto' Until Proved Fashionable*. https://www.essence.com/beauty/black-hair-cultural-appropriation-fashionable/

32 Natural Hair Discrimination FAQ. (2016). *NAACP Legal Defense and Educational Fund*. https://www.naacpldf.org/natural-hair-discrimination/

33 Diaz, J. (2022, March 18). The House passes the CROWN Act, a bill banning discrimination on race-based hairdos. *NPR*. https://www.npr.org/2022/03/18/1087661765/house-votes-crown-act-discrimination-hair-style

34 "Natural Hair Discrimination FAQ," 2016.

35 Garcia, S. (2018, May 14). *The Durag, Explained—The New York Times*. https://www.nytimes.com/2018/05/14/style/durag-solange-met-gala.html

36 "Natural Hair Discrimination FAQ," 2016.

37 Payne, T. (2018, June 21). *Kim Kardashian West Responds to the Backlash Over Her Braids | Glamour*. https://www.glamour.com/story/kim-kardashian-braids-explanation

38 Young, 2020.

39 Bravo, J. (Director). (2016). *Atlanta: "Juneteenth."* Hulu. https://www.imdb.com/title/tt5853556/

40 Browne, R. (2016, August 23). *Donald Glover's Community*. Vulture. https://www.vulture.com/2016/08/donald-glover-atlanta.html

41 Wappel, D. (2021, September 21). *High Concept vs. Low Concept: What's the Difference?* Arc Studio. https://www.arcstudiopro.com/blog/high-concept-vs-low-concept-whats-the-difference

42 Seimetz, A. (Director). (2018, March 22). Atlanta: "Helen." In *Atlanta*.

43 Berg, A. (Director). (2013, January 8). New Girl: "The Cabin." In *New Girl*.

44 Russo, A. (Director). (2011, September 28). Happy Endings: "Blax, Snake, Home." In *Happy Endings*.

45 This idea is reminiscent of Jerry's summer camp friend, dubbed "Summer George," from the *Seinfeld* episode "The Junk Mail."

46 Glover, D. (Director). (2016, October 11). Atlanta: "B.A.N." In *Atlanta*.

47 Rachel Dolezal was the president of the Spokane, Washington chapter of the National Association for the Advancement of Colored People (NAACP). She resigned in 2015 following national controversy over her racial identity. Dolezal identified as Black despite being born to White parents, sparking outrage about potential fraud, racism, and appropriation. McGreal, C. (2015, December 13). Rachel Dolezal: "I wasn't identifying as black to upset people. I was being me." *The Guardian*. https://www.theguardian.com/us-news/2015/dec/13/rachel-dolezal-i-wasnt-identifying-as-black-to-upset-people-i-was-being-me

48 *U.S. Census Bureau QuickFacts: Atlanta City, Georgia*. (2021). U.S. Census Bureau. https://www.census.gov/quickfacts/atlantacitygeorgia

49 Massey, D. S., & Denton, N. A. (1988). The dimensions of residential segregation. *Social Forces, 67*(2), 281–315. https://doi.org/10.2307/2579183

50 Frey, W. H., & Myers, D. (2000, Census). *Segregation: Dissimilarity Indices.* CensusScope. https://censusscope.org/us/m520/chart_dissimilarity.html

51 Mitchell, B., Franco, J., & Richardson, J. (2018). *HOLC "redlining" maps: The persistent structure of segregation and economic inequality.* https://doi.org/10.13140/RG.2.2.21841.48486

52 Jackson. (2021, August 17). *What Is Redlining? - The New York Times.* https://www.nytimes.com/2021/08/17/realestate/what-is-redlining.html

53 Mitchell, Franco, & Richardson, 2018.

54 Loh, T. H., Coes, C., & Buthe, B. (2020, December 16). Separate and unequal: Persistent residential segregation is sustaining racial and economic injustice in the U.S. *Brookings.* https://www.brookings.edu/essay/trend-1-separate-and-unequal-neighborhoods-are-sustaining-racial-and-economic-injustice-in-the-us/

55 *1960 Census of the Population: Supplementary Reports: Race of the Population of the United States, by States: 1960* (PC(S1)-10). (1961). U.S. Census Bureau. https://www.census.gov/library/publications/1961/dec/pc-s1-10.html

56 Frey, W. H. (2020, July 1). *The nation is diversifying even faster than predicted, according to new census data.* https://www.brookings.edu/research/new-census-data-shows-the-nation-is-diversifying-even-faster-than-predicted/

57 Schneider, M. (2021, August 12). *Census shows US is diversifying, white population shrinking | AP News.* https://apnews.com/article/census-2020-house-elections-4ee80e72846c151aa41a808b06d975ea

58 Frey, 2020.

59 Williams, A., & Emamdjomeh, A. (2018, May 10). *Segregation map: America's cities 50 years after the Fair Housing Act of 1968—Washington Post.* The Washington Post. https://www.washingtonpost.com/graphics/2018/national/segregation-us-cities/

60 Small, L. (Director). (2018, January 16). *Katt Williams "Great America."* North American Entertainment.

61 Roeder, A. (2014, August 4). *Zip code better predictor of health than genetic code.* News. https://www.hsph.harvard.edu/news/features/zip-code-better-predictor-of-health-than-genetic-code/

62 Ducharme, J., & Wolfson, E. (2019, June 17). *How Your Zip Code Could Affect Your Lifespan | Time.* https://time.com/5608268/zip-code-health/

63 Phelan, J. C., & Link, B. G. (2015). Is racism a fundamental cause of inequalities in health? *Annual Review of Sociology, 41*(1), 311–330. https://doi.org/10.1146/annurev-soc-073014-112305

64 Braveman, P., & Gottlieb, L. (2014). The social determinants of health: It's time to consider the causes of the causes. *Public Health Reports, 129*(Suppl 2), 19–31. https://www.ncbi.nlm.nih.gov/pmc/articles/PMC3863696/

65 Nurius, P., Uehara, E., & Zatzick, D. (2013). Intersection of stress, social disadvantage, and life course processes: Reframing trauma and mental health. *American Journal of Psychiatric Rehabilitation*, 16. https://doi.org/10.1080/15487768.2013.789688

66 Hawkley, L. C., Lavelle, L. A., Berntson, G. G., & Cacioppo, J. T. (2011). Mediators of the relationship between socioeconomic status and allostatic load in the Chicago Health, Aging, and Social Relations Study (CHASRS). *Psychophysiology*, 48(8), 1134–1145. https://doi.org/10.1111/j.1469-8986.2011.01185.x

67 Nurius, Uehara, & Zatzick, 2013.

68 Brown, T. H., Richardson, L. J., Hargrove, T. W., & Thomas, C. S. (2016). Using multiple-hierarchy stratification and life course approaches to understand health inequalities: The intersecting consequences of race, gender, SES, and age. *Journal of Health and Social Behavior*, 57(2), 200–222. https://doi.org/10.1177/0022146516645165

69 Lee, H., & Hicken, M. T. (2018). Racism and the health of White Americans. *The American Journal of Bioethics*, 18(10), 21–23. https://doi.org/10.1080/15265161.2018.1513607; Phelan & Link, 2015.

70 Jones, C. P. (2000). Levels of racism: A theoretic framework and a gardener's tale. *American Journal of Public Health*, 90(8), 1212–1215. https://www.ncbi.nlm.nih.gov/pmc/articles/PMC1446334/

71 Bonilla-Silva, 2001.

8   Sociology of Health and Illness

This chapter explains how we socially define health and illness. Using comedic examples alongside historical evolutions of medical classifications, this chapter showcases how the definition of illness evolves, how society stigmatizes illness, and how individuals engage in impression management when dealing with ill health. This chapter uses examples from standup and television to show how mental health is discussed in comedy and analyzes the veracity of the *sad clown paradox* – a purported phenomenon in which people assume comedians are deeply depressed people – using a sociological approach. This chapter draws on the contributions of symbolic interactionism, gender as performance, stigma visibility, feminist theory, postmodernism and Jean Baudrillard, critical theory, and Erving Goffman. Concepts include medicalization, constructionist theories of deviance, interactionism, labeling theory, network burden, falseness, repressiveness, and invisible disabilities. This chapter returns to sociological explanations of deviance to discuss illness and its social consequences. From there, the chapter delves into a discussion on performed authenticity as it relates to mental health.

Physical Health and Stigma Visibility with Tig Notaro

In the prior chapter, we used The Gardener's Tale to describe how social forces – specifically, segregation – impact one's health and self-perception. In this chapter, we expand on those concepts as we discuss the sociological analysis of health and illness. Comedians and their works provide a great entry point for understanding how mental and physical health become pieces of our self-identity. Definitions of health and illness impact the way the world sees us, labels us, and allows us to move through the world. In this section, we will tie sociological concepts related to physical health, gender performance, and stigma visibility to the comedy of Tig Notaro.

Symbolic interactionism refers to how individuals interact with one another based upon shared symbols.[1] Breast tissue is common among all humans; yet, breasts have become a symbol of adult womanhood.[2] Breasts are a symbol. Consider, now, how the visual appearance of breasts relates to "doing gender." Recall, **doing gender** refers to the idea that gender is not a biological construct

DOI: 10.4324/9781003469537-9

but is socially constructed and must be performed.[3] We discussed earlier how the performance of gender includes factors such as wearing clothes and engaging in behaviors which are socially defined as "masculine" or "feminine." Such clothing and behaviors are symbols. Society has also assigned meaning to body parts. Breasts, hips, hands, jaw lines, and height are all examples of body parts which have gendered meanings associated with them.

Breast cancer is the most common cancer for women in the United States aside from skin cancers, and 13 percent of women develop breast cancer during their lifetimes.[4] Thirty-three percent of patients diagnosed with stage I or II breast cancer receive a mastectomy, which is the complete removal of breast tissue. Patients may undergo a single mastectomy (one breast) or double mastectomy (both breasts). Yet, views of women's bodies do not necessarily take this into account. Regardless of health status, women are often expected to have breasts and styled hair (both of which can be lost while battling cancer).[5]

Not all mastectomized patients undergo breast reconstruction surgery; about sixty-three percent do.[6] The utility of using breasts as a symbol of womanhood is shaky. Breast cancer survivors who identity as women have to grapple with how to present themselves as "women" without this socially important symbol of womanhood.[7]

There is potential for stigma and harassment if there is misalignment between one's gender performance and biological sex.[8] Let us define some terms. **Sex** is assignment of a biological classification, usually assigned at birth, based primarily on reproductive organs. **Gender identity** is one's own sense of their gender and the labels they attach to it. These may change over time. **Gender expression** is how one socially presents their gender.[9] As this relates to breasts, consider how the social experiences of mastectomized women may compare and contrast to the experience of trans people for whom bodily symbols do not align with their gender identity. (Note: these are not mutually exclusive categories. Trans people get breast cancer, too.)

Sociologist Erving Goffman makes a distinction between **discredited individuals** (those who cannot conceal what brings them stigma, like someone is visibly physically disabled) compared to **discreditable individuals** (those who can conceal their stigma, like someone suffering from depression or someone with a stigmatized sexual identity).[10] Discreditable individuals often feel pressure to hide the stigmatized parts of their experiences or identities.

Sociologists Lisa R. Miller of Indiana University and Eric Anthony Grollman of the University of Richmond extend upon Goffman's discredited/discreditable individuals framework into the realm of physical health. They refer to the degree to which someone holds a visible stigmatized status as **stigma visibility**.[11] They posit that individuals with greater stigma visibility face more discrimination and hostile treatment relative to individuals who can better conceal their stigmatized status. They argue that non-conformance to gender norms is a form of stigma visibility. For example, trans individuals, non-binary individuals, or women who have undergone mastectomies (without subsequent breast reconstruction surgeries) fall into this group. We can use comedy to break down the idea that one's status as a "woman" or a "man" is biologically defined by bodily features which hold socially symbolic meaning.

To consider how biological features are tied to social norms of sex or gender status, let us turn to comedian Tig Notaro (born in Jackson, Mississippi, 1971). Notaro made headlines with her 2015 HBO special *Boyish Girl Interrupted*. Notaro is known for her deadpan style and flat, calculated delivery, which she applies to both silly and serious topics. Those silly and serious topics are often sandwiched together. In *Boyish Girl Interrupted*, after material about getting a chocolate ice cream mustache in Las Vegas, trying to hire a Santa Claus impersonator, and her girlfriend meeting her family in Mississippi, Notaro confesses to the crowd she had been diagnosed with bilateral breast cancer and underwent a double mastectomy to remove all her breast tissue. After her material about breast cancer and her double mastectomy, Notaro takes her shirt off. She performs the rest of her special topless and does so without commentary about her (now naked) chest.[12]

Notaro's special was novel for the way it usurped traditional views of women's bodies. Traditionally held views of sex and gender in the United States consider breasts part of what it means to be a "woman." Notaro talks about this in *Boyish Girl Interrupted* when she tells a story of going through security at an airport. Even before she had her double mastectomy, Notaro was used to being mistakenly identified as man. But, as Notaro said in her bit, that misgendering was amplified after her surgery (she did not have reconstructive surgery).

As Notaro explains in this bit, a TSA agent at the airport decides Notaro needed a pat down for extra security. So he calls for a "female assist." This means that the guard was calling for another guard (a woman) to conduct the pat down for Notaro (the female traveler). Notaro then describes how the female TSA agent began patting her down and was surprised and confused when she did not feel any breasts underneath Notaro's shirt. The female agent then walks over to have a conversation with the original TSA agent. Notaro could overhear them discussing whether or Notaro was, indeed, a woman. Notaro tells this story with her signature, hilarious wit. In his joke, Notaro highlights the question: Is she still a woman without breasts? Certainly. The butt of the joke is the TSA agent, not Notaro. By removing her shirt, Notaro challenged the idea that she needs to be ashamed of her breastless chest or that it changes anything about her as a person or as a woman.

Consider how Notaro's gender presentation fits into the "doing gender" framework. Notaro presents as more masculine than is proscribed by traditional gender norms. She keeps her hair short, wears minimal (or no) makeup, and wears clothing that may be considered gender neutral or masculine. For the TSA agent, the combination of these symbols – hair, limited makeup, clothing, no breasts – caused confusion. Consider if a woman who presented as more traditionally "feminine" was in the same position. If a woman with long hair, a face of makeup, and a traditionally feminine outfit presented with no breasts – how do you think the TSA agent would have responded? If you think the TSA agent would have understood this person was a "woman," regardless of the breasts, think about how that relates to your understanding of gender. Gender is a combination of symbols. Breasts are one symbol, but they are not the only symbol. Notaro challenges the idea that changes to her physical form make her any different as a performer or as a person than she was before the bilateral mastectomy.

The "shock" of seeing Notaro perform with her shirt off challenges the audience to reckon with that shock. *Why* is it so shocking and novel to see a breastless woman on stage? Notaro offered no apology and no explanation. This lack of apology for her body is novel in a society in which women's personhood can often be defined by their physical forms. So who is Notaro without breasts? As her performance in *Boyish Girl Interrupted* dares audiences to realize, Notaro is the same person she always was.

Notaro made it okay to talk about her cancer, but also gave space for her to be the same Tig Notaro her fans have always known. She is not the butt of the joke; in fact, there is no joke at all when it comes to her breasts. The hope is that anyone watching *Boyish Girl Interrupted* who, like Notaro, has scars on their chest, will see Notaro perform topless and that act will make them feel more normal, accepted, and like life post-surgery is going to be okay. The special was nominated for an Emmy Award in 2016 and the special's album recording was nominated for a Grammy Award in 2017. Comedy allows comedians to talk about difficult subjects in certain ways that may otherwise be off-limits.

Grief with Eugene Mirman

Boyish Girl Interrupted is a great example of how features of one's physical form – such as breasts – are tied to one's sex or gender identity in the United States. Beyond this point, Notaro's special highlights how comedy can be used to break the silence around difficult or taboo subjects like cancer, death, and grief, and to breathe and laugh through them.

Notaro is not the only comedian who has discussed cancer openly on stage. There are many. To name just two: Comedian Marina Franklin (born in Chicago, Illinois, 1986) also talked about her breast cancer diagnosis on stage, and comedian Eugene Mirman (born in Moscow, Russia, 1974, but was largely raised in Lexington, Massachusetts) talked about supporting his wife through treatment of breast cancer, though he ultimately lost her to it.

Mirman provides an example of what laughing through grief looks like. Mirman is an absurdist alternative comedian. He created the Eugene Mirman Comedy Festival, which featured alternative comedians and ran from 2008 to 2017. The 2019 documentary, titled *It Started as a Joke*, details the festival's history and was filmed during the final years of the festival's run.[13]

The documentary introduces Mirman's family and shows his wife, Katie, living with a terminal breast cancer diagnosis. Audiences of the comedy festivals and the documentary showcasing them see Mirman reckon with his wife's terminal diagnosis on stage while developing his material year after year as her condition worsens. Mirman's material grapples with his own grief and attempts to provide a release valve for others. In one of his bits that develops throughout each year of the festival, Mirman workshops cancer sympathy cards on stage. He personally found that commercially available sympathy cards never accurately reflected his grief.

The cards Mirman created, however, were weird and whimsical. As an example: one of his cards read: [front] "Terminal illness?" [inside] "More like bus terminal!" (Mirman, 2019). As Mirman reads the card's inner text, you can see that the surprise suspended the audience from sadness, even if for just a moment. After presenting that card, Mirman laughs. Through his chuckles, he admits to the audience: "That doesn't make any sense. I'm just at a complete loss and very, very sad" (Mirman, 2019). It is a public display of grief, an expression of trust, and a moment of connection between Mirman and everyone watching him. Consider if this type of public display of grief would be considered "normal" or "acceptable" in other professions. Consider how the role of comedian may have granted Mirman space to process his emotions – with sadness and whimsy in front of strangers – in ways not afforded by other professions and spaces.

The Sad Clown Paradox

Notaro and Mirman bare their chests onstage (in Notaro's case, literally) as they talk about dark times in their lives. An old joke goes: "A comedian walks into a psychologist's office. The psychologist says: 'Lie down and tell me everything you know.' I haven't been able to get an appointment since. He's been doing my act in Philadelphia."[14] The joke pokes fun at the commonly held belief that comedians are often sad and depressed. This idea that those tasked with making us laugh are harboring deep sadness is known as the **sad clown paradox**. The sad clown paradox, in most people's understanding, stems from the idea that depressed people are more likely to enter the profession of comedy than nondepressed people. Something about experiencing depression draws one to comedy.

In social statistics, this is what is known as a causal pathway. From this theory, a social statistician would draw the sad clown paradox using a diagram like Figure 8.1.

As shown in Figure 8.1, the sad clown paradox posits a **causal pathway** in which one factor (depression) leads to another factor (becoming a professional comedian). This belief is propped up by the many examples of famous comedians who suffered at the hands of depression (Marc Maron), anxiety (Aparna Nancherla), addiction (Robin Williams), eating disorders (Gilda Radner), self-harm (Naomi Ekperigin), bipolar disorder (Taylor Tomlinson), or other mental health disorders. Sadly, some of these comedians ultimately died from suicide or overdose because of their condition. Robin Williams, Freddie Prinze,

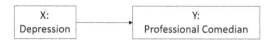

Figure 8.1 Causal Pathway Applied to the Sad Clown Paradox

and Richard Jeni died of suicide, while John Belushi and Chris Farley died of overdose.[15]

There is not much evidence to suggest there is a direct causal pathway between depression and becoming a professional comedian. So let us think like a sociological researcher. What are some other possible ways to understand the sad clown paradox? Let us take a look at social norms. Instead of the idea that people experiencing depression are more likely to enter professional comedy than nondepressed people (the causal pathway, discussed above), let us consider if there are different social norms within the field of professional comedy which may explain the sad clown paradox.

As it relates to social norms, observations of the sad clown paradox may exist because comedians have the platform and ability to discuss their mental health struggles in ways not afforded to people in most professions. Often, people only feel comfortable discussing their mental health struggles in the back stage due to stigma and norms of professionalism in many people's workplaces. Comedy as performed in standup or in television and movies has different norms than, say, working as an attorney. Your attorney may be depressed, but they may not tell you about it. Your favorite comedian, however, may put their depression at the center of their performance. Consider Eugene Mirman, discussed in the prior section.

In this case, it is not that experiencing depression is leading someone to a specific profession (comedy). Instead, one's profession impacts whether someone experiencing depression openly talks about their experiences of depression. This is called a **moderated pathway**. From this theory, a social statistician would draw the sad clown paradox using a diagram like Figure 8.2.

As shown in Figure 8.2, the sad clown paradox posits a **moderated pathway**, in which the causal pathway between one factor (depression) and another factor (talking about depression), is moderated by a third factor (whether someone is a professional comedian). While this is looking at one's profession (specifically, whether they are a professional comedian), you can imagine this pathway being mediated by a host of other factors – including one's age, gender, culture, and religion, among others.

The moderated pathway makes sense but let us not stop there. Remember, the scientific method challenges us to ask the right questions and be confident in our study design. It can be helpful to brainstorm different frameworks, vet their pros and cons – and possibly combine them – before moving forward with your study. To practice this one more time, let us consider another

Figure 8.2 Moderated Pathway Applied to the Sad Clown Paradox

pathway which may help us understand the sad clown paradox. To get some ideas, let us review some literature on the relationship between professional comedians' intelligence and their ability to turn dark feelings and experiences into quality comedic output.

A seminal study conducted by psychotherapist Samuel S. Janus in 1975 is oft quoted by scholars when discussing the sad clown paradox.[16] Janus' study analyzed the link between comedians' use of humor with personality traits. His data came from interviews and psychological tests conducted with fifty-five nationally known, professional comedians who had been in the profession for a minimum of ten years. The sample consisted of fifty-one men and four women. On these subjects, Janus performed an IQ test (Wechsler Adult Intelligence Scale), personality assessments (Machover Human Figure Drawing Test, graphological analysis), and questions pertaining to earliest memories and recurring dreams.[17]

Janus' sample had above-average intelligence (average IQ score in the sample was 138) and a majority (80 percent) had been in some form of psychotherapy. Janus' findings indicate that comedy provides a pathway of relief for those with a history of suffering. The comedians' strong cognitive abilities allowed them to find the light in their life's darkness and use their words and their wit as protest against suffering.

Dr. Deborah Serani is a clinical psychologist and author of the 2012 book, *Living With Depression*. She has extensive experience working with performers who suffer from depression and other mental health conditions. Serani sees humor as a depression defense mechanism.[18] Serani notes that comedians' intelligence allows them to identify what is funny about their sad or dark situations and spin it up for humor. There are two elements present in this theory. First, mining the saddest, darkest moments of your life offers a trove of comedic material. Second, making that material funny is difficult. Thus, it is implied that exceptional comedic talent or exceptional intelligence is necessary to make the material work. The talent is a gift that enables them to find light in the darkness.

Let us put take Janus' and Serani's conclusions into a causal diagram. If a comedian's ability to produce "good" comedy out of their emotional suffering is based upon their intelligence, we would say the relationship between depression and producing good comedy is mediated by intelligence. A social statistician would draw the sad clown paradox using a **mediated pathway** diagram like Figure 8.3. This model focuses specifically on the relationship between depression and producing "good" comedy among professional comedians. Your **population** is professional comedians.

As shown in Figure 8.3, the sad clown paradox posits a **mediated pathway** for professional comedians in which the causal pathway between one factor (depression) and another factor (producing good comedy) is mediated by another factor (one's level of intelligence). In other words, the link between depression and being a "good" comedian is one's ability to use their cognitive abilities to create meaningful art.

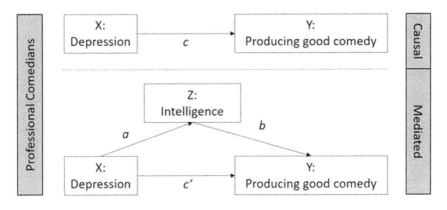

Figure 8.3 Mediated Pathway Applied to the Sad Clown Paradox

Top panel of Figure 8.3 (causal model): The primary causal pathway is path *c*. This is the pathway of interest: depression → producing good comedy. This is the pathway without consideration of the mediator.

Bottom panel of Figure 8.3 (mediation model): The **total effect** of the mediated pathway is the sum of the direct effect (*c'*) (depression → producing good comedy) and the indirect effect (*a*b*) (depression → intelligence → producing good comedy).

The **direct effect** is path *c'*. The direct effect quantifies the variability in the dependent variable (producing good comedy) with a one-unit change in the independent variable (depression), when controlling for the mediator variable (intelligence).

The **indirect effect** is the product of paths *a* and *b*. To calculate the indirect effect, you first quantify the variability in the mediator variable (intelligence) with a one-unit change in the independent variable (depression) (path *a*). You then quantify the variability in the dependent variable (producing good comedy) when the independent variable (depression) is held constant and there is variability in the mediating variable (intelligence) equal to the amount the mediating variable changes with a one-unit increase in the independent variable (path *b*, while controlling for *c'*).

The pathways described here (causal, moderated, and mediated) are just three examples of the myriad ways sociological researchers test hypotheses using statistics. They are briefly introduced here to help you practice visualizing how variables are related in social life. These various pathways are also used to help you consider the importance of thinking about *how* you measure things. For example, if you were conducting a study about the sad clown paradox, how would you measure depression? Would you ask respondents if they have ever received a clinical diagnosis for depression (e.g., "Yes" or "No")? Would you ask respondents about a set of possible depressive symptoms from which you can create a composite score (e.g., 0–20 on a depressive scale)? An important consideration when discussing or testing the sad clown paradox, according to Dr. Rami Kaminski, psychiatry professor at Columbia University School of Medicine, is that being funny and being happy are not synonymous.[19]

Stigma and Mental Illness with Maria Bamford

Maria Bamford, introduced earlier in this book, uses her comedy to destigmatize mental health struggles. Bamford has a surrealist, bizarre, interactive, clever, and funny comedic style. Her comedy is truly unique. Two of her comedy specials, *The Special Special Special* (2012) and *Old Baby* (2017), omit the traditional standup stage for collections of small, intimate gatherings.

Much of Bamford's comedic work centers on the interplay between other people in her life, such as her parents and a caricaturized version of herself. Her humor is less about punchlines and more about her tonal changes as she quickly transitions between characters, often playing up the helplessness felt between both her and those who love her.[20]

Bamford has never shied away from talking about mental illness openly, something which is a relatively recent phenomenon in the United States. Mental illness was long stigmatized and is only recently starting to become normalized in mainstream society (though remains highly stigmatized in many communities). To cite one of her jokes from her 2013 special, *Ask Me About My New God!*, "People don't talk about mental illnesses the way they do other illnesses. If I was like, 'Wow, apparently Steve has cancer.' It's like, 'F**k off! We all have cancer, right?'" (Bamford, 2013).[21] This was a pretty novel take at the time, and is playing off the too-common experience of folks who express feelings of stress, anxiety, or depression being met with responses akin to "Oh yeah? Guess what, we're all stressed!" The same type of response is not common if someone shared their experiences with physical illness. Here, Bamford touches on something sociological. Why were physical illnesses labeled as something worthy of recognition and sympathy from family and friends, while mental illnesses were written off as trivial or unworthy of attention? Classifications such as "important or not," and "real or not" are social classifications, not medical classifications.

Sociology has contributed an important concept to medical literature known as medicalization. **Medicalization** is the process in which some elements of life become pathologized (meaning they become part of the medical domain) when they were not before.[22] It is an important area of sociological study because it highlights how a "medical condition" is partly a social construction. To draw a comparison in physical health, obesity is a medicalized condition in the physical health space. Obesity was declared a medical disease by the American Medical Association in 2013.[23] The decision to define obesity as a disease was based upon myriad factors, including reducing stigma, acknowledging the genetic and biological factors contributing to obesity, and increased resources for research, prevention, and clinical care. There are strong parallels between the medicalization of obesity and mental illness. As with obesity, the medicalization of mental illness serves to reduce stigma, acknowledge the genetic and biological causes of mental illness, and increase resources for research, treatment, and care.

The American Medical Association's decision to identify a condition by its genetic and biological causes is a social act. We can see this in the reverse as well. The *Diagnostic and Statistical Manual of Mental Disorders (DSM)*, published by the American Psychiatric Association (APA), serves to classify mental disorders using a set of standard definitions and criteria.[24] Homosexuality was defined as a mental illness in the first edition of the *DSM*, published in 1952. This served to codify heteronormative behavior as healthy, natural, and the norm, and anything else as illness and deviance to correct. Recall this book's discussion of the ways powerful institutions create deviance by establishing norms and regulations. The *DSM* served as rulebook for what is normal behavior and what is illness. Homosexuality remained listed as a mental illness in the *DSM* through 1974, following many years of challenges from gay rights activists and a vote by the APA to declassify homosexuality as a mental illness in 1973.

Let us now look at Bamford's joke again using the lens of medicalization: "People don't talk about mental illnesses the way they do other illnesses. If I was like, 'Wow, apparently Steve has cancer. It's like, 'F**k off! We all have cancer, right?'" (Bamford, 2013).[25] Bamford's joke compares the trivialization of mental illness to the prioritization of physical health and exposes how the cultural perception and treatment of illness is socially constructed. Bamford's material reframes the conversation around mental illness as something just as real as cancer. She sets the stage for comedians who came up after her to talk about their own struggles with mental health.

Intersectionality and Mental Health

Social norms on mental health struggles vary by culture and community. **Intersectionality** refers to how one's experiences and social treatment differ depending upon intersecting features of their identity – such as race, ethnicity, sex, gender, and cultural background. The way mental illness is labeled and stigmatized, or discussed and accepted, varies by such features. Not all cultures understand mental health struggles in the same way, nor are they applied to individuals in the same way depending on features such as race, ethnicity, sex, and gender.

Comedian and actress Aparna Nancherla (born in Washington, DC, 1982 to parents who immigrated from India), often draws her comedic material from her (sometimes dueling) identities as a South Asian woman and someone who struggles with anxiety and depression. In a 2020 interview on the *Good One* podcast, Nancherla explained that mental health is not often talked about or explored in minority or immigrant communities. Nancherla notes that discussions of mental illness are becoming more common in comedy, but are still stigmatized – particularly in minority communities.[26] But Nancherla sees her identity as the driver of her comedic voice; anxiety and depression are part of her story.

Nancherla is one of the favorite comedians of comedian and writer Naomi Ekperigin (born in Harlem, New York City), who wrote for *Broad City* and *Difficult People* and has her own thirty-minute special on Netflix's *The Standups*.

Ekperigin has great admiration for the way Nancherla openly talks about her struggles with depression. But the two comedians come from very different backgrounds, families, and communities. It took Ekperigin some time to figure out how to package her jokes about her mental health struggles in a way that fit audiences' perceptions of her. Ekperigin knows that audiences see her as a confident, sassy, and bold Black woman comedian. But she also struggles with her mental health and its damaging effects on her confidence and energy.[27]

Ekperigin was featured on the podcast *The Hilarious World of Depression* in 2018. Ekperigin tells the host, John Moe, about how she first experienced depression and self-harming behaviors as a teenager while she was attending the Dalton School in New York City, which is a prestigious, private, and overwhelmingly White college preparatory school. As a Black teenager, Ekperigin believed that depression was an illness reserved for White people. It was a privilege to worry about your own emotions. In her understanding at the time, you could only worry about your own emotions if you did not have to worry about more tangible problems – like if you could pay your bills that month. Ekperigin did not see herself represented in cultural representations of people struggling with mental health issues like depression. Depression was a privilege. For Ekperigin, the cultural expectation was that she needed to emotionally pull herself up by her bootstraps.

Ekperigin is making a difference for others like her by talking about her mental health struggles on stage. During a 2016 standup set on *Late Night with Seth Meyers*, Naomi joked about her previous dependence on alcohol (she is now sober) and her ongoing struggles with overeating behaviors.[28] Seeing a Black woman on national television jokes about her own struggles with mental health and addiction makes it more normal. For teenagers out there listening, Ekperigin offers them an antidote to the idea that mental health struggles are only the problems of White people.

The degree to which mental illness is understood, accepted, and openly discussed varies by generation, religion, sex, gender, and place, among countless other factors and intersections therein. Women of color, like Nancherla and Ekperigin and countless others not discussed here, are breaking expectations by talking about their mental health onstage. Men, trans folks, and nonbinary folks all face different challenges than the women discussed here. But as more people from a diversity of backgrounds have the platform to share their stories in their own voices, there is hope for more people to feel understood, represented, and get the support they need when they are struggling.

Constructionist Theory of Deviance with You're the Worst

The television series *You're the Worst* plays with form to dig in on mental health struggles. Playing with form is a clever way for comedic television creators to draw audiences in with employing silly and fun content, then to hit audiences with boundary-pushing messages. Running for five seasons (2014–2019) on *FX*, *You're the Worst* follows four main characters with the classic romcom setup: the primary romantic couple, Gretchen and Jimmy (played by Aya Cash and Chris Geere, respectively), with their side kicks, Lindsay and Edgar (played by Kether Donohue and Desmin Borges, respectively). Gretchen and Jimmy are individually troubled and complex, but the core tension of the show rests on their shared struggle to bond and feel secure in their romantic relationship. Most of the episodes focus on the characters' wild and silly antics. But without warning, some *You're the Worst* episodes can hit audiences with something completely different.

Gretchen suffers from depression, which is made clear throughout the show but not often discussed. But as it happens for real-life sufferers, Gretchen experiences waves of crippling depression. There is an episode arc in season 2 (episodes 9–11) that takes audiences along for the ride as Gretchen's world closes in. The first of this arc is an episode called "LCD Soundsystem" (season 2, episode 9).[29] It was filmed in an entirely different tone; darker, slower, and more somber than the show's usual bright, silly LA vibes. Viewers follow along on Gretchen's journey as she lives out her life for a day as though she were her neighbors, Lexi and Rob. She spies on them, holds their daughter (thanks to persuading their nanny to let her do so at the local drugstore), and "borrows" (read: steals) their dog for the day. She seems truly happy this day. That is, until the end of the episode. Gretchen is invited into Lexi and Rob's home (a kind invitation following her return of their "lost" dog). Jimmy ultimately joins the group, and following a shared drink, Rob confides in Gretchen he is considering divorcing Lexi. Gretchen's blissful state is shattered. We are witness to the shattering of Gretchen's expectations that others are happy, and maybe if even some things in her life were different, she could be happy too.

The latter two episodes of this arc, titled "A Right Proper Story" and "A Rapidly Mutating Virus," dig deeper into Gretchen's spiral. We see her go days and days without leaving the couch. We see her pull a gun on two unknown women in a parking lot following a fight between the women and Gretchen's group. This moment feels tense and shocking and scary to the viewer. But later, Gretchen admits to a friend she felt *bored* during the altercation. This moment showed viewers who may not have personal experience with depression that what they may see, feel, or experience in response to an event is different for someone battling depression.

Gretchen's behavior in these episodes feels sad, scary, and unsettling. Certainly not "normal" or "okay." Her behaviors would be defined as "deviant" according to mainstream social norms. So who defines what is "normal" behavior?

Constructionist theories of deviance seek to explain how people or behaviors become deviant in the first place. The **constructionist theory of deviance** asserts that deviant behaviors are socially constructed and serve to maintain a particular social order. The unit of focus for constructionist theorists is primarily institutions and powerful elites who are in the position to codify deviant behavior. In short: *who makes the rules?*

Constructionist theorists see deviance not as real and objective, but instead as a social construction devised to maintain a particular social order. This can be relatively straightforward for sociology students to understand using historical examples. Take interracial marriage. Interracial marriage (also called miscegenation) was illegal in many states in the United States until 1967, following the Supreme Court decision in *Loving v. Virginia.*[30] Prior to this ruling, people who engaged in miscegenation in states outlying the practice were classified as deviant. Anti-miscegenation laws were a part of a large ecosystem of laws designed by White people in positions of power to maintain racial segregation in the United States. Recall, **racial segregation** refers to social or physical separation of racial and ethnic groups. We can see that interracial marriage was not an objectively deviant phenomenon but was constructed as deviant by those in power and then codified by the institutions they control.

Interactionist theories are a set of theories that fall under the constructionist umbrella. **Interactionism** asserts that society is a product of all the small, everyday social interactions that occur between people.[31] In this way, interactionism focuses on small interactions. For example, those interactions could include those between you and your friends or your family, your employer, or members of your church. We respond to information and context through actions and behaviors, and those actions and behaviors form the information and context to which other people respond. We both respond to and create society. (So do comedians, and we will come back to this.)

A key element of the interactionist understanding of deviance is known as labeling theory. Labeling theory was first discussed in 1963 by sociologist Howard Becker (born in Chicago, Illinois, 1928) and is closely tied to symbolic interactionism. Recall that symbolic interactionism understands people interact with one other based on shared symbols and meanings.[32] **Labeling theory** posits that individuals behave in accordance with the labels other people apply to them.[33] Labels are applied by social control agents, who may be psychiatrists, police officers, or newscasters. Labels serve to maintain the status quo. By labeling someone as "deviant," it becomes socially acceptable – or even desirable – to punish or ostracize them. An important component of labeling theory is the way people internalize their labels. People who are called "deviants" may begin to see themselves as such. They may not think they are worth more than their label. Consider how this relates to the concept of internalized racism introduced in the prior chapter.

Attached to labels is the concept of **stigma**. Sociologist Erving Goffman's 1963 book, *Stigma: Notes on the Management of Spoiled Identity,* details how individuals who have been given negative labels are restricted in their ability to achieve social acceptance.[34] Examples of groups of people to whom negative labels may have been applied are people who are unsheltered, currently or formerly incarcerated, engage in sex work, are physically disabled, or have a mental health disorder. Recall, Goffman defines **discredited individuals** as those who cannot conceal their stigmatized feature, like a physical disability. He defines **discreditable individuals** as those who can conceal their stigmatized feature, like someone suffering from depression. Discreditable individuals may feel social pressure to hide such features due to internalized shame or fear of harassment.

In the decades since Goffman's seminal work on stigma was published in 1963, much sociological research has been conducted studying the social determinants of mental health status. Indeed, sociological studies of mental health have helped inform on the social correlates and the upstream causes of mental illness. Recall, as introduced in the prior chapter, sociologists have found that **cumulative burden** and **stress proliferation** (these terms refer to the compounding effects of things like harassment, financial instability, living in an unsafe neighborhood, or environmental hazards. Marginalized groups experience these stressors at over-representative rates) are associated with mental health status.[35] Sociologists have also been instrumental in quantifying and identifying the pathways through which social bonds are linked to mental health status.[36] Sociologists have analyzed how stigma impacts the ability of people with mental illness to share information about their condition to others or to seek the help they need.[37-39]

Taken together, sociologists use data to understand causes, consequences, and disparities therein on the topic of mental health. Thankfully, there is an increased tendency toward understanding and acceptance of mental health struggles today compared to the past.[40] Results from a 2019 APA survey indicate 87 percent of respondents believe "having a mental health disorder is nothing to be ashamed of."[41] But the trends toward greater understanding and acceptance are not necessarily true for all cultures or communities, nor does it necessarily extend to other mental health conditions, such as schizophrenia. In the same 2019 APA survey, although many of those respondents said a mental health disorder is nothing to be ashamed of, 33 percent agreed with the statement, "people with mental health disorders scare me." Limited representation and a lack of understanding breeds fear and mistrust and defines those with mental health issues as "the other." Conversely, better representation and information foster understanding and breed connection.

Taken together, Goffman's discussions of stigma and the sociological understandings of the way we socially define mental health can help us understand why and how individuals suffering from a mental health disorder may feel compelled to conceal their disorder from others. Stigma has harmed people who suffer from mental illness, and mental illness is still largely misunderstood. That is why creators who put their mental health status at the center of their work are driving positive social change. In doing so, these creators educate their audiences about how they experience their illness (think about the *You're the Worst* examples) and the social response to their illness (think about Maria Bamford's "We all have cancer!" joke).

Showing what it feels like to navigate the world as someone who experiences depression adds humanity to people suffering from mental illness. This really influences how people suffering from mental illness are able to engage fully with society, do so comfortably, and do so in a way that allows them to feel seen and understood. Recall, in the 2019 APA survey, 33 percent agreed with the statement, "people with mental health disorders scare me." There is fear in the other. That otherness stems from being labeled, stigmatized, and viewed as deviant. This concept of fear resulting from otherness is one which we will return to repeatedly in the following chapters.

Before moving on from *You're the Worst*, let us discuss one more example from the show, demonstrating for audiences what it feels like to experience a mental health struggle. **Post-Traumatic Stress Disorder** (PTSD) is a mental illness triggered by a scary or horrific event or a set of recurring events. Symptoms of PTSD center on visualizations of the events' occurrence (like flashbacks) and chronic anxiety.[42] PTSD can be a debilitating illness and is experienced by 4 percent of men in the United States.[43]

However, PTSD is largely misunderstood. One of the most prevalent symptoms of complex PTSD is shame.[44] Shame associated with a mental illness like PTSD stems from a misunderstanding of its causes, both from the sufferer and from their loved ones, who may assume the sufferer did something wrong to bring this upon themselves or that suffering from PTSD is a choice.[45] "They should just snap out of it!" is a common and harmful refrain often used in this situation by people who do not understand the complexity of the disorder.

While PTSD is complex, serious, and largely misunderstood, there is opportunity for media representations of the illness to educate audiences about its causes and consequences. There is a two-episode arc in season 3 of *You're the Worst* (episodes 4 and 5) that does this. The first of the arc, titled "Men Get Strong," focuses on Gretchen helping Jimmy fast-forward through all the steps of the grieving process following the loss of his father. To do this, Gretchen takes Jimmy on a "sadness tour," using Edgar as their driver. Stops on the tour include crashing a funeral, going to a paint-your-own-pottery class where they watch other fathers and sons bonding, and a British pub (Jimmy's dad was British). While the plot may sound somber, it is delivered in the typical *You're the Worst* light, fun, and zany style.

The next episode, titled "Twenty-Two" retells the same story from Edgar's perspective. Edgar has PTSD, stemming from his time serving in the Army. In this episode, we see where Edgar goes in between the rides he gives to Jimmy and Gretchen. We see him drinking straight liquor in a reservoir before climbing up to a busy highway and clearly, although without dialogue, consider walking into traffic. There is both silence and deafening noise in this scene.

When Edgar picks up Jimmy and Gretchen (and, audiences remember the comedic relief in the prior episode), we see the world through Edgar's perspective; his vision is jumpy, narrow, and there is a ringing in his ears. The world looks different through his eyes. The effectiveness in showing the two perspectives across "Men Get Strong" and "Twenty-Two" comes from remembering the times Edgar is not shown in the first episode of the arc. In that first episode, we saw Edgar drive Jimmy and Gretchen from stop to stop when they "Call an Edgar" (a riff on calling a rideshare, such as a Lyft or an Uber), as soon as they are ready for a pickup. But as we realize later, we did not think much about his character at all.

As with the episodes told from Gretchen's perspective during her episodes of severe depression, the juxtaposition of the fun antics in "Men Get Strong" to the high stress, insular retelling of the same story in "Twenty-Two" shows viewers how differently two people can experience the same events. In this juxtaposition, *You're the Worst* shows audience what their world looks, feels, and sounds by elevating the perspective of someone battling mental illness. A perspective which is largely ignored, misunderstood, or vilified.

"Madness" with Crazy Ex-Girlfriend

Comedy is an artform centered around elevating alternative perspectives. Now, let us walk through examples from other creators who employ another form of comedy to meet the same goal. Musical comedy is comedy that includes song and dance, often paired with other elements of theatrical performance like costumes and sets. I highlight musical comedy here for two primary reasons. One, musical theater allows for incongruity (recall incongruity theory) to happen quickly. Comedy happens when the visual on screen does not match the tone or the words of the song. It is comedically efficient because it happens fast, with little need for explanation. Two, musical comedy provides an example of the ways in which comedy varies in form and style, but is united by perspective. Comedy is not defined by form, platform, or tone, but is instead defined any artistic performance that offers a view of the world through a non-traditional lens.

Let us return to the musical comedy series *Crazy Ex-Girlfriend* (recall "The Sexy Getting Ready Song" discussed earlier in this book), created by Rachel Bloom and Aline Brosh McKenna. First, we will discuss how the show highlights important sociological points about how "normal" feelings and behaviors are highly gendered in the United States. Second, we will discuss how mental health status is further defined in accordance with one's intersecting identities, including how sex and gender intersect with race, ethnicity, social class, religion, and sexuality.

As the show's title somewhat flippantly implies, *Crazy Ex-Girlfriend* puts mental health issues right at the forefront. The main character, Rebecca Bunch is a flawed heroine; she has depression, anxiety, OCD, borderline personality disorder, suicidality, and is so cripplingly focused on her ex-boyfriend that she acts in wildly unacceptable and sometimes illegal ways. *Crazy Ex-Girlfriend* pushes the envelope by making a complicated, nuanced character like Rebecca challenge what is considered socially normative and "acceptable" behavior; particularly as it relates to media portrayals of mental illness and romantic relationships. Like in *You're the Worst*, *Crazy Ex-Girlfriend* adds to the television landscape the perspective of someone who knows what it means to live with mental illness. The show uses songs and musical performances to showcase the character's inner thoughts in a way that juxtaposes them against the "normal" scene from which the musical comedy cuts away. In doing so, audiences have a front-row seat to each character's inner monologue. We can see Rebecca's and other characters' anxieties, insecurities, and longing to be loved. Consider how this ties to the voiceover and bathroom mirror scenes discussed in *Insecure*, which gave viewers a window into Issa's back stage.

Like in *Insecure*, *Crazy Ex-Girlfriend* presents us both the character's front stage and back stage. The normal scenes show us the former, and the musical cutaways show us the latter. In the back stage, we walk through the sociological themes of labeling and stigma related to deviant status (e.g., we see characters grapple with how others see them as it relates to their mental health, sexuality, bodies, their choices, and their behaviors). Through the juxtaposition of the front stage and back stage, we see how characters engage in impression management to try to adhere to socially normative expectations.

Crazy Ex-Girlfriend shows audiences what is normally invisible by using musical cutaways that provide windows into each character's internal dialogue. There is a juxtaposition between what characters do (Dance! Twirl! Wear sequins!) and what they say ("I'm sad!"), which allows for comedically efficient incongruity. As one example of what this looks like, we can refer to the song "I'm So Happy 4 U," written to appear in season four, episode five (episode title: "I'm So Happy For You"). The song was ultimately cut from the episode, but it is worth describing here as it succinctly personifies many of the musical comedy techniques endemic to the *Crazy Ex-Girlfriend* songbook.

Immediately preceding the song, two of Rebecca's closest friends, Heather and Valencia, break the news to Rebecca that they are moving out of town. Rebeca instantly feels sad, anxious, and self-critical for where she is in her own life while her friends move forward in theirs. Yet Rebecca feels the pressure to be outwardly supportive of her friends. Cue the music and a window into Rebecca's inner monologue. We see Rebecca dancing with neon pretzels then jumping out of a giant cake while wearing a hot-pink jumpsuit. She is surrounded by falling balloons and singing to her friends, praising their happy news in upbeat tones. But between praises and twirls, she sings about her own insecurities and self-doubt.[46]

Seeing Rebecca sing, twirl, and dance surrounded by neon and balloons while she is clearly sad and anxious reflects the way we often must hide our own emotions in order to support or appease others. Songs like "I'm So Happy 4 U" highlight the juxtaposition between the pressures the character feels to present in a certain way in the front stage, no matter how they feel in the back stage. This pressure and internal struggle is something normally invisible to audiences, and the light, bubbly, musical style of *Crazy Ex-Girlfriend* makes these struggles feel real, understandable, and even fun.

Our constructionist and symbolic interactionist lenses will help us analyze how perceptions of mental illness are informed by socially proscribed feminine and masculine behaviors. Let us start with a bit of history about hysteria. **Hysteria** was a condition that historically only applied to women. Coming from the Latin word *hystericus*, which means "of the womb," the term hysterical was to describe women exhibiting what others deemed as neurotic or uncontrolled behavior.[47] Similarly, *loony* was derived from "lunacy."

The term lunacy was used to described monthly "periods of insanity" tied to women's menstrual cycles (the *luna* in these words implied these periods were tied to cycles of the moon).

Regina Barreca (1988) describes in a compilation of essays, titled *Last Laughs: Perspectives on Women and Comedy,* that men are seen as authentic in their emotions, whereas women are "crazy" or "shrill."[48] Audiences, then, tend to find women's experiences are unnatural and threatening. Being a woman, then, is a barrier to being seen and respected in comedy.

Recall Dr. Stephanie Brown's analysis of authenticity in comedy. As discussed in the section on the Louis C.K.-ification of comedy, men's experiences are treated as "the norm" and are broadly left unchallenged or unquestioned. Building onto this point, Barreca and Brown discuss how the lack of assumed authenticity granted to women comedians is a consequence of how social norms attach value to women's emotional states. This matters greatly in comedy. If a male comic tells a joke about experiencing something outrageous, the audience is likely to believe him and be along for the twists and turns leading toward a punchline. If a woman's story sounds outrageous, the audience is not automatically on board. And the way comedy works – if the audience does not get on board in the beginning, it is incredibly difficult to bring them along for the ride. This will become clearer in the discussion of Hannah Gadsby's 2018 Netflix special *Nanette* later in this book.

Different value judgments are assigned to men and women based upon differing social expectations of what is considered acceptable behavior by sex.[49] Labeling women as shrill or hysterical for expressive behaviors is a tool that serves to coerce quiet and compliant behavior by the more dominant, powerful group (men).

The title of the show, *Crazy Ex-Girlfriend,* satirizes the idea that women expressing their emotions or advocating for their emotional or romantic needs may be labeled as crazy. Rebecca's behavior is intentionally exaggerated beyond normal behavior in her pursuit of rekindling her love with her ex-boyfriend, Josh (by ex-boyfriend, we mean teenage summer camp fling). Examples of those behaviors include intentionally clogging her garbage disposal so Josh will come over to fix it, staging break-ins, forging coupons for free drinks about to expire, and pawning a family ring to afford a plane ticket to Hawaii so she can run into him there. The list goes on.

Most women do not go to such lengths to trick men into love. Applying the label crazy to a girlfriend, or ex-girlfriend, is a tool to coerce submissive behavior by women. *Crazy Ex-Girlfriend* leans into the stereotype of women communicating their emotional needs as crazy behavior and spins it up through song, dance, and humor. This serves to challenge the notion that the behaviors for which women may be labeled as crazy are behaviors in pursuit of what women deserve, including love, honesty, emotional support, and the power to use their own voice.

To understand the way labeling women as crazy is a tool of coercion, we must understand the concept of gaslighting. **Gaslighting** refers to manipulation from one person to make another person question their own sanity, judgment, and experiences. It is used as a form of social control.[50] The origins of the term come from a 1944 film titled *Gaslight*. In the film, a husband manipulates his wife slowly over a long time until he eventually he convinces her she is crazy. His goal is to make her vulnerable enough so that he can steal from her.[51] If women are told they are crazy for asking for, say, exclusivity in a relationship, the goal from the gaslighting partner is to enable and excuse their own non-monogamous behaviors as normal and the woman's wishes as deviant. It is a way of forcing compliance.

Crazy Ex-Girlfriend illustrates how labeling folks as crazy serves as a coercive force to compel socially normative behavior and to suppress deviant behavior. In doing so, the show engages an intersectional lens to showcase how mental health status intersects with sex, sexual identity, race, culture, and socioeconomic status to influence what is considered normative versus deviant behavior. In addition to different stress and trauma exposures by one's social identity and socioeconomic class, society dictates different emotional processing mechanisms for people based on social group. Honest portrayals of the intersections between gender, race, and socioeconomic status matters in relation to how we experience mental illness. Think back to Naomi Ekperigin's early experiences of depression, wherein she believed depression was reserved for White people. She did not have examples of Black women like her experiencing what she was experiencing, and it shaped her perceptions of her own illness.

Crazy Ex-Girlfriend shows people of various racial, ethnic, and cultural backgrounds, educational and occupational prestige, sexual identities, and religions all struggle in their own ways. The show's musical theater component allows audiences to see the juxtaposition between what different characters, influenced by their intersectional identities, present in the front stage versus what they feel and experience in the back stage. This is a particularly effective way to showcase that different groups have different levels of shame or stigma surrounding mental illness, which makes it more difficult for some people to express their feelings or share their struggles.

Let us return to our discussion of PTSD as one example of the way one's identity impacts mental health, focusing specifically on gender differences. In media, PTSD is often more associated with men; specifically with veterans and war-based trauma. This is the case with the example from *You're the Worst*, discussed earlier. PTSD in women is infrequently covered by the media, even though 10 percent of women in the United States suffer from PTSD.[52] For men, women, trans, and non-binary people alike, childhood trauma, sexual trauma, intimate partner violence, serving in war, witnessing violence, and other traumatic events all are triggers for PTSD. The likelihood of experiencing these events varies by one's social status and gender identity. For example, women, trans, and non-binary people are more likely to be victims of sexual abuse than are men, and cismen are more likely than other sex and gender groups to serve in war.[53-55] But differences in exposure do not fully account for the disparate prevalence of PTSD for women and men.[56] Studies specifically focusing on women and men show women are twice as likely as men to develop PTSD symptoms following a traumatic event.

In communities which emphasize traditional gender roles (wherein men have more power and influence than other sex and gender groups), studies find that women have higher rates of PTSD.[57] Women in these communities are more susceptible to violence and coercion than women in communities which afford more social and political freedom (which puts women living in traditional communities at a greater risk of PTSD). These studies focused specifically on comparison between ciswomen and cismen, but we may infer that trans and non-binary people are at further risk of PTSD in communities that are unwelcoming of their identities.

Studies also find that stress and trauma coping strategies differ between men and women based on socially proscribed norms. In response to stress, men tend to exhibit more "fight or flight" behavior, while women tend to exhibit more "tend and befriend" behavior (as in seeking out love and support from others). These different coping strategies matter in situations where tending and befriending results in staying in dangerous situations, such as staying with an abusive partner.

Depictions of mental illness in media often reinforce these social norms.[58] Portrayals of men with mental illness focus on their anger and aggression in line with socially normative perceptions of masculinity, and portrayals of women with mental illness tend to depict passivity and vulnerability in line with socially normative perceptions of femininity. Media depictions often fail to account for the ripple effect that occurs for women outside the stressful or dangerous situation. Women experience higher **network burden** than do men, as women provide more emotional, social, and tangible support for friends and family members experiencing their own stress or hardship.[59] This takes an emotional toll, and the mental and physical impact of providing such support is largely invisible in media.

Let us bring this back to *Crazy Ex-Girlfriend*. The show has a large ensemble cast composed of characters grappling with mental health issues; strains in romantic, friendship, and family ties; discovering one's true sexual identity; parenting; family; and faith. *Crazy Ex-Girlfriend* handles these topics with care and portrays them in ways more reflective of people's lived experiences. For example, we see a middle-aged man realize and accept his bisexuality, and we see a middle-aged, married mother decide to have an abortion. These are real stories rarely portrayed on television. Other shows on television have certainly touched on these topics, like sexuality and reproductive choice, but often only portray them through the lens of young or unidimensional characters. We see male characters grapple with how they are "supposed" to exhibit only a very narrow range of emotional responses to suffering. For example, it is socially normative in the United States to teach boys and men that they can be angry, but they cannot be sad. They can yell, but they cannot cry.[60] Showing sadness, or even putting forward displays of love and affection, makes men appear soft or feminine in the public American consciousness.

We can take an example from a male character, Josh, to see how socially proscribed norms of masculinity can influence the way someone processes emotions internally and in conjunction with social norms. The song "Angry Mad" (season 1, episode 17) showcases Josh's inner voice as he grapples with the sadness of discovering his crush and his best friend have entered a sexual relationship.[61] The song takes place in Josh's karate dojo. Clad in his *gi*, Josh sings about his heartache while simultaneously executing the kicks and punches of a trained fighter. The image shows audiences that to express his emotions, Josh feels compelled to simultaneously perform an overt display of masculinity. The juxtaposition of Josh's emotional and physical behaviors remind audiences of the social pressure placed on men to hide the expression of their natural emotions.

Performing Authenticity with Bo Burnham

Another example of musical comedy which centers on mental health struggles is Bo Burnham's 2021 Netflix special, *Inside*. In this section, we first discuss how Burnham's career highlights the importance of understanding and leveraging the Internet as a young comedian today. Second, we see how *Inside* exemplifies how comedy is based on shared understanding; in this case, that shared understanding is tied to experiencing a specific event (living through the height of the COVID-19 pandemic from home) among a specific Internet-savvy generation. Third, we discuss how *Inside* is a postmodern comedy special which engages hyperreality elements to show that comedy is a performance. Fourth, we will consider what fan and critic receptions to *Inside* tell us about the assumed authenticity of Burnham as a performer.

Let us start with some background on Burnham (born in Hamilton, Massachusetts, 1990). Burnham became a viral sensation as a teenager when he began posting his original, comedic songs on YouTube. Burnham leveraged the Internet in ways not done before, in terms of both platform (YouTube) and content (aimed purposefully at a young, Internet-savvy generation). Audiences at home loved it. Consider how Burnham's early success was largely outside the realm of comedy gatekeepers and instead pumped into homes by tweens and teens too young to go to comedy clubs. Burnham could make comedy that spoke to him and his generation without needing buy-in from older or more traditional gatekeepers.

From there, Burnham's rise as a young comedic star can only be described as meteoric. Burnham performed comedy all over the world, released three hour-long comedy specials (*Words, Words, Words* (2010), *what.* (2013), and *Make Happy* (2016)), and wrote and directed his own film, *Eighth Grade*, all before turning thirty. Burnham won an Independent Spirit Award for his work on that film. After *Make Happy*, Burnham announced he was taking a break from performing live due to an anxiety disorder. He has spoken openly about dealing with depression, anxiety, and experiencing anxiety attacks during live performances. After much improvement in his mental health, Burnham announced to the world in January 2020 that he was ready to start performing again and would begin working on a new special.

Then, in the spring of 2020, the COVID-19 pandemic hit. A primary prevention strategy for the spread of COVID-19 was for people to stay at home, if their work or other personal obligations allowed it. There was a huge shift during the pandemic toward remote work and social interaction to online spaces. In the early days of the pandemic, many workplaces and industries were shut down in the United States. For example, restaurants, gyms, and movie theaters were closed to in-person service, and many workplaces, schools, and religious services transitioned to an online format.

Depending upon one's occupational position and health status, the early days of the COVID-19 pandemic impacted lives very differently. Those who worked in the restaurant or retail space found their positions were cut or their hours were cut drastically. Others, like those who worked in essential industries like healthcare, grocery, or delivery services, perhaps kept their working hours and incomes, but attended work with a new fear of contracting the virus. Others had the privilege of keeping their positions and their incomes by conducting their work remotely. For many, this was certainly not a walk in the park. Parents and caretakers navigated working from home *while* watching their children and helping them with school or taking care of sick or ailing family members, perhaps in the face of language barriers or physical space limitations (like apartments too small for Zoom school and Zoom business meetings to be happening at the same time). It was a confusing, scary time for many, and it was also a time of isolation and disruption to routines that kept people's physical and mental health in check.

This is where Burnham found himself at the start of the COVID-19 pandemic. He was stuck inside. He channeled his energy into a self-written, directed, produced, staged, lit, costumed, and edited one-man musical comedy special titled *Inside*, which debuted on Netflix in May 2021. The result of Burnham's year-long effort is a ninety-minute epic journey through his personal and, in many ways, a broader collective experience navigating isolation (although as detailed above, not universal). Specifically, those personal but relatable experiences include overdosing on social media and the Internet, reckoning with issues of social justice as a White person of privilege, and especially mental health issues and suicidal ideation.

Burnham structures *Inside* to follow the evolution of Burnham's mental and physical states as the pandemic and his isolation go on for longer and longer. We see Burnham's hair grow longer and his facial hair and clothing become more unkempt. The tone and content of the songs evolve as well. The early songs in *Inside* focus primarily on Burnham's celebrity and his own role as a comedian. For example, the second song in *Inside*, titled "Comedy," poses questions which have been long asked, including when it is appropriate to joke following tragic events.[62] The song is fun and cheeky, much in line with the first part of *Inside*. Burnham writes about his self-reflection and White guilt during the height of the COVID-19 pandemic and Black Lives Matter protests which followed the murder of George Floyd in 2020, although Burnham mentions neither the pandemic nor the movement by name during the special. There is an expectation that his audience will understand the references, given the broad awareness of these events at the time of *Inside*'s release.

In *Inside*, Burnham acknowledges he is a talented White guy who wants fame and money, while simultaneously sharing with his audience that he is unsure if he deserves either. But he also nods to the fact that the Internet and the fast and expansive way in which creators and art are criticized plays into how he presents himself in the special. Specifically, during the Internet-trope-filled song titled "Welcome to the Internet," Burnham breaks out into a montage where he mimics a Twitch streamer filming an Internet reaction video. Burnham gets stuck in a seemingly infinite reaction. First, he reacts to his own song, then he reacts to that reaction of his song, then he reacts to his reaction of his reaction of his song. Here, Burnham nods to the fact that everything he puts forward on *Inside* is a performance for the Internet age; one in which creators react to their expected reactions and create content accordingly.

As an example of how Burnham effectively critiques social media norms in *Inside*, we can turn to the song "White Woman's Instagram." This song is a compilation of beautifully composed and on-the-nose descriptions of a generic White woman's Instagram account. The twist in the song is a bridge sequence wherein the White woman, who Burnham was just roasting, pays tribute to her late mother in a deeply personal, reflective, and beautiful post. Burnham then swiftly switches back to satirizing the seemingly trivial Instagram posts of young White women. The song "White Woman's Instagram" highlights Burnham's deep understanding of the Internet and the fact that we are all performers on social media. It's easy to poke fun (and so many artists and commentators do) but Burnham juxtaposes the trivial with the humanity and emotions often hiding behind the scenes.

Consider how "White Woman's Instagram" relates to the postmodernism. **Postmodernism** is marked by individuality and freedom of expression. Recall our earlier example of paintings. A painting from the modern era – an era which emphasized rationality over individuality – tended to be more direct representations of life. Picture a still-life painting of a bow of fruit. An apple looks like an apple. Paintings in the postmodern era became more abstract. An apple looks like sadness. Burnham leaned into a postmodern style of art with *Inside*. He creatively used the images, music, and words of *Inside* – and creative juxtapositions of those media – to express complicated experiences and emotions.

The song also tells us something about *Inside*, itself. It makes use of the Internet and digital media spaces to curate a performance. The project seems well-suited for streaming. Its intended audience is those who would get his in-jokes. Refer to the sociological concept of **shared norms**. For his audience to understand *Inside*, they need to understand the Internet and social media. Burnham needed to meet them online.

There is real emotion underneath Burnham's songs and images, but it is still edited and curated for an audience. Jean Baudrillard called such false realities **simulations**. The postmodern era is rife with simulations. Media which are presented as "real" but are heavily curated or edited meet this definition.

Baudrillard viewed simulations with a negative lens. Indeed, companies sell people products through unrealistic simulations. However, we can expand Baudrillard's concept of simulations into the realm of postmodern art – like comedy. Burnham uses a simulation to convey emotion. Burnham's own emotions are brought to the forefront in dark, fantastical sequences and a monologue about his mental health as he spirals toward, what he tells us, is his lowest point.[63]

Burnham succeeds at making his isolated year and personal spiral into something relatable to many, largely by clinging onto the touches to reality the Internet provided him. To many folks who were in similar privileged positions as Burnham, this was a year of tumultuous change on the outside, and yet, a year of numbing monotony on the inside. As such, some of the rawest moments of *Inside* are when we see Burnham seemingly tortured by, but still clinging to the project of making this special. Images show what is normally behind the scenes; cords everywhere, Burnham setting up lighting (and the lighting falling down), Burnham hunched over his laptop with editing software open on his screen. It looks tiresome and lonely. But Burnham also tells us – the audience – in a monologue that he desires to keep working on the special forever. As the monologue implies; without the project, he has nothing left.

The monologue warrants discussion for the way it breaks the fourth wall of the special. Yes, *Inside* is a postmodern portrait of Burnham's year in lockdown. But it is also a project. It is not an unedited livestream into his life. It is a crafted performance. This is an artistic project goes on until Burnham feels it is complete, in the same way a painter adds brush stroke after brush stroke until the final brush stroke completes the piece. While we watch *Inside*, we feel we are inside Burnham's world. This close feeling happens concurrently as we see Burnham set up his stage. We see him set up lighting and rearrange furniture; we see him hunch over his laptop as he edits footage. It is an example of hyperrealism. *Inside* feels so real because the audience feels included in its creation. We are invited into the back stage. But of course, the back stage is itself staged.

I ask you to consider whether Burnham's *Inside* represents a simulation and/or falseness. A key distinction between a simulation (postmodernism) and falseness (critical theory) is the message. One form of a **simulation** is the postmodern expression of one's real experiences and emotions through hyperbolic means. For example, through scripting, lighting, staging, and editing, Burnham can create the *feeling* of loneliness he experiences inside his own mind. He uses a simulation, *Inside*, to convey these feelings. If audiences saw his real, unedited life, Burnham's feelings would not be as clear.

Falseness, however, presents an entirely false narrative. According to critical theorists, falseness is a technique used by mass media to sell products. It is not about emotion; it is about money. Compare *Inside* to the comedy of Louis C.K. discussed earlier in this book.

Inside presenting itself as clearly and intentionally staged sets up an important point about comedy in that it is first and foremost a *performance*. Burnham's special breaks the fourth wall from the traditional structure of a comedy special that many audiences have come to expect; one where comics get on stage, often with no frills, lighting, or changing of camera angles, to entertain us with comedic material. The notion of comedians as truth tellers has come to define the content and tone of many comedians' material today. We as audience members have largely come to value comedians as truth tellers. But comedians are performers. The only way to truly be authentic is to acknowledge that. Burnham, with *Inside*'s behind the scenes views, does just that.

Burnham did no interviews in preparation for the release of *Inside*. Burnham has previously stated "celebrity is the enemy of comedy." It would be harder for audiences watching *Inside* to experience Burnham's feelings of isolation if we could see he has a larger home with many rooms, outside of the tiny, rectangular box that encompasses *Inside*. Burnham did not show us what his life looks like; he showed us what it *feels* like. Or at least a spun-up version of what it feels like. Burnham's comedy and his public control of its narrative serve as a reminder that comedy is performance.

Burnham's mainstream success affords him generous leeway in creating his art and great understanding and forgiveness from audiences in its reception. The way Burnham's centers his feelings in his work was largely viewed positively by audiences and the media critics. Headlines from around the time of the special's release included: "'Inside,' Reviewed: Bo Burnham's Virtuosic Portrait of a Mediated Mind,"[64] "'Bo Burnham: Inside' Review: A Brilliant Pandemic-Era Special About Trying to Be Funny in Sad Times,"[65] and "Bo Burnham: Inside review – this is a claustrophobic masterpiece,"[66] among countless others praising Burnham's creative achievement. It was received as an authentic portrait of his mental and emotional state.

When audiences empathize with a performer, they open themselves up to engage with, relate to, and be welcoming of their art. What is "normal" or even "exemplary" behavior depends on who is doing it. This discussion ties back to earlier discussions around whose experiences are considered "neutral" and "authentic." Recall, Dr. Rebecca Krefting's and Dr. Danielle Fuentes Morgan's descriptions of how White men's experiences are considered "neutral" and the stories of women and people of color are seen as "niche."[67] Similarly, Dr. Stephanie Brown described how White men's experiences are viewed as "authentic" while the stories of women and people of color need to be validated.[68] We will explore this idea more in the next section.

Truth and the Rise of the Docu-Comedy

Many comedy fans have come to view comedians as truth tellers, despite the reality that comedy is a performance. This era was shepherded in long before Burnham, but Burnham's place in history as a comedian who came up during the digital boom is important here. Because of the digital boom, there are now so many ways in which comedians can, and perhaps feel compelled to, "prove" their truth through digital images, videos, and social media posts. Let us dig into what these digital avenues mean for the modern comedy land-scape in which truth and comedy are often conflated. Specifically, this section will dig into the recent rise of docu-comedies, and the rise of docu-comedies will help us conceptualize why many viewers understood *Inside* more as a documentary than a work of crafted art.

Docu-comedies refer to comedy specials which feature interstitial documentary-style footage, generally of the comic's personal life. These may include interviews with family members or clips from childhood home videos. One example of this style is Yvonne Orji's 2020 HBO special, *Momma, I Made It!* This special intermixes footage from her live comedy performance at the Howard Theater in Washington, DC with footage from a recent trip home to Lagos, Nigeria. In Orji's special, much of her material focuses on comparisons between Nigerians and Americans. For example, Orji tells a joke in her special about the way Nigerians give directions. Then, documentary footage cuts to her receiving directions from a Nigerian woman in Lagos which aligns with the de-scription given in Orji's joke.[69] Incorporating documentary footage into one's comedy special can be a way to prove the authenticity of the comic's jokes.

Other examples include Jenny Slate's 2019 Netflix special, *Stage Fright,* and Whitmer Thomas' 2020 HBO special, *The Golden One*; both of which interweave the live standup performances with footage of the comics inter-acting with their families. In the specials by Slate and Thomas, both comics focus on personal traumas and anxieties. Showing the audience intimate con-versations between them and their families validates those features of their background and identity.

Vulture comedy writers Jesse David Fox and Kathryn VanArendonk re-corded a discussion on docu-comedy specials for Fox's podcast, *Good One*. Both argue that the use of documentary footage to validate a standup performance ignores that those pieces of footage are also constructed and un-dermines standup as an artform. Archival footage, such as home videos from childhood and documentary footage, were carefully chosen. Interviews with friends or family members were scheduled and setup with mics and lighting. Docu-comedies show real words said by real people, but they are ultimately still scripted, edited, and designed to fit a particular narrative. In short, its constructed; like all retellings of history are constructed.[70]

According to Fox, there are two problems with this framework. The first problem is that it seeks to define "true" as that which is an "accurate" his-tory of someone's life. However, the pieces you *choose* to highlight do not necessarily accurately encapsulate a person's whole history, and, the narrative around which you present those pieces impact its reception. The second problem, as Fox argues, is that we should not be judging art on its "accuracy." Accuracy should not be the goal of art. This is certainly a postmodern (and post-comedy) perspective on art. But if creating a moving and expressive postmodern piece of work is the marker of "good" art today, we must consider *who* has the necessary presumed credibility to create "good" art. If not everyone is equally believed, then not everyone has the ability to be a "great" artist. Others may feel the need to validate their own experience. Consider how this relates to the alternative comedy movement and the Louis C.K.-ification of comedy discussed earlier in this book.

Let us connect this to sociological discussions of health and illness. We have discussed the stigma associated with mental illness, but we have not yet discussed the visibility (or lack thereof) of mental illness and the way it impacts someone's life. Sociologists refer to illnesses one cannot see as **invisible disabilities**. These can include conditions or impairments such as mental illness or chronic back pain.[71] Individuals who need accommodation for their conditions (such as those related to school deadlines or work schedules, or those who seek understanding from friends, family, or partners), then need to make decisions regarding how, when, and to whom they disclose information about their conditions. With invisible disabilities more so than visible disabilities, there may be fears from the individual about to disclose their condition regarding if they will be stigmatized or believed. Remember Bamford's joke: "Wow, apparently Steve has cancer. It's like, 'F**k off! We all have cancer, right?'" (Bamford, 2013).[72] Someone may feel additional pressure to provide evidence for their mental health struggles relative to someone suffering from a more visible limitation. Comedians engaging outside interviews or documentary footage, then, may be attempting to validate experiences that are invisible to the naked eye.

Let us see how this works in Jenny Slate's (born in Milton, Massachusetts, 1982) 2019 Netflix special, *Stage Fright*. The title of Slate's special refers to an admission she makes during the show that she has stage fright. She has anxiety both on and off stage but you would never know it based on the way Slate presents herself to her audience. She bounces onto the stage, giggles, and carries herself with an appearance of confidence. But it is known that how someone presents on the outside is not necessarily how they feel on the inside. By marrying her standup material with documentary footage, a viewer may assume that Slate is trying to provide evidence for who she really is beneath the bubbly surface.

One of the Slate's jokes in *Stage Fright* focuses on her childhood fear of ghosts. While this specific example may seem to some like normal childhood fears, it sets the backdrop for Slate's adult anxieties. Slate explains to her audience that she was raised in a haunted home (she then acts out the impact on her personality through exaggerated body shakes; eyes and mouth opened wide).[73] Slate explains that prior owners had died in the home. As she details, the home is not the *fun kind* of haunted where you break out the tarot cards and drink rosé with your girlfriends. It is *scary* haunted. Slate gives examples – such as a young, bleeding boy asking if he missed the picnic – marked with her signature performative flair for each of the ghosts.

Immediately after this joke, the special cuts to B-roll footage of the interior of the home, shot in ominous tones and set to foreboding music. The voiceover is Slate's father speaking in a serious and chilling voice. He factually recounts his own experience seeing a ghost in the shape of a man floating up the stairs in their home. In a review of *Stage Fright* written for *Vulture*, VanArendonk writes of this transition. She notes that Slate's comedic description of the events was, to her, one of the best and most moving parts of the entire special. To then have Slate's father give his autobiographical description immediately after the joke, the joke loses a bit of its "energy" and "magic."[74]

VanArendonk first acknowledges Slate's strong comedic performance of her childhood experiences. Slate took her childhood experiences, mined them for emotional truth, and delivered them to her audience complete with characters, voices, and her signature charm. However, as VanArendonk identifies, the cut to the documentary footage drains some of this charm away. In *Stage Fright*, it seems that providing evidence that Slate's fears and anxieties are real was the motivation for the documentary footage here. Recall, Slate started the joke by saying her entire personality (which she acts out as anxious and jumpy) is based upon the fact that she was raised in a haunted house. Providing evidence that her ghostly fears were real – her dad experienced them, too, after all – implies to audiences that all her fears are real. They are not childhood make-believe.

Let us return to Fox's second point regarding that autobiographical accuracy is not the basis on which art should be judged. Fox questions whether art should be judged based upon how accurately it reflects reality is an important question when discussing what defines modern comedy. He and VanArendonk go on to discuss how they feel comedy should be judged. Fox and VanArendonk believe relying on documentary footage prioritizes truth in comedy over comedians creating an art.[75] Instead, they believe the art of standup is a comedian's ability to arrive at truth through constructing an environment. By environment, here, I refer to the selected information, points of comparison, areas of emphasis, tone, and any features of the built environment (such as the stage) which set the scene for the audience.

Recall from earlier in this book that, according to Ramy Youssef, comedy does not need to be factually true, but instead should be emotionally true. VanArendonk touches on the same points as Youssef in her analysis of docu-comedy specials. She explains that realism is often conflated with a record; something objective, accurate, and real. Yet records like history are not objective. They reflect particular viewpoints the history-keepers deemed important to save. This is true for historical accounts of past events and it is true for comedians.

Fox and VanArendonk's statement that comedy is an artform in which the ultimate goal is to find and create emotional truth inside a staged performance is a sociological take on comedy that acknowledges that truth itself is constructed. Everything is a performance. Even documentary footage that says: "Here you go, it's true!" values objective truth over someone's ability to craft an experience that truly conveys their experiences, emotions, and unique perspectives. This behavior overvalues the status quo and the mainstream ways of thinking about the world, and undervalues lesser-understood experiences which require translation for their audiences. Reconsider the *Stage Fright* example. The notion that Slate should have to prove her anxiety through documentary footage, versus telling us about it in her own words, is a burden not required of all comedians.

Recall how Dr. Stephanie Brown noted that "authenticity" was assigned to performers based upon their position within the social hierarchy. White men were assumed to be more credible than women or people of color.[76] Given this, it is understandable that a comedian may choose to infuse their comedy special with documentary special. Particularly a comedian whose personal narratives may not be viewed as "authentic." There is an added burden to "prove" the veracity one's own experiences.

What emotional burdens does this value system of comedy place on comedians? We heard from comedians in this chapter, including Aparna Nancherla, Naomi Ekperigin, and Jenny Slate, who choose to talk about mental illness because it is a part of their life. But, must performers talk about their struggles on stage? Many struggles can be difficult or re-traumatizing to discuss at all, let alone on stage in front of a room full of strangers. As we continue to discuss the ways identity and intersectionality impact audience reception to material about stigmatized topics like mental illness, we must acknowledge that performers' identities can carry unequal burden and unequal reward.

With this discussion in mind, let us revisit this book's definition of comedy. Comedy, as defined here, is an artform in which the performer shares a non-traditional perspective with their audience and provokes disruptions in normative ways of thinking. That does not *necessitate* sharing one's traumas. Comedians certainly *can*, but it is not required. Comedians can mine their personal histories to talk about their traumas directly, they could satirize social systems which led to those traumas, and/or they could discuss fun and trivial topics which give them moments of levity and release from those traumas (or, of course, choose to have nothing to do with trauma whatsoever). The point is that a comedian's emotional truth is whatever they want and choose to focus on. This is an important point about truth in general; truth and history in society are constructed, too. The way we tell history and share news is largely dependent upon who writes and retells those narratives (recall this book's earlier discussion of the consolidation of news media outlets). How each comedian sees the world, and how they craft their retelling of what they see for their audiences, is the "art" of comedy.

So, when I say comedy is conveying emotional truth in a staged environment, what I mean is that what comedians owe their audience is their voice and their perspective on any subject they deem interesting or important. Comedians are people who inherently tell their own stories using their personal lens. Their sets are formed by first asking themselves: Which of my stories do I deem important enough to tell on stage? Which of these stories am I ready to tell on stage? Which elements of these stories deserve my focus? What were the lessons these stories taught me? The way comedians answer these questions becomes the art. Each comedian will answer these questions differently, and that is what makes each comedian's voice unique and provides opportunity for surprise. This is also what allows for audiences to experience surprise, laughter, anger, or connection. If everyone saw the world the exact same way, there would be no surprise endings or comedic twists because we would all see them coming. You need more than truth to make comedy because comedy is an artform that pulls truth apart.

Summary

This chapter walked through examples of how a sociological toolkit can be applied to the sociology of health and illness. This chapter used sociological explanations of deviance to discuss social conceptualizations of health and illness, how they evolve, and how they are presented in media. This chapter analyzed the sad clown paradox using methods and approaches employed by sociologists and social statisticians. We walked through comedic examples from television that highlight the perspectives of people suffering from mental illness and discussed how conceptions of mental illness and associated behaviors are highly gendered in the United States. From there, we discussed the concept of performed authenticity and what it means to be "truthful" in comedy.

Discussion Questions

8-1: Define <u>sex</u>, <u>gender identity</u>, and <u>gender expression</u>. How does the sociological idea that body parts are social "symbols" tie to all three of these concepts.

8-2: <u>Interactionist theory</u> asserts we both respond to and create society through our interactions with others. Using the comedic examples provided in this chapter, highlight an example that demonstrates how this works.

8-3: Define <u>discredited individuals</u>, <u>discreditable individuals</u>, and <u>stigma visibility</u>. How do these concepts relate to <u>socialization</u>, <u>deviance</u>, and <u>presentation of the self</u>?

8-4: Do you agree with the underlying assumption of Maria Bamford's joke that physical illness and mental illness are not treated the same way? Why or why not? Consider how social norms vary by place, culture, and time. Compare answers with your classmates and discuss any differences.

8-5: Do you think Naomi Ekperigin's understanding of mental health struggles as only the problems of White people relates to "stereotype threat"? Why or why not?

8-6: Why and how would a sociologist want to use an <u>intersectional</u> lens to understand how someone experiences a physical or mental health condition?

8-7: How does Charles Horton Cooley's concept of the <u>looking-glass self</u> relate to <u>labeling theory</u>?

8-8: Do you believe Burnham's *Inside* represents a <u>simulation</u>? What about <u>falseness</u>? In both cases, justify your answer. Be specific about the distinctions between the two concepts and how or why *Inside* meets, or does not meet, their definitions.

8-9: With a classmate, discuss how Jenny Slate's *Stage Fright* relates to Stephanie Brown's analysis of authenticity in comedy. Consider if and how the need to "prove" the veracity of one's own experiences (i.e., by using documentary footage in a comedy special) may be detrimental to one's co-medic expression. Do you think about the long-term career repercussions of comedians who need to battle for audiences' trust?

8-10: Do you think comedians should be required to talk about their strug-gles on stage, lest they be considered "inauthentic"?

Notes

1 Blumer, H. (1986). *Symbolic Interactionism: Perspective and Method*. University of California Press.
2 Champagne, A. M. (2018, August 14). Beauty and The Breast: Mastectomy, Mate-riality & the Iconicity of Gender. *Regular Session: Culture and Identity*. American Sociological Association 2018 Annual Meeting, Philadelphia, PA. https://www.academia.edu/90953049/Beauty_and_The_Breast_Mastectomy_Materiality_and_The_Iconicity_of_Gender_by_Anne_Marie_Champagne
3 West, C., & Zimmerman, D. H. (1987). Doing gender. *Gender and Society, 1*(2), 125–151. https://www.jstor.org/stable/189945
4 *Breast Cancer Statistics | How Common Is Breast Cancer?* (2022, January 12). https://www.cancer.org/cancer/breast-cancer/about/how-common-is-breast-cancer.html
5 Lingshan, S., Ang, E., Ang, W. H. D., & Lopez, V. (2017). Losing the breast: A meta-synthesis of the impact in women breast cancer survivors. *Psycho-Oncology*. https://onlinelibrary.wiley.com/doi/abs/10.1002/pon.4460
6 Susini, T., Renda, I., Giani, M., Vallario, A., Nori, J., Vanzi, E., Innocenti, A., Russo, G. L., & Bianchi, S. (2019). Changing trends in mastectomy and breast re-construction. analysis of a single-institution experience between 2004-2016. *Anti-cancer Research, 39*(10), 5709–5714. https://doi.org/10.21873/anticanres.13770
7 Champagne, 2018.
8 West & Zimmerman, 1987.
9 Pfeffer, C. A., & LaRossa, R. (2010). "Women's work"? Women partners of transgender men doing housework and emotion work. *Journal of Marriage and Family, 72*(1), 165–183. https://www.jstor.org/stable/27752562
10 *Stigma*. (1986). https://www.simonandschuster.com/books/Stigma/Erving-Goffman/9780671622442
11 Miller, L. R., & Grollman, A. (2015). The social costs of gender nonconformity for transgender adults: Implications for discrimination and health. *Sociological Forum, 30*(3), 809–831. https://www.jstor.org/stable/43654134

12 Karas, J., & Notaro (Directors). (2015). *Tig Notaro: "Boyish Girl Interrupted."* https://www.imdb.com/title/tt4920096/

13 Clem, J. S., & Druckerman, K. (Directors). (2019, March 10). *It Started as a Joke* [Documentary]. Left/Right, Pretty Good Friends.

14 Christensen, J. (2017, March 1). *The sad clown: The deep emotions behind stand-up comedy.* CNN. https://www.cnn.com/2017/03/01/health/sad-clown-standup-comedy-mental-health/index.html

15 Neporent, L. (2014, August 12). *What's the Deal With Comedians and Depression?* ABC News. https://abcnews.go.com/Health/deal-comedians-depression/story?id=24945911

16 Christensen, 2017; Janus, S. S. (1975). The great comedians: Personality and other factors. *The American Journal of Psychoanalysis, 35*(2), 169–174. https://doi.org/10.1007/BF01358189

17 Janus, 1975.

18 Neporent, 2014.

19 Christensen, 2017.

20 Corbett, S. (2014, July 17). *The Weird, Scary and Ingenious Brain of Maria Bamford—The New York Times.* https://www.nytimes.com/2014/07/20/magazine/the-weird-scary-and-ingenious-brain-of-maria-bamford.html

21 Bamford, M. (2013). *Ask Me About My New God!* Comedy Central Records. https://music.apple.com/us/album/ask-me-about-my-new-god/1590944891

22 Conrad, P. (1992). Medicalization and social control. *Annual Review of Sociology, 18,* 209–232. https://www.jstor.org/stable/2083452

23 Kyle, T. K., Dhurandhar, E. J., & Allison, D. B. (2016). Regarding obesity as a disease: Evolving policies and their implications. *Endocrinology and Metabolism Clinics of North America, 45*(3), 511–520. https://doi.org/10.1016/j.ecl.2016.04.004

24 Uyeda, R. L. (2021, May 26). *How LGBTQ+ Activists Got "Homosexuality" out of the DSM.* JSTOR Daily. https://daily.jstor.org/how-lgbtq-activists-got-homosexuality-out-of-the-dsm/

25 Bamford, 2013.

26 *Good One: Aparna Nancherla's Anxiety.* (2020, May 12). https://podcasts.apple.com/us/podcast/aparna-nancherlas-anxiety/id1203393721?i=1000474326857

27 *Hilarious World of Depression: Naomi Ekperigin Brings In Her Baggage, Unpacks It.* (2018, December 10). https://www.hilariousworld.org/episode/2018/12/10/naomi-ekperigin-brings-in-her-baggage-unpacks-it

28 Late Night with Seth Meyers (Director). (2016, September 30). *Naomi Ekperigin Stand-Up Performance.* https://www.youtube.com/watch?v=UB7wnsJSLCw

29 Falk, S. (Director). (2015a, November 4). You're the Worst: "LCD Soundsystem." In *You're the Worst.*

30 *Loving v. Virginia.* (1967). LII / Legal Information Institute. https://www.law.cornell.edu/supremecourt/text/388/1

31 Baumeister, R. F., & Twenge, J. M. (2001). Personality and Social Behavior. In N. J. Smelser & P. B. Baltes (Eds.), *International Encyclopedia of the Social & Behavioral Sciences* (pp. 11276–11281). Pergamon. https://doi.org/10.1016/B0-08-043076-7/01779-4

32 Blumer, 1986.

33 Becker, H. S. (1963). *Outsiders: Studies in the Sociology of Deviance.* Free Press Glencoe.

34 *Stigma,* 1986.

35 Thoits, P. A. (2010). Stress and health: Major findings and policy implications. *Journal of Health and Social Behavior, 51 Suppl,* S41–S53. https://doi.org/10.1177/0022146510383499

36 Umberson, D., & Montez, J. K. (2010). Social relationships and health: A flashpoint for health policy. *Journal of Health and Social Behavior, 51*(Suppl), S54–S66. https://doi.org/10.1177/0022146510383501

37 Markowitz, F. E. (2005). Sociological Models of Mental Illness Stigma: Progress and Prospects. In *On the stigma of mental illness: Practical strategies for research and social change* (pp. 129–144). American Psychological Association. https://doi.org/10.1037/10887-005

38 Payton, A., & Thoits, P. (2011, March). *Medicalization, Direct-to-Consumer Advertising, and Mental Illness Stigma.* https://www.researchgate.net/publication/258188441_Medicalization_Direct-to-Consumer_Advertising_and_Mental_Illness_Stigma

39 Pescosolido, B. (2013, January 16). *The Public Stigma of Mental Illness: What Do We Think; What Do We Know; What Can We Prove? – Bernice A. Pescosolido, 2013.* https://journals.sagepub.com/doi/abs/10.1177/0022146512471197

40 Pescosolido, B. A., Halpern-Manners, A., & Luo, L. (2021, December 21). *Trends in Public Stigma of Mental Illness in the US, 1996-2018 | Depressive Disorders | JAMA Network Open | JAMA Network.* https://jamanetwork.com/journals/jamanetworkopen/fullarticle/2787280

41 *Americans Becoming More Open About Mental Health* (p. 2). (2019). [Survey]. American Psychological Association. https://www.apa.org/news/press/releases/apa-mental-health-report.pdf

42 *Post-traumatic stress disorder (PTSD)—Symptoms and causes.* (2022). Mayo Clinic. https://www.mayoclinic.org/diseases-conditions/post-traumatic-stress-disorder/symptoms-causes/syc-20355967

43 Vernow, D. (2019, October 8). *PTSD is More Likely in Women Than Men | NAMI: National Alliance on Mental Illness.* https://www.nami.org/Blogs/NAMI-Blog/October-2019/PTSD-is-More-Likely-in-Women-Than-Men

44 López-Castro, T., Saraiya, T., Zumberg-Smith, K., & Dambreville, N. (2019). Association between shame and posttraumatic stress disorder: A meta-analysis. *Journal of Traumatic Stress*, 32(4), 484–495. https://doi.org/10.1002/jts.22411

45 Saraiya, T., & Lopez-Castro, T. (2016). Ashamed and afraid: A scoping review of the role of shame in post-traumatic stress disorder (PTSD). *Journal of Clinical Medicine*, 5(11), 94. https://doi.org/10.3390/jcm5110094

46 *"I'm So Happy 4 U"—Crazy Ex-Girlfriend (feat. Rachel Bloom).* (2019). https://www.youtube.com/watch?v=nSTJ9xwNV0M

47 Nunn, G. (2012, March 8). *The feminisation of madness is crazy | Media | The Guardian.* https://amp.theguardian.com/media/mind-your-language/2012/mar/08/mind-your-language-feminisation-madness

48 Barreca, R. (1988). *Last Laughs: Perspectives on Women and Comedy.* Routledge. https://www.routledge.com/Last-Laughs-Perspectives-on-Women-and-Comedy/Barreca/p/book/9781032226217

49 Nunn, 2012.

50 *Gaslight Definition & Meaning—Merriam-Webster.* (2022). https://www.merriam-webster.com/dictionary/gaslight

51 Cukor, G. (Director). (1944, May). *Gaslight.* https://catalog.afi.com/Catalog/moviedetails/1552

52 Vernow, 2019.

53 Das, J. (2021). *Gender Issues in Society: Myths, Reality and Responsibility.* Krishna Publication House.

54 Hill, M. L., Nichter, B., Na, P. J., Norman, S. B., Morland, L. A., Krystal, J. H., & Pietrzak, R. H. (2021). Mental health impact of the COVID-19 pandemic in U.S. military veterans: A population-based, prospective cohort study. *Psychological Medicine.* https://www.cambridge.org/core/journals/psychological-medicine/article/mental-health-impact-of-the-covid19-pandemic-in-us-military-veterans-a-populationbased-prospective-cohort-study/BE7E49DD813ADF49A38742145C1F395C

55 Vespa, J. E. (2020). *Those Who Served: America's Veterans from World War II to the War on Terror.* 18. https://www.census.gov/library/publications/2020/demo/acs-43.html

56 Birkeland, M., Blix, I., Solberg, Ø. S., & Heir, T. (2017, December 1). *Frontiers | Gender Differences in Posttraumatic Stress Symptoms after a Terrorist Attack: A Network Approach.* https://www.frontiersin.org/articles/10.3389/fpsyg.2017.02091/full

57 Vernow, 2019.

58 Ferster, H. (2019). *Crazy Women and Crazier Men: Mental Illness and Gender in Television Shows and Fan Conversations.* 75.

59 Sever, I., Somer, E., Ruvio, A., & Soref, E. (2008). Gender, distress, and coping in response to terrorism. *Affilia, 23*(2), 156–166. https://doi.org/10.1177/0886109908314317

60 West & Zimmerman, 1987.

61 *Angry Mad—Crazy Ex-Girlfriend Cast feat. Vincent Rodriquez III.* (2016, May 20). https://www.youtube.com/watch?v=osu9j3kPaZw

62 *Bo Burnham: Inside (TV Special 2021)—IMDb.* (2021). https://www.imdb.com/title/tt14544192/

63 *Bo Burnham: Inside (TV Special 2021)—IMDb,* 2021.

64 Syme, R. (2021, June 5). *"Inside," Reviewed: Bo Burnham's Virtuosic Portrait of a Mediated Mind | The New Yorker.* https://www.newyorker.com/culture/on-television/inside-reviewed-bo-burnhams-virtuosic-portrait-of-a-mediated-mind

65 Kohn, E. (2021, May 30). *'Bo Burnham: Inside' Review: Netflix Special Is Pandemic-Era Genius | IndieWire.* https://www.indiewire.com/2021/05/bo-burnham-inside-review-netflix-1234641131/

66 Logan, B. (2021, May 31). Bo Burnham: Inside review – this is a claustrophobic masterpiece. *The Guardian.* https://www.theguardian.com/stage/2021/may/31/bo-burnham-inside-review-netflix

67 Krefting, R. (2014). *All Joking Aside: American Humor and Its Discontents.* Johns Hopkins University Press.

68 Brown, S. (2018). Open Mic? Gender and the Meritocratic Myth of Authenticity in the Cultural Production of Stand-Up Comedy (Dissertation). *University of Illinois at Urbana-Champaign.*

69 *Yvonne Orji: "Momma, I Made It!"* (2020). HBO. https://www.hbo.com/movies/yvonne-orji-momma-i-made-it

70 *Good One: Docu-Comedy Specials with Kathryn VanArendonk.* (2021, September 30). https://podcasts.apple.com/us/podcast/docu-comedy-specials-with-with-kathryn-vanarendonk/id1203393721?i=1000537092666

71 Evans, H. (2016). Disability, Identity, and the Law: A Phenomenological Study of Living with Acquired, Invisible Impairment. *Undefined.* https://www.semanticscholar.org/paper/Disability%2C-Identity%2C-and-the-Law%3A-A-Study-of-with-Evans/27a909dc241dffd9533a82fb88f5ea825e6d3e47

72 Bamford, 2013.

73 *Jenny Slate—Stage Fright.* (2019). https://www.netflix.com/title/81027753

74 VanArendonk, K. (2019, October 22). *Review: Jenny Slate's 'Stage Fright' Netflix Comedy Special.* https://www.vulture.com/2019/10/jenny-slate-stage-fright-netflix-comedy-review.html

75 *Good One: Docu-Comedy Specials with Kathryn VanArendonk* (2021).

76 Brown, 2018.

9 The Performance of Trauma

This chapter builds upon earlier discussions of sociological concepts related to the marginalization of people based upon intersections of their sex, gender, sexuality, and race. This chapter provides examples of how members of marginalized groups have long been excluded, assaulted, or made the butts of the joke, and discuss what audiences are paying for when they pay to laugh at someone's pain. We expand upon earlier discussions of "alternative spaces" to examine how marginalized comedians have engaged digital platforms to carve out new avenues for success and perform innovative styles of comedy in the Internet era.

Drawing on the research of Darnell Hunt and Ana-Christina Ramón, this chapter discusses the rise of YouTube and streaming services as antidotes to the current landscape of concentrated power in that they have the potential to expand opportunities for the inclusion of diverse voices and challenges to the status quo. Informed by postmodernism and the work of sociological theorists bell hooks and Patricia Hill Collins, this chapter discusses approaches for rising up against oppression. Sociological concepts include identity contingencies, internalized stigma, exclusion, identity politics, the invisibility of racism, and the matrix of oppression.

Postmodernism and the Performance of Trauma with Hannah Gadsby

Figure 9.1 highlights the "Digital Boom" era of comedy, roughly spanning 2000-Present. This era provides rich sociological information about postmodernism, subcultures, and how new social structures may work against, and work for, existing social hierarchies. In the next section, we will dive specifically into the sociological significance of this era in comedy's history.

Let us jump into Hannah Gadsby's (born in Burnie, Tasmania, Australia, 1978) 2018 Netflix special, *Nanette*. For those of you unfamiliar with the special, it is a big deal. It defines many aspects of modern comedy. One of the noteworthy and unique aspects of *Nanette* is the way Gadsby talks about painful and traumatic experiences in their life.[1] Comedians often call upon pain and trauma but in *Nanette*, Gadsby refuses to be the butt of the joke.

Usually, comedians lean silently upon the form of standup comedy to engage in social decoding, critique, and commentary. There are many examples

DOI: 10.4324/9781003469537-10

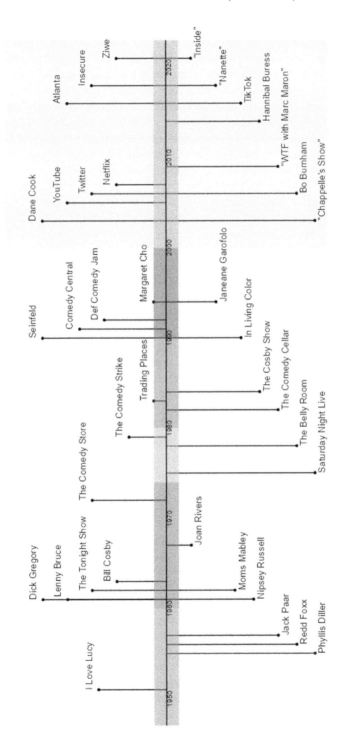

Figure 9.1 The Digital Boom Timeline

covered so far in this book which do exactly this. Comedians translate their experiences through metaphors or spin up a story's inconsistencies or absurdities to uncover its emotional truth. Gadsby, however, does not translate or soften their experiences and trauma. Gadsby breaks the fourth wall by explicitly telling the audience what they are doing in their performance. They first tell a joke, then tell the audience the differences between what they said and what they *did not say* in that joke.

Gadsby lets it sink in for their audience that their standup career is built upon airing their trauma for the entertainment of strangers. Their performance rhetorically asks why audiences show up – and pay on entry – to be entertained by someone else's pain. Gadsby breaks down the illusion implicitly accepted among some comedy audiences that comics enjoy being the butt of the joke or that they enjoy being laughed at. Gadsby offers the truth: comics use the backdrop of a standup set to share their story and make their voices heard to a group of people who might otherwise not be listening.

A pivotal moment in *Nanette* centers on Gadsby recounting how they used to tell a joke about when a man almost beat them up. In the joke, Gadsby describes chatting with the man's girlfriend at a bus stop late in the evening. The man immediately became angry at Gadsby. Based on their somewhat masculine presentation, he assumed Gadsby was a man and assumed Gadsby was hitting on his girlfriend. The man shoves and yells at Gadsby, screaming at them and calling them pejorative terms. The girlfriend intervenes, telling the man to stop because Gadsby is a woman. The man responds to this new information. He apologizes to Gadsby and assures them he does not "hit women" (Gadsby, 2018).[2] Gadsby relieves the tension of this story for the audience when they deliver a punchline about how this guy's "good" policy should certainly be extended to not hit *anyone*. Laughter from this jokes stems from the incongruity between who the audience originally pictured the man to be (a violent, bigoted person) with who he ultimately was (a man guided by principles who was simply ignorant about Gadsby's identity).

But then Gadsby does something different from what most comedians do during their standup specials. Gadsby dissects the frog. She walks the audience through *how* they crafted the joke and *why* it deviates from reality. The "why" is important because, as Gadsby explains, the punchline of that joke is not representative of what truly happened. The man did not apologize and give an assurance he does not "hit women." He *does* hit women. Badly. And that's exactly what happened to Gadsby. But they explain to the audience that they tell the joke the way they did because they are good at controlling tension in a room. Gadsby explains that they are a good comedian because they can artfully craft stories which set up tension, release it, and get laughs in the right places.

Gadsby shows the underbelly of what being a good comedian means for marginalized folks. They explain that to break the tension in that joke, they could not tell her audience about what really happened when the man learned Gadsby was a woman. The man did not apologize. He continued to verbally attack them and then he physically assaulted them. He beat them up. And not a single person intervened on Gadsby's behalf.

Consider the identity contingencies Gadsby describes here. Recall, **iden-tity contingencies** are the circumstances one must battle due to their social identity – such as age, race, sex, gender, sexuality, or intersections therein – and may include physical barriers, threats, harassment, or assault. Identity contingencies have both physical and psychological impacts. Physically, iden-tity contingencies determined the physical spaces where it is safe or accept-able for people to enter – such as which bathroom individuals are allowed to use based upon their physical sex or gender identity. Psychologically, identity contingencies can stoke fear and shame, among other consequences.[3]

Consider the weight of Gadsby's craft. To get laughs, they can share the part of their truth in which they were mistaken for a man and threatened at a bus stop. But they could not be truthful about what came next. Like Donald Glover's televi-sion series *Atlanta*, Gadsby engages elements of **hyperreality** in this *Nanette*. Re-call that hyperreality refers to an audience's inability to decipher what is real from what is simulated. Gadsby makes their audience question their own knowledge and feelings about the harassment incident as told in the original joke.

This is a burden heightened for marginalized people and for anyone who needs to break tension on stage, when tension did not break in their real life. Gadsby explains this further. They note that they did not report this incident to the police or seek medical attention. They tell the crowd they did not report the incident because they felt it was what they were worth. Gadsby explains that people like them have always been taught their existence is shameful, and others – like the man who beat her up – have been taught they have permission to hate them.[4]

Here, Gadsby effectively conveys to the audience that their assault was not a one-off incident. This is their life. This is something they have experienced be-fore and something they will likely experience again. They explain that because they are not feminine, and therefore not correctly performing being a woman, many think they deserve punishment for their deviance. This is an example of enforcing normative behavior through coercion. Attempting to force everyone to adhere to binary gender expectation means those who are marginalized due to their sexuality or gender identity have come to expect harassment and assault.

Gadsby is describing their experiences with **internalized stigma**. As in our earlier discussion of internalized racism, the internalization of any form of oppression is to take on oppressive messages about yourself and begin to believe them. You begin to see yourself the way others see you and/or blame yourself for the oppression and harm to which you are subjugated. Consider how this relates to earlier discussions of Howard Becker's **labeling theory**, which posits that individuals internalize the labels that are applied to them and begin to see themselves as worth less than others because of their labeled or stigmatized status. Labels contribute to the maintenance of the status quo by punishing and discrediting individuals for behaviors and/or features of their identity which do not align with dominant social norms.

Gadsby is reacting to social norms which label and stigmatize marginalized individuals. And it also criticizes comedy – their own artform – for covering up tragedy. *Nanette* is a unique special for the way it looks in on itself. Consider the sociological imagination Gadsby uses here. Their comedic perspective in *Nanette* is not just shining a light on society using comedy. Their comedic perspective in *Nanette* is using comedy to shine a light on society and on how comedy does not always shine a light on society. *Say that ten times fast.*

In the special, Gadsby explains that they are not going to cut the tension of these types of situations anymore. The audience needs to experience the tension that folks like them experience every day of their lives; the marginalization, fear, and constant threat of danger. The way Gadsby made a joke from real experience, shared that joke, then explained why they structured the joke that way is powerful art. They made their experience *felt*. They took reality, flipped it on its head, then flipped it back over because that was the most emotionally effective way to have their story heard. They broke the tension, then they pieced it back together.

Consider how Gadsby's comedy is an inverse of the comedy of Louis C.K. in many ways. Many considered C.K. the godfather of truth-telling comics for sharing the bad thoughts in his head that he would "never" act on. Except, as the public now knows, he *did* act on them. Dangling those falsehoods in front of his audience was performative and self-congratulatory. It served himself and his image. Gadsby, meanwhile, had to soften their truth for the audience to make their material palatable for *the audience*, not to serve themself. When they lift the veil, it is vulnerable, real, and revelatory. They did not do it to sell tickets. In fact, they thought it might end their career.

Because of this, many critics did not see *Nanette* as comedy. This is a common critique of *Nanette*. Many called it a one-woman show, a TED Talk, or a lecture.[5] Gadsby satirizes these critiques in their subsequent special, *Douglas*.[6] Toward the end of *Douglas*, Gadsby tells a series of jokes which are visually aided by a PowerPoint presentation of Renaissance paintings. Gadsby moves through the slides as if they were giving an art history lecture. The jokes are funny, historically accurate, and in true Gadsby form, their jokes are commentary on the world while also being jokes about jokes. Like Andy Kaufman before them, Gadsby plays with the audience's expectations for what happens at a standup special.

Alexis Sobel Fitts, then-senior editor at *WIRED* magazine, held up *Nanette* as textbook comedy for the way it uses form, narrative, and comedic decoding to engage in social commentary. *Nanette* cannot be genre-breaking for comedy (as some critics defined it) because it *is* comedy.[7] I agree with Fitts' assessment. The definition of comedy used throughout this book asserts comedy is commentary which depicts the world through a new lens. In *Nanette*, Gadsby does this twice. They use their comedic perspective to make jokes about their personal experiences; then, they use it to comment on their own jokes. To say this is not comedy is to ignore what comedians do as artists, performers, and social commentators, and to ignore that art evolves. If comedians comment on the world, eventually comedians will comment on comedians commenting on the world.

Criticisms lodged against *Nanette* are holding comedy to an older, narrower standard. Comedy inherently changed with the advent of the Internet.

Jesse David Fox speaks about how YouTube and the Internet fundamentally shifted the function of comedic storytelling and the relationship audiences have with comedians.[8] He argues that that invention of YouTube is to comedy what the invention of photography was to film and painting. Before photography, artists attempted to accurately represent life. Paintings looked more like photographs. But once cameras were able to take photographs, the painting artform needed to evolve. It became more abstract and more impressionistic. To Fox, this same transition happened in comedy. **Post-comedy** refers to the transition from comedians building a set based on jokes anyone could deliver, to sets based more on their perspective and personality. Comedy, too, became more impressionistic. The expectations and norms associated with traditional standup comedy in a night club are dismantled.

To see how comedy evolves and to understand how comedy's evolution helps us understand what comedy is, I want to raise a comparison between *Nanette* and Dane Cook's 2006 special *Vicious Circle*. This comparison was raised by comedy journalist Fox in an episode of his podcast *The Specials*. Fox and his co-hosts rail against *Vicious Circle* for its use of misogyny, homophobia, clapter, and what they consider to be lazy joke writing. In many ways, *Vicious Circle* is nearly the exact comedic opposite of *Nanette*. If you attempted to find an example for whatever is the opposite of clapter, that would be *Nanette*. Yet, the two specials share similarities.

The first similarity: both specials were exactly what audiences wanted from comedy at their time. Let us go back in time to Dane Cook's (born in Cambridge, Massachusetts, 1972) era of extreme popularity. Cook was a rockstar comedian at the time he released *Vicious Circle*. Cook had gathered a large and dedicated following using social media and he was a pioneer for leveraging the Internet for comedic success. Because of his beloved persona, his *Vicious Circle* audience laughed, clapped, hooted, and hollered at just about anything he said.

The second similarity between the two specials is what they can teach us about comedy. Specifically, that comedy does not need to be funny all the time. As Fox argues, both *Vicious Circle* and *Nanette* show that comedy is not composed of non-stop humor. Instead, there are moments in every comedic performance of "in between" time where the comedian is telling a story, setting up context, or giving the setup for the next joke's payoff.[9]

Even in *Vicious Circle,* which is a comedy special that was tailor-made for laugher, hooting, and hollering, the audience is not literally laughing the entire time. There are the parts in between the jokes. Fox extends this point to say that, in *Nanette*, most of the performance was this "in between" part. Fox's argument is an astute one. I argue most comedy fans and critics would agree that comedy does not necessitate you laugh the entire time. There is time in between punchlines. There are always elements of storytelling, setup, and transition; and those elements are still considered integral to comedy. Gadsby and Cook divide their time differently between those two parts of comedy.

So while there are similarities between Gadsby's and Cook's specials, there are certainly large differences. The primary difference is the way Gadsby has long been made to be the butt of the joke. Jokes like those made by Cook. In *Nanette*, Gadsby tells their audience they are will no longer cow down or self-deprecate to make others feel comfortable.[10]

Streaming Services on Diversity and Opportunity

On *The Specials* podcast, Fox explains how Netflix opened avenues for comedians not welcomed by comedy club audiences using *Nanette* as an example. Fox argued that *Nanette* may be the biggest comedy special of all time and it likely would not have been nearly as successful were it not for streaming. He attributes its success to three primary factors: the reach of Netflix as a platform, the international element afforded by the fact that Gadsby is not American (they are Australian), and that Gadsby's joke structure and pacing allows for multiple entry and exit points. By entry and exit points, he means that people can relate to various elements of their story without having to relate to all of it. They can join in and jump out of their jokes throughout the special because they weave in accessible elements all along the way. In this, Gadsby shows their skill as a brilliant comedian. They reach broad audiences (making their comedy universal) without losing the specifics of their experiences. This is something streaming affords. People have access to more content and can "try" more things.

The amount of content accessible to us has swelled in recent years due to the rise of streaming services like Amazon Prime Video, HBO Max, Hulu, Netflix, and others. A benefit of creating a show or movie for streaming is its viability is not directly tied to its ratings.[11] In the traditional media landscape, a show's ratings determined its success and lifespan. It needed to perform well for the masses. Streaming services provide a "gift baskets of content," however, meaning they need subscribers to buy the general access to the streaming service (the "basket"), but it does not really matter which of their offerings they like the best or watch the most. In the gift basket model, having a variety of content is good business. It behooves the streaming service to have a diversity of content to draw in a diversity of subscribers who can enjoy whatever subset of content they desire. Like we just discussed with YouTube, having content not directly tied to its ratings or profitability opens up opportunities for creators who might otherwise be shut out from having their voices heard.

For this reason, some streaming services have bought the distribution rights to older sitcoms still desired by some key audiences (including Black audiences) like *Sister, Sister* and *Moesha*. Both shows are sitcoms from the 1990s starring Black women (Tia and Tamera Mowry in *Sister, Sister*, and Brandy Norwood in *Moesha*). Streaming services also create their own content, and streaming has afforded greater representation for Black writers, producers, and actors; whom had long been shut out from creating content or pigeonholed into projects deemed suitable for mainstream (read: White) audiences.

Indeed, streaming platforms afford creators greater freedom in their content and widen the media offerings compared to those on network television.

Netflix, in particular, revolutionized the game. They were the first streaming service and enjoyed a decades-long monopoly on it. While traditional broadcasting networks tried to appeal to the widest and most general audiences, Netflix considered diversity of content as a strength.[12] Netflix created content for audiences often overlooked and underserved by traditional broadcasters and movie studios. Netflix secured contracts with Black creators (like Kenya Barris, Ava DuVernay, and Shonda Rhimes), women creators (like Liz Flahive, Jenji Kohan, and Carly Mensch), and creators of content aimed at LGBTQ+ audiences (like RuPaul). For example, *Orange is the New Black* was one of the Netflix's first original productions. It had a woman creator, starred women of color, and featured LGBTQ+ characters. The show was not necessarily a fit for broadcast, but it found its home and its audience at Netflix. Netflix did not always uphold inclusive values, but it did prove there was a large audience for content created by and for overlooked communities.

To see if, and to what degree, streaming increase the diversity of actors, directors, and writers in film, relative to theatrically released films, we can refer to the *Hollywood Diversity Report*. Authored by Dr. Darnell Hunt and Dr. Ana-Christina Ramón, the *Hollywood Diversity Reports* have been released annually since 2014. In these reports, the authors analyze the top English-language films released during the prior calendar year based on global box office and total U.S. household ratings. The reports allow readers to understand the diversity of the cast and creators of these films and track such measures over time.

In response to the changing film distribution landscape, Hunt and Ramón began analyzing streaming and theatrical films separately in the 2023 edition of the *Hollywood Diversity Report*. Results from the *Hollywood Diversity Report 2023, Part 1: Film* indicate that people of color and women have greater representation in the lead acting, writing, and directing credits in streaming films than in theatrical films.[13] However, there is still much ground to cover. Below, I share some findings from the report:

Lead Actors: People of color represented 33.3 percent of lead actors in streaming films (66.7 percent White), compared to 21.6 percent of lead actors in theatrical films (78.4 percent White). While streaming services are doing better than theatrical films in this regard, progress remains before there is equal representation to the U.S. population (43.1 percent people of color). Women were lead actors in 48.5 percent of streaming films (50.5 percent male, 1 percent non-binary), compared to 38.6 percent of theatrical films (60.2 percent male).

Directors: People of color were directors of 23.0 percent of streaming films (77.0 percent White), compared to 16.8 percent of theatrical films (83.2 percent White). Women were directors of 25.0 percent of streaming films (75.0 percent male), compared to 14.6 percent of theatrical films (85.4 percent male).

Writers: Films with a writer of color composed 20.0 percent of streaming films (80.0 percent White), compared to 12.4 percent of theatrical films

(87.6 percent White). Films with a female writer composed 36.0 percent of streaming films (64.0 percent male), compared to 27.0 percent of theatrical films (73.0 percent male).

While these roles are reported here separately, they are inextricably linked. Consider, for example, that Hunt and Ramón highlight that among streaming films with a writer of color, more than 75 percent also had a director of color.

Consider how you, as a sociological researcher, would measure representation. Is it just share of positions? What about level of opportunity? Hunt and Ramón also considered a film's budget. Streaming films tend to have smaller budgets and be less profitable than theatrical films. This remains a disadvantage to people of color and women. For example, 35.4 percent of streaming films had budgets less than $10 million (the lowest reported budget category), compared to 14.6 percent of theatrical films, while 9.4 percent of streaming films had budgets greater than $100 million (the highest reported budget category), compared to 16.9 percent of theatrical films.

Even within streaming films, there are disparities in budgets. On the low end of the budget spectrum, the report shows 40.6 percent of films with a director of color had budgets less than $10 million, compared to 35.5 percent of films with a White woman director and 28.1 percent of films with a White male director. On the high end of the budget spectrum, the report shows 12.5 percent of films with a director of color had a budget greater than $100 million, compared to 0 films with a White woman director and 15.6 percent of films with a White male director.

Overall, results highlighted in the report indicate streaming films afford more opportunities for people of color and women in lead acting, directing, and writing credits than do theatrical films; yet, more progress is needed before there is proportional representation and equal financial backing of those opportunities.

Let us return to Netflix. In addition to its impact on television and film, the streaming platform also changed the landscape of standup comedy specials. Netflix has produced hundreds of comedy specials; many of them featuring comedians from around the world and/or performed in languages other than English (including Arabic, Dutch, French, German, Hindi, Italian, Korean, Portuguese, Spanish, Swedish, and Turkish). Vir Das, introduced earlier in this book, was the first Indian comedian to have a standup special on Netflix in 2017, titled *Abroad Understanding,* and filmed five more comedy specials for Netflix by the end of 2022.[14] This is an example of **globalization**, defined as the expansion of culture and media across the globe. Similar trends have occurred in the music industry with the rise of streaming platforms like Spotify and iTunes.[15] Music preferences have become more global, and audiences are listening to more non-mainstream artists as access to music has become less tethered what is played on the radio (and what got played on the radio was largely determined by record labels, which limited the ability of independent artists to make it on air).[16]

A 2021 study published in "Humanities and Social Sciences Communications" found increased segmentation of the music market on Spotify and iTunes across the years 2017–2020.[17] This means there was growing diversity in the songs, artists, and labels streamed on the platforms over the five years of the study period. Like Netflix, Spotify and iTunes provide a platform for a wide array of content, knowing its audience is out there. With streaming, creators and audiences alike are no longer forced to assimilate to the mainstream media that was available through traditional broadcast or radio networks. With streaming, more cultures and subcultures can thrive.

Consider, again, Hannah Gadsby's special *Nanette*. For so long, mainstream platforms – including comedy club stages and television spots – were only available to White men. However, Netflix put *Nanette* front and center on their home page and the special was covered widely by the press. The promotion was not niche; it was mainstream. And the mainstream nature of *Nanette's* viewership means the special had ample opportunity for impact. Members of marginalized communities, like Gadsby, have always had brilliant comedic voices, but major platforms have not always been available to them.

While the rise of streaming services opens opportunities for a great diversity of voices and content, it is not a panacea for the inequities in comedy and media seen in other platforms. Netflix has opened a lot of doors that otherwise would have remained closed, but Netflix still reflects social stratification in its content and practices. Take it from comedian and actress Mo'Nique (born in Woodlawn, Maryland, 1967). In 2017, Mo'Nique called for a boycott of Netflix after she was offered a fraction of what Dave Chappelle, Chris Rock, and Amy Schumer were paid for their comedy specials. Mo'Nique was offered $500,000 for a special. Dave Chappelle received $20 million for each of the three specials he delivered that year, Chris Rock earned $20 million for his shows, and Schumer collected $13 million for *The Leather Special* (which she renegotiated with Netflix following their initial $11 million offer, citing sex-based inequalities in pay based upon Chappelle's and Rock's compensation).[18] Mo'Nique has since become a vocal critic of the rampant racism and sexism Black women experience in the comedy space.

It is important to use an intersectional lens to see who is getting access to these opportunities and how much they are compensated for their art. Even on streaming services, power, fame, and money are consolidated at the top. Even if two comedians have access to the same opportunities (a Netflix comedy special), if one is compensated more highly for it, it may influence current and future monetary, social, and professional valuations. Recall this book's discussion regarding how people are valued in the United States based upon their social status and monetary resources. Compensation matters. While YouTube and streaming services are moving the comedy world toward equity, there is still more ground to cover.

Streaming services acknowledge there is a hunger from audiences for more diverse content. It is profitable for these companies to make content for more niche audiences from a diversity of creators. Yet, these streaming services still operate under a capitalist system. They own the means of the productions:

the streaming platforms. There is pressure to make a larger profit for themselves by exploiting the labor of workers.

Recall, **labor unions** protect writers and actors through collective bargaining agreements. Two of these labor unions include the Writers Guild of America (WGA) and Screen Actors Guild and American Federation of Television and Radio Artists (SAG-AFTRA). The WGA is a consortium of two labor unions representing writers across media platforms – including television, film, the Internet, and radio. SAG-AFTRA represents workers across a diversity of media positions – including actors, singers, news writers and broadcasters, and program hosts, among others. The WGA and SAG-AFTRA helped establish contracts between workers and major studios to ensure fair labor and compensation practices in media production.

However, streaming opened up a whole new world. Consider the structure of residuals. A residual is the payment an artist receives after the initial compensation they receive for their work. The initial compensation, for example, would cover an actor's wages for filming an episode of a television show. Residual payments pay that actor every time the television episode is re-aired. On network television, re-airing of an episode (a "rerun") may occur somewhat regularly, but certainly not anywhere near the scale of views on streaming services.

In the new world of streaming, a minimum residual payment amount was not yet contractually agreed upon between the labor unions and the major studios. Studios took advantage of that by undercutting and underpaying writers and actors. A **false consciousness** existed for creators, wherein they were lauded for their show's success through positive reviews and awards. They were deemed "successful." Yet, they were not getting paid (at least, not well) on residuals. Things began to change when false ideologies were broken through what Karl Marx deemed **class consciousness**. Writers and actors began sharing their residual checks online, on platforms such as X (formerly known as Twitter). For example, actress Jana Schmieding showed one of her quarterly residual payments for her work on FX's *Reservation Dogs*. It was for three cents.[19]

In 2023, both WGA and SAG-AFTRA called for a **labor strike**.[20] Residual payments are just one of the fair labor demands being asked by the unions. Artists demanded better working conditions and limitations put in place against the use of artificial intelligence in script writing. WGA and SAG-AFTRA reached deals with major studios and streaming platforms, and ended their strikes on September 27, 2023 and November 9, 2023, respectively.

Subculture, the Internet, and Social Media

Like the entertainment industry and society in general, comedy has long been a White man's club. Having such a narrow view of comedian sensibilities and a firm grip on power has long shut other comedians out of the limelight through **formal exclusion** (like relegating Black comedians to the Chitlin'

Circuit and not giving stage time to women or people of color), or through **informal exclusion** (like labeling women comedians as unfunny, too crass, or too old; or labeling Black comedians as too vulgar). When the power is concentrated, it allows for unchecked freedom on what stories are told about those without the power. In more specific words: racist, misogynistic, xenophobic, and homophobic jokes go unchecked.

In this section, we will talk about the power of the Internet and digital platforms like YouTube to see how they can facilitate leveling the comedic playing field. Let us start with an example detailed in Kliph Nesteroff's 2021 book, *We Had a Little Real Estate Problem*, which elevates stories of Native Americans in comedy.[21] In the book, Nesteroff discusses a comedy troupe featuring Sterlin Harjo (born in Holdenville, Oklahoma, 1979). Harjo details going to an audition calling for Native American actors with his father, only for them to discover that the roles were stereotypes of Native Americans. He recalls going into auditions and seeing other actors playing to the part; one notable person, Harjo recalls, was wearing a choker and using baby oil to give his skin a sheen. Harjo would question what it really meant to be Native American. So Harjo decided to make comedy highlighting the absurdity of this situation: the idea that Native Americans were engaging in their own exploitation for the benefit of White directors and producers.

Harjo and four of his friends had a comedy troupe called the 1491s – named for the year before Christopher Columbus landed on the Americas. They self-produced a video mocking these stereotypic characterizations of Native Americans. One member (Dallas Goldtooth) dressed in a loin cloth, one member (Migizi Pensoneau) in a fur coat, one member (Bobby Wilson) sported a pair of red underwear, and one member (Thomas Ryan RedCorn) wore nothing but a plastic turtle positioned in front of his groin.[22] The 1491s had great fun making the video; they could not stop laughing the whole shoot. They felt like they had tapped into making content that was *for* and *by* their community.

Harjo explained that they were competing against a notion that there was no interest in contemporary images of Native Americans. That notion was a barrier from comedians and actors like Harjo making it on screen. Directors and producers, like the ones Harjo and his dad encountered at the audition, were gatekeepers of traditional avenues for television and movies. But Harjo and his friends had access to the Internet. They uploaded their video to YouTube – where there were no gatekeepers telling them they do not belong in comedy – and their video hit ten thousand views in mere hours. Students at the school where Harjo worked broke through the school's firewall to be able to watch and share the video. The 1491s' contemporary comedy smashed stereotypes of Native Americans as savages, or as "overly peaceful and passive." Their video's instant success was evidence that there is an appetite for comedy for and by Native American people. For Native American people watching the 1491s' video at home, it likely mattered greatly they were not the butt of the joke.

Harjo went on to co-create the critically acclaimed television series, *Reservation Dogs* (FX on Hulu, premiering 2021), alongside Taika Waititi (born in Raukokore, New Zealand, 1975). The series is set on a reservation in Oklahoma and centers on the lives of four Native American teenagers navigating friendship, family, dreams, and loss. *Reservation Dogs* made history as the first television series to ever be written and directed entirely by an Indigenous team of creators.[23] With the series, Harjo continued his comedic vision of telling Indigenous stories from Indigenous perspectives; one where Native American people are not the butt of the joke. Having an entertainment industry that better represents the population allows audiences who share a life experience or set of life experiences with a performer to connect with their stories, feel accepted, and feel less alone.

Finding a Community with TikTok

Without buy-in from the entertainment industry, people make their own spaces. Earlier in this book, we discussed physical alternative spaces – such as comedy shows held in coffeehouses, theaters, and laundromats during the alternative comedy movement of the 1990s. In this section, we describe online communities as avenues for acceptance.

Let us first review how sociologists discuss **mass media** as an agent of **socialization**.[24] As one example, children learn language and model behaviors after characters on television programs like *Sesame Street*. With the advent of new forms of media, including smartphones and social media, the reach of media as an agent of socialization has expanded over time. Children and adolescents are spending more time connected to media devices than ever before.[25] A study by Common Sense Media found an increase in total digital consumption among tweens (8–12-year-olds) and teens (13–18-year-olds) increased by 17 percent in just two years, between 2019 and 2021. The 2021 values for screentime totaled nearly nine hours per day for teens and just over five and a half hours per day for tweens.[26] Those tweens and teens are consuming their media over a variety of devices, including smartphones, tablets, computers, television, and a diversity of digital platforms therein.

For tweens and teens who are LGBTQ+, they may not see themselves represented in mainstream media. Recall this book's earlier discussions of **queer theory**. Queer theory scholars posit that sex, gender, and sexuality are not determined by biological features. Queer theory scholars ask for broader and more holistic understandings of one's sex, gender, and sexuality – which are separated from biological features of sex and are more reflective of the individual's self-understanding. They ask for great flexibility in our understandings of what it means to be a woman, man, or non-binary person, and in our sexual preferences and expressions. In this vein, queer theory scholars champion the deconstruction of the false binaries used to maintain a patriarchal and heteronormative social order.

Queer theory criticizes the idea that there are any stable elements of one's identity.[27] Sexuality is fluid and can change throughout the life course, and meaning tied to one's sexuality as gay, straight, or other identities can vary from person to person. For example, a man who identifies as straight may still enjoy sex with men. An important feature of queer theory is that it focuses attention on social dynamics between the LGBTQ+ community and other groups in society, versus focusing on individuals. Specifically, queer theory understands that LGBTQ+ folks have been marginalized by mainstream society and ignored by, or misrepresented in, mass media.

Online communities which are safe and tailored to these folks' experiences become important spaces for support and offer new agents of socialization. As an example, let us draw on the 2020 digital pride issue of *Paper* magazine, an independent magazine focused on fashion and culture based in New York City.[28] *Paper* brought together many talented LGBTQ+ comedians to talk about their work over video call (the event was originally planned as an in-person photo shoot but was moved to an online conversation due to the COVID-19 pandemic). The focus of the conversation was on how long-marginalized comedians created their own alternative spaces on the Internet to create comedy on their terms for their audiences. Alternative spaces often come with the added bonus of an alternative audience more likely to enjoy the niche humor these comedians offer.

Several of the comedians on the *Paper* call discussed how the Internet also makes it easier for fans to find these performances. Audiences who may be too far away, too young, too old, those facing physical limitations or those limited in money, childcare, transportation, and a host of other factors that inhibit their ability to come out to a comedy show, may have better access to the Internet.

Comedian Benito "Benny Drama" Skinner (born in Boise, Idaho, 1993) stated he wants his work to speak to kids growing up in areas that may not accept or understand them, so they know there is a place for them to live authentically and be celebrated for it. He wants to give them hope.[29] His characters are based on icons he loved growing up but had to admire in secret. His parodies of those pop and LGBTQ+ icons come from a place of love, the way you might parody a good friend.

Skinner and the other comedians on the call are engaging in what sociologists would call identity politics. **Identity politics** refers to how groups like the LGBTQ+ community use their collective power to say: "This is who we are, we will not assimilate." A great example of identity politics in action is the history of LGBTQ+ Pride (commonly known as Gay Pride). LGBTQ+ Pride is a movement focused on promoting the visibility, equality, acceptance, and respect of LBGTQ+ people and communities in society.[30] The grounding force of this movement is in the promotion of respect and reduction of stigma for LGBTQ+ people and their lifestyles. Some of the drivers of this movement include Gay Pride parades (public displays of pride and acceptance) and other grassroots activism efforts aimed at full acceptance and equality for LGBTQ+ people and communities.

These comedians acknowledge the strain that exists between making the comedy they want and their desire to "make it" in the industry. To remedy this strain, many of these comedians have redefined what success means to them. Their following was largely built through online platforms, such as Twitter, Instagram, TikTok, or by creating and posting their web series or podcasts. Skinner notes that he has moved away from the idea that the only marker of success is making it onto *Saturday Night Live* (as he jokes, when are you making it onto *SNL* is what uncles will continue asking you on holidays).[31] Skinner has certainly found success online. Thanks in large part to his viral videos depicting drag astrology characters, he amassed 1.4 million Instagram and 1.1 million TikTok followers by December 2021.[32]

With a greater emphasis on social media and the Internet as a stage for comedy, some of the same fracturing has occurred online. "Alternative" subareas are now popping up in popular platforms. For example, many LGBTQ+ comedians have found their home on alternative "Alt" TikTok.[33] On Alt TikTok, there is community, recognition, and celebration for people who have been long rejected by mainstream society.

The increased fracturing of media allows for more tailored experiences. While there used to be only a handful of channels and popular television programs that children and adolescents could watch, that is no longer the case. Today, there is greater representation of voices on television and online where children and adolescents can experience socialization. This continues to be done through mass media such as television and movies available one streaming channels, but also through peer networks on social media. They can find people who look and talk like themselves. As some YouTubers and TikTokers show their audiences; it is okay to be *you*.

Intersectional Lenses in *A Black Lady Sketch Show*

Let us discuss another example of the importance of finding your community using *A Black Lady Sketch Show*, a sketch comedy series which premiered on HBO in 2019. The show has Robin Thede (born in Spencer, Iowa, 1979) at the helm as creator, producer, showrunner, and co-star. *A Black Lady Sketch Show* immediately made its point of view clear as a sketch show created by, written by, and starring Black women.[34,35]

In the first of what later became a recurring sketch, "Courtroom Kiki," the celebration of Black women is at the fore. The sketch shows characters entering a courtroom as a civil case which is set to begin. The judge (played by Yvette Nicole Brown) takes the bench, followed by court stenographer (Gabrielle Dennis), bailiff (Bresha Webb), attorney for the defense (Quinta Brunson), and the plaintiff (Issa Rae) and her attorney (Robin Thede). The women look around and, to their surprise and glee, acknowledge they are all Black women. Brunson's character shouts: "It's a Black lady courtroom!" (*A Black Lady Sketch Show*, HBO, 2019).[36] The scene's humor is generated from the quick and frequent swings from formal legal procedures to the women's bursts of celebration.

For example, Judge Kiki asks if all the women want to go to lunch after the evidential hearing. Later, she call the attorneys, bailiff, and stenographer to the bench; but instead of discussing legal procedure, they discuss their alma maters, share their sorority affiliations ("AKA; first and finest" says Judge Kiki), and take a selfie. The sketch is fun and silly, but the underlying message is an important one; Black women have long been excluded from positions of power. And for those who make it through the door, they are often the only Black woman in the room.

The sketch highlights the privilege of others who may not notice the race or sex makeup of the spaces in which they work. It is a privilege to not notice race or sex. A courtroom full of White men is so normal for men in that space it may not even catch their attention. By focusing "Courtroom Kiki" on the glee of being a group of powerful Black women in a powerful space, it signals how unique of an experience this is for the characters.

"Courtroom Kiki" is an effective sketch for showcasing the sociological concept of the invisibility or racism. The **invisibility of racism** refers to the ways White privilege and institutional racism function relatively silently in daily life.[37] Compared to personal acts of racism or discrimination, which are easier to highlight, the structural ways racism and discrimination form daily life are harder to flag as social problems which deserve action, due to their relative invisibility.

The sketch shows how Black women's lived experience is not like those of White people. It shows these characters' immense joy when experiencing something so "normal" which White people, particularly White men, may take for granted. A show created, written, and performed by Black women like *A Black Lady Sketch Show* shines a light on the way racism is often hidden in the dark by contrasting the darkness with bright spots of joy.

Podcasting with 2 Dope Queens

We cannot talk about how the Internet opened up new avenues for comedians to find success, find their audiences, and be themselves without talking about podcasts. As a bit of background on the rise of podcasting, we will begin with podcaster, standup comedian, actor, and writer Marc Maron (born in Jersey City, New Jersey, 1963). Maron was a pioneer in comedy podcasting. At the 2011 Montreal *Just for Laughs* comedy festival (the largest international comedy festival in the world), Maron delivered the keynote address. In his speech, Maron told the crowd he was asked to give the address because he – and his podcast – represents the future of the industry.[38] Maron hosts *WTF with Marc Maron*, a weekly podcast that has been running since 2009 and receives an average of 220,000 downloads per episode (with a cumulative total of 600 million downloads between September 2009 and April 2021).[39]

By stating he represents the future of the industry, Maron foreshadows the rising importance of the podcasting platform in comedy. Comedy podcasts feel almost ubiquitous now. They are incredibly popular to fans and provide a low barrier to entry for comedians. To get started with a very bare-bones podcast, all you need is a phone (or other recording device) and the ability to upload to the Internet. During the COVID-19 pandemic, comedy podcasts grew; aided by their location flexibility and remote-friendliness, during a time when in-person standup comedy came to a halt.[40]

Consider potential parallels between podcasts today with the early days of produced storytelling in the home. Radio's popularity rose quickly in the late 1920s and early 1930s. It was a shared experience. Radio dramas (audio performances distributed over radio wave) were incredibly popular pieces of at-home entertainment. Families would gather around the radio to tune in to programs such as Orson Welles' *The War of the Worlds*, which was widely considered to be one of the most popular radio dramas in the U.S. history.[41] The following day, people would gather to talk about the stories at work, school, religious services, or in other places of socialization. Radio's immense popularity as a form of entertainment quickly waned in the 1950s, however, with the popularization of the television. This new platform changed the media landscape.

The early days of radio were marked by mainstream content. People were largely all listening to the same thing. Podcasts today, in comparison, are much more diverse. There are millions of them. Podcasts allow creators to find their own voice and skirt some of the gatekeepers present in more mainstream media or broadcast networks. Phoebe Robinson and Jessica Williams exemplify how creators can start their own podcasts and why that is socially meaningful. The comedic duo has myriad successful projects, with one of their most well-known being their podcast, *2 Dope Queens*.

Robinson (born in Bedford, Ohio, 1984) is a comedian, podcaster, television writer, best-selling author, and was a writer for *Girl Code* (MTV) and consultant for *Broad City* (HBO). In a 2015 Huffington Post article titled "Jessica Williams and Phoebe Robinson Want Comedy to Stop Ignoring Black Women," Robinson expressed frustration with her repeated experience being the only Black woman in a writer's room.[42] Robinson and Williams were then on a mission to increase opportunities for Black women in comedy and on television. There are a lot of voices and experiences being ignored.

The other half of the duo, comedian, actress, and podcaster Jessica Williams (born in Los Angeles, California, 1989), became the youngest senior correspondent for *The Daily Show with Jon Stewart* when she joined the show in 2012. Speaking from her experience of working in late night television (which is incredibly White and male), Williams noted there is a hunger from audiences for new voices and new perspectives. She feels so much of the content in media, coming from the White male perspective, feels "recycled." It was important to Robinson and Williams to change that, and the duo worked to create more opportunities for women of color to break into an industry that has long shut them out.

To this end, Robinson and Williams created *Blaria LIVE!*, a standup show that ran in Brooklyn, New York, and Washington, DC. The name of the live show nods to Robinson's blog, *Blaria* (the name stemming from Black + Daria, with *Daria* referencing the MTV animated sitcom which ran from 1997 to 2002). In their live shows, Robinson and Williams talk about their lives as young Black women living in New York City. While their material is based on their personal experiences, diverse audiences find it funny, relatable, and fresh. Indeed, audiences find great meaning in seeing Black women on stage being their smart, funny, witty, and real selves.

The show translated into a successful podcast, *2 Dope Queens*. The WNYC-produced podcast, taped live at Union Hall in Brooklyn, New York, was hosted by Robinson and Williams and ran from 2016 to 2018. The show skyrocketed to the very top of the iTunes charts in the first week it launched. The podcast became a platform for its diverse panel of guests to discuss topics related to issues often not covered by more mainstream outlets. It gave their guests – largely composed of folks not often represented in media, unless relegated to a side character or stereotype – a platform to tell their own stories from their own perspectives. As Williams explained, the goal of *2 Dope Queens* was to pass the microphone and let their guests be the "stars of their own stories" (Williams, 2015).

Let us connect this to sociological theory. Early feminist theoretical contributions were based upon the experiences of White women. Consider Mary Wollstonecraft, introduced earlier in this book. The experiences and humanity of Black and Brown women were excluded. More recent scholarship engages intersectional perspectives. Dr. bell hooks was at the forefront of **intersectional feminism** and **radical feminism**. hooks' work details the unique experiences of Black women as they navigate life while battling intersecting and compounding forms of racism and sexism. As a radical feminist scholar, hooks called for the dismantling of social structures which subjugate and financially disadvantage women, particularly Black women.

Black women, like Williams and Robinson, answered hooks' call. They carve out their own spaces to speak in their own voices, celebrate their successes and experiences, and, make their own money. Podcasting allows for that. Podcasting is a new medium with fewer gatekeepers than more traditional forms of media. Yet, it should be noted, White men like Maron are often still considered the "faces" of the medium.

Satirizing Late Night with Ziwe

Another comedic example which centers a Black woman's perspective on issues of race and racism is the series created by Ziwerekoru "Ziwe" Fumudoh (born in Lawrence, Massachusetts, 1992). Two of Fumudoh's earliest writing credits were for late night talk shows starring prominent comedians; *The Rundown with Robin Thede* (BET, 2017–2018) and two seasons of *Desus & Mero* (Showtime, 2018–2020).

During this period of her life, Fumudoh started her own show, *Baited with Ziwe*, which she premiered on YouTube in 2017. During the COVID-19 pandemic, in 2020, Fumudoh transitioned the show to Instagram Live. The premise of *Baited with Ziwe* centered on Fumudoh inviting on non-Black individuals (in the beginning, her friends) as guests and "baiting" them into making racially insensitive statements or ignorant gaffes.[43] One of the most publicized examples such gaffes came from a 2020 episode featuring food writer and chef Alison Roman, which occurred just one month after Roman received public backlash for disparaging comments she made about Chrissy Teigen and Marie Kondo – both of whom are Asian women; Roman is White – by calling them "sellouts" for launching their popular product lines.[44] While a guest on *Baited with Ziwe*, Fumudoh asked Roman if she could name five Asian people off the top of her head. Roman, embarrassingly, could barely pull it off (and with ample time allowed by Fumudoh).[45]

Recall, Dr. Amber Day noted the rise of parodic news programs in the years leading up to the writing of her book (2012).[46] Parodic news shows continued to evolve in form since the time of Day's writing. Parodic news shows today often lean harder into the postmodern. Like their predecessors before them, they rely less on monologues, impersonations, or sketches, and lean harder into deconstructing the news, giving jarring interviews of public figures or celebrities, and drawing an even finer line between what is "real" and what is "fake." As Day noted, the rising number, and changing nature, of parodic news programs is tied to the expansion of the Internet. More people now have access to the Internet, video recording devices, and platforms for posting content (e.g., Instagram and TikTok) than ever before. Such technologic advances have made it easier and more accessible to post satirical content that matches the pace of the rapid news cycle. They are less scripted productions. They are meant to shock, awe, and entertain.

The success of *Baited with Ziwe* opened new opportunities for Fumudoh. Her next show, *Ziwe*, premiered on Showtime in 2021. Produced by the production company A24, the show leans heavily into fun colors, animations, and comedic chyrons. Fumudoh explains that her show's style – which is very pink and "feminine" – was designed to counter the "masculine" aesthetic of traditional late night programs which feature men in suits sitting behind a desk.[47] The set includes teen-boppy portraits of Michelle Obama and Oprah Winfrey and Fumudoh's wardrobe choices are bright and feminine.

Although airing on premium television, *Ziwe*, appears designed for the Internet era; with the interviews being less of a flowing conversation designed to be consumed in full to understand the context, and more of meme-able soundbites and clips. The comedy of *Ziwe* comes from Fumudoh trying to trap her guests into saying something unsavory. Fumudoh puts her guests in situations where they struggle with what is the "right" choice to make or to force an on-the-spot decision or a statement which they may later regret. The point is to make them uncomfortable. *Ziwe* seeks to put privileged guests in the shoes of Black people and people of color who are constantly forced to make difficult choices to live and succeed in a world designed by and for White people.

Recall, Dr. Patricia Hill Collins is an important feminist scholar who detailed the origins of **Black feminist thought** in her book, *Black Feminist Thought: Knowledge, Consciousness and the Politics of Empowerment* (1990). Collins discusses in the book that intersecting experiences of oppression form a **matrix of oppression,** under which people are subordinated and denied opportunities based upon their intersecting identities.[48]

Fumudoh explained in a 2020 *New York Times* interview that, as racism is one of the most dominant challenges in her life, she wants to use her platform to move society, and herself, toward a place of healing. In doing so, Fumudoh's goal is not to "cancel" any of her guests, but to highlight systemic drivers of racism and oppression. Fumudoh wants to "push back" on society and expose inequalities in the discomforts that are often hidden from view.[49] Even for White guests of the show who identify as "woke" or as "allies" still exist in a system of race-based privilege, and that privilege provides comfort. Suspending the guest's comfort is the point.

Fumudoh describes the way the murder of Trayvon Martin fundamentally shaped her point of view as a Black person in the United States and as a comedian.[50] For those unfamiliar, Martin was a Black seventeen year-old who was fatally shot by George Zimmerman (who was twenty-eight years-old) in Sanford, Florida, in 2012.[51] Martin and his father were in town visiting his father's fiancée, and Martin was returning home to his father's fiancée's house after visiting a convenience store. Zimmerman saw Martin walking through the neighborhood and dubbed him "suspicious." Zimmerman began following Martin and ultimately fatally shot him in the chest. Police initially did not press charges against Zimmerman, who claimed self-defense, even though Martin was unarmed and there was tape of the 911 responder telling Zimmerman not to follow Martin. But following national outcry, Zimmerman was later charged with second-degree murder and manslaughter. However, a jury acquitted Zimmerman of the charges in July 2013.

The Zimmerman trial shattered Fumudoh's previously held understanding of the world which she had described as "rose colored."[52] Fumudoh talks about how her socialization impacted her worldview. She grew up in Massachusetts during the era when President Barack Obama led the nation. There was a permeating message of a "post-racial" America disseminated across the nation marked by feelings of hope, change, and Obama's motto of "Yes We Can." But, in July 2013, that was shattered. Fumudoh was shocked when Zimmerman was acquitted of any wrongdoing. She describes this as a moment that shifted her understanding of the U.S. social structure.

The second time Fumudoh's worldview was first shattered was when she went to college. Fumudoh explains that even though she had attended an incredibly prestigious private boarding school for high school (Phillips Academy in Andover, Massachusetts), she was completely unaware of important African American history. Until Fumudoh went to college and took elective courses, she had never heard about the Scottsboro Boys, Emmett Till, Assata Shakur, Fannie Lou Hamer, or the Black Panthers. Fumudoh said, it "broke her brain" that these figures were omitted from her education and left holes in her knowledge of Black culture, history, and context. Fumudoh is quoted as saying that she had to take time to reflect on her understanding of the world; to question what she was taught as "truth."

What Fumudoh explains here is why, I believe, comedians are important agents in the fight against oppression. Comedians are more accessible to more people than are the type of college elective courses that broke Fumudoh's brain. As much I want every person to have access to a sociology course in K-12 school or postsecondary education, that reality is incredibly limited. In much of the country, there are restrictions in place (and at the time of this writing, even more are being enacted with more severity) around talking about race in K-12 classrooms.[53] College is prohibitively expensive, and aside from cost, there are additional access restrictions making attending college untenable for a large part of the population.[54] Of course, not everyone desires to attend college or to take these types of courses. Fumudoh's comedic point of view is incredibly accessible. As a performer, she can be found on YouTube, Instagram, TikTok, and Showtime, and as a featured guest on podcasts and magazines. Her writing can be found in news publications and on television shows. She is accessible.

Summary

This chapter used a sociological lens to discuss the impact of pivotal performances sharing experiences of trauma related to sex and sexuality – notably, Hannah Gadsby's *Nanette*. We then discussed more recent examples of how marginalized comedians created unconventional spaces for their comedy on the Internet. By diving deeper into these spaces – focusing largely on LGBTQ+ comedians inhabiting online spaces – we learn sociological lessons about what it means to be an outsider from the mainstream and an insider in one's own community. For many, carving out their own paths are the only ways they will be successful or be safe. The chapter showed examples of how comedians found their communities on the Internet or through social media, and leveraged those communities to make their voices heard, foster connection, and achieve comedic success.

This chapter discussed the use of YouTube as a platform for sharing one's voice without limitation from gatekeepers and the rise of streaming services in expanding opportunities for non-mainstream creators and content. However, there is still work to be done to ensure equal access and compensation for comedians of different identities and backgrounds. This chapter concluded by discussing comedic examples from sketch comedy, podcasting, and satirical news programs – created by Black women – which allow for exploration of sociological concepts – including intersectionality and the matrix of oppression. We will expand on these concepts in the next chapter.

Discussion Questions

9-1: Consider the <u>identity contingencies</u> Hannah Gadsby described in their everyday life *and* their work as a comedian.

9-2: Do you think <u>postmodern</u> comedy specials like Gadsby's *Nanette* would have existed without the rise of streaming? Use sociological theories to justify your answer.

9-3: Draw on results from *Hollywood Diversity Report 2023, Part 1: Film* to discuss the impact of streaming on opportunity through the lens of <u>structural/functionalism,</u> including <u>functions</u> and <u>dysfunctions.</u>

9-4: What are your views of <u>globalization</u> in terms of media? Do you think having access to international media is beneficial to people living in the United States? Do you think having access to content produced in the United States is beneficial to people living in other countries? Justify your answer using sociological concepts. Consider if you agree or disagree with <u>Karl Marx</u>'s views on globalization in your answer.

9-5: Define <u>formal exclusion</u> and <u>informal exclusion.</u> In the United States, do you think *formal* exclusion is more common, or less common, today than in the past? What about *informal* exclusion?

9-6: Do you think the role of <u>mass media</u> as an <u>agent of socialization</u> has changed with the proliferation of the Internet? Why or why not?

9-7: With a classmate, discuss how the sketch from *A Black Lady Sketch Show* highlights the <u>invisibility of racism.</u>

9-8: Do you think creating a podcast like *2 Dope Queens* is an example of what <u>bell hooks</u> would consider an act of dismantling the racist and sexist social structures which subordinate and financially disadvantage Black women? Why or why not?

9-9: First, explain how Ziwe Fumudoh taking time to reflect and question what she knew to be "true" is an example of the <u>sociological imagination</u> at work. Second, explain how you think this type of exercise does, or does not, fuel her comedic work.

9-10: Do you think that Fumudoh's interview technique on her show, *Ziwe*, represents <u>parrhēsia</u>? Why or why not?

Notes

1 WIRED Staff. (2018, July 31). Seriously, We Really Need to Talk about Hannah Gadsby's "Nanette." *WIRED*. https://www.wired.com/story/hannah-gadsby-nanette-discussion/

2 *Hannah Gadsby: Nanette*. (2018). https://www.netflix.com/title/80233611

3 Steele, C. M. (2010). *Whistling Vivaldi: How Stereotypes Affect Us and What We Can Do*. W. W. Norton & Company.

4 *Hannah Gadsby: Nanette*, 2018.
5 Berman, J. (2018, July 13). 'Nanette' Is the Most Discussed Comedy Special in Ages. Here's What to Read About It. *The New York Times*. https://www.nytimes. com/2018/07/13/arts/television/nanette-hannah-gadsby-netflix-roundup.html
6 Parry, M. (Director). (2020, May 26). *Hannah Gadsby: "Douglas"* [Comedy]. Irwin Entertainment.
7 WIRED Staff, 2018.
8 *The Specials: Hannah Gadsby's "Nanette."* (2022, January 20). https://www. patreon.com/posts/1-year-ep-hannah-61430355
9 *The Specials: Dane Cook's "Vicious Circle."* (2021, January 5). https://www. patreon.com/posts/dane-cooks-45819346.
10 *Hannah Gadsby: Nanette*, 2018.
11 Giorgis, H. (2021, September 13). *"The Unwritten Rules of Black TV."* The Atlantic. https://www.theatlantic.com/press-releases/archive/2021/09/october-2021-issue-press-release/620054/
12 Rose, S. (2022, February 5). *Stream big: How Netflix changed the TV landscape in 10 years*. The Guardian. https://www.theguardian.com/media/2022/feb/05/ stream-big-how-netflix-changed-the-tv-landscape-in-10-years
13 Hunt & Ramón, 2023.
14 Kozell, I. (2017, April 25). Vir Das Has an 'Abroad Understanding.' *Vulture*. https://www.vulture.com/2017/04/vir-das-has-an-abroad-understanding.html
15 Bello, P., & Garcia, D. (2021). Cultural Divergence in popular music: The increasing diversity of music consumption on Spotify across countries. *Humanities and Social Sciences Communications*, 8(1), 1–8. https://doi.org/10.1057/ s41599-021-00855-1
16 Leight, E. (2019, September 10). *How Labels Use Pay-for-Play to Get Songs on the Radio*. Rolling Stone. https://www.rollingstone.com/music/music-features/pay-for-play-how-labels-pay-songs-radio-871457/
17 Bello & Garcia, 2021.
18 Mo'Nique takes on Amy Schumer in a row over Netflix. (2018, January 25). *BBC News*. https://www.bbc.com/news/newsbeat-42817623
19 Archie, A. (2023, July 27). Actors Take to the Internet to Show Their Residual Checks, with Some in the Negative. *NPR*. https://www.npr.org/2023/07/27/ 1190336979/actors-strike-residuals-sag-aftra-wga
20 Barnes, B., Koblin, J., & Sperling, N. (2023, July 13). Hollywood Actors Join Writers on Strike, Bringing Industry to a Standstill. *The New York Times*. https:// www.nytimes.com/2023/07/13/business/media/sag-aftra-writers-strike.html
21 Nesteroff, K. (2021). *We Had a Little Real Estate Problem* (First Simon & Schuster hardcover edition). Simon & Schuster.
22 As a layer of unintentional comedy: their shoot location was the Little Earth of United Tribes housing project where Harjo was working on a multi-year mural. He had not realized the location rented out space to a Sunday school over the weekends. This made for an unfortunate run-in between the scantily clad comedy troupe and the Sunday school teachers and students (Nesteroff, 2021).
23 *Sterlin Harjo says "Reservation Dogs" gives audiences permission to laugh*. (2022, September 19). https://www.npr.org/2022/09/19/1123452609/reservation-dogs-sterlin-harjo-native-stories
24 Genner, S., & Süss, D. (2017). Socialization as Media Effect. In Patrick Rössler, Cynthia A. Hoffner, & Liesbet van Zoonen (Eds.), *The International Encyclopedia of Media Effects* (pp. 1–15). John Wiley & Sons, Ltd. https://doi.org/ 10.1002/9781118783764.wbieme0138
25 Moyer, M. W. (2022, March 24). *Kids Are Using Social Media More Than Ever, Study Finds—The New York Times*. https://www.nytimes.com/2022/03/24/well/ family/child-social-media-use.html

26 *The Common Sense Census: Media Use by Tweens and Teens.* (2021). Common Sense. https://www.commonsensemedia.org/sites/default/files/research/report/8-18-census-integrated-report-final-web_0.pdf

27 Grzanka, P. (2019). *Queer Theory.*

28 Goldfine, J. (2020, June 30). *This Generation of Comedy Is Queer.* PAPER. https://www.papermag.com/queer-comedy-portfolio-2020-generation-2646300928.html?rebelltitem=18#rebelltitem18?rebelltitem=18

29 Mzezewa, T. (2021, May 29). Benito Skinner Is All about Drama. *The New York Times.* https://www.nytimes.com/2021/05/29/style/benito-skinner-is-all-about-drama.html

30 Fern, C. (2018, June 14). *Pride Events Encourage Acceptance of LGBTQ Community.* VOA. https://www.voanews.com/a/pride-events-encourage-acceptance-of-lgbtq-community/4439555.html

31 Goldfine, 2020.

32 Bernardini, G. (2021, December 22). *Viral Star Benny Drama Talks Impersonating Celebs, Avoiding "Low Blows" (EXCLUSIVE).* Distractify. https://www.distractify.com/p/benny-drama-kardashians; Goldfine, 2020.

33 Sung, M. (2020, June 21). *The stark divide between "Straight TikTok" and "Alt TikTok."* Mashable. https://mashable.com/article/alt-tiktok-straight-tiktok-queer-punk

34 The stars and guest stars of *A Black Lady Sketch Show* are acting and comedy powerhouses, including Angela Bassett, Ashley Nicole Black, Yvette Nicole Brown, Quinta Brunson, Nicole Byer, Laverne Cox, Gabrielle Dennis, Patti LaBelle, Laci Mosley, Tia Mowry, Kyla Pratt, Issa Rae, Raven-Symoné, Amber Riley, Kelly Rowland, Wanda Sykes Skye Townsend, Gabrielle Union, and Bresha Webb.

35 Zinoman, J. (2022, April 27). 'A Black Lady Sketch Show' Has the Most Exciting Comics (and the Silliest). *The New York Times.* https://www.nytimes.com/2022/04/27/arts/television/a-black-lady-sketch-show.html

36 HBO (Director). (2019, September 8). *A Black Lady Sketch Show: Courtroom Kiki.* https://www.youtube.com/watch?v=MSElx7C1vLY

37 Apata, G. O. (2020). *'I Can't Breathe': The Suffocating Nature of Racism.* https://journals.sagepub.com/doi/full/10.1177/0263276420957718

38 Grihalva, J. (2012, July 18). *Tracing the Birth of the Comedy Podcast Boom.* https://www.vulture.com/2012/07/tracing-the-birth-of-the-comedy-podcast-boom.html

39 Garney, M. (2021, April 12). *"WTF With Marc Maron" awarded the Governors Award—CNN.* https://edition.cnn.com/2021/04/12/entertainment/marc-maron-wtf-podcast-award/index.html

40 James, B. (2021, December 15). *The 10 Best Comedy Podcasts of 2021.* https://www.vulture.com/article/best-comedy-podcasts-2021.html

41 *War of the Welles: The story behind the most famous radio drama of all time | CBC Radio.* (2018, October 31). https://www.cbc.ca/radio/ideas/war-of-the-welles-the-story-behind-the-most-famous-radio-drama-of-all-time-1.4884766

42 Finley, T. (2015, September 28). Jessica Williams and Phoebe Robinson Want Comedy to Stop Ignoring Black Women. *HuffPost.* https://www.huffpost.com/entry/jessica-williams-and-phoebe-robinson-want-comedy-to-stop-ignoring-black-women_n_56094683e4b0af3706dcca22

43 Hawgood, A. (2019, March 15). *Ziwe Fumudoh uses humor to push racial buttons—The New York Times.* https://www.nytimes.com/2019/03/15/style/ziwe-fumudoh-comedian-desus-mero-showtime.html

44 Ducharme, M. (2021, May 6). *Ziwe interviews: From Caroline Calloway to Alison Roman, the Showtime star's most uncomfortable moments.* https://slate.com/culture/2021/05/ziwe-interviews-caroline-calloway-alison-roman-showtime.html

45 Jeffery, L. (2021, May 6). A Lightning Round with Ziwe, Late-Night's Newest Host. *PBS*. https://www.pbs.org/newshour/arts/9-quick-questions-with-ziwe

46 Day, A. (2011). *Satire and Dissent: Interventions in Contemporary Political Debate*. Indiana University Press. https://iupress.org/9780253222817/satire-and-dissent/

47 Blake. (2021, May 6). *Ziwe wants to shake up late night. Even if it makes you uncomfortable*. Los Angeles Times. https://www.latimes.com/entertainment-arts/tv/story/2021-05-06/ziwe-showtime-instagram-live-late-night-comedy

48 Collins, P. H. (1990). *Black Feminist Thought: Knowledge, Consciousness, and the Politics of Empowerment*. Hyman.

49 Garcia, S. (2020, July 9). *Ziwe Fumudoh Asks: 'How Many Black People Do You Know?'—The New York Times*. https://www.nytimes.com/2020/07/09/style/ziwe-fumudoh-asks-how-many-black-people-do-you-know.html

50 Blake, 2021.

51 *Trayvon Martin Shooting Fast Facts*. (2022, February 14). CNN. https://www.cnn.com/2013/06/05/us/trayvon-martin-shooting-fast-facts/index.html

52 Blake, 2021.

53 Defending Our Right to Learn. (2022, March 10). *American Civil Liberties Union*. https://www.aclu.org/news/free-speech/defending-our-right-to-learn

54 Kelchen, R., Goldrick-Rab, S., & Hosch, B. (2017). The costs of college attendance: Examining variation and consistency in institutional living cost allowances. *The Journal of Higher Education*, 88(6), 947–971. https://doi.org/10.1080/0022 1546.2016.1272092

10 Race and the Social Thriller

This chapter expands upon earlier discussions of the sociological study of race and racism. We draw on the contributions of Jonathan P. Rossing, Eduardo Bonilla-Silva, W.E.B. Du Bois, and Peter L. Berger. Sociological concepts discussed in this chapter include critical race humor, color-blind racism, virtue signaling, the color line, debunking, and multiple consciousness. This chapter provides examples from modern comedians and creators which teach audiences about the omnipresence and social impact of racism in the United States.

Critical Race Humor

Dr. Jonathan P. Rossing, associate dean of the College of Arts and Sciences at Gonzaga University, defines **critical race humor** as a form of comedy that explores the institutional, structural, and cultural forces which enforce systems of racial oppression in society.[1] According to Rossing, "Racial truth-telling and criticism artistically angled through humor has the potential to defy dominant practices and ideologies that promote the erasure of material realities of race" (Rossing, 2014). Rossing used Richard Pryor's (born in Peoria, Illinois, 1940) comedy as a case study to describe how humor has long been employed as a tool for social criticism. We will discuss Richard Pryor's comedy and legacy later in this chapter.

In his analysis of Pryor's comedy, Rossing engages the concept of **parrhēsia** to define how Pryor utilizes humor to stand up to injustice and rattle the status quo. Recall, parrhēsia refers to speaking truth to power without concern over the potential consequences. In this, we can see how critical race humor directly challenges racism by exposing systems of oppression and their long-reaching impacts.

This chapter links sociological concepts of race and racism to examples from comedians who employ critical race humor and engage parrhēsia. First, this chapter describes how sociology helps us understand institutional nature of racism. Second, this chapter covers the "social thriller" film genre, notably exemplified by the movie *Get Out* (2017), to explain how and why media representations of racism developed through a comedic lens helps White audiences understand the systemic and pervasive nature of racism in everyday life. Third, this chapter shows examples of

DOI: 10.4324/9781003469537-11

standup comedy bits spanning decades, covering topics like police brutality, to highlight how much work is still needed to combat racism and inequality. In doing so, we discuss the media's role in spreading messages of activism and awareness.

Through these examples, this chapter provides creative examples from comedians which effectively demonstrate the causes, consequences, and omnipresence of racism in the United States. These examples will bolster our sociological understanding of the way race and ethnicity are socially salient categories for the ways people are treated in society.

The Social Thriller Genre and *Get Out*

Alexis Sobel Fitts wrote in *WIRED* magazine that comedy is a practice designed to "question its own existence" (Fitts, 2018).[2] What Fitts means here is that comedy is a form that can be utilized to engage in social commentary, even more so than a practice utilized to elicit laughs. The form of comedy allows creators to share what it feels like to be an underdog and to be marginalized, oppressed, and scared for your life. If this is the definition of critical race humor; the line between drama, comedy, and horror becomes very fine.

We can see how fine that line is by discussing the 2017 film, *Get Out*.[3] *Get Out* was written and directed by filmmaker, comedian, and actor Jordan Peele (born in New York City, New York, 1979). Peele first became known for his comedic work – specifically, the sketch comedy show *Key & Peele*, briefly introduced earlier in this book. Peele co-created, wrote, and starred in the series alongside co-creator Keegan-Michael Key (born in Southfield, Michigan, 1971). *Key & Peele* was lauded for its comedic chops and its tackling of tough issues like racial stereotypes and race relations. The show ran on Comedy Central for five acclaimed seasons (2010–2016).

Following the end of *Key & Peele* in 2016, Peele debuted as a film director with *Get Out* in 2017. *Get Out* follows Chris Washington (played by Daniel Kaluuya), a Black man, as he meets the family of his White girlfriend (played by Allison Williams) for the first time. *Get Out* uses horror tropes traditionally reserved for demons, the spiritually possessed, and wild psychopaths, and uses them to highlight the pernicious and omnipresent evils of racism and White privilege. Some of these tropes include suburban settings meant to evoke juxtaposing feelings of kind with creepy, comfort with control, and unassuming banality with unorthodox medical experiments.[4]

The film is a masterfully crafted commentary on race, racism, and the threats experienced by Black people even from "woke" White folks. Recall our introduction to Dr. Eduardo Bonilla-Silva, an important scholar of **critical theories of race and racism**. In his book *Racism Without Racists: Color-Blind Racism and the Persistence of Racial Inequality in the United States* (2003), Bonilla-Silva describes the omnipresent problem of racism in the United States. Racism is systemic. It is entrenched within the very fiber of our social systems. Racism, therefore, would perpetuate even in the absence of personally mediated racism.[5]

Bonilla-Silva defined the concept of **color-blind racism**. "Color-blindness" occurs when individuals purport to "not see race." In other words, such individuals believe they do not treat people differently based upon their race and navigate the world as if they are color-blind. As explained by Bonilla-Silva, however, color-blindness is not the absence of racism. It is, in fact, a new form of racism. Color-blind racism maintains White hegemony by assuming racial equity has been achieved. It allows White people to not question their own biases, actions, or privilege. It stalls progress toward greater equality because it falsely claims that we are already equal.

Refer to this book's earlier description of the "Juneteenth" episode of *Atlanta*, wherein a rich White man appropriates Black art and culture for his own benefit and to the detriment and discomfort of Black folks at his party. We see similar social commentary in *Get Out*. For example, we can turn to the scene where Chris first meets Rose's father, Dean (played by Bradley Whitford). In this scene, Dean tells Chris, with a bold mix of sincerity and self-satisfaction, that he would have voted to re-elect President Barack Obama for a third term as president, if that were possible.[6]

It is a beautifully succinct piece of writing. In this one moment, the viewer is introduced to the type of family Chris is meeting, as Dean instantly and proudly engages in virtue signaling. **Virtue signaling** occurs when someone shares or displays a social or political belief with the specific intent of receiving admiration for their righteousness. The creative weight of the film starts with these signals of virtue and "wokeness" which quickly and seamlessly slide into horror. As Chris settles into the home of his girlfriend and her seemingly "woke" family, the Armitages, the film takes dark and thrilling turns. Chris and other Black people are not safe in the Armitage home or in their community. The film displays how these racist horrors are pernicious and structural.

Highlighting the structural forces of racism is a sociological way to structure a film. Peele particularly showcases his sociological point of view in the final scene of *Get Out*. In the final moments of the film, we see Chris almost successfully escape from the Armitage home after killing everyone in the family except for Rose. In the driveway, Rose, who is lying on the ground bleeding from a gunshot wound, tells Chris she loves him and begs him for forgiveness. Chris hovers over Rose. He has the opportunity to kill her but refrains from doing so. Then, we see headlights; it looks like a police car. The audience tenses up because we know what is about to happen. Chris is certainly about to be pinned for the deaths of the Armitages; there is no way his story will be believed. He will be taken from one oppressive place and brought to another: prison. The audience has learned that the latter is no safer for Chris than the former.

Peele wrote several versions of the final scene. In the original ending, after the police car pulled up in the driveway, the audience watches as Chris is arrested by the police. Producer Sean McKittrick referred to this original ending as the "sad truth" ending.[7] The team ultimately switched out the "sad truth" ending for one of the alternative versions they shot.

In the final ending that made it to wider theatrical release, there is relief; a thrilling and comedic twist occurs after the car pulls up in the driveway. As the camera pans along the body of the car, the audience sees the letters "TSA" painted along the car's body. Audiences instantly know it is the not the police who just arrived at the scene but Chris' friend Rod (played by Lil Rel Howery), who works as a TSA agent at the local airport. Rod shows up just in time to save Chris from this nightmare. After nearly two hours of terror, the film ends with a bit of hope. The final scene gives audiences some comedic relief, thanks to a stellar performance by Howery as Rod, as well as a visible representation of the importance of Black friendship in an unjust and unsafe world.

For its masterful writing, acting, and directing, *Get Out* was chosen as one of the top ten films of 2017 by the American Film Institute, *Time Magazine*, and the National Board of Review. Peele won an Academy Award for *Best Original Screenplay* (plus three other Academy Award nominations: *Best Picture*, *Best Director*, and *Best Actor* for Kaluuya). Yet, a controversy ensued when *Get Out* was nominated for a Golden Globe in 2017 as its nomination was in the "comedy or musical" category instead of the (more prestigious) "drama" category.

The controversy raises the question – should a film which centers on exposing the omnipresent danger of racism be labeled as a comedy?[8] This is a fundamental question I struggle to answer. If Hannah Gadsby's *Nanette* is comedy, isn't *Get Out*? But if *Get Out* is a comedy, then what are audiences paying to laugh at? Peele has stated in interviews that a "comedy" label may often be applied to a project to "trivialize" the seriousness of its content or message. His film is about racism. That is nothing to trivialize or laugh at. It is about real suffering.[9]

During a guest appearance on *The Late Show*, Peele told host Stephen Colbert that he submitted *Get Out* in the documentary category. To Peele, the film is a documentary because the movie portrays truth.[10] Indeed, Peele has stated *Get Out* is his story and his truth.[11] *Get Out* is incredibly successful at making audiences understand pieces of what it is like to be a Black man every single day in the United States, like Gadsby's *Nanette* does for LGBTQ+ people. Particularly, parts of their experiences were previously unchallenged in mainstream media, like the dangers of "woke" White liberals. Peele and Gadsby exist in a world where people have not yet figured out what to do with their art.

Peele has also described the film as a "**social thriller**" – a term he coined and which gained attention following the release of *Get Out*. A social thriller combines elements from the genres of horror and psychological thriller – and I argue, comedy – to shine a light on society's flaws and oppressive social systems.[12]

See a genre guide (Figure 10.1) which showcases some of the common elements of these three major movie genres (in black), and how Peele's social thriller genre fits into their existing structure (in gray). The film *Get Out* does not simply fall into any one of these categories. Particularly, society as a villain is an important marker which precludes *Get Out* from falling directly into horror (in which the villains tend to be very clear) or into psychological thriller (in which much of the tension comes from the illusive nature of the true villain's identity).

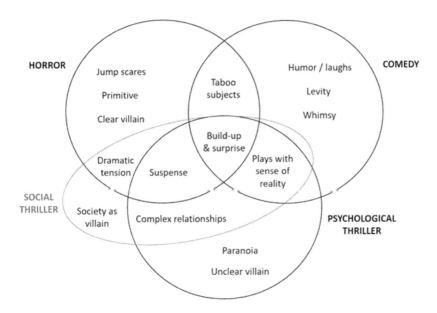

Figure 10.1 Common Trait Venn Diagram of Horror, Comedy, Psychological Thriller, and Social Thriller Movies

Watching *Get Out* for the first time, many may think the film fits into the psychological thriller category because of Chris' complex relationships with the Armitage family and the twisting and terrifying confusion about who is villainous and who is deserving of trust. But the underlying message is not about the Armitage family or their friends and neighbors as individual actors. They are creations and maintainers of an unjust society which privileges White people and abuses Black people like Chris. Peele sees the villains of racism through an institutional lens. In doing so, Peele engages critical race humor.

Showcased by the film's ending (when Chris nearly escapes the Armitage's home as headlights pull up in the driveway), the genre social thriller is apt. It is very much a commentary on the villainous nature of social structure, more so than individual actors. *Get Out* and films with similar goals (e.g., *Sorry to Bother You*, discussed previously) show what society looks like if you are seeing it through a non-dominant lens. Show what it feels like to be someone without all the power.

While not a *comedy*, I argue *Get Out* is successful at showing the harm of racism from seemingly good-intentioned folks because it is the *work of a comedian*. For example, think back to Bonilla-Silva's concept of **color-blind racism**, which occurs when individuals believe they "do not see race."[13] Bonilla-Silva argues that color-blind racism is a new form of racism which maintains White hegemony by purporting society has achieved racial equity. Color-blind racism allows White people to not question their privilege. Getting people to question their question their own "color-blindness" is exactly what Peele does with *Get Out*. Comedy is all about getting people to question their own biases, assumptions, privileges, and views of the world. So, while *Get Out* is not a comedy, it was made by a skilled comedian – and I see that as instrumental to the film's effectiveness in portraying difficult subjects in a captivating way.

Comedians are adept at using their sociological imagination to see the world like an outsider. This outsider perspective makes better art, comedy or otherwise. Peele's objective in the writing and directing of *Get Out* was for Black people's stories to be told, for those experiences to be taken seriously, and to alert audiences to the omnipresence of racism, White privilege, and White supremacy. Peele cleverly paired his background as a comedic writer, his status as social observer, and knowledge of horror tropes to showcase that story in a new way that audiences could not ignore.

Def Comedy Jam and the Color Line

Figure 10.2 again highlights the "Alternative, Def Comedy Jam, & Sitcoms" era of comedy, roughly spanning 1990–2000. In the next section, we will discuss the sociological significance of *Def Comedy Jam* in comedy's history. Specifically, we will discuss how comedians showcased on *Def Comedy Jam* – a predominantly Black program – were underappreciated, vilified, and marginalized by mainstream outlets.

Def Comedy Jam was a television program filmed live in New York which aired Friday nights on HBO from 1992 to 1997. It was an important showcase for predominantly Black comedians. However, the show's importance to the comedy landscape was underappreciated by many in the mainstream news media. *Def Comedy Jam* comics often did not fit within the expected norms of what comedy was supposed to be in terms of material, language, volume, physical performance, and who was performing it. As such, *Def Comedy Jam*'s performers were viewed as deviants by some outlets.[14]

For example, an article printed in the Sunday edition of the *New York Times* on July 31, 1994, written by John J. O'Connor, was oh-so-cleverly titled "The Curse of Incessant Cursing."[15] O'Connor first describes the way *Def Comedy Jam* was lauded for the national exposure it gave to Black comics who otherwise would have been excluded from television opportunities. But, O'Connor quickly turns to his criticism of *Def Comedy Jam*'s language. He admonishes the comedians for their use of curse words and "street talk" (as he describes, this would be the "diplomatic term"), and what he perceives as a "foul attitude" (O'Connor,1994). While perhaps giving cursory nods to its strengths, critics of *Def Comedy Jam* like O'Connor focused almost exclusively on what they viewed as its faults. *Def Comedy Jam* performers were labeled, stigmatized, and viewed as deviants.

Let us, instead, focus on *Def Comedy Jam*'s strengths and successes. First: the wealth of comedic talent showcased on the program was extensive. The bench was *deep*. A shortlist of comics that appeared on *Def Comedy Jam*

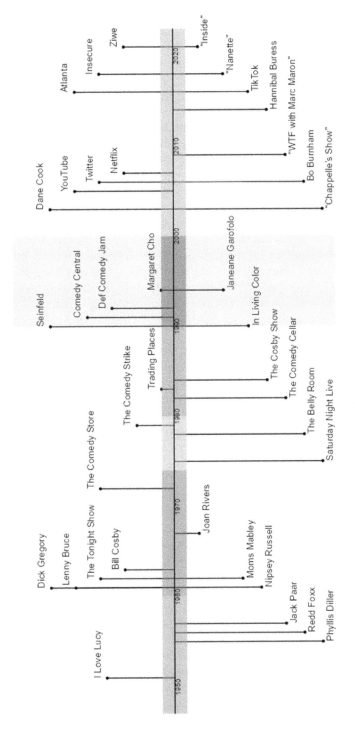

Figure 10.2 Alternative, *Def Comedy Jam*, and Sitcoms Timeline

includes Jamie Foxx, Adele Givens, Steve Harvey, Bernie Mac, Mo'Nique, J.B. Smoove, Sommore, and Chris Tucker.[16] Second, *Def Comedy Jam* performers were known for delivering material that excited, engaged, and surprised audiences. They gave audiences a good time. As an example of a *Def Comedy Jam* performance, consider a wildly popular recurring bit from COCO the Comedian (hailing from Highland Park, Michigan). She would stash a glass, liquor bottle, ice cubes, and all the other makings of a cocktail in her blouse tucked under or between her breasts. She would take the ingredients out, one-by-one, and make herself a drink while simultaneously telling her jokes. It was brilliant, hilarious, and the essence of physical and risqué comedy for which *Def Comedy Jam* performers came to be known.

The women of *Def Comedy Jam* deserve a special spotlight both for their comedic chops and for the way their experiences differed from those of the male comedians. Women comedians who participated in *Def Comedy Jam* had a chance to discuss their experiences in a panel that took place in 2017 for *Def Comedy Jam 25,* the recorded 25th anniversary event celebrating the launch of *Def Comedy Jam.*[17] The host of the panel was comedian, actress, and *Def Comedy Jam* alum Tiffany Haddish (born in Los Angeles, California, 1979), who asked Adele Givens (born in Chicago, Illinois, 1960) about the origin of her catchphrase: "such a lady." Givens explains her catchphrase was born from experiencing a double standard wherein men were allowed to be loud and brash, but the women were expected to be "ladylike." Givens leaned into her outsider status as a brash woman in comedy by delivering her crass jokes, then letting her audience know that yes, she was a lady.

Givens continued with her brash comedy. Givens did not agree that men should be able to get away with more on stage. Givens told *Billboard* magazine in a 2018 interview that, in traditional comedy clubs, she would follow men whose whole sets were composed of graphic material. After her set, however, club owners would tell her – and only her – that she needed to "tone it down."[18] Talking about her sexuality and personal experiences – graphic or not – was part of what it meant to be a woman and a performer to Givens. She refused to change herself for what traditional comedy clubs. But *Def Comedy Jam* was a space where Givens and other comedians with similar comedic sensibilities were encouraged *not* to tone it down. On *Def Comedy Jam*, Givens and her comedy thrived. Givens went on to perform on the show more times than any other comedian during the show's run.[19] Not just women comedians but all comedians.

Consider how *Def Comedy Jam* relates to W.E.B. Du Bois' theoretical framework of the **color line**. Recall, the color line refers to the physical, political, and psychological barriers separating Black and White folks based upon skin color.[20] Now consider if and how having your own space to thrive ties to the work of Du Bois. In *The Souls of Black Folk* (1903), Du Bois described how Black people could break free from the psychological barriers limiting their potential. He described how Black people could break free from seeing themselves in the way White people saw them. How do you think the comedians who thrived while performing on *Def Comedy Jam* exemplify this point? Consider if and how having the space to speak in your own voice can help shatter a dominant worldview.

Symbols with Roy Wood Jr.

To discuss another example of how standup comedy can break apart a dominant worldview, let us turn to comedian Roy Wood Jr. (born in New York City, New York, 1978). In his 2017 special, *Father Figure*, Wood Jr. uses his comedic perspective to enter a national conversation about race and American symbols. *Father Figure* was released in 2017, the year the national conversation over NFL quarterback Colin Kaepernick's peaceful protests reached a peak. Kaepernick frequently knelt during the national anthem to protest police brutality and racial injustice. He would not stand for the anthem and flag of a nation which oppresses Black and Brown people.[21]

In 2017, Kaepernick filed an official grievance against the National Football League over allegedly colluding to edge him out of an NFL contract for his protest. The context of this national conversation around how and if people should unify around the national anthem is present in Wood Jr.'s special, in which he talks about Black people's relationship to music. He states that patriotic songs do not exist in Black music because Black people's painful relationship with the United States prevents them from having a patriotic song that is honest.[22]

Wood Jr., whose comedic style is loud, animated, and fun, belts out impressions of traditional African songs about freedom in their homelands. Wood Jr. joyfully sings as he claps and dances. As Wood Jr. explains, these were the joyous and patriotic songs African people sang in their traditional homelands. However, once enslaved people were stolen from their traditional lands and brought to America on slave ships, the music changed. Wood Jr. begins to mimic sad blues music and solemnly air-play the harmonica; a musical nod to the sadness and hardship experienced by enslaved people.

Wood Jr.'s jokes juxtapose patriotic songs written and performed by White people (who may feel safe and free in the United States) to music created by Black people. He sets up this juxtaposition to make a broader point about Black people's relationship to "American" music and symbols. "American" is in quotes, here because the term is often used to represent one specific idea of American values that are largely White and Christian, while of course, the United States contains multitudes. American symbols are not universal. Wood Jr. jokes that White people can write patriotic songs because they are the ones that have a fun, peaceful, free life in the United States. He then delivers lines from "God Bless the U.S.A." about how American pride stems from being free.[23] The underlying message is immediately clear when watching the special. The image of Wood Jr., a Black man discussing the plight of Black folks in the United States while singing about freedom as the foundation for American pride, reveals the misguidedness of Kaepernick's critics.

Recall this book's introduction to syllogisms. A syllogism is a logical argument in which two premises share one common conclusion. For example: "Cobras are snakes" and "all snakes are reptiles" imply that "cobras are reptiles." Now place Wood Jr.'s joke in this framework: "American pride is grounded on freedom" and "Black people are not free" does not logically imply that "Black people should have American pride." Of course, many Black people *do* have American pride. But that does not take away from the fact that Black, Brown, and Indigenous people do not enjoy the same freedoms and liberties as do White people in the United States.

Recall that sociologist Peter L. Berger defined the goal of structuralism as **debunking**.[24] Debunking is the process of breaking apart the false narratives put forward by those in power which aim to hide their true intentions or means. Let us consider the example of folks, like Colin Kaepernick, who protest police brutality and the oppression of Black people in the United States, who then are torn down in the media for being "unpatriotic" or "ungrateful." Sociologists like Berger may argue that the labeling of Kaepernick and his compatriots are "unpatriotic" or "ungrateful" serves to maintain the status quo. By vilifying those who critique police brutality, for example, people in power attempt to exempt themselves from listening to their demands. It is like saying, "*Don't listen to that guy! We're the good ones! HE'S the one who hates America!*"

This was the current state of affairs when Wood Jr. entered the chat. He used his comedy special to debunk the false narratives put forth by those in power. His bit effectively showed, "*No, Kaepernick is not unpatriotic for kneeling during the national anthem. He has a real point he is trying to make.*" Audiences can see that the national anthem never represented the Black American experience, which was founded on the enslavement of Black people and the genocide and oppression of Indigenous people and people of color. In bringing this understanding to light, Wood Jr. is engaging in a sociological act.

Father Figure is full of examples of debunking – beginning with Wood Jr.'s very first bit in the special. Wood Jr. starts his special in the middle of a sentence (starting his special with "But ..."), which is perhaps a nod to his special's place within the political landscape.[25] Wood Jr. starts with an inquiry about how – if symbols of racism are removed – is he supposed to identify which spaces are safe and which are threatening? He gives the example of stopping for gas in an unknown area in the middle of the night. A Confederate flag hanging in a gas station window is a good indication he should keep driving and find another gas station. It highlights how removing the symbols of racism does not eradicate racism itself, which is systemic, pervasive, scary, and dangerous.

Post-Comedy with Jerrod Carmichael

Wood Jr.'s Confederate flag bit dovetails with a plot line from the television series, *The Carmichael Show*, which ran on NBC for three seasons (2015–2017). *The Carmichael Show* was created by and starred standup comedian, writer, actor, producer, and filmmaker Jerrod Carmichael (born in Winston-Salem, North Carolina, 1987). *The Carmichael Show* was a multi-camera sitcom focusing on tough subjects while skipping the laugh track and keeping takes with poor audience reactions (which, in traditional multi-cam sitcoms with live studio audiences, are reshot in favor of takes with better audience reactions). Carmichael's comedic approach is sociological in the way he strives to shake up people's way of seeing the world.

Carmichael hired a sociologist as a series consultant for *The Carmichael Show*. UCLA sociology professor and director of African American Studies, Dr. Darnell Hunt (introduced earlier in this book), helped Carmichael and writing staff successfully tackle tough social issues. The series is raw and real. Like Carmichael's standup, the series takes tough stances and challenges White liberal mindsets. In other words, he *trolls* them (meaning, he makes controversial or inflammatory statements to provoke emotional reactions).

A prime example of this trolling comes from the episode titled "Gender" (season one, episode four). The episode's cold open begins with Jerrod arguing *for* keeping Confederate flags on buildings, while Jerrod's parents – Joe and Cynthia – disagree. Joe's perspective is based on growing up in an earlier generation; he feels it is long overdue for these hateful symbols to be removed. But Jerrod retorts that he would rather *know* if a business is actively racist so he could avoid walking into that venue and have his "pie spat at" (*The Carmichael Show*, NBC, 2015).[26] This is a perspective that makes complete sense coming from Jerrod's character; yet, a Black character arguing *for* keeping up the Confederate flag is one which may also surprise or confuse White viewers at home.

Indeed, Carmichael creates art which forces people to question their own understanding of the world. Carmichael strives to not listen to or be a part of a political echo chamber.[27] He brings a different perspective to a wide (and often controversial) range of topics and leans into pushing buttons in ways most performers might avoid. He did this in *The Carmichael Show* and his three HBO standup specials – *Love at the Store* (2014), *8* (2017), and *Rothaniel* (2022) – among other creative projects.

For example, topics covered in Carmichael's second comedy special, *8*, including race, family, Donald Trump, climate change, and animal rights. During *8*, Carmichael asks audiences a lot of questions about their lives or who they're dating. Classic crowd work. But Carmichael also engages in a lot of call-and-response. He ends sentences, with "Right?" and waits for the audience to answer. He makes eye contact with specific audience members and holds its. He points to people as if one line is specifically for them. It feels like it is less of a performance and more of a conversation. In one piece of crowd work, Carmichael points to a specific audience member and engages him in a moment of connection about how being Black in the United States is exhausting. Intermixed with seemingly off-the-cuff jokes, Carmichael speaks with this audience member about how being Black in the United States takes work and it wears you down.[28] The way Carmichael handles this crowd work –

deeply engaged, seriously yet jokey – it feels like a conversation he might have with a friend. He uses his crowd work to make the special feel casual, intimate, and unscripted.

Carmichael wanted *8* to feel uncomfortable, visceral, and intimate, and he certainly achieved that. And he also wanted *8* to feel raw and real. For the audience at home, he absolutely achieved that too. But much like we discussed with Burnham's *Inside*, the filming of *8* was not "real" in the way viewers at home might expect. It was a crafted performance, and the live audience members were unwittingly part of that performance.

Jeffrey Gurian, columnist for *The Interrobang*, wrote about his experience attending the taping of *8*. Gurian describes how Carmichael repeated lines over and over to get different audience reactions and often stopped during his performance to speak directly to production staff.[29,30] The way Gurian described the taping, it was more akin to the taping of a scripted television show than a live comedy show. For some people, this may seem antithetical to the idea of a comedy special who believe that the comedy specials you see on television are records of a live event. But that is the not the perspective held by Carmichael. He is creating art in which the live audience takes part in its creation for the benefit of audiences at home.

On an episode of *The Specials* podcast, co-hosts Jesse David Fox and Kathryn VanArendonk discuss *8* with guest host Dr. Danielle Fuentes Morgan (introduced earlier in this book). They discuss how good art evokes new feelings in you when you revisit it again and again. Good art can do this because what you see in art, if done well, is a reflection of how you see yourself and how you see the world. So, as your own perspective changes in relation to evolving social norms or changing social, geographic, or political context, so too does your view of that art. Based on this point, they make the distinction between art and entertainment. A lot of standup comedy strives to be entertaining. You watch it once, enjoy it, and do not necessarily revisit or reevaluate it. But *8* is striving to be art. It is meant to make you reevaluate the performance and reevaluate your reaction to it.

Expanding on Carmichael's body of work will help us elucidate how his goal is to make art, which is a distinction from a goal of making entertainment. Carmichael pushes boundaries that make people repeatedly question their own thoughts and reactions. To do this effectively, Carmichael must set a particular tone for his performance. And the uncomfortable, drawn out, manufactured performance of his special is what achieved that tone for him. His raw and intimate performance is just the opposite of what it seems.

Carmichael's comedy fits into the realm of **post-comedy**. Recall that post-comedy refers to comedy becoming more impressionistic, alongside other forms of art in the postmodern era. The norms and expectations associated with traditional standup comedy are dismantled. Standup no longer looks a certain way or sounds a certain way. It is more based on comedic perspective than on a set of hard rules. For Carmichael, his comedy is art designed to provoke an emotional response.[31] Like an impressionist painting, the taped version of *8* was never meant to be a live recording of the evening. It was meant to convey Carmichael's artistic vision, and it certainly achieved that.

Carmichael's follow-up special, *Rothaniel* (HB0, 2022) has many similarities to *8* but was much more personal. In *Rothaniel*, Carmichael comes out as a gay. Sitting on a folding chair on stage at New York's Blue Note Jazz Club, Carmichael explains that he never thought he would come out. He comes from a long line of hypermasculine Black men.

The special evokes the thinking of W.E.B. Du Bois and his discussion of **double consciousness**. Black folks must hold their dual identities of being Black and being American simultaneously. While, for White people, their race and American identity feel, essentially, synonymous. Black Americans, however, must juggle what it means to be Black and be American – which may often be at odds with one another. Du Bois' believed the remedy for double consciousness is the deconstruction of the ideology around what it means to be "American." He believed in the expansion of what it looks like or feels like to be American. He believed Black folks should not have to shirk their cultures or traditions to assimilate into "American" life. Instead, we should view African, Caribbean, and other cultural histories and traditions *as* essential parts of American life.

Scholars have expanded Du Bois' work in more recent years to account for the diversity of experiences within the Black community. For example, scholars have expanded the concept of **multiple consciousnesses** to describe the experiences of people of color who identify as LGBTQ+.[32] LGBTQ+ people may feel pressure to "police" their own behavior in certain spaces. For Black and Brown LGBTQ+ people, social or cultural norms which prioritize hypermasculinity may shape the acceptability – or lack thereof – of certain behaviors. The experiences of LGBTQ+ depend upon other features of one's identity and social setting.[33] We see that internal conflict in Carmichael's *Rothaniel*. He discusses what it means to be a Black and gay man growing up in a hypermasculine family.

In addition to coming out as gay, Carmichael's special is centered around coming out with all his personal secrets. He begins the set by telling the audience they do not even know his real first name. It is not Jerrod; that is his middle name. His first name has long been a secret, a name he would get removed from his bank cards and his high school yearbooks (the latter he accomplished through twenty-dollar bribes to classmates). From the material about his name, he tells his origin story. He goes into detail about secrets kept by his grandfathers and his father.

The special is incredibly personal. By watching *Rothaniel*, the audience feels like they are present for a life-changing moment for Carmichael. The exact moment when Carmichael frees himself from his long-kept secrets. This is a crafted feeling. In the first part of the special, Carmichael delivers tightly crafted jokes and stories with confidence and energy. But later, as Carmichael talks about his strained relationship with his parents and his own struggles with his identity as a gay man, we see the things become looser and more vulnerable. Carmichael takes long pauses. He shifts uncomfortably in his seat, often hunching over and obscuring his face from the camera. Carmichael speaks directly with the audience. They give him love and support. They ask him questions, which Carmichael answers. The audience transforms from being witnesses to a performance to being central players within it. And this is the point.

Rothaniel plays with the comedic form. The second half of the special goes long stretches without laughs. Yet in the end, Carmichael looks directly into the camera and delivers one big, planned punchline that ties the whole special together. He reestablishes himself as the performer and signals to us that everything that just happened was part of the performance.

To set the imagery of the special a bit more, let us talk about who directed it: Bo Burnham. Burnham has a comedy special production philosophy that breaks from tradition. Historically, comedy specials were filmed recordings of one person standing in place and delivering their comedy just like they would at a comedy club. Burnham, however, has spoken about how comedy specials should be more like high-ticket concerts.[34] The production should evoke emotions. These effects ensure the special feels intimate, raw, and visceral.

Burnham's signature is all over the cinematographic and editing choices. Early in the special, the camera is pointed up toward Carmichael's face, which is lit with warm tones on his skin and bright colors in the background. But once the special shifts to more of a vulnerable exchange between Carmichael and the audience, the lighting and framing change. Carmichael is under a harsh, white spotlight. The colorful background turns dark.

The spotlight placed on Carmichael as the performer, just as the performance falls apart, says so much about what post-comedy is, and how comics like Carmichael and Burnham play with the form. Think about it this way: the initial lighting and framing feel intimate. You feel like you are in the room. The performance is scripted, but it is meant to feel the opposite. It is meant to feel loose, natural, and real. What Carmichael and Burnham do in the latter part of the performance highlights how vulnerability is a performance, too. It is all a performance. At his most intimate and vulnerable, Carmichael is spotlighted. It is a reminder that this is not an intimate conversation between friends that happens to be caught on camera. It is a piece of art. One which was planned, edited, and produced by some of the biggest names in the business. They are intentionally showing their hand.

If we know anything else about Burnham from our discussion of *Inside*, it is that he knows how to create art that provokes specific moods and feelings. Even though you know his work represents scripted performances, watching his work still feels like you are looking through a window into a real, intimate experience. In this regard, Burnham and Carmichael operate very similarly (and in addition to being regular collaborators, they are also very close friends).

One of the Burnham's oft-cited inspirations for his work is the magic duo Penn & Teller, whom he admires for how they could explain a trick directly to the audience, then later, still "awe" the crowd with it anyway.[35] For those unfamiliar, Penn & Teller are a long-running magic duo who started performing together in the 1970s and have had long-running success as Las Vegas headliners and television personalities. Part of their act often includes revealing a secret about how their illusion is about to be performed. Yet, they are so good at their performance that the audience will fall for the illusion.

This is what is happening in *Rothaniel*. All the clues that tell us this is a crafted and produced special are right in front of our eyes. The special is bookended by breathtakingly beautiful shots of Carmichael walking to and from the Blue Note in the falling snow. It is so beautiful; it almost does not matter that it was not snowing in New York City the night Carmichael filmed *Rothaniel*.[36] The lighting, the colors, the framing; they flow with the material. The audience at home is shown from beginning to end that *Rothaniel* is a masterfully produced film, yet Carmichael and Burnham still trick us into thinking it is a raw documentary. If Penn & Teller watched *Rothaniel*, I imagine they would be proud.

Omnipresence of Racism with Richard Pryor

Figure 10.3 highlights the "SNL & Richard Pryor" era of comedy, roughly spanning 1974–1980. In the next section, we discuss the comedic career and legacy of Richard Pryor through a sociological lens.

Carmichael pushes boundaries and provides comedic perspectives not often represented in comedy. In this, Carmichael's comedy evokes parallels to the work of Richard Pryor. Pryor is considered by many to be the greatest comedian of all time. The genius of his comedic performance came with his voices and his characters. Pryor used characters, voices, and big movements to tell stories and convey messages about his life and experiences. Pryor originally had trouble breaking into the mainstream with this material.

In addition to the content of his work which focused on marginalized members of society, Pryor's comedic style was very visual. It had to be both seen and heard to be intelligible. But because Pryor was Black, he was shut out from the television performances that White comedians or Black comedians with material less offensive to White sensibilities, like Bill Cosby (born in Philadelphia, Pennsylvania, 1937), had access to.[37]

In his early days, a White agent specifically told Pryor to mimic Cosby's tone and style. Cosby was one of the first Black comedians to reach White and mainstream audiences. One of the reasons Cosby achieved mainstream success in his standup career, some argue, was because he did not talk about race in his material. He defended his choice of material, largely focusing on childhood recollections and observations, as a way to gain favor with White audiences. It should be noted that one of the other Black comedians to reach White and mainstream audiences was Dick Gregory (born in St. Louis, Missouri, 1932), who *did* lean into race-focused material. But Cosby's career took off like a rocket.

Pryor's agent's advice was based on his belief that Cosby was a Black performer with whom White folks felt comfortable; someone they would

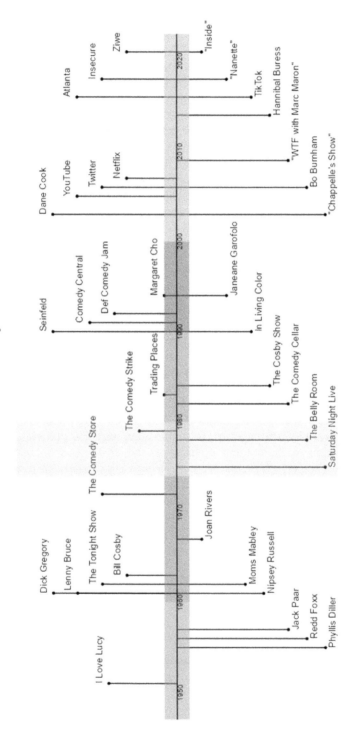

Figure 10.3 SNL and Richard Pryor Timeline

welcome onto their television screens and into their homes. (Of course, this statement has a cruel irony knowing what we know now about Cosby's predatory behavior).[38] But Pryor took his agent's advice, and his material from the 1960s was tailored to White sensibilities. His "family friendly" act was void of political or racial commentary. This led to Pryor finding mainstream success in the 1960s; he booked appearances on the *Ed Sullivan, Mery Griffin,* and *Johnny Carson* shows, and performed in front of largely White audiences in Las Vegas.[39]

But Pryor felt bound by the cutesy style he modeled after Cosby that led to his mainstream success. He went through a period of personal trouble (including a cocaine habit and complications with the law and the Internal Revenue Service) and he ultimately broke down during one of his Las Vegas performances in 1967. Pryor explained his break was caused by frustration. Pryor felt frustrated and trapped by the way he was limited as an artist because of how the world treated him as a Black man. He no longer wanted to box himself in to cow down to White preferences.

After that, Pryor's comedy was truly his own. He started using profanity. He leaned into political and racial commentary and counterculture ideals. His comedic material centered on characters otherwise left out from media representation, satirizing their treatment in society. Pryor's characters often played into the fears or stereotypes commonly held by White folks – with his Black characters being "failures" or "dangerous." The way Pryor acted out these characters inspired audiences and critics came to refer to Pryor's act as "theater." This new comedic style developed by Richard Pryor and Lily Tomlin (born in Detroit, Michigan, 1939) was dubbed the "theater of the routine" (Felton, 1974).[40] "Theater of the routine" referred to how Pryor's and Tomlin's comedy transcended the need for laughter. Instead, these comics focused on uncovering the blemishes and struggles of common people in society. Their material discussed life's highs and lows, its beauty and sadness. Consider how the "theater of the routine" relates to earlier discussions about *if* comedy necessitates constant laughter.

Pryor's comedy albums earned three consecutive Grammy awards for "Best Comedy Album" for *That N——'s Crazy* (1974), ... *Is It Something I Said?* (1975), and *Bicentennial N——* (1976). Pryor's bodily movements cannot be seen on the albums, of course, but his characters, jokes, and voices shine through. When Pryor had the opportunity get his comedy specials taped and released in a visual medium, his comedy really stood out. His 1979 comedy special, *Richard Pryor Live in Concert,* is lauded as one of the best comedy specials in history.

Let us dig in to some of Pryor's work. We can start with Pryor's role as the host of *Saturday Night Live* during its first season in 1975. NBC executives were initially resistant to signing on Pryor to host. Lorne Michaels was so set on Pryor that he resigned following the executives' decision to not hire Pryor. The NBC executives eventually caved and Michaels returned to *SNL*. Once Michaels got the greenlight to hire Pryor as a host, Michaels flew out to meet with Pryor in Florida to discuss the specifics of the deal. Pryor said he would only agree to host if *SNL* hired a Black actor (Thalmus Rasulala), a Black writer (Paul Mooney), and a Black musical guest (Gil Scott-Heron) for the episode, in addition to Pryor's girlfriend (Kathy McKee) and ex-wife (Shelly). Michaels agreed to Pryor's terms.[41]

In Pryor's episode of *SNL*, race was at the forefront. In one sketch, which most sources say was written by Mooney, but apparently Chevy Chase also claims to be the writer, Chase interviews Pryor for a janitorial position and includes a game of "word association" in the interview process. It starts simply. Chase says "tree" and Pryor responds with "dog." But it moves quickly into racial epithets.[42] In describing writing the sketch, Mooney said that having Chase call Pryor the "n-word" on broadcast television was simply putting into words what White Americans *thought* every time they saw a Black comedian like Pryor on screen. The point of the sketch was to shine a light on how Black people know how White people perceive them.

The concept of this sketch was reiterated years later in a sketch which aired on Richard Pryor's own comedy variety series, *The Richard Pryor Show*, which premiered in 1977. In one sketch, "The First Black President," Pryor's character is a Black U.S. president at a press conference (as this was 1977, there had not yet been a Black president in the United States). After Pryor speaks on his satirical policy platforms (such as promising more Black quarterbacks in the NFL), a White reporter asks the president if his [the president's] mother will be his [the reporter's] housecleaner following the end of the presidential term.[43] The underlying message of this question is that no matter how successful a Black person may be, they will always be seen the same way by a White audience. A Black person's professional success does not allow them to escape from racism.

The Richard Pryor Show aired on NBC but Pryor's relationship with NBC at this time was incredibly tense. Pryor felt restricted in what he could say and do on the network, limiting his ability to put his true self on screen. Pryor was rightly concerned. His first ideas for sketches, which took stabs at his relationship the network, were cut. For example, Pryor's idea for the series' opening sketch was for Pryor's body to be seen undergoing an operation implanting the brain of "an inoffensive White guy" (to visualize Pryor's image of the operation, think: Frankenstein's monster). The sketch was scrapped. Instead, the opening sketch showed a naked Pryor (with no visible genitalia, like a Ken doll) as he jokingly tells the audience he did not need to give up anything to compromise with NBC.

Pryor's motive for centering his comedy around discussions of race was to foster connection between people. He did not see talking about race as a divisive force, but as a connective one. In 1998, Richard Pryor won the inaugural Mark Twain Prize for American Humor. Pryor notes in his acceptance speech that a motivation for his comedy was to lessen people's hatred toward each other.[44] He achieved this by allowing audiences to understand the life circumstances of his characters. Pryor did not simply rattle off jokes in a character's voice; he breathed life into them.

In his 1974 album (titled *That N——'s Crazy*), Pryor asked why the everlasting experience of police brutality causes Black people to "go mad." In this bit, he walked the audience through the different experiences of a White person and a Black person being pulled over by the cops. After playing the part of a White person getting pulled over – with a light and casual quality to them – he transitions to the experience of a Black person getting pulled over. In a classic line, Pryor slowly enunciates every word while telling the police officer he is reaching into his pocket for his license. The bit killed. Pryor said so much with how he delivered that line; that was the genius of Pryor's comedic perspective.

That was 1974. A lot has changed in society and in comedy since then. But the police brutality leveled against Black people (and comedians commenting on it) has not. Let us look at a more recent joke that pays homage to Pryor's 1974 set which was performed by standup comedian, actor, and *SNL* writer and *Weekend Update* host, Michael Che (born in New York City, New York, 1983). Che made *SNL* history when he became co-head writer of *SNL* in 2017, becoming the first Black head writer in the show's history.[45] In his 2016 Netflix special, *Matters*, Che tells the audience that his brother is a police officer. Che has trouble "turning off" his fear of, and learned behaviors for interacting with, police officers when he sees his brother every year at Thanksgiving. Che's punchline may sound familiar to Pryor fans, as he slowly enunciates every word while telling his brother he is reaching across the table for the potatoes.[46]

Something remarkable about Che's bit is that it is both classic and contemporary. You do not need to know this pays homage to Pryor to understand this joke in 2016. An article by culture critic at large Jason Zinoman in the *New York Times* places this in context: "Look at stand-up comedy and you'll find more than sixty years of jokes about police brutality. What's not funny is how little they've changed."[47] The jokes are still here because the reality of police brutality leveled against Black people is still here, too.

Summary

This chapter discussed critical race humor, which refers to how humor can be a tool for social criticism. We connected this form of humor to parrhēsia; speaking truth to power, no matter the consequence. This chapter showcased examples of comedians who employ critical race humor and parrhēsia in their work – including Jordan Peele, Jerrod Carmichael, and Richard Pryor.

The discussion of the social thriller genre, exemplified by the movie *Get Out*, highlighted how and why media representations of racism developed through a comedic lens help White audiences understand the systemic and pervasive nature of racism in everyday life. Through comedic examples of standup comedy bits about police brutality, this chapter highlighted how much work still needs to be done to combat racism and inequality and the role the media plays in spreading messages of activism and awareness.

These examples were selected to highlight the institutional causes and omnipresent dangers of racism in the United States. This is part of the comedic perspective. In the next chapter, we will explore what happens when a comedian's perspective is corrupted. Using a sociological lens, we will discuss how power and platform can become turned into a vehicle for maintaining the status quo.

Discussion Questions

10-1: Compare and contrast the myth of meritocracy with Eduardo Bonilla-Silva's concept of color-blindness.

10-2: Define virtue signaling. With a classmate, discuss examples of virtue signaling you have seen or experienced. What connections do you see between virtue signaling and color-blind racism?

10-3: Consider Jordan Peele's argument that *Get Out* can be considered a documentary. Using sociological theories – such as mass media, simulations, and postmodernism – consider what is or is not defined as a "documentary."

10-4: Do you think it matters what genre a film is placed in by media, critics, and/or awards shows? Why or why not? Consider sociological concepts related to language, value, and social power.

10-5: How do you think the existence of *Def Comedy Jam* relates to W.E.B. Du Bois' concept of the color line?

10-6: Do you consider color-blind racism, as defined by Bonilla-Silva, to be an example of falseness and/or repressiveness, and as defined under critical theory?

10-7: Consider how comedians who curse are received in the media by comparing Lenny Bruce and comedians featured on *Def Comedy Jam*. Use sociological theories to explain how or why the receptions differ between these comedians.

10-8: Discuss double consciousness using the comedic examples of Roy Wood Jr. Do you think his comedy debunks the narrative being told about Colin Kaepernick's protest? Why or why not?

10-9: Does Jerrod Carmichael's comedy effectively engage parrhēsia? Provide examples and justification for your view. Discuss *8* and *Rothaniel* using sociological concepts – including postmodernism and multiple consciousnesses.

10-10: How are the sketches described from *The Richard Pryor Show* – including the "word association" sketch and the "First Black U.S. President" sketch – examples of critical race humor? Do you think these sketches are examples of effective satire?

Notes

1 Rossing, J. P. (2014). Critical Race Humor in a Postracial Moment: Richard Pryor's Contemporary Parrhesia. *Author*. https://scholarworks.iupui.edu/handle/1805/7069

2 WIRED Staff. (2018, July 31). Seriously, We Really Need to Talk about Hannah Gadsby's "Nanette." *WIRED*. https://www.wired.com/story/hannah-gadsby-nanette-discussion/

3 Peele, J. (Director). (2017, February 24). *Get Out*. Universal Pictures, Blumhouse Productions, QC Entertainment.

4 Romano, A. (2017, March 7). *How Get Out deconstructs racism for white people*. Vox. https://www.vox.com/culture/2017/3/7/14759756/get-out-benevolent-racism-white-feminism

5 Bonilla-Silva, E. (2003). *Racism without Racists: Color-Blind Racism and the Persistence of Racial Inequality in America*. Rowman & Littlefield Publishers.

6 Peele, 2017.

7 Chitwood, A. (2018, February 22). *Get Out Filmmakers Explain Why They Changed the Ending*. https://collider.com/get-out-alternate-ending-explained/

8 Nast, C. (2017, November 16). *Is Get Out Really a Comedy? Don't Ask Jordan Peele*. Vanity Fair. https://www.vanityfair.com/hollywood/2017/11/jordan-peele-get-out-golden-globes-comedy

9 Kohn, 2017.

10 The Late Show with Stephen Colbert. (2017, November 15). *Jordan Peele Crashed A "Get Out" College Course*. https://www.youtube.com/watch?v=vKbyfdJXoDg

11 Kohn, E. (2017, November 15). Jordan Peele Challenges Golden Globes Classifying 'Get Out' As a Comedy: 'What Are You Laughing At?' *IndieWire*. https://www.indiewire.com/2017/11/jordan-peele-response-get-out-golden-globes-comedy-1201897841/

12 Harris, J. Y., Hunter. (2018, February 22). *How Get Out, the First Great Movie of the Trump Era, Got Made*. Vulture. https://www.vulture.com/article/get-out-oral-history-jordan-peele.html

13 Bonilla-Silva, 2003.

14 Zinoman, J. (2016, November 11). Why 'Def Comedy Jam' Gets No Respect. *The New York Times*. https://www.nytimes.com/2016/11/12/arts/television/why-def-comedy-jam-gets-no-respect.html

15 O'Connor, J. J. (1994, July 31). The Curse of Incessant Cursing. *The New York Times*. https://www.nytimes.com/1994/07/31/arts/television-view-the-curse-of-incessant-cursing.html

16 Zinoman, 2016.

17 Horvitz, L. J. (Director). (2017, September 26). *Def Comedy Jam 25* [Documentary, Comedy].

18 LeDonne, R. (2018, September 25). *Adele Givens Explains How She Ended Up on Kanye West & Lil Pump's 'I Love It' – Billboard*. https://www.billboard.com/music/rb-hip-hop/adele-givens-i-love-it-kanye-west-lil-pump-8476899/

19 Horvitz, 2017.

20 Du Bois, W. E. B. (1899). *The Philadelphia Negro*. University of Pennsylvania Press.

21 Wyche, S. (2016, August 27). *Colin Kaepernick explains why he sat during national anthem*. https://www.nfl.com/news/colin-kaepernick-explains-why-he-sat-during-national-anthem-0ap3000000691077

22 Hartman, S. (Director). (2017, February 3). *Roy Wood Jr. "Father Figure."* https://www.youtube.com/watch?v=QgN6hpnFMPg

23 Greenwood, L. (1984). *God Bless the U.S.A.* MCA Nashville.

24 Berger, P. L. (1963). *Invitation to Sociology: A Humanistic Perspective*. Anchor.

25 Hartman, 2017.

26 *The Carmichael Show: "Gender."* (2015). NBC. https://www.imdb.com/title/tt4893038/

27 Weiner, J. (2016, March 2). Jerrod Carmichael Goes There. *The New York Times.* https://www.nytimes.com/2016/03/06/magazine/jerrod-carmichael-goes-there.html

28 *Jerrod Carmichael: "8."* (2017). https://www.hbo.com/movies/jerrod-carmichael-8

29 Gurian, 2016.

30 *The Specials: Jerrod Carmichael's "8,"* 2022.

31 Fox, J. D. (2018, September 4). *How Funny Does Comedy Need to Be?* Vulture. https://www.vulture.com/2018/09/post-comedy-how-funny-does-comedy-need-to-be.html

32 Triple-Consciousness: The Souls of Intersectional Folx. (2017, July 31). *Young Invincibles.* https://younginvincibles.org/triple-consciousness-souls-intersectional-folx/

33 "Invincible Voices - Triple-Consciousness," 2017.

34 *Good One: Bo Burnham's Can't Handle This.* (2021, May 19). https://podcasts.apple.com/ca/podcast/bo-burnhams-cant-handle-this/id1203393721?i=1000415049394

35 Telford, T. (2018, July 12). *Bo Burnham made a movie to work out his anxiety. It ended up explaining our Instagram age.* The Washington Post. https://www.washingtonpost.com/entertainment/bo-burnham-made-a-movie-to-work-out-his-anxiety-it-ended-up-explaining-our-instagram-age/2018/07/12/86d40f08-8384-11e8-8553-a3ce89036c78_story.html

36 *The Specials: Jerrod Carmichael's "Rothaniel."* (2022, May 31). https://www.patreon.com/posts/jerrod-rothaniel-67169206

37 McPherson, J. (1975, April 27). The new comic style of Richard Pryor. *The New York Times.* https://www.nytimes.com/1975/04/27/archives/the-new-comic-style-of-richard-pryor-i-know-what-i-wont-do-says-the.html

38 Madani, D. (2021, July 1). *60 women accused Bill Cosby. His conviction had been considered a big win for #MeToo.* https://www.nbcnews.com/news/us-news/60-women-accused-bill-cosby-his-conviction-had-been-considered-n1272864

39 McPherson, 1975.

40 Felton, D. (1974, October 10). *Richard Pryor, Lily Tomlin & the Theatre of the Routine—Rolling Stone.* https://www.rollingstone.com/culture/culture-news/richard-pryor-lily-tomlin-the-theatre-of-the-routine-177111/

41 Peisner, D. (2018). *Homey don't play that!: The story of In Living Color and the black comedy revolution.*

42 Wilson, D. (Director). (1975, December 13). *Saturday Night Live*: "Richard Pryor/Gil Scott-Heron." NBC.

43 Moffitt, J. (Director). (1977, September 13). *The Richard Pryor Show*: "Episode #1.1." NBC.

44 Kilian, M. (1998, October 21). Richard Pryor Has Humor Rewarded with Mark Twain Prize. *Chicago Tribune.* https://www.chicagotribune.com/news/ct-xpm-1998-10-21-9810210141-story.html

45 Rao, S. (2017, December 13). *Michael Che is "SNL's" First Black Head Writer.* https://www.colorlines.com/articles/michael-che-snls-first-black-head-writer

46 *Michael Che "Matters."* (2016). https://www.imdb.com/title/tt6209400/

47 Zinoman, J. (2020, June 17). How Richard Pryor Changed the Way Comedy Sees Police Brutality. *The New York Times.* https://www.nytimes.com/2020/06/17/arts/richard-pryor-police-brutality.html

11 Corruption of Comedy

Using a sociological perspective, this chapter discusses how one's sociological imagination can be corrupted and how appropriation of an "underdog identity" by those in power serves to maintain the status quo. First, in this chapter, we discuss the early stages of Dave Chappelle's career to highlight how the comedic perspective can be an effective tool for highlighting the inescapability of racism and inequality in the United States. Second, we discuss Chappelle's more recent work to exemplify how increasing fame, money, and power can corrupt one's comedic perspective. This chapter draws on the work of Ralf Dahrendorf, W.E.B. Du Bois, and critical theorists. Sociological concepts discussed in this chapter include in-groups and out-groups, positions of authority, White privilege, appropriation, and respectability politics.

The Corruption of Comedy Through Success with Dave Chappelle

We cannot talk about comedic commentary of racism in the United States in the modern era without talking about Dave Chappelle (born in Washington, DC, 1973). Chappelle's comedy career began at age fourteen when he started performing at clubs in Washington, DC. A primary focus of Chappelle's comedy has long been the pervasiveness of racism to which Black people have been subjected in the United States.

Important to Chappelle's comedic perspective was his understanding of race as a socially constructed performance. As Dr. Danielle Fuentes Morgan writes in her book, *Laughing to Keep from Dying* (2020), Chappelle's comedy specifically satirized simplistic performances of race.[1] He satirized the way simplistic understandings of entire groups of people flattened them into one narrow image and flummoxed people when anyone existed outside those narrow bounds. This was a common theme in his series, *Chappelle's Show*, a sketch comedy series which ran on Comedy Central 2003–2006, which Chappelle co-created alongside comedian Neal Brennon.

For example, in the first episode of *Chappelle's Show*, audiences are introduced to the character Clayton Bigsby, a blind man, in a fake episode of the PBS show *Frontline*. The fake-*Frontline* documents Bigsby's life as a White supremacist. The comedy of the sketch comes from what the audience knows

DOI: 10.4324/9781003469537-12

but Bigsby does not: he is Black.[2] Bigsby's fellow White supremacists fervently agree with his beliefs, but ... not him? Or maybe they do? The sketch asks: what does it mean if a Black man cannot see he is Black and therefore does not perform his race accordingly? It showcases the way people do not know how to respond to someone who does not fit neatly into one box or who does not properly perform their race.

Let us go back in time to before *Chappelle's Show* premiered. We will use an example from one of the Chappelle's comedy specials, *Killin' Them Softly* (2000), as an example of his early comedic contributions to the sociological examination of race and ethnicity in the United States. *Killin' Them Softly* was his first-hour-long comedy special, premiering on HBO in 2000.[3] If you are only familiar with Chappelle's more recent comedy, *Killin' Them Softly* looks and feels very different.

In the special, Chappelle uses voices to perform characters and tell stories that effectively convey messages about his personal experiences. Those stories are meant to be more emotionally true than factually true. One of the Chappelle's biggest laughs (and there are lots of big laughs) in the special comes from him describing the difference in the relationships with the police between White people and Black people. As Black people are more often targeted, brutalized, and murdered by the police relative to White people, Black people learn early in life to adjust their behavior around police offers to aid in safety and self-preservation.

Chappelle begins telling a story about being lost in New York City with a White friend after they both had smoked some marijuana. They see some police officers. The friend, whom Chappelle names Chip for the purpose of this story, is excited to see the police officers and goes up to them to ask for directions (while also *confessing* he is high as justification for his directional confusion). Chappelle tells his audience that a Black man would not dare speak to a police officer while high. He jokes about being hesitant to speak to a police officer while tired, lest they confuse the symptoms of being tired with those of being a dangerous man, high on PCP, who needs to be taken down through physical force. In the bit, he uses voices and characters (one of whom, "Officer Johnson," is a character who makes later appearances in Chappelle's work) to convey a compelling story about his reality as a Black man in the United States. The bit is funny, gripping, and effective.

Chappelle's bit brings to life the results of sociological studies detailing how, and to what extent, people of color are subjected to more interactions with, and greater surveillance from, police officers than their White counterparts. A 2016 study conducted by Seton Hall Law School's Center for Policy and Research analyzed all traffic violation tickets issued to unique drivers in Bloomfield, New Jersey, during a twelve month period preceding the study (N = 9,715).[4] In 2016, the population of Bloomfield was 60 percent White, 18.5 percent Black, and 24.5 percent Latinx. While the population was 60 percent White, 78 percent of the traffic violation tickets in Bloomfield were given to Black and Latinx drivers.

The researchers found that, of the tickets that noted the location of the traffic violation, 88 percent were given in just one-third of the city, the areas nearest Newark and East Orange. Findings indicate that the racial disparities in traffic ticketing in Bloomfield are largely due to Bloomfield Police Department's targeting the areas of the city that neighbor Newark and East Orange, which have predominantly Black and Latinx populations. The researchers referred to the large police presence in these areas as a "wall" formed against the Black and Brown residents of Newark and East Orange.

This phenomenon of Black drivers being profiled for alleged traffic violations is so rampant that it has a name: **driving while Black**. Being targeted for driving while Black results, in part, from police officers' targeting of certain areas which are predominantly inhabited by Black or Brown residents. Further, being targeted for driving while Black stems from explicit, systemic regulations dictating police activity. To take another example from the state of New Jersey, police training memos (which were released in 2000) instructed police officers to use the race of a vehicle's occupants as part of their calculus in "occupant identifiers for a possible drug courier" stop.[5] To put this type of traffic stop in more lay terms, police officers can pull someone over if there appears to be evidence of the vehicle carrying drugs. One of the visual signs of this, the memo indicates, is the vehicle having Black occupants. The violation here is quite literally driving while Black.[6]

Through these increased traffic stops, Black and Brown folks are more likely to have their plates or their licenses checked (which could result in a parole violation, car insurance violation, or immigration charge) and a search conducted of their person or their car.[7]

Such searches may result in police officers finding evidence of arrestable offenses, such as drug possession. Let us talk about what would then happen next, focusing on the unfair sentencing of drug offenses disproportionately affecting Black communities. One of the most notable stains on our country's history is certainly the **war on drugs**. The name was coined by the media to represent a set of policies first enacted during the Nixon administration (in 1971, Nixon declared drugs "public enemy number one") and continued to expand in later Administrations.[8] The war on drugs created lengthy federal sentencing minimums for the possession, sale, or trafficking of illegal substances, and extreme sentencing disparities for crack compared to powder cocaine.

It was widely known at the time these laws were drafted that crack was more common in Black communities compared to its more expensive sister, powder cocaine, which was more common among White and more affluent communities.[9] The sentencing disparity was 100-to-1. Yes, *one hundred* to *one*. Meaning, possessing five grams of crack *or* five hundred grams of powder cocaine received the same minimum sentence of five years in federal prison. The war on drugs effectively criminalized Black communities.[10] There were many reports of police officers planting crack on Black people they were arresting so they would receive a harsher sentence, or to arrest them in the first place. With this context, consider the bit detailed earlier wherein Chappelle shared his fear a police officer may allege he was on PCP and would use that to justify the use of physical force to restrain him. His fear was valid.

It is important to understand the devastating consequences these harsh and disparate drug laws had on marginalized communities. Ava DuVernay's documentary, *13*th, covers the war on drugs. The title of the documentary refers to the 13th Amendment of the United States which abolished slavery. However, as the documentary argues, the control of Black people did not end with the ratification of the 13th amendment. That subjugation simply took a new form: mass incarceration. During the Reagan administration, spending on drug enforcement tripled compared to spending levels in 1981. There was public buy-in for this war on drugs which stemmed in large part from a media narrative pushing the idea that the United States was under attack from a generation of "**super predators.**" The term implied there was an entire generation of young Black men that were "animals" and needed to be locked up.

Recall mass media's heavy influence on social systems, especially when harping on people's fears. People bought into social policies framed as those designed to keep society safe. This included policies aimed at arresting and jailing Black adults and children like the Central Park Five. The Central Park Five case (also known as the Central Park jogger case) was a criminal case following the 1989 rape and murder of a 28-year-old White woman who had been attacked while jogging in New York City's Central Park. Five boys aged fourteen to sixteen, all of whom were Black or Hispanic, were convicted of the woman's murder.[11] The boys served out their sentences, which ranged between six and thirteen years, before their convictions were vacated in 2002 after another man confessed to the attack.

The boys' innocence was clouded in their trials by racial bias throughout the investigation and court proceedings. And there was a lot of pressure from the public to imprison these young predators to "keep society safe." The Central Park Five's trials were highly publicized. In 1989, Donald Trump, head of a real estate empire at the time, took out ads in all the major newspapers in New York City (*The Daily News, The New York Post, New York Newsday,* and *The New York Times*) urging for the return of the death penalty in response to the attack. While the ad does not name any of the Central Park Five defendants specifically, it refers to them as a collective "roving band of wild criminals."[12] These were teenagers he wanted put to death. Trump was able to use his power, influence, and money (the ads reportedly cost $85,000 in 1989, which is roughly $210,000 in 2023) to spread that message loud and wide. Being labeled as super predators changed the entire course of these boys' lives.

There were lasting consequences of naming an entire generation of Black men and boys as super predators and locking them up with harsh sentences for small crimes (or in the case of the Central Park Five, and many others like them, crimes they did not commit). Not only did the individuals who were targeted suffer the stigmatization and the systemic restriction of future opportunities which stems from having a criminal record, their families and communities suffered too.[13] Black men were removed from families and communities. They were thereby stripped of their opportunities to financially and tangibly contribute and to serve as support systems, mentors, or role models for those in their network. They were gone. This perverse political, legal, and social history is all wrapped up in Chappelle's bit.

The Alienation of Fame

The political, legal, and social weight of comedy is a part of the comedic perspective of Keith and Kenny Lucas (the Lucas Brothers), who were introduced earlier in this book. The Lucas Brothers analyze the roots of why a joke is funny and why personal stories matters. Before their stand-up careers (and acting, writing, and producing careers following that) took off, the brothers both studied philosophy in college and attended law school (Kenny at New York University and Keith at Duke University). They left law school with one week left to focus on their stand-up careers.

I talk about the Lucas Brothers' educational background because it helps contextualize their comedy. They love philosophy. They talk about it on stage, in their written work, and during interviews. The Lucas Brothers are essentially philosophy professors performing in comedy club basements, on mainstages, and on television (with the power of Netflix behind them). That is a power most professors will never get.

While the Lucas Brothers most closely identify as philosophers in their work, I personally see them first and foremost as sociologists. The brothers' material focuses extensively on societal issues like systemic racism. They contextualize the systems and institutions that perpetuate racism, White privilege, and White supremacy. Their wildly popular 2017 Netflix special, *On Drugs* (complete with pop-art portraits of Richard Nixon tiled across the stage backdrop) talked about policies stemming from the war on drugs.

The Lucas Brothers have more recently discussed how much they, and their stand-up, have changed since releasing *On Drugs*. Particularly, they feel they had not yet confidently found their comedic voice at this point in their careers. They were going through personal struggles (the brothers almost broke up as a comedy duo at this time), but have since grown as individuals, as a duo, and as comedians.[14]

Even with that disclaimer in mind, there are still many gems in *On Drugs* that aid in understanding sociological concepts. For one, I will refer to a joke in which the brothers describe an incident in which they were suddenly stopped by a police officer. They were rightfully fearful. But, they quickly realized that the police officer only wanted a selfie, as he recognized them for their roles in the film *22 Jump Street*. The Lucas Brothers then joke that the crisis of police brutality could be ended by Jonah Hill offering every Black man in America a small role in one of his movies.[15]

The joke highlights several important sociological concepts. First, comedy can help elucidate the omnipresence of police brutality experienced by Black and Brown people in the United States. When approached by a police officer, the Lucas Brothers were immediately afraid. The second thing this joke highlights is the way that fame can change the equation. They were no longer just young Black men, they were celebrities. They were in positions of power. That completely changed their interaction with the police.

The Lucas Brothers have discussed in interviews not just how fame changed their interactions with police officers, but also, how fame changed their careers. They discuss this on a 2021 episode of *The Last Laugh* podcast with host Matt Wilstein. The brothers tell Wilstein that during 2016–2018, they were arguing regularly and considered breaking up their comedic duo. They attribute much of their tension to their different professional and artistic goals.[16] The brothers explain gaining fame and notoriety affected their comedic practices. They were no longer able to live in "the margins" of society where they could covertly observe the social norms and behaviors existing around them. When people notice you, and act differently around you because of your fame or status, your ability to silently and objectively observe the world diminishes. The spotlight of fame inhibited them from observing the world as outsiders and in engaging in their artform as they previously could. When the Lucas Brothers felt that lens slipping away, they lost sight of their shared comedic vision.

Dave Chappelle's Public Transformation

Let us expand on this idea of losing one's comedic vision. Earlier, we discussed Chappelle's skill as a comedian which he used in his early work to teach audiences about racism. He built his career by weaving his experiences and observations into stories that spoke volumes about race and racism in the United States.

Chappelle's brash comedy has long-pushed boundaries. Unfortunately, more recently, he has done this in ways not always worth celebrating. The most notable (although certainly not the only) example is Chappelle's special, *The Closer*, which arrived on Netflix in early October 2021.[17] There was an immediate reckoning for Chappelle's overtly transphobic material in the special. Netflix employees staged a walkout over the company's handling of *The Closer*.[18] Think-pieces, reviews, and social media posts lambasted Chappelle as a comedian who no longer weaves his experiences and his identity into stories to highlight injustice.[19,20]

To dig into *The Closer,* we will start with a story Chappelle tells about an experience he had at a gay bar in Texas. Chappelle got into a verbal altercation with a man (who was gay and White), which almost came to blows. Chappelle explains that, right before things turned physically violent, the man took out his cellphone to call for the police. In Chappelle's words, this man was "gay" until he wanted to be "White again" (Chappelle, 2021).[21] Chappelle notes that this behavior is a major gripe he has with the LGBTQ+ community. He, seemingly, believes that all LGBTQ+ people are White and that they seamlessly float between minority and majority status when it best serves their interests.

Let us deconstruct this a bit more. First, as he expressed in *The Closer*, Chappelle sees the marginalization of the LGBTQ+ community and the Black community as in conflict and in competition for the scarce resource of safety and protection. To Chappelle, LGBTQ+ folks get to call the police and he as a Black man does not. Chappelle certainly is not wrong that Black people are not af-forded safety and protection from the police. Calling the police is a scary and po-tentially life-threatening act for Black people and other marginalized groups. But Chappelle is wrong to wholly pit LGBTQ+ communities and Black communities against each other. First, these communities are not mutually exclusive; there are indeed many Black and Brown members of LGBTQ+ communities.

Second, while Chappelle correctly understands that Black people are more likely to experience police victimization than White people, he is ignoring the extent to which sexuality and gender identity matter. According to statistics shared by the Anti-Violence Project, transgender people experience police physical violence at 3.7 times the rate of cisgender people.[22] Intersections in these identities further elucidate inequalities in police violence victimiza-tion. Transgender people of color are victims of police physical violence at six times the rate of their White cisgender counterparts. The failings of our institutions to protect all people regardless of race, sex, sexual orientation, sexual identity, religion, nationality, and every other facet of one's identity are a failing for everyone. Chappelle pits Black and LGBTQ+ communities against each other (which are not mutually exclusive) as if only one group can receive safety and protection from police violence. But systemic protec-tions against discrimination, harassment, and injustice from police violence would benefit all marginalized groups. It is not a zero-sum game.

I want to call attention to sociological terms that can help us break down Chappelle's views in *The Closer* a bit more: in-groups and out-groups. Recall that **in-groups** refers to the groups to which an individual belongs and, often, a person's in-group can play a large part in their identity. **Out-groups** refers to groups to which a person does not belong and a person may deem mem-bers of out-groups as outsiders. Sociological research shows that fear, ten-sion, and aggression can arise from members of in-groups when they feel an out-group may harm the in-group's interests. Chappelle, like everyone, holds many overlapping identities that should not be limited to one in-group. But in response to *The Closer*, the viewer can see Chappelle believing the interests of what he sees as his out-group (the trans community) to be threatening to the interests of what he sees as his in-group (the Black community). But, of course, these communities are not mutually exclusive. They overlap.

Recall Ralf Dahrendorf's description of how both consensus *and* conflict are present in society, validating the theoretical contributions of both structural/ functionalists and conflict theorists.[23] Dahrendorf believed power resides in **positions of authority**, not within individual holding those positions. Chap-pelle's position of power is being a *celebrity*. This is a valuable status. Consider how his comedy is compensated. Netflix paid Chappelle $24.1 million for *The Closer* (2021).[24] For comparison to another major comedy special, put out by another hugely famous comedian, Netflix paid Bo Burnham $3.9 million for *Inside* (2020). If money is a symbol of value, Chappelle's words are considered as highly valuable. His words then become part of the public discourse.

Chappelle's transformation from someone who punches up to someone who punches down can be directly attributed to his success according to multiple critics.[25] They argue that Chappelle is no longer seeing the world through the lens of an outsider. He is now in a position of authority. In an article titled "Dave Chappelle the Comedy Relic," which appeared in *Vulture* in late October 2021, Dr. Danielle Fuentes Morgan discusses the public backlash to *The Closer* and Chappelle's evolution as a comedic figure. Morgan, who teaches courses on African American culture, literature, and comedy at Santa Clara University, explains that most of her students were born after the year 2000. This means that they were born after Chappelle's special, *Killin' Them Softly*, was released.

In prior academic years, when Morgan introduced her students to Chappelle's early specials like *Killin' Them Softly* (2000) or *For What It's Worth* (2004), she noted that her students liked and admired Chappelle's material reacting to political injustices like racism and policing.[26] They found him funny. But this positive response from her students has changed in recent years. Today, as Morgan explains, her students no longer find Chappelle politically relevant. Morgan does not see this as a consequence of his age; she notes other comedians who have enjoyed lengthy careers (she lists Tig Notaro, Leslie Jones, Marc Maron, and Paul F. Tompkins) who continue to feel relevant to their fans.

Morgan's points draw our attention to the way Chappelle's comedy has changed. In his early days, he punched up. Today, he is punching down. Chappelle's more recent work lacks nuance and critical reflection of the way society classified people into narrow groups. More specifically, his more recent comedy lacks a necessary intersectional perspective; which results in divisive and often hateful work (to draw on Richard Pryor's Mark Twain Prize acceptance speech as a visualization, Chappelle's comedic career scooted closer to hatred from humor). As Chappelle's work evolves, he shows audiences that he fails to understand different life experiences among members of Black communities based on factors such as sexuality and social class. He fails to validate struggles of communities other than his own.

Morgan equates the shift not only to Chappelle's changing material, but also to changes in how her students perceive his entire persona. *Killin' Them Softly* is not just a relic of another era but of a different man. Morgan notes that the majority of Chappelle's standup work (which she defines as what the public can access) has been created in the past five or six years. Netflix and YouTube have made Chappelle's recent works incredibly accessible. In many ways, the moves comics make today have larger and more immediate impact than those they made pre-Internet. Today, the world sees and responds to every move a comedian makes in nearly real time. There is great responsibility in that.

Appropriation of the Underdog Identity

In this section, we will expand upon how holding a position of authority corrupts the comedic perspective. This book has consistently argued two things: first, a comedic perspective is an outsider perspective. Second, the profession of comedy has long been an old White boys club (alternatively speaking, an *insider's* club). It is important to understand how those two ideas co-exist. To do this, we need to talk about Henry Beard (born in New York City, New York, 1945) and Doug Kenney (born in West Palm Beach, Florida, 1946). Beard and Kenney were Harvard undergraduates in the 1960s and both wrote for its humor magazine, *The Harvard Lampoon*. Beard, Kenney, and their contemporaries came up in comedy at a time when television was relatively new. They went on to create *The National Lampoon*, a national humor magazine which ran from 1970 to 1998 which they created alongside Robert Hoffman. Kenney also went on to write, produce, and star in many large television and film projects. Two of his most notable films are the 1978 film *Animal House* (starring John Belushi) and the 1980 film *Caddyshack* (starring Chevy Chase and Rodney Dangerfield).

The transition of comedy from being an artform primarily consumed in comedy clubs to being widely available on television and movie screens had a large impact on the profession. Previously, comedians performed in comedy clubs and occasionally put out a comedy record. Only certain comedians had access to the type of widespread, mainstream consumption that the expansion of film and television afforded.

For the generation of kids and teenagers who came of age during the 1960s and 1970s, the comedians they saw on television were the only comedians they may have ever known. Recall our earlier discussions of Moms Mabley's and Richard's Pryor's careers, for example, to remember which comedians had early and easy access to television stages. The comedy available on television – which was new and exciting to this young generation – was offered to audiences almost entirely devoid of any historical context.

Comedians who made it to television still presented themselves as underdogs (recall Rodney Dangerfield, for example). To the kids and teenagers watching at home, there was a conflation of what it meant to be a "comedian" with what it meant to be an "underdog." Understanding the history and sociology of comedy is important. On an episode of *The Specials* podcast, comedian Dave Schilling explains comedy was created for minorities to freely express the details of their oppression by the system in a safe space. Comedy started as an underdog sport.[27] Schilling goes on to detail what he describes as the erasure of the "ethnic" origins of comedy in favor of one that is White, male, and elite. Comedy moved toward the money and lost its intersectional perspective. Hurdles were thrown in the way of comedians who did not fit this White, male, and elite mold.

White privilege is the relative advantages afforded to White people which stem from the subjugation of Black people and people of color.[28] An important feature of White privilege is the ability to not think about one's own race. Doors have not been slammed in front of you because of your race. As such, for White people, the omnipresence of racism and the salience of one's race as a guiding social structure are easy to misunderstand or ignore. When you do not see the doors slammed in others' faces, it is easy to assume you made it to the table (when others did not) because of your skill or merit.

Schilling explains that the art of comedy is jeopardized when privileged folks like Beard and Kenney act as though – by the pure act of being comedians – they, too, are underdogs. In sociological terms, Schilling describes the appropriation of comedy by White, male, and elite people like Beard and Kenney. Recall our discussion of **cultural appropriation**. As a refresher, cultural appropriation is the unacknowledged adoption (read: theft) of the practices, behaviors, or forms of one group by another usually more powerful group. This appropriation of the underdog identity that began to occur in the 1960s and into the 1970s had a profound and lasting impact. *The Harvard Lampoon*, *The National Lampoon*, and *Saturday Night Live* and all served to take comedy out of nightclubs and into avenues where there was money to be made. This really changed the game; this marketability made comedy seem cool and made it desirable to young, affluent, White men.

The timing and context matter greatly here. This generation of comedians was coming up in tandem with the first generation of children who were, as some argue, "raised by television."[29] These comedians' popularity and ubiquity on television gave young audiences the false idea that these comedians *invented* comedy. The false idea that it was a new artform, one created by these men. In short, these comedians appropriated comedy. They appropriated everything but the burden of comedians who came before them.

Some of the major comedians leading up to this time were comics sharing their perspectives as underdogs and speaking truth to power, like Richard Pryor. So when the Beards and Kenneys of the world entered comedy in the 1960s and 1970s, they adopted the identity of an underdog. They took inspiration from the underdog and rabble-rousing comedians who came before them but they failed to understand their own privilege.[30]

By entering comedy – a profession of underdogs – Beard, Kenney, and their contemporaries assumed that meant they too were underdogs. First, they failed to understand how their privilege offered them the opportunity to enter comedy through a door not open to most (e.g., to write for the *Harvard Lampoon*, you must attend Harvard University). Second, they failed to see how privilege made their life experiences very different from those of, say, Richard Pryor. And this limited their comedic perspective.

Comedy, #MeToo, and Bill Cosby

It is dangerous for a monoculture to exist wherein a small set of cultural icons have too much unchecked power and can silence and discredit other's voices. One's success, money, and power can influence public perception, buy trust, and cover up criminal behavior. Here, we will review the legacy of a major figure in the world of comedy: Bill Cosby.

Before Cosby, the first Black comedian to play to White audiences was Dick Gregory. Gregory did not avoid talking about race. He talked about racism on stage, right in the faces of White audiences. He has been described as the "Jackie Robinson" of club comedians for the way he broke racial barriers in White clubs. His first big gig to White audiences was when he played the Playboy Club in 1961 (the Playboy Club, truly, plays an important role in comedic history for the diversity of comedians who played there).

As an example of the way he opened up spots for other Black comedians is his appearance on *The Jack Paar Show* (which was rebranded as *The Tonight Show* when Johnny Carson took over in 1962). *The Jack Paar Show* famously showcased many comedians (including Black comedians) but Gregory recognized that Jack Paar only invited White comedians to come sit on the couch and chat after their set. Gregory refused to perform on the show unless Paar agreed to invite him over to the couch. This broke down barriers for other Black performers who came after him.

The height of Gregory's fame was the era in which Cosby came up in comedy. Gregory was big and he put race front and center in his comedy. When Cosby first started performing comedy, he also talked about race in his act. Then he got new management. They recommended he stop talking about race, racism, and oppression and adopt are more "White-friendly" style. And White audiences and mainstream media ate it up. The media referred to Cosby as "raceless," implying that he was amenable to audiences of different racial backgrounds (specifically referring to the fact that he was amenable to White people).[31] This classification was intended as a compliment. By adopting a "cutesy" style and avoiding talking about race in his comedy, Cosby was non-threatening to White audiences. In this way, per comedian and comedy historian Wayne Federman, Cosby was "not Dick Gregory."[32] Cosby leaned into the status quo, whereas Gregory challenged it.

There were many barriers for Black comedians to get on television during this time. Almost all the gatekeepers on television (such as talk-show hosts, television and film directors and producers) were White and mostly men. It was hard for a Black performer to get airtime of any kind. So it was groundbreaking when Cosby was cast as one of the leads of *I Spy*, playing Alexander "Scotty" Scott. *I Spy*, which aired on NBC from 1965 to 1968, was the first television drama series in the United States to feature a Black lead actor. This matters because not only was he a Black actor in a lead role, Cosby's character Scotty was smart, accomplished, and talented.

Prior representations of Black characters in media were largely stereotypical or degrading. For example, at this same time, *Amos & Andy* was still on air. *Amos & Andy* was a radio program centered around two Black characters (initially voiced by White actors) that ran from 1943 to 1960, first as *The Amos 'n' Andy Show*, and later as *Amos 'n' Andy's Music Hall*. The show has been criticized for its racial stereotypes and racist tropes. The radio program was adapted for television, with *The Amos 'n' Andy Show* running on CBS 1951–1953. The NAACP almost immediately campaigned to have the show taken off the air for being a libelous and fabricated depiction of Black personhood.[33] Now, consider Cosby as Scotty on *I Spy*. His character was a Rhodes scholar and spoke multiple languages. With this role, audiences looked up to Cosby as a role model.[34]

I Spy launched Cosby's television career. He went on to have various successful children's programs. For example, Cosby hosted the "Picture Pages" segment on the program *Captain Kangaroo*. *Captain Kangaroo* was an educational children's television program that aired on weekday mornings on

CBS from 1955 to 1984 (for those unfamiliar with the program, *Sesame Street* is an apt comparison). "Picture Pages" was a recurring segment on the show wherein Cosby, as himself, would teach interactive math and drawing lessons to preschool-aged children. The lessons moved through puzzle booklets which were available to the public for purchase.

Cosby was also the creator, host, and lead voice actor of *Fat Albert and the Cosby Kids* (hereafter referred to as *Fat Albert*), which ran on CBS from 1972 to 1985. *Fat Albert* was a children's cartoon centered around kids in a low-income, predominantly Black area of Philadelphia. It added representation to a landscape that largely ignored Black communities either entirely or without any nuance or insider understanding. Something unique and important about *Fat Albert* was that the title character had an entire group of Black friends. This was unlike other representations of Black characters on television at the time (or still today) which commonly featured only one Black "sidekick" to a White lead character. Further, those Black characters were commonly written or drawn as if they were White characters with darker skin. On *Fat Albert*, however, there was better representation of what it looked like and felt like to be Black in the United States.

One of the Cosby's biggest television legacies is *The Cosby Show*, which ran on NBC for eight seasons from 1984 to 1992. The show centered around the Huxtable family, headed by obstetrician Cliff (played by Cosby) and attorney Clair (played by Phylicia Rashad) Huxtable, with their five children, in Brooklyn Heights, New York. The show was groundbreaking at the time for many reasons. To begin, it was the first mainstream sitcom to showcase an upper-class Black family headed by highly educated professionals. The popularity of *The Cosby Show* among mainstream audiences, including White audiences, is important to note. The show was rated number one by the Nielsen ratings for five consecutive seasons. It is one of the only two sitcoms in history (the other being *All in the Family*) to be number one for five seasons.[35]

Audiences looked up to the Huxtables in *The Cosby Show*. Their house was a "monument to Black excellence" (Bell, 2022).[36] As comedian and television host W. Kamau Bell put it, White audiences would simply enjoy the show for its storyline and jokes. But Black audiences would also see the art on the wall, hear music playing the background, and recognize them as the work of Black artists.

A goal of W.E.B. Du Bois, as expressed in *The Souls of Black Folk*, was to show Black people that they were not limited to seeing themselves as White people saw them. They could break free from the psychological limitations imposed upon them and live a fuller, richer life. Consider Du Bois' beliefs alongside critical theory and its description of mass media. Recall that critical theorists see culture as a coercive societal force. Mass media, like widely popular mainstream television programs, are powerful agents of socialization.[37] Cosby stood at the top of television for decades and hit multiple generations of television audiences. He was an iconic, powerful, and admirable figure in the in the United States, but particularly for Black Americans. Before Cosby's rise, Black folks had largely been excluded from television or were represented using racist tropes and narrow understandings of Black people's lives and experiences. Cosby centered his work on the Black experience and Black excellence and sent it out to the masses. Such positive displays on a popular television series played an important role on socialization.

However, the role of Cosby in celebrating the lives and experiences of Black folks began to have cracks in the veneer. The first downward turn in Cosby's public persona was the reception to his "pound cake" speech. This refers to a speech given by Bill Cosby on May 17, 2004, during an NAACP Legal Defense Fund awards ceremony in Washington, DC, to commemorate the 50th anniversary of the *Brown v. Board of Education* 1954 Supreme Court decision that ended the legal racial segregation of public schools. In the speech, Cosby lodges criticism directly toward the Black community and their failure to "live up to" the life they believed in and fought for during the civil rights era of the 1950s and 1960s. He cites false statistics about soaring high school dropout rates and makes broad claims about men running away being fathers and women feeling no embarrassment for being pregnant without a husband (as Cosby implies: they should be).

The speech is known as the pound cake speech for a line in his speech that first compares Black people who were imprisoned during the civil rights era, whom he considers to be admirable advocates for social justice, to Black people who are incarcerated today (referring to 2004, when the speech was delivered). Cosby describes how, in his view, Black people are committing too many crimes. He says Black people are stealing small items like Coca-Cola and pound cake. When a Black person is shot by the police, instead of the community getting angry, Cosby believes that they should instead ask why the person was holding pound cake.[38]

As the message implies, Cosby is of the opinion that Black people have caused their own oppression through selfish, irresponsible, and dangerous acts. To Cosby, traumatic physical injury or death at the hands of the police is an appropriate punishment for stealing pound cake.[39] Incarceration and police brutality are a result of their choices and behaviors, not systemic racism. The pound cake speech does not consider whether a different way of life is equally respectable, nor does it consider any structural barriers inhibiting the ability of people to achieve his touted goals.

In W. Kamau Bell's 2022 Showtime documentary *We Need to Talk About Cosby*, Bell describes the content and tone of the pound cake speech sociologically.[40] He notes that the speech is an example of respectability politics. **Respectability politics** is a form of discourse or political rhetoric employed by prominent figures (like political or religious leaders, successful business people, renowned academics, and famous actors or celebrities) who are members of a marginalized group to police behavior among their own group members.[41]

Tenets of respectability politics include defining what is good versus what is deviant behavior; encouraging behaviors which align with the White, mainstream, status quo; and asking members to steer away from behaviors stereotypic of their group. Inherent in messages of respectability politics is the idea that marginalized people are responsible for their own oppression. In the pound cake speech, Cosby positioned himself as a moral authority who looked down upon Black people as a group. This was a huge deal. For so long, Cosby was an icon of Black excellence in an era largely void of positive Black representation. This had a big impact on folks who looked up to Cosby. Cosby transitioned from "America's Dad into America's Angry Grandpa" (Bell, 2022).[42] To Bell and others who grew up in an era led by Cosby as an icon of Black excellence, the pound cake speech really matters for how Cosby was understood as a public figure.

As Bell acknowledges in the documentary, the pound cake speech was likely not as pivotal for White folks during this era or even for Black folks of younger generations. He notes that a White documentarian, for example, may not even include the pound cake speech in their telling of Cosby's legacy.[43] Bell understands that identity and perspective shape how a story is told. What you notice depends on your context and past experiences. What you consider an important detail inside the broader narrative matters, and how you present that detail constitutes your comedic perspective.

We can apply that same understanding to Cosby's public takedown for allegations of sexual assault. Cosby was, allegedly, a serial sexual predator who drugged and raped *at least* sixty women over the course of decades.[44] Allegations were lodged against Cosby and his predatory behavior was known by people in the industry. Yet, very little happened to Cosby or his career because of these allegations. For example, he received major deals from NBC during this time. The alleged horrific abuses these women experienced were not enough to cause a stir in the public consciousness. Cosby's elite image provided him an air of protection against deviant labels. He could perform deviant and horrific acts and still receive trust and admiration from the masses.

Until 2014. Enter comedian and actor Hannibal Buress (born in Chicago, Illinois, 1983). An October 2014 set by Burress took the comedy world by storm after it was recorded by an audience member on their cell phone and posted on YouTube. In this set, Buress spoke of the numerous rape allegations lodged against Cosby. People argue that part of the reason Buress' set took off was because he did *not* focus specifically on the rape allegations. He flipped the script by focusing on Cosby's hypocrisy.

Mimicking a conversation between Cosby (using an imitation of his signature voice) and a Black audience, Burress goes back and forth between Cosby telling them to "pull their pants up" and lauding himself for not cursing onstage, with the audience lobbing back the evidence that he is a rapist.[45] Recall that after the pound cake speech, part of Cosby's public persona included talking down to Black people for what he considered inappropriate behavior. In Buress' bit, the foundation of Cosby's high horse – and his respectability rhetoric – looks pretty wobbly when juxtaposed against allegations of such horrific abuse.

Comedians are trained to look for hypocrisy and for any incongruity between one's words and one's actions. That is what Buress' comedic lens allowed him to do. This narrative of hypocrisy effectively woke up audiences and the public. To Bell, he believes that Buress' socialization mattered for his comedic perspective on Cosby's hypocrisy. Buress is younger than Bell; he grew up in a different generation. He likely watched *The Cosby Show* as reruns but as Bell argues, that is not the same thing as growing up with *Cosby Kids, Fat Albert,* and *The Cosby Show* as appointment television. As such, Bell believes that Buress and other young Black people have less "patience" for Cosby's hypocrisy than do Black people in his own generation.[46]

Bell's observation is important for the way we understand the role of celebrity and media on how we see the world. Because Bell grew up in a time dominated by one view of Cosby as "America's Dad" and an icon of Black excellence, he saw him predominantly in that light. Because Buress grew up in a different generation that was less Cosby-dominant, his perspective allowed him to see Cosby's behavior through an outsider's lens. He could look at Cosby's behavior more objectively.

Cosby had skirted sexual misconduct accusations for years, but things finally broke open after Buress' set. Following the set going viral in 2014, Cosby was accused of sexual misconduct, ranging from rape, sexual battery, drug-facilitated sexual assault, attempted sexual assault, and child sexual abuse.[47] A trail began in 2015 for his drugging, sexual assault, and aggravated indecent exposure of Andréa Constand, which allegedly occurred in 2004. In 2018, he was convicted and sentenced to a prison term of three to ten years.[48] However, Cosby's conviction was overturned in 2021 when a judge declared the original trial a mistrial.[49]

Buress does not like talking about this set, or Cosby in general, in interviews. He did not perform this set with the intention of transferring its virality into personal notoriety or to mark himself as an overtly political comedian. But Buress' set *did* go viral thanks to an audience member's choice to record it on their cell phone and upload it to YouTube. YouTube has become a powerful facilitator of change. The advent of YouTube represents a pivotal shift in the way comedy is disseminated and consumed. People no longer need to go to a comedy club to see comedy. Suddenly, they can just open their laptops or cell phones. For years, Cosby's dominance in the mainstream media landscape protected him from legal liability for his actions. Gatekeepers like NBC kept giving Cosby deals because he was making them money. But Buress' fresh perspective served to challenge the status quo, disrupt those in power, and change the world.

Summary

This chapter provided examples of what happens when comedic viewpoints are corrupted or underdog identities are appropriated. This chapter used these examples to showcase the importance of continuing to view the world as a sociologist – by always using the lens of an outsider. At the end of this chapter, readers should understand how conflict theory relates to the corruption of comedy through success.

Comedians with great levels of authority through fame, power, and money have the freedom to act in ways that may be harmful to those with less power, often with little legal or financial consequence. While earlier chapters in this book served to discuss how comedians are underdogs and outsiders whose art serves to challenge the status quo, this chapter highlighted exceptions (as in comedians whose comedic perspective is corrupted or appropriated) to prove the rule. These comedic examples should challenge and deepen your understanding of the core sociological principles they are meant to represent – including in-groups and out-groups, intersectionality, identity, perspective, social status, and social power.

Discussion Questions

11-1: Use <u>labeling theory</u> to discuss the media narrative of Black youths as <u>super predators</u> and of Black men "abandoning" their families. Consider the motivation for, and consequences of, the mass media coverage that put forward the false narrative that the paternal absenteeism in Black men was a personal failing, while mass incarceration was systemically and forcefully removed large swaths of Black men from their families and communities by political and legal systems.

11-2: Discuss Chappelle's line in *The Closer* wherein he states that a man is "gay" until he wanted to be "White again" using sociological concepts. Consider <u>privilege</u>, <u>intersectionality</u>, the <u>matrix of oppression</u>, <u>in-groups</u> and <u>out-groups</u>.

11-3: Do you agree that to be a celebrity is to be in a <u>position of power</u>? Consider if you believe celebrities can enforce compliance to rules and social norms. Justify your answer using sociological concepts, including those related to <u>social status</u> and <u>mass media</u>.

11-4: Do you agree or disagree with the idea that White, privileged, male comedians – like Henry Beard and Doug Kenney – <u>appropriated</u> comedy? Why or why not? Discuss the role of <u>White privilege</u> in their professional success.

11-5: Think about how shows like *Fat Albert* and *The Cosby Show*, which aired during the 1980s, stood in contrast to the <u>super predator</u> narrative spouted by news media outlets at the same time. Consider how this frames your understanding of their cultural impact.

11-6: Consider Cosby's public persona and the roles he played on television (like Alexander "Scotty" Scott and Dr. Cliff Huxtable) as compared to his personal life using Erving Goffman's <u>dramaturgical theory of the self</u>.

11-7: Do you see parallels between Cosby's pound cake speech and Chappelle's comedy in *The Closer*? Consider <u>respectability politics</u> and the corruption of comedy through success.

11-8: Compare the underlying message of Cosby's pound cake speech to the *Family Matters* episode titled "Good Cop, Bad Cop" discussed earlier in this book. Discuss how media portrayals of Black figures, in these examples, serve to maintain the status quo using Eduardo Bonilla-Silva's concept of color-blindness.

11-9: How does the media narrative of super predators relate to respectability politics?

11-10: Do you agree with W Kamau Bell's belief that Hannibal Buress' youth allowed him to have a different perspective on Bill Cosby's hypocrisy than did folks of the prior generation? Why or why not? Can you think of similar examples, in your own life, of how you may perceive a public figure differently than someone of an on older or younger generation based on their behavior or persona? Tie your answers to socialization, social norms, and mass culture.

Notes

1 Morgan, D. F. (2020). *Laughing to Keep from Dying: African American Satire in the Twenty-First Century*. University of Illinois Press.
2 *Was Clayton Bigsby the Best "Chappelle's Show" Skit Ever?* (2018, October 31). Rare. https://rare.us/rare-humor/clayton-bigsby-the-best-chappelle-show/
3 Lathan, S. (Director). (2000, July 26). *Dave Chappelle: "Killin' Them Softly"* [Comedy].
4 Denbeaux, M., Kearns, K., & Ricciardelli, M. J. (2016). *Racial Profiling Report: Bloomfield Police and Bloomfield Municipal Court*. https://doi.org/10.2139/ssrn.2760382
5 Genner, S., & Süss, D. (2017). Socialization as Media Effect. In *The International Encyclopedia of Media Effects* (pp. 1–15). John Wiley & Sons, Ltd. https://doi.org/10.1002/9781118783764.wbieme0138
6 Heumann, M., & Cassak, L. (2007). *Good Cop, Bad Cop: Racial Profiling and Competing Views of Justice* (3rd edition). Peter Lang Inc., International Academic Publishers.
7 Denbeaux, Kearns, & Ricciardelli, 2016.
8 DuVernay, A. (Director). (2016, October 7). *Documentary: The 13th*. Netflix. https://www.netflix.com/title/80091741
9 Palamar, J. J., Davies, S., Ompad, D. C., Cleland, C. M., & Weitzman, M. (2015). Powder cocaine and crack use in the United States: An examination of risk for arrest and socioeconomic disparities in use. *Drug and Alcohol Dependence, 149*, 108–116. https://doi.org/10.1016/j.drugalcdep.2015.01.029
10 DuVernay, 2016.
11 Central Park Five: The True Story behind When They See Us. (2019, June 12). *BBC News*. https://www.bbc.com/news/newsbeat-48609693
12 Wilson, M. (2002, October 23). Trump Draws Criticism for Ad He Ran After Jogger Attack. *The New York Times*. https://www.nytimes.com/2002/10/23/nyregion/trump-draws-criticism-for-ad-he-ran-after-jogger-attack.html
13 DuVernay, 2016.
14 *The Last Laugh: The Lucas Brothers Crash the Oscars!* (2021, April 12). https://podcasts.apple.com/us/podcast/the-lucas-brothers-crash-the-oscars/id1456474041?i=1000516898470

15 *Lucas Brothers "On Drugs."* (2017). Netflix. https://www.netflix.com/title/ 80117484

16 *The Last Laugh: The Lucas Brothers Crash the Oscars!* (2021).

17 Lathan, S. (Director). (2021, October 5). *Dave Chappelle: "The Closer"* [Comedy]. Netflix Worldwide Entertainment.

18 Legaspi, A. (2021, October 21). *Netflix Employees Walk Out to Protest Dave Chappelle's "The Closer."* Rolling Stone. https://www.rollingstone.com/tv-movies/ tv-movie-news/netflix-employees-supporters-walkout-dave-chappelle-the-closer-1245366/

19 Lewis, N. (2021, October 14). Dave Chappelle Accomplished Exactly What He Wanted to. *Slate*. https://slate.com/culture/2021/10/dave-chappelle-the-closer-netflix-controversy.html

20 Romano, A. (2021, October 23). *What Dave Chappelle gets wrong about trans people and comedy—Vox*. https://www.vox.com/culture/22738500/dave-chappelle-the-closer-daphne-dorman-trans-controversy-comedy

21 Lathan, 2021.

22 *Hate Violence Against Transgender Communities*. (2017). National Coalition of Anti-Violence Programs. https://avp.org/wp-content/uploads/2017/04/ncavp_transhvfactsheet.pdf

23 Dahrendorf, R. (1959). *Class and Class Conflict in Industrial Society*. Routledge, UK.

24 Shaw, L. (2021, October 13). Netflix Staff Raised Concerns about Dave Chappelle Special Before Release. *Bloomberg*. https://www.bloomberg.com/news/articles/ 2021-10-13/netflix-staff-raised-concerns-about-dave-chappelle-special-before-release

25 Lewis, 2021; Rude, M. (2021, March 23). *Trans People Four Times as Likely to Face Violent Crime as Cis*. https://www.advocate.com/crime/2021/3/23/trans-people-four-times-likely-face-violent-crime-cis

26 Morgan, D. F. (2021, October 21). *Dave Chappelle the Comedy Relic*. Vulture. https://www.vulture.com/article/dave-chappelle-the-comedy-relic.html

27 *The Specials: Mo'Nique's "One Night Stand."* (2021, March 3). https://www. patreon.com/posts/moniques-one-48267073

28 Bonilla-Silva, E. (2001). *White Supremacy and Racism in the Post-Civil Rights Era*. Lynne Rienner Publishers.

29 Nachman, G. (2003). *Seriously Funny: The Rebel Comedians of the 1950s and 1960s*. Pantheon Books.

30 *The Specials: Mo'Nique's "One Night Stand"* (2021).

31 McPherson, J. (1975, April 27). The New Comic Style of Richard Pryor. *The New York Times*. https://www.nytimes.com/1975/04/27/archives/the-new-comic-style-of-richard-pryor-i-know-what-i-wont-do-says-the.html

32 Bell, W. K. (Director). (2022). *We Need to Talk about Cosby* [Documentary]. https://www.imdb.com/title/tt16378210/

33 Von Schilling, J. A. (2003). *The Magic Window: American Television, 1939-1953*. Haworth Press.

34 Bell, 2022.

35 The Editors of Encyclopaedia Britannica. (2024, February 5). The Cosby Show. *Britannica*. https://www.britannica.com/topic/The-Cosby-Show

36 Bell, 2022.

37 Genner & Süss, 2017.

38 Cosby, B. (2004). Dr. Bill Cosby Speaks at the 50th Anniversary Commemoration of the "Brown v. Topeka Board of Education" Supreme Court Decision, May 22, 2004. *The Black Scholar*, 34(4), 2–5. https://www.jstor.org/stable/41069098

39 Moyer, J. Wm. (2015, July 7). How Bill Cosby's 2004 'Pound Cake' speech exploded into his latest legal disaster. *The Washington Post*. https://www.washingtonpost. com/news/morning-mix/wp/2015/07/07/how-bill-cosbys-2004-pound-cake-speech-exploded-into-his-latest-legal-disaster/

40 Bell, 2022.

41 Pitcan, M., Marwick, A. E., & Boyd, D. (2018). Performing a vanilla self: Respectability politics, social class, and the digital world. *Journal of Computer-Mediated Communication, 23*(3), 163–179. https://academic.oup.com/jcmc/article/23/3/163/4962541?searchresult=1

42 Bell, 2022.

43 *The Last Laugh: W. Kamau Bell: 'We Need to Talk About Cosby.'* (2022, January 31). https://podcasts.apple.com/bz/podcast/w-kamau-bell-we-need-to-talk-about-cosby/id1456474041?i=1000549618171

44 Bell, 2022.

45 Zuckerman, E. (2014, October 20). Hannibal Buress calls Bill Cosby a "rapist" in stand-up set. *EW*. https://ew.com/article/2014/10/20/hannibal-buress-calls-bill-cosby-a-rapist-in-stand-up-set/

46 *Black on the Air: W. Kamau Bell on "We Need To Talk About Cosby."* (2022, January 22). https://podcasts.apple.com/ca/podcast/w-kamau-bell-on-we-need-to-talk-about-cosby/id1234429850?i=1000548699725

47 Ioannou, F., Mathis-Lilley, B., Hannon, E., & Wilson, L. (2018, April 26). A Complete List of the Women Who Have Accused Bill Cosby of Sexual Assault. *Slate*. https://slate.com/culture/2018/04/bill-cosby-accusers-list-sexual-assault-rape-drugs-feature-in-women-s-stories.html.

48 Bowley, G., & Coscarelli, J. (2018, September 25). Bill Cosby, Once a Model of Fatherhood, Is Sentenced to Prison. *The New York Times*. https://www.nytimes.com/2018/09/25/arts/television/bill-cosby-sentencing.html.

49 Cosby's attorneys appealed the conviction claiming criminal charges should not have been brought forward by District Attorney Kevin Steel in 2015 because Cosby had made a non-prosecution agreement with a prior District Attorney, Bruce Castor, when Cosby provided testimony in a civil case with Constand in 2005. The 2021 judge agreed with Cosby's legal team and deemed the unsealing of Cosby's 2005 testimony in which he detailed his sexual assault of Castor for the 2015 trial as the wrong decision. As such, the judge declared a mistrial. Dale, M., & Richer, A. D. (2021, June 30). EXPLAINER: Why Bill Cosby's conviction was overturned. *AP NEWS*. https://apnews.com/article/why-was-bill-cosby-conviction-overturned-2a65ec25c153fbd1c24b1c58a2b6e583

Conclusion

Sociology can be a framework for fostering stronger human connections and a tool for social change. I believe the same can be true for comedy. This book concludes by using comedy to visualize how understanding one another better affords opportunity for joy, hope, and connection. Even in the face of tragedy, comedy asserts that knowing someone understands you or shares your experience gives hope that things will be okay.

Connection with Jo Firestone

Something the 2020 COVID-19 pandemic taught many of us – through loss – is that there is connection in experiencing things together. The height of comedy as a connection can be seen in Jo Firestone's 2021 Peacock special, *Good Timing*. The special chronicles Firestone (born in St. Louis, Missouri, 1986), a New York City-based standup comic known for her chaotic and whimsical energy, as she teaches a group of sixteen senior citizens how to write and perform standup comedy. Firestone began teaching this workshop at New York City's Greenwich House in early 2020, right before the COVID-19 pandemic hit and forced the group to convene over Zoom.[1]

What was supposed to be a thirteen-week class turned into a year-and-a-half-long project. The group continued to meet over Zoom and bonded over their shared love of comedy. According to Firestone, aside from the students' age (which ranged from mid-60s to late-80s), they have little in common. They have different life experiences, religions, racial identities, ethnic identities, relationship statuses, and varying levels of comfort onstage. The uniting force is their love of laughter. The special shows the first in-person class back after the long Zoom run, interviews between Firestone and the students, and the group's first live performance in front of a live theater audience in June 2021.

The way comedy creates connection and brings joy is particularly evident in the interviews Firestone conducts with her students. When Firestone interviews one of the married couples in the class, Rebecca and Orlando Dole, she asks the couple if they remember their first date (in a style which evokes memory of the couple interviews in the 1989 movie, *When Harry Met Sally*). They do. Orlando explained that Rebecca needed someone to come over and

DOI: 10.4324/9781003469537-13

fix her loft bed. Rebecca continues the story, saying that Orlando came over to fix the bed and he told a joke which made her laugh. She fell in love with him right then. Many of the students speak about how comedy brings people together. For the Doles, it started a romantic relationship.

Bibi Elvers, one of the oldest members of the group at age eighty-eight, speaks to Firestone (who was thirty-four years old at the time) about how comedy unites the two of them. Firestone asks Elvers what makes her laugh; Elvers responds that she laughs at everything. She sees humor as a survival strategy. Finding humor in the every day is something she does for herself. Elvers changes pace and expresses to Firestone the gratitude she has for her. Elvers explains that she feels as though there is no generational divide between the two of them. What Elvers means is that comedy allows them to connect in a way that glosses over their age difference. They are simply two comedians who love to laugh. In an interview with the *NY Post*, Firestone explained that she feels energized being with people who genuinely enjoy making one another laugh.[2]

As *Good Timing* shows, the love of comedy is a beautiful thing. And that love is what allowed the workshop to survive the transition to Zoom and extend beyond the original thirteen-week run time. While teaching a comedy workshop during the COVID-19 pandemic, Firestone saw her students were motivated to find light and joy during dark and difficult times. So much of what connected these people to Firestone and to each other is the way they all listened to one another. When these folks opened Zoom every week, in the name of comedy, they were able to share their stories and no longer feel so alone.

Laughter as Medicine, Sociology as Hope

Comedy can be a source of hope during times of challenge and tragedy – even for people who did not have that same relationship to comedy in previous eras of their life. For example, Jason Zinoman, comedy writer for the *New York Times*, saw his view of comedy evolve during the COVID-19 pandemic. His relationship to comedy became more "sentimental" and he became more open to "dumb laughs." He became more receptive to the concept of laughter as medicine.[3] And that's the beautiful thing about comedy. It changes, and our relationship to it changes. We revisit the same comedy again and again, potentially with new interpretation, or we look for new styles of comedy during different phases of our lives. As this book describes, the demographics, perspectives, messages, and forms of comedy change with time. And so does its individual purpose. Sometimes we want comedy to challenge us but sometimes we want comedy to distract us from the realities of our world.

And the same can be said of sociology. Sociological theories have expanded and evolved over time. We, too, need a flexible and growing understanding of our social world. For me, the process of writing this book expanded my worldview. As my knowledge of comedy grew deeper and wider through my research, so did my understanding of sociology. Sociology is about discovery and seeing the world through a new lens. As the world changes, so too do our frameworks for understanding it. They evolve, expand, and adapt. And that's what makes them survive.

Sociology and comedy are both about discovery. It is the job of both sociologists and comedians to be tour guides for our social world. To uncover what is hidden, question the status quo, and offer a voice to the voiceless. Comedy can help us better understand one another, which, in turn, affords opportunity for joy, hope, and connection. Even in the face of tragedy, knowing someone understands and hears you can provide hope that things will be okay.

Notes

1 Miller, J. (Director). (2021, November 3). *Good Timing with Jo Firestone*. Park City Television. https://www.youtube.com/watch?v=i6OrjH-gN5A
2 Fleming, K. (2021, October 14). Seniors don pasties in 'Good Timing with Jo Firestone' stand-up special. *New York Post*. https://nypost.com/2021/10/14/seniors-make-dirty-jokes-in-good-timing-with-jo-firestone/
3 *The Specials: Bo Burnham's "Inside."* (2021, June 11). https://www.patreon.com/posts/bo-burnhams-52399908

Index

Milton Keynes UK
Ingram Content Group UK Ltd.
UKHW020859280724
446158UK00008B/41